Spera™

• *Volume Three* •

JOSH TIERNEY

DIALYNAS • GANDY • GODBEY • ZHAO • BOSMA

ARCHAIA ENTERTAINMENT LLC
WWW.**ARCHAIA**.COM

Written by
JOSH TIERNEY

Illustrated by
MICHAEL DIALYNAS
MEG GANDY
CORY GODBEY
AMEI ZHAO
SAM BOSMA

Character Designs and Cover Art by
AFU CHAN

Edited by
REBECCA TAYLOR

Design by
SCOTT NEWMAN

Archaia Entertainment LLC
Jack Cummins, *President & COO*
Mark Smylie, *CCO*
Mike Kennedy, *Publisher*
Stephen Christy, *Editor-in-Chief*
Mel Caylo, *Marketing Manager*
Scott Newman, *Production Manager*

Published by **Archaia**

Archaia Entertainment LLC
1680 Vine Street, Suite 1010
Los Angeles, California, 90028
www.archaia.com

ARCHAIA™
NEW STORIES. NEW WORLDS.

SPERA Volume Three. Original Graphic Novel Hardcover. September 2013. FIRST PRINTING.

10 9 8 7 6 5 4 3 2 1

ISBN: 1-939867-01-0
ISBN 13: 978-1-939867-01-8

TABLE of CONTENTS

OUR HEROES' PASTS AND CURRENT STATUSES

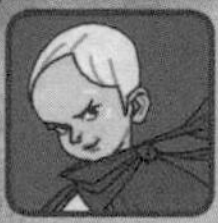

PIRA
PRINCESS ◇
LV 12 SPT 64
EXP 12058
HP 154/154
MP 36/36

Pira is the exiled princess of the **Starless Kingdom**. After years of disagreeing with her mother, the **Evil Queen**, Pira decided to disobey her mother's final order by rescuing her friend, **Princess Lono**, from the Starless' impending invasion. With the help of the fire spirit **Yonder**, Pira and Lono fled to the land of **Spera**, looking to rebuild their shattered lives by becoming adventurers in a strange new land.

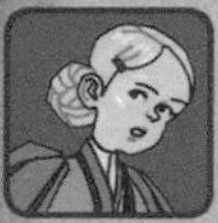

LONO
PRINCESS ◇
LV 11 SPT 72
EXP 11836
HP 86/86
MP 157/157

Lono is the exiled princess of the **Plain Kingdom**, former neighbour to the Starless. Her father, the **Good King**, was murdered in the **Court of the Starless** by Pira's mother, marking the beginning of the **Starless Invasion**. In order to live, Lono was forced to leave her kingdom behind; now only death and fire awaits her there.

After a lengthy stay in the city of **Kotequog**, home of the **Adventurer's Guild**, Lono and Pira headed to the harbour town of **Nethans** in search of more treasure-hunting missions...

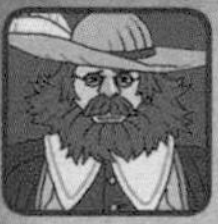

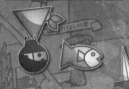

YONDER
FIRE SPIRIT ◇
LV 37 SPT 84
EXP 37863
HP 875/875
MP 316/316

Yonder is a mysterious fire spirit who alternates between the forms of a red-bearded man and large, flaming dog. He is the lifelong friend of Pira, and served as the hiding place for Pira's magic green sword during their days as Starless. Yonder is haunted by ominous dreams involving Pira, her sword and an uncertain future.

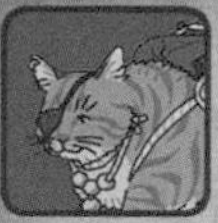

CHOBO
WARRIOR ◇
LV 23 SPT 53
EXP 23576
HP 383/383
MP 10/10

Chobo the warrior tabby is the star of a series of books in a faraway kingdom. He accompanies Pira, Lono and Yonder under the agreement that all treasure shall be shared between them. What Chobo does with his share of the treasure, however, is unknown.

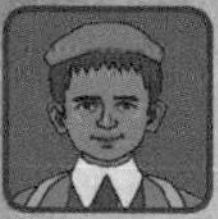

ADEL
STUDENT ◇
LV 9 SPT 30
EXP 9367
HP 77/77
MP 42/42

Adel is a student from the walled town of **Hammer**. He met Pira and Lono as Hammer was being violently attacked by a werewolf; Pira proceeded to make short work of the monster, and the trio then worked together to solve the mystery of the werewolf's existence.

It is now summer break, and Adel has asked Pira and Lono to join them on one of their adventures...

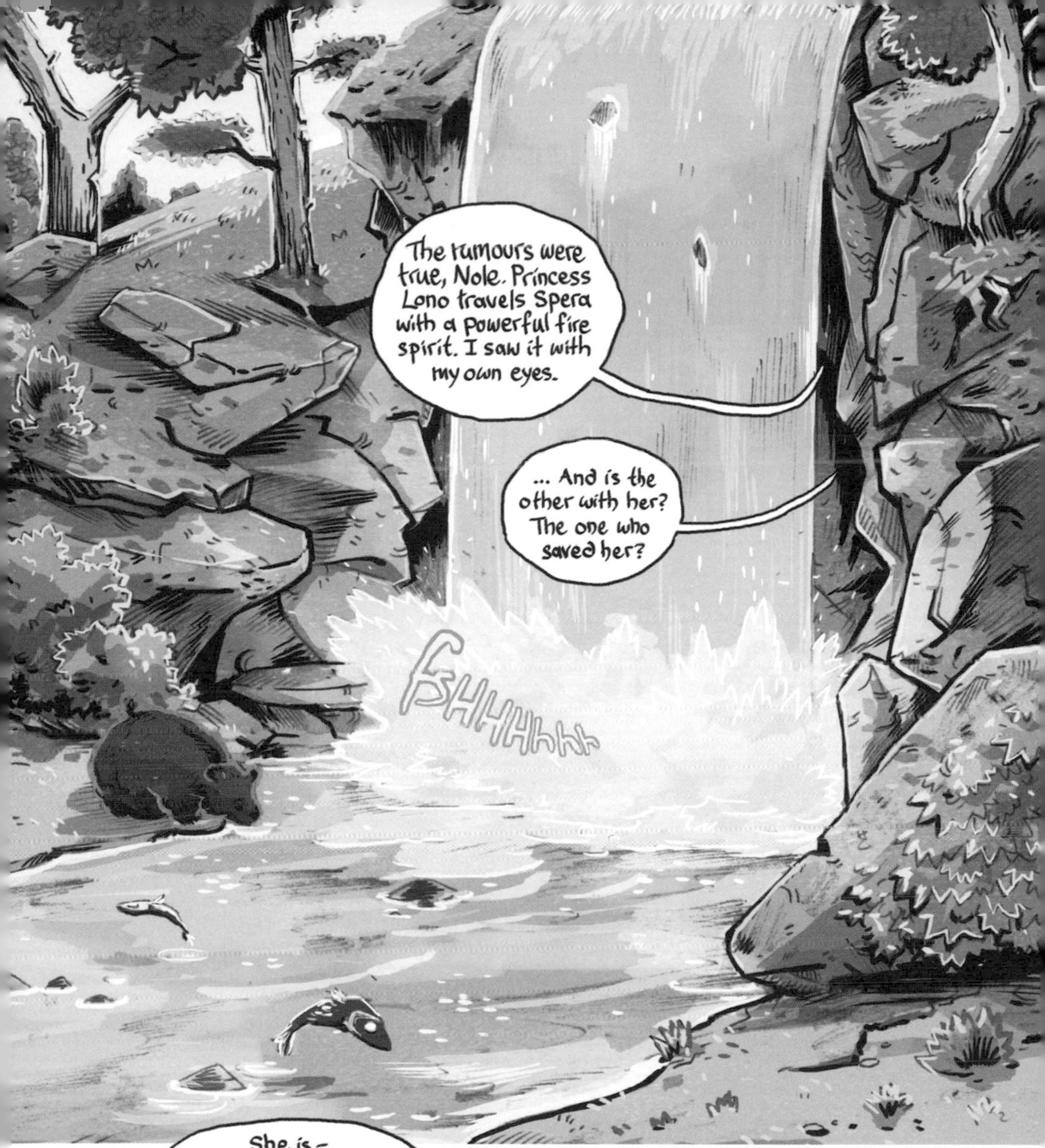
The rumours were true, Nole. Princess Lono travels Spera with a powerful fire spirit. I saw it with my own eyes.
... And is the other with her? The one who saved her?
FSHHHhhh

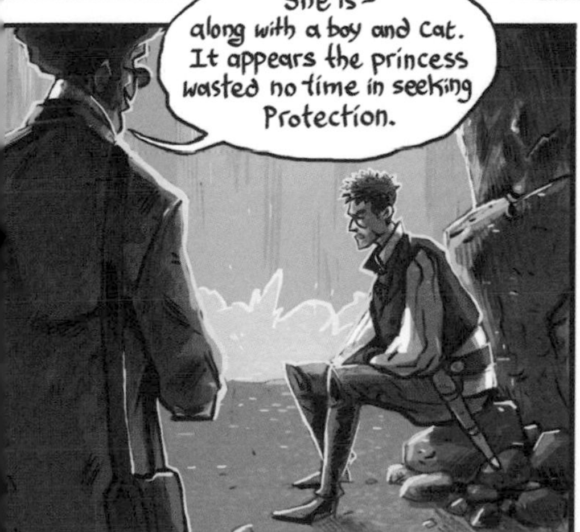
She is - along with a boy and cat. It appears the princess wasted no time in seeking Protection.

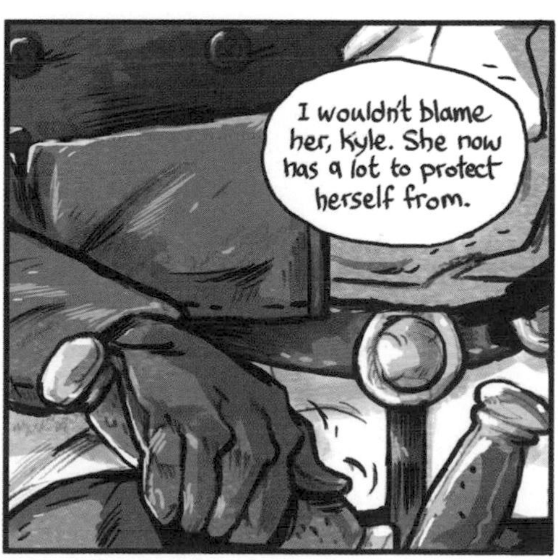
I wouldn't blame her, Kyle. She now has a lot to protect herself from.

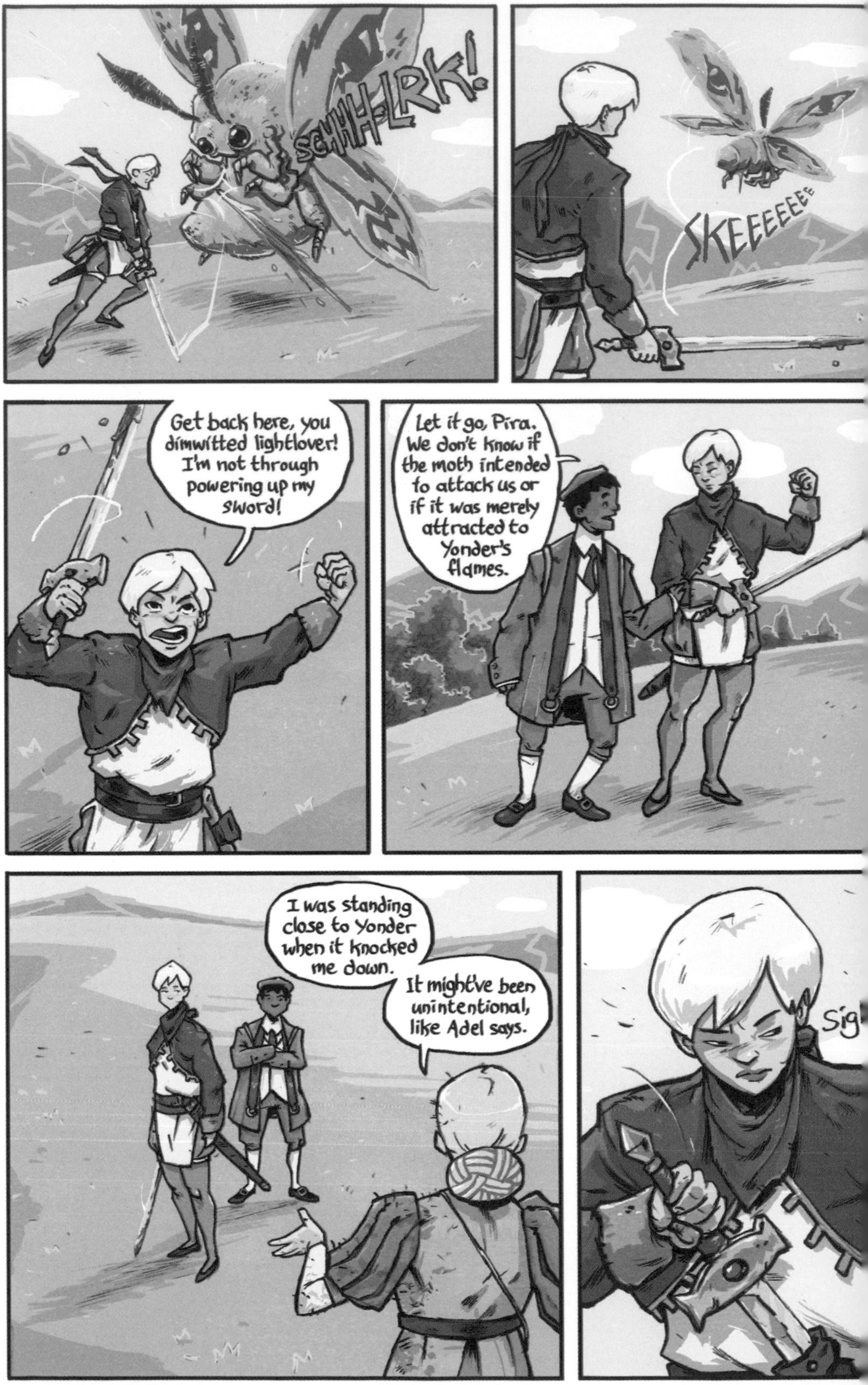
SCHHH-LRK!
SKEEEEEEE
Get back here, you dimwitted lightlover! I'm not through powering up my sword!
Let it go, Pira. We don't know if the moth intended to attack us or if it was merely attracted to Yonder's flames.
I was standing close to Yonder when it knocked me down.
It might've been unintentional, like Adel says.
Sig

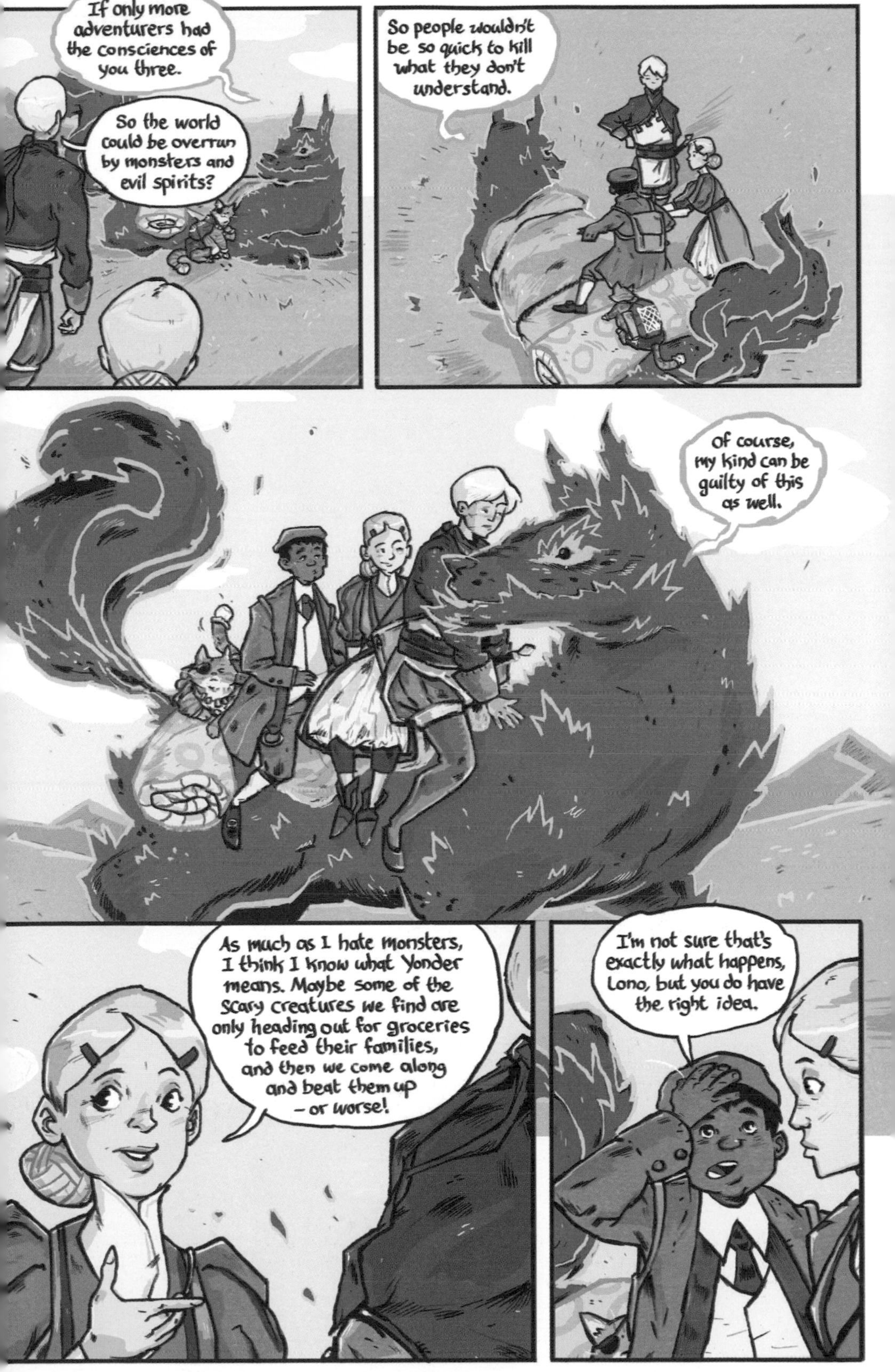
If only more adventurers had the consciences of you three.
So the world could be overrun by monsters and evil spirits?
So people wouldn't be so quick to kill what they don't understand.
Of course, my kind can be guilty of this as well.
As much as I hate monsters, I think I know what Yonder means. Maybe some of the scary creatures we find are only heading out for groceries to feed their families, and then we come along and beat them up —or worse!
I'm not sure that's exactly what happens, Lono, but you do have the right idea.

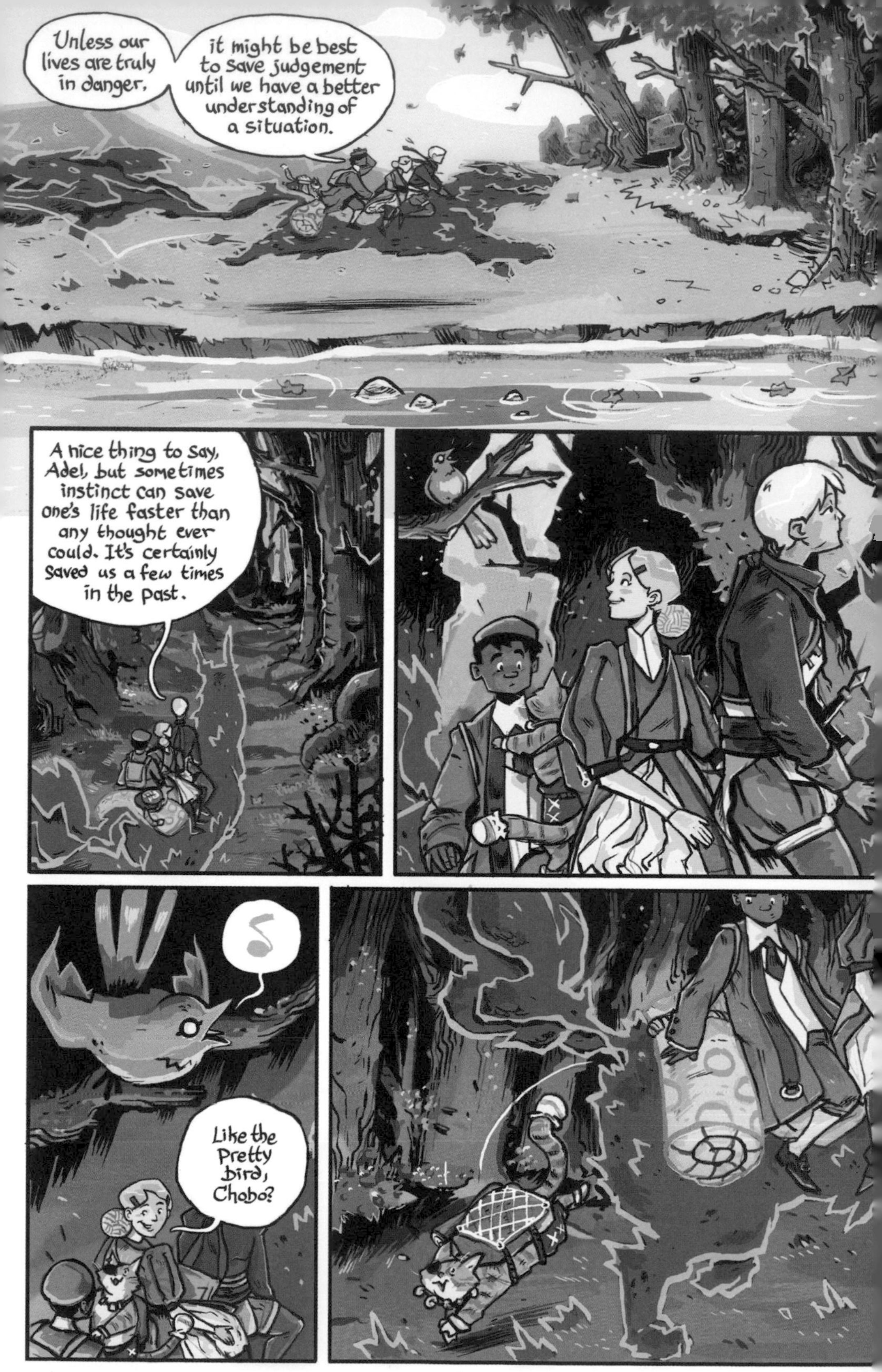
Unless our lives are truly in danger,
it might be best to save judgement until we have a better understanding of a situation.
A nice thing to say, Adel, but sometimes instinct can save one's life faster than any thought ever could. It's certainly saved us a few times in the past.
Like the Pretty bird, Chobo?

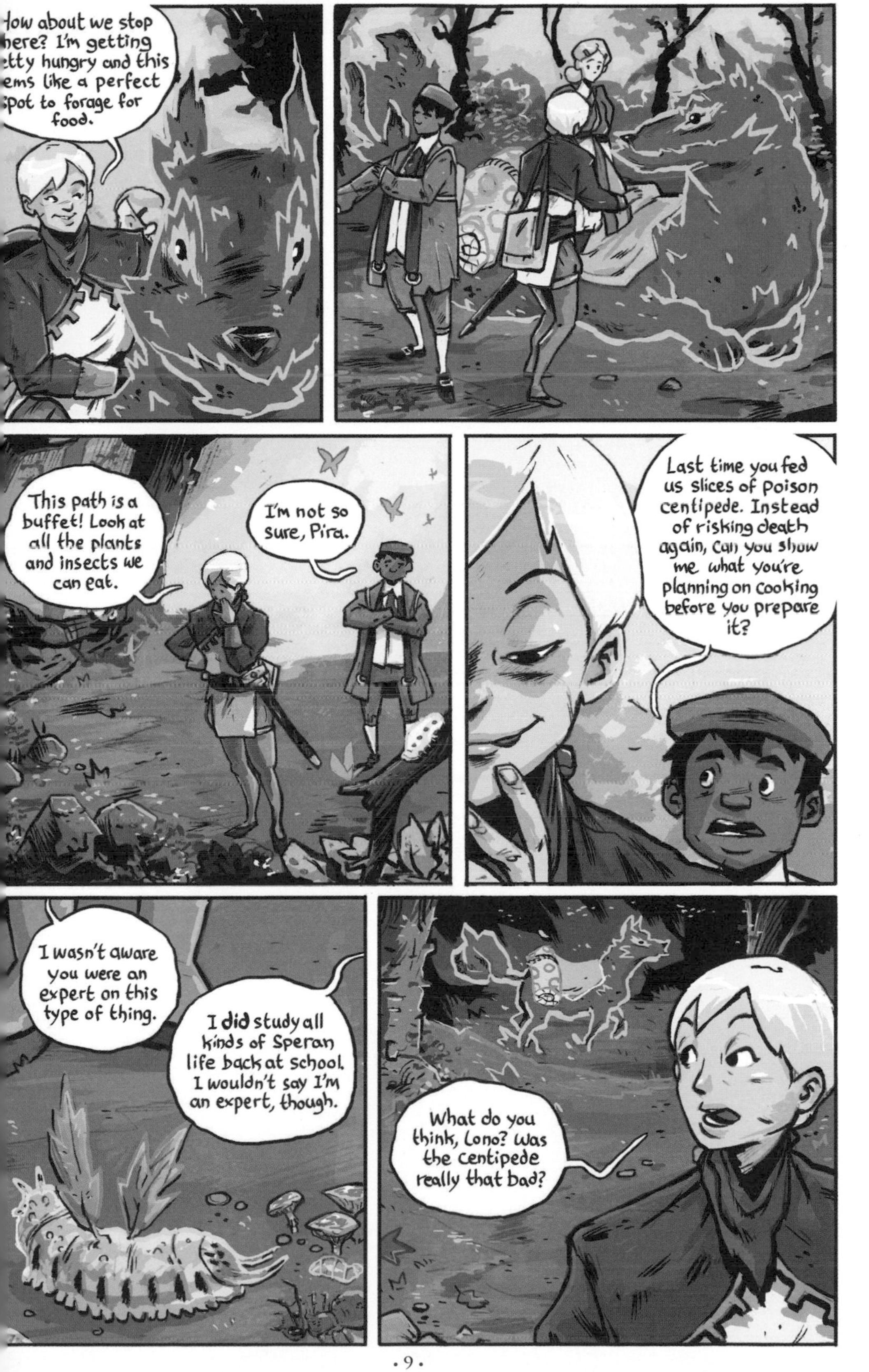

How about we stop here? I'm getting pretty hungry and this seems like a perfect spot to forage for food.
This path is a buffet! Look at all the plants and insects we can eat.
I'm not so sure, Pira.
Last time you fed us slices of poison centipede. Instead of risking death again, can you show me what you're planning on cooking before you prepare it?
I wasn't aware you were an expert on this type of thing.
I did study all kinds of Speran life back at school. I wouldn't say I'm an expert, though.
What do you think, Lono? Was the centipede really that bad?

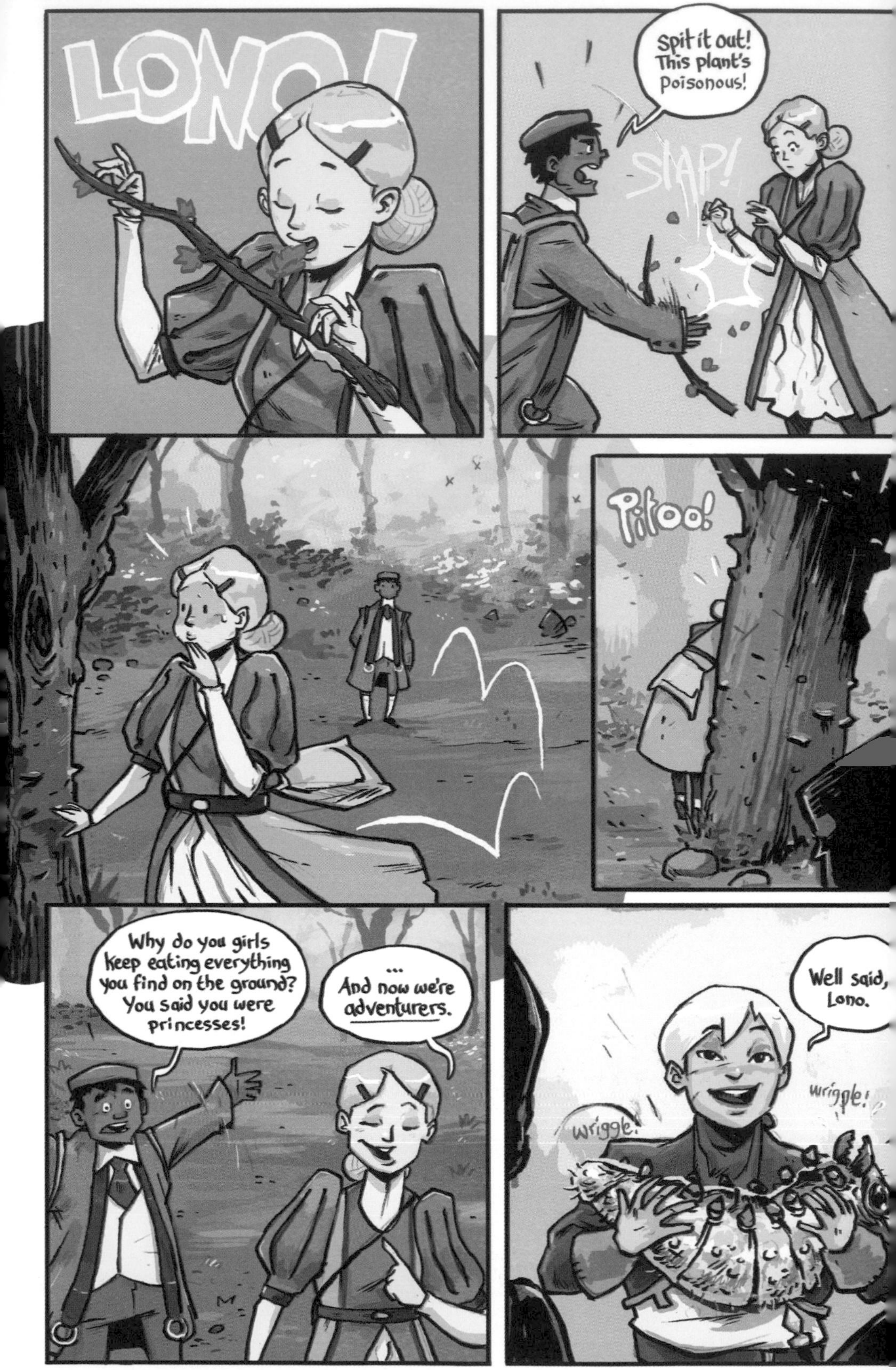
LONO!
Spit it out! This plant's poisonous!
SLAP!
Pitoo!
Why do you girls keep eating everything you find on the ground? You said you were princesses!
... And now we're adventurers.
Well said, Lono.
wriggle!
wriggle!

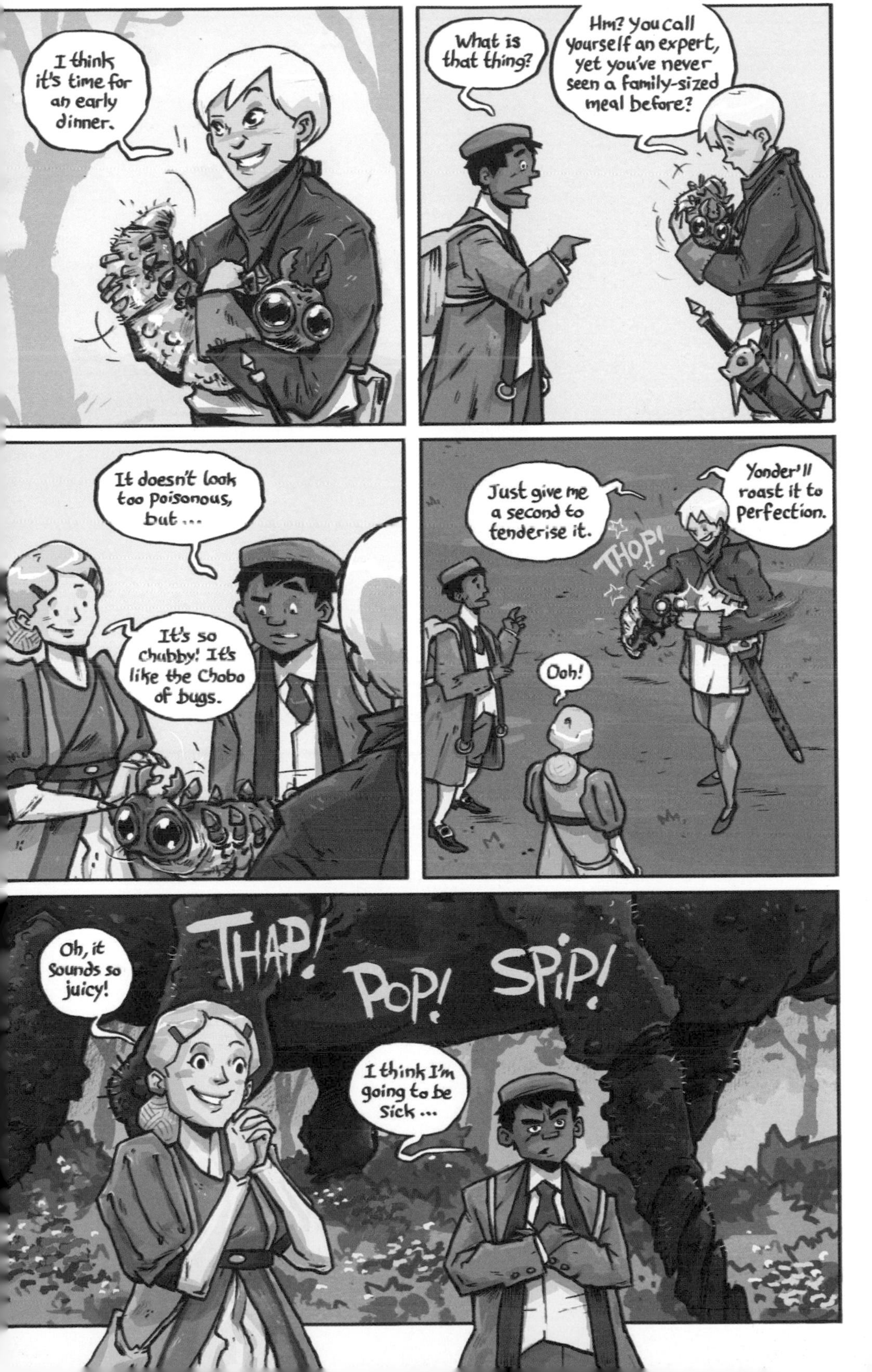
I think it's time for an early dinner.
What is that thing?
Hm? You call yourself an expert, yet you've never seen a family-sized meal before?
It doesn't look too poisonous, but ...
It's so chubby! It's like the Chobo of bugs.
Just give me a second to tenderise it.
Yonder'll roast it to perfection.
THOP!
Ooh!
THAP! POP! SPIP!
Oh, it sounds so juicy!
I think I'm going to be sick ...

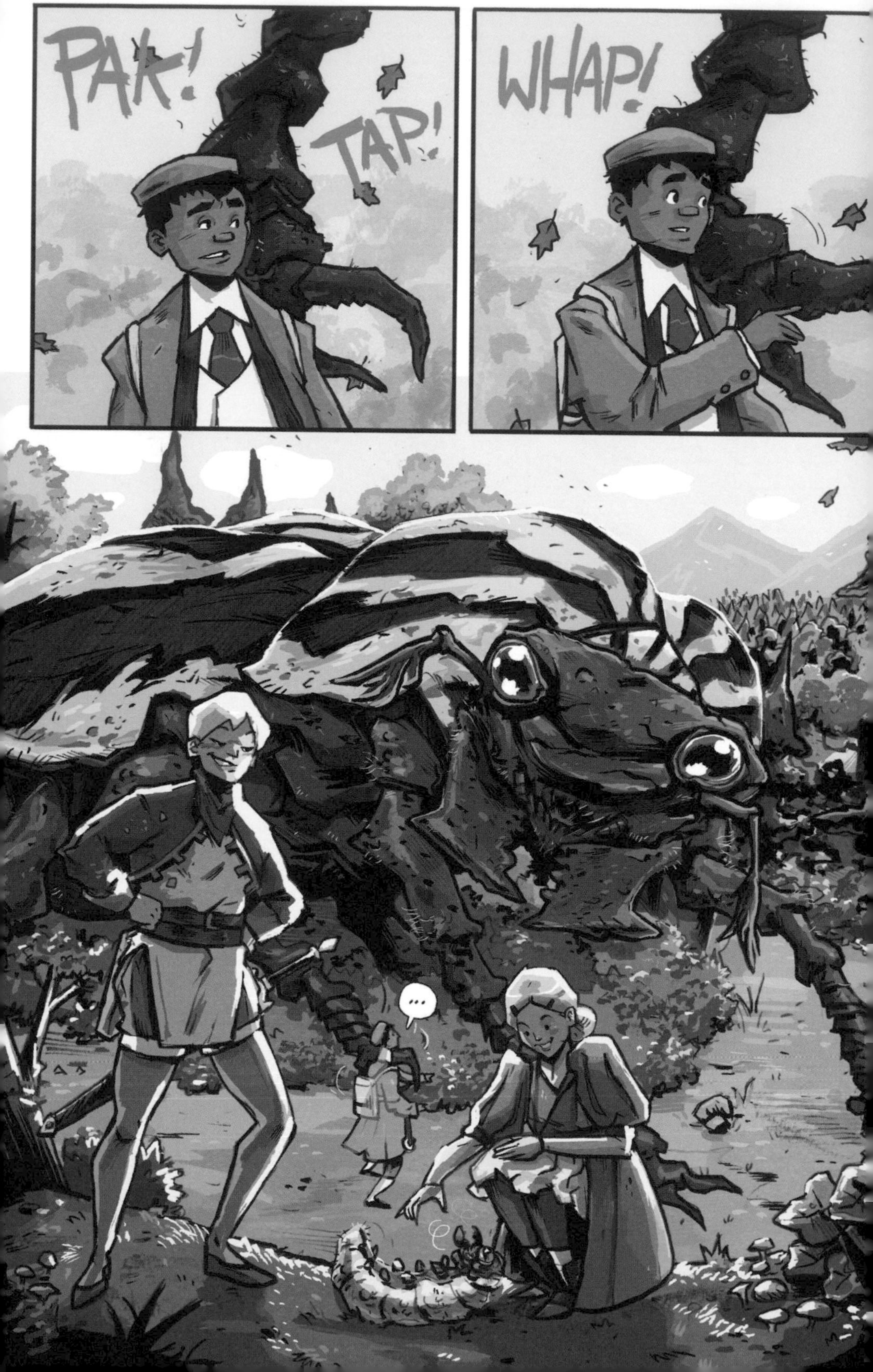
PAK!
TAP!
WHAP!
...

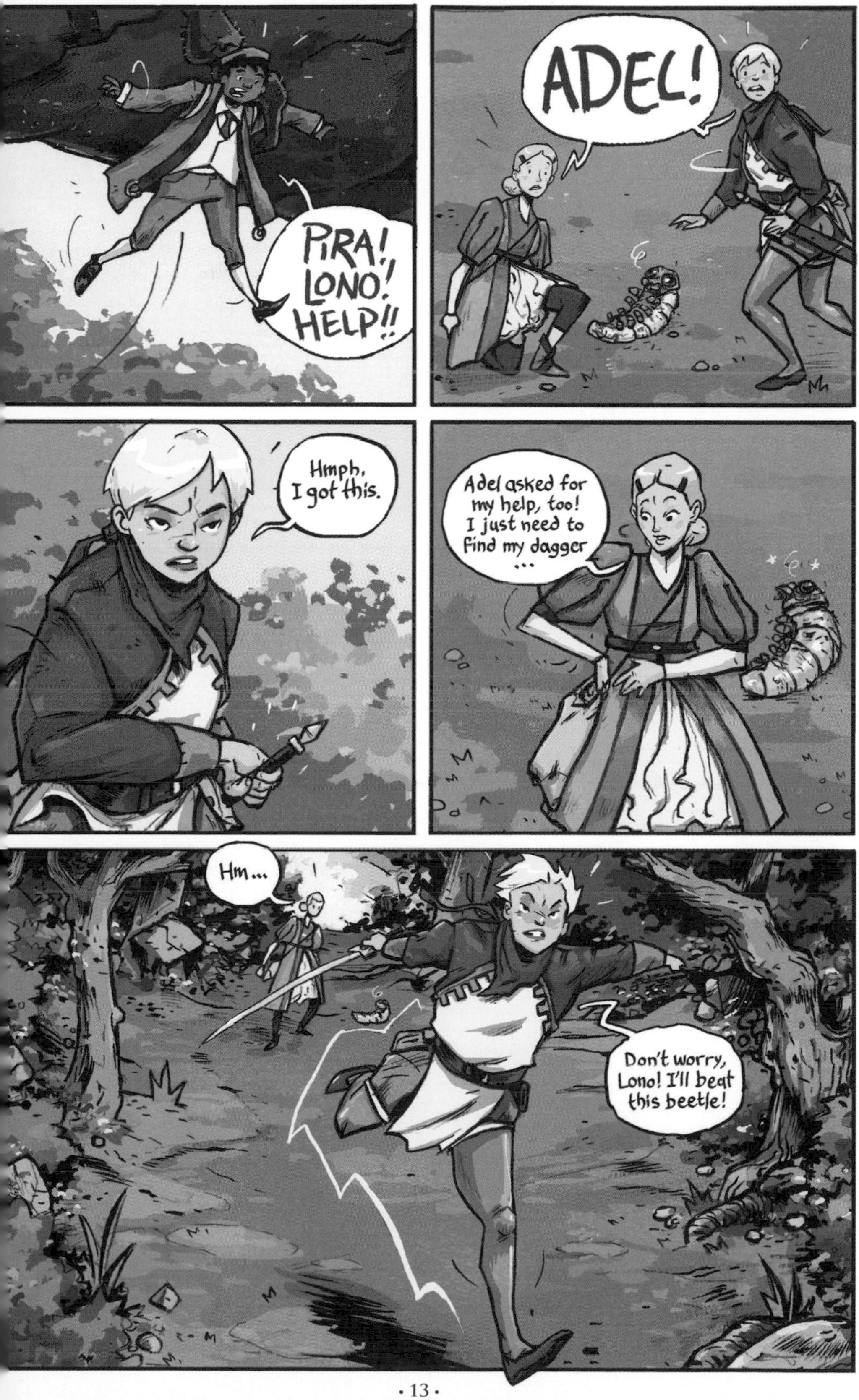
PIRA! LONO! HELP!!
ADEL!
Hmph, I got this.
Adel asked for my help, too! I just need to find my dagger ...
Hm...
Don't worry, Lono! I'll beat this beetle!

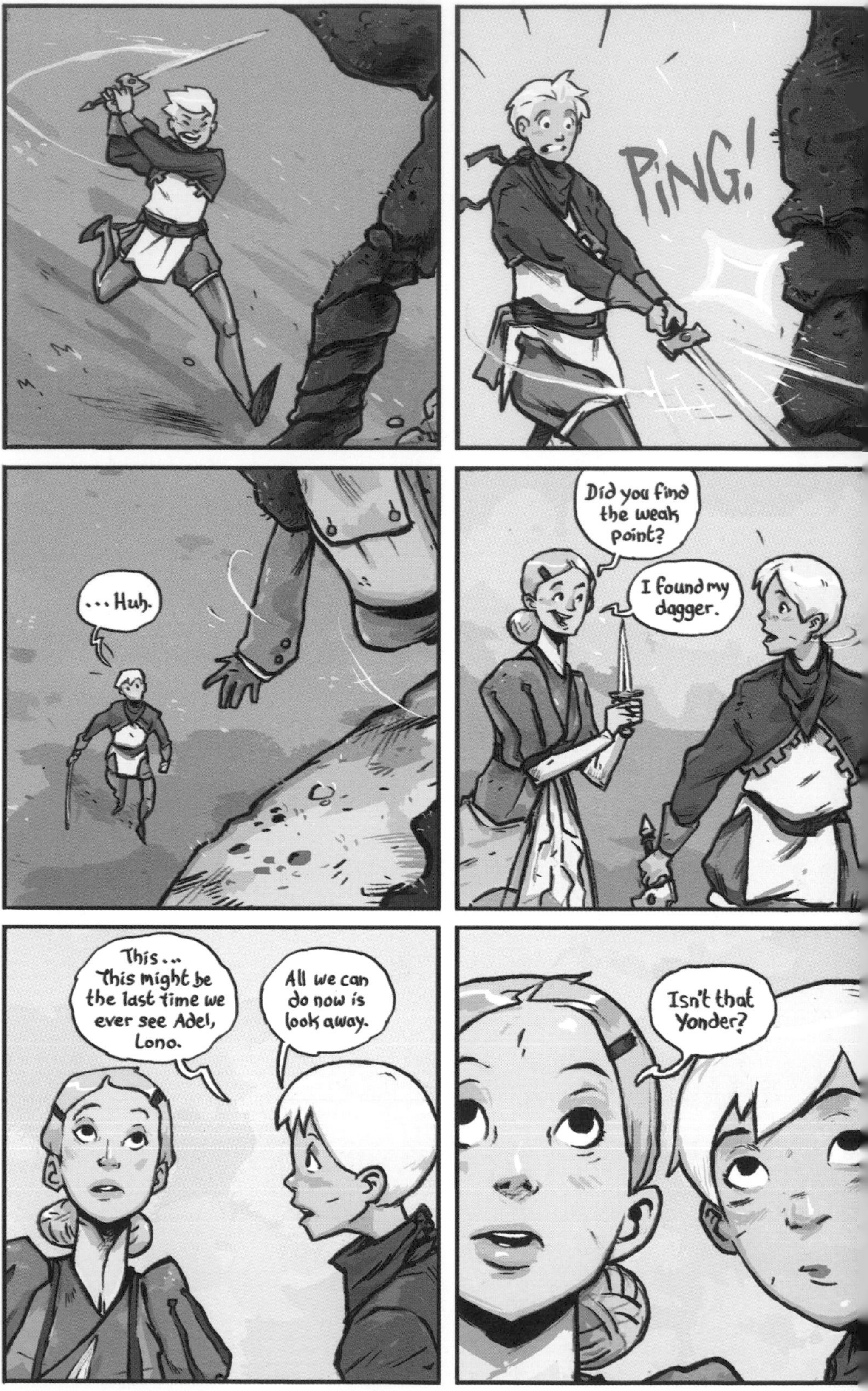
PING!
...Huh.
Did you find the weak point?
I found my dagger.
This... This might be the last time we ever see Adel, Lono.
All we can do now is look away.
Isn't that Yonder?

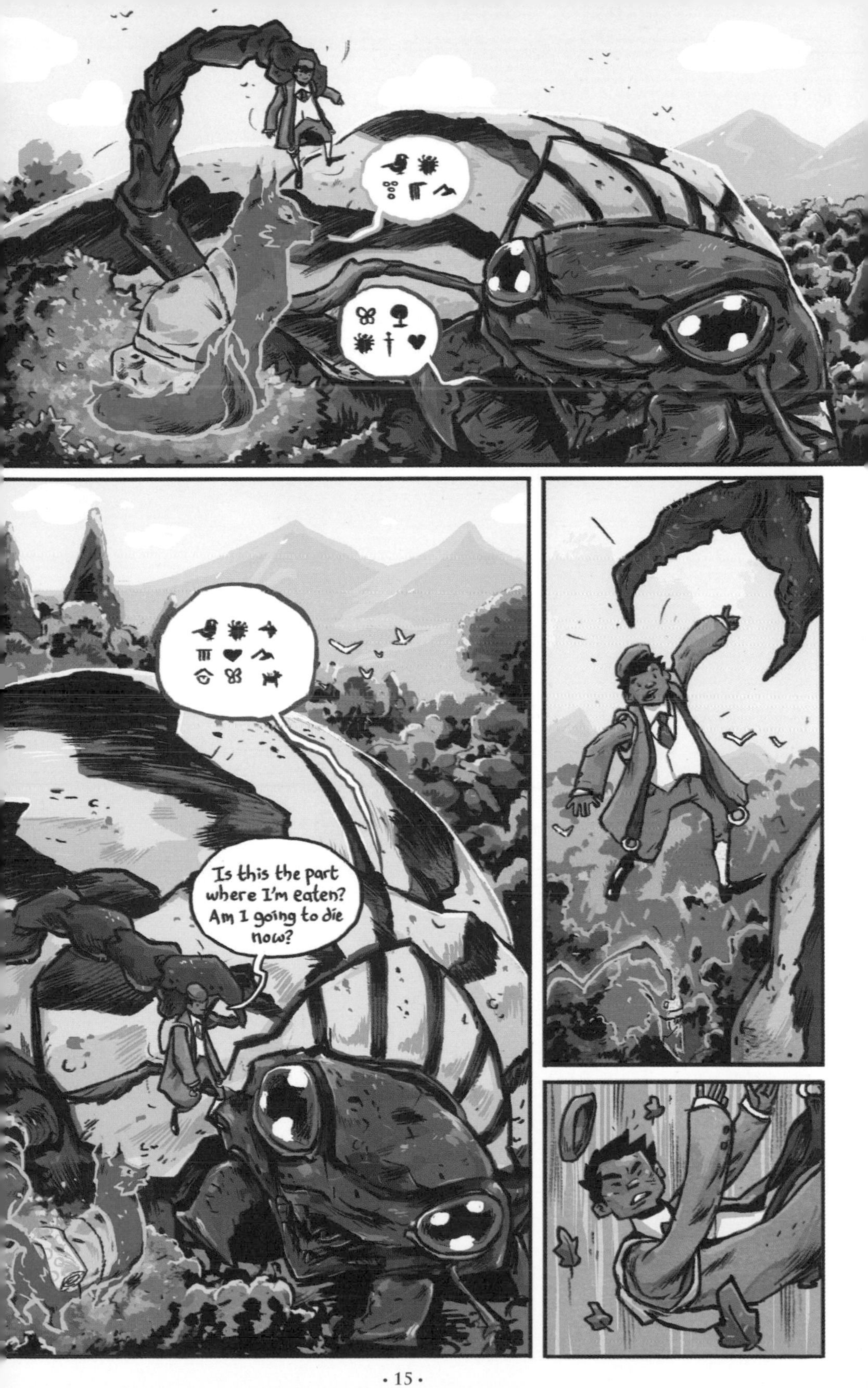
Is this the part where I'm eaten? Am I going to die now?

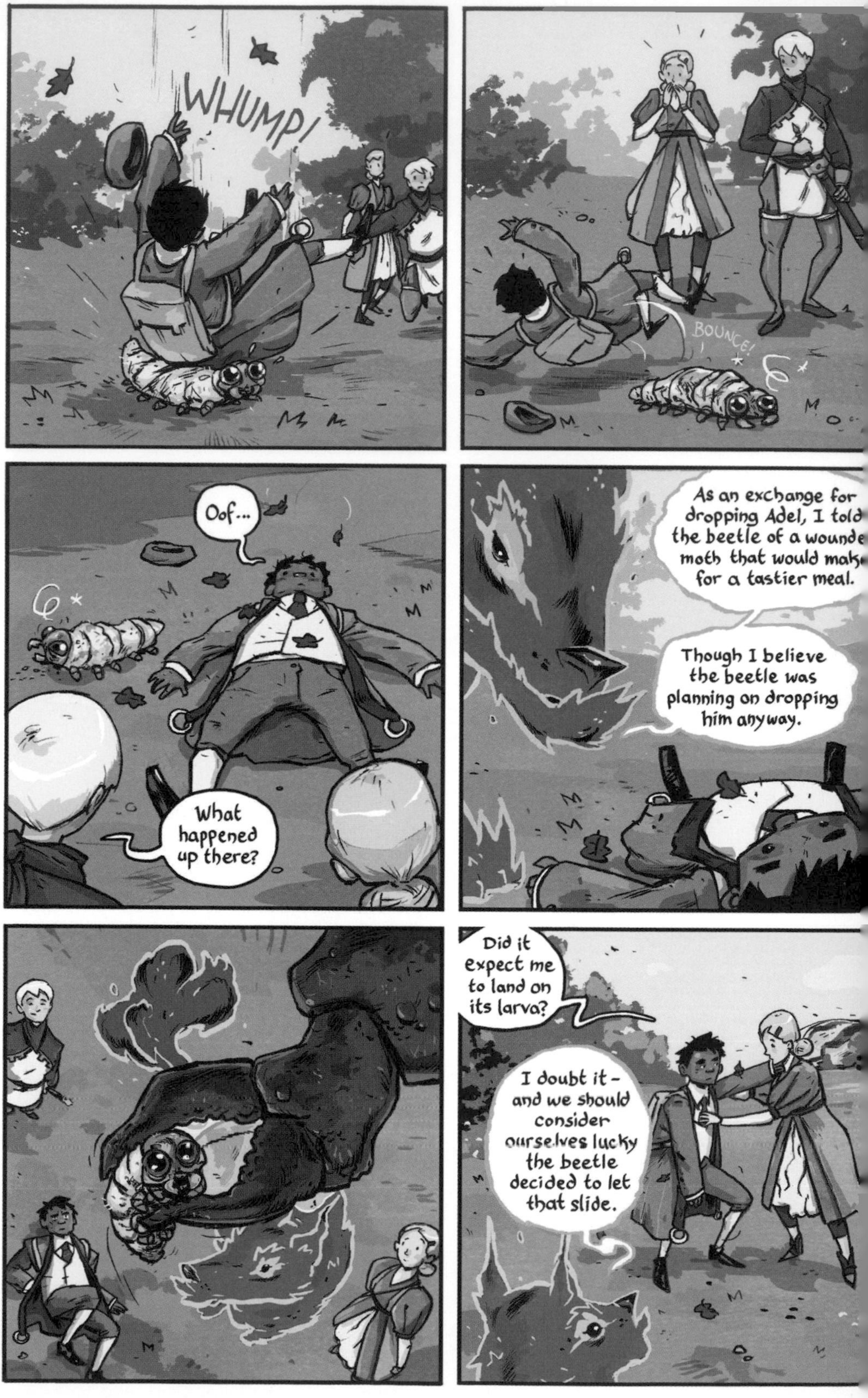
WHUMP!
BOUNCE!
Oof...
What happened up there?
As an exchange for dropping Adel, I told the beetle of a wounde moth that would mak for a tastier meal.
Though I believe the beetle was planning on dropping him anyway.
Did it expect me to land on its larva?
I doubt it - and we should consider ourselves lucky the beetle decided to let that slide.

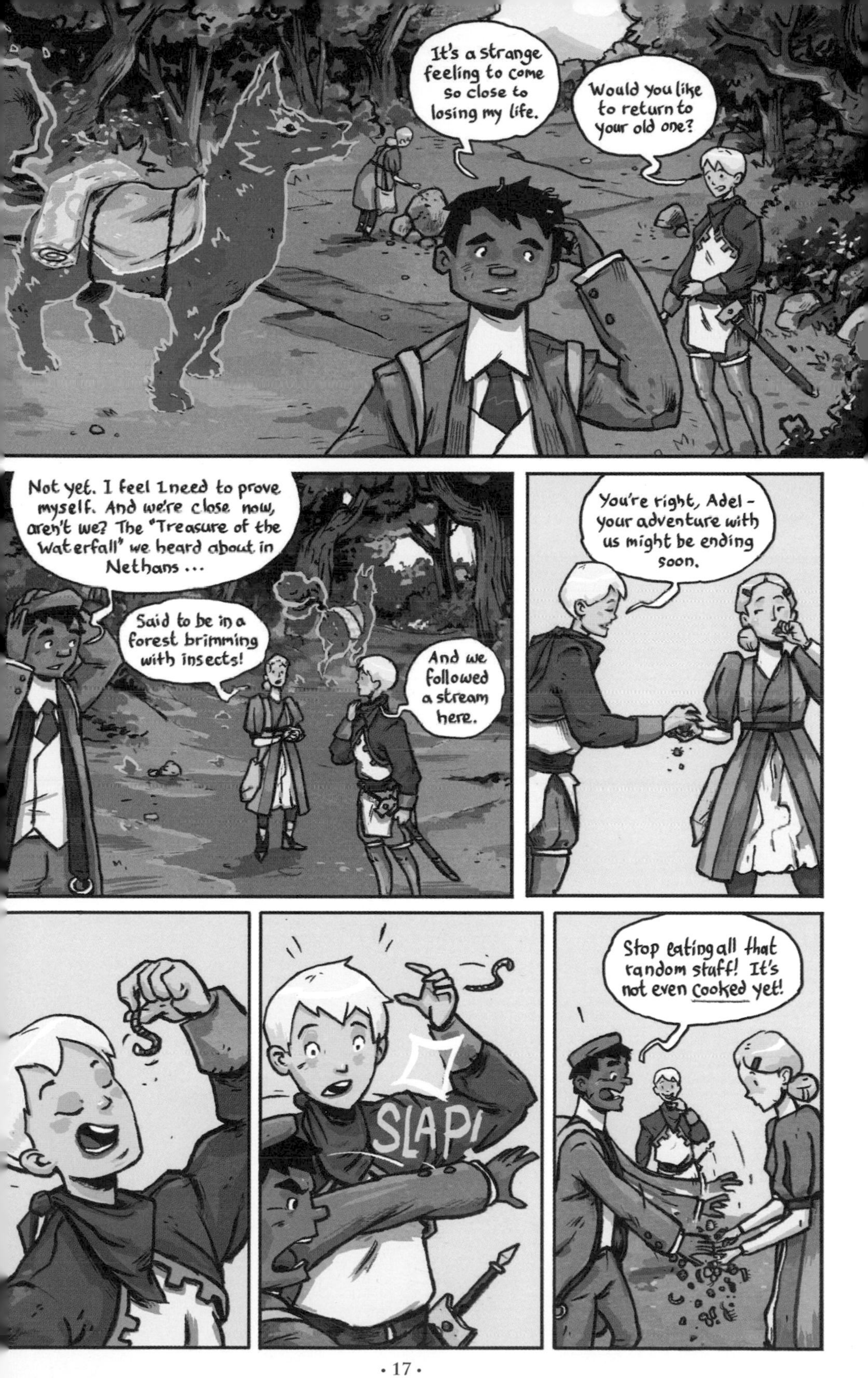
It's a strange feeling to come so close to losing my life.
Would you like to return to your old one?
Not yet. I feel I need to prove myself. And we're close now, aren't we? The "Treasure of the Waterfall" we heard about in Nethans ...
Said to be in a forest brimming with insects!
And we followed a stream here.
You're right, Adel - your adventure with us might be ending soon.
SLAP!
Stop eating all that random stuff! It's not even cooked yet!

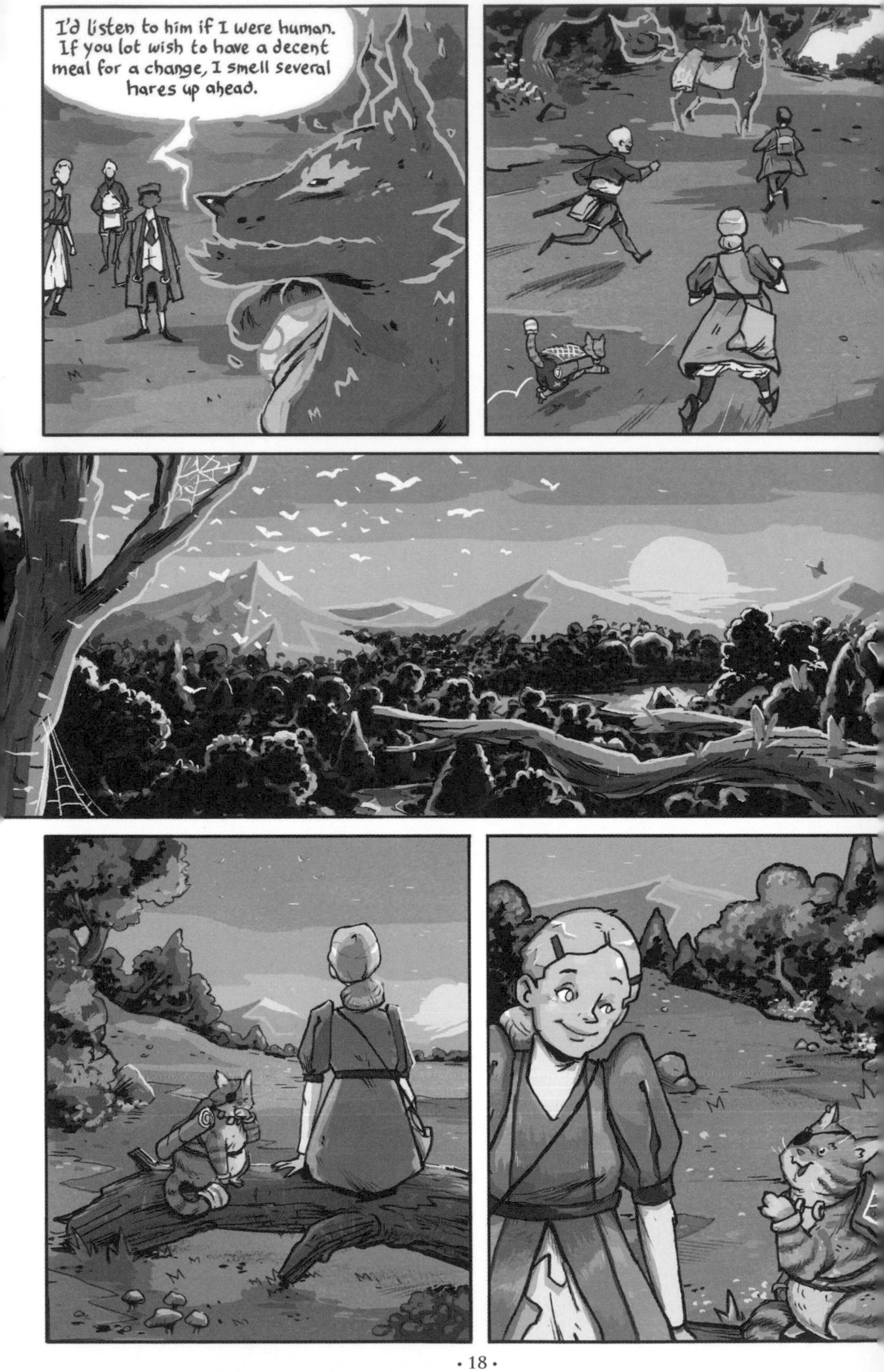
I'd listen to him if I were human. If you lot wish to have a decent meal for a change, I smell several hares up ahead.

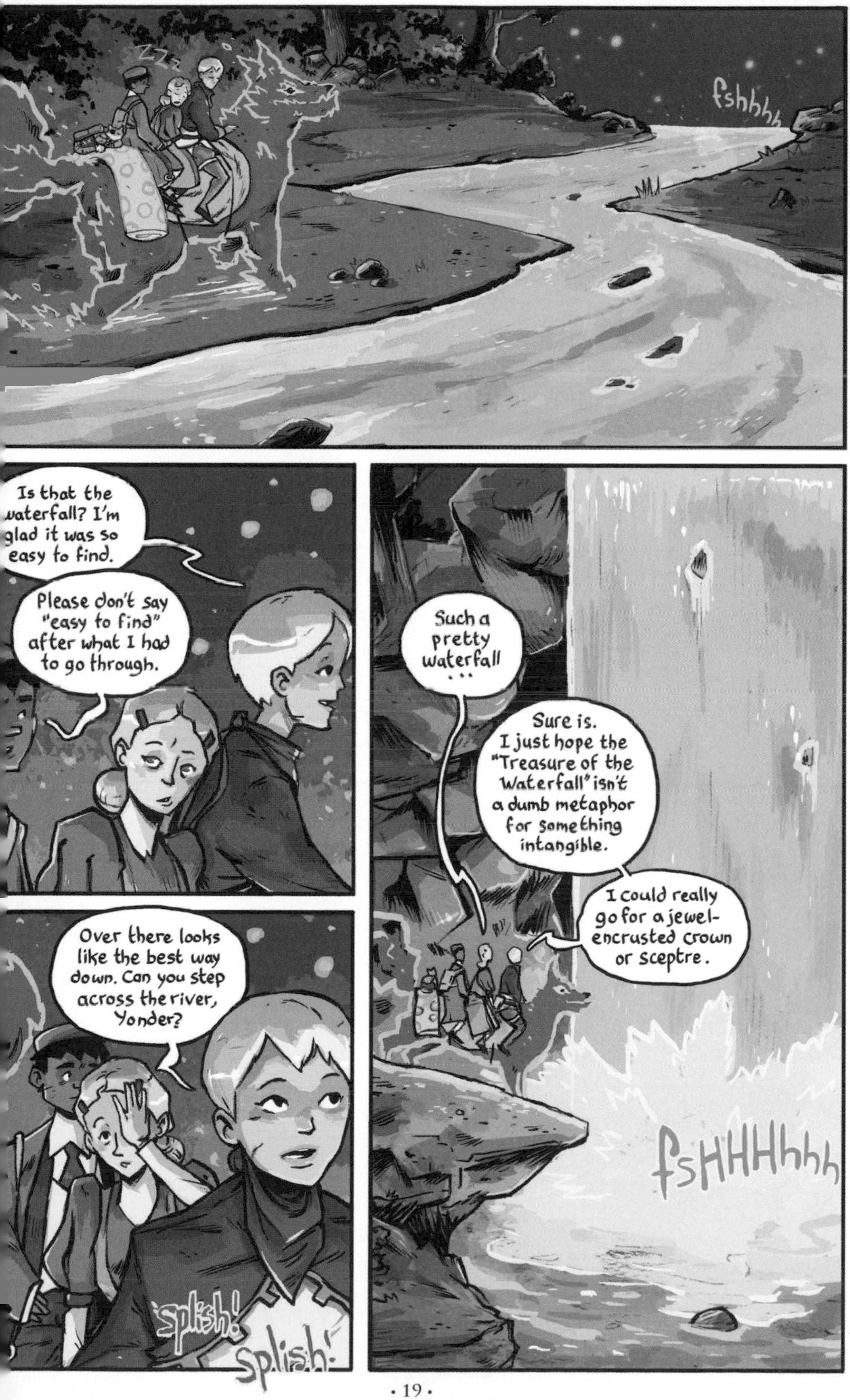
fshhhh
Is that the waterfall? I'm glad it was so easy to find.
Please don't say "easy to find" after what I had to go through.
Over there looks like the best way down. Can you step across the river, Yonder?
splish!
splish!
Such a pretty waterfall . . .
Sure is. I just hope the "Treasure of the Waterfall" isn't a dumb metaphor for something intangible.
I could really go for a jewel-encrusted crown or sceptre.
fsHHHhhh

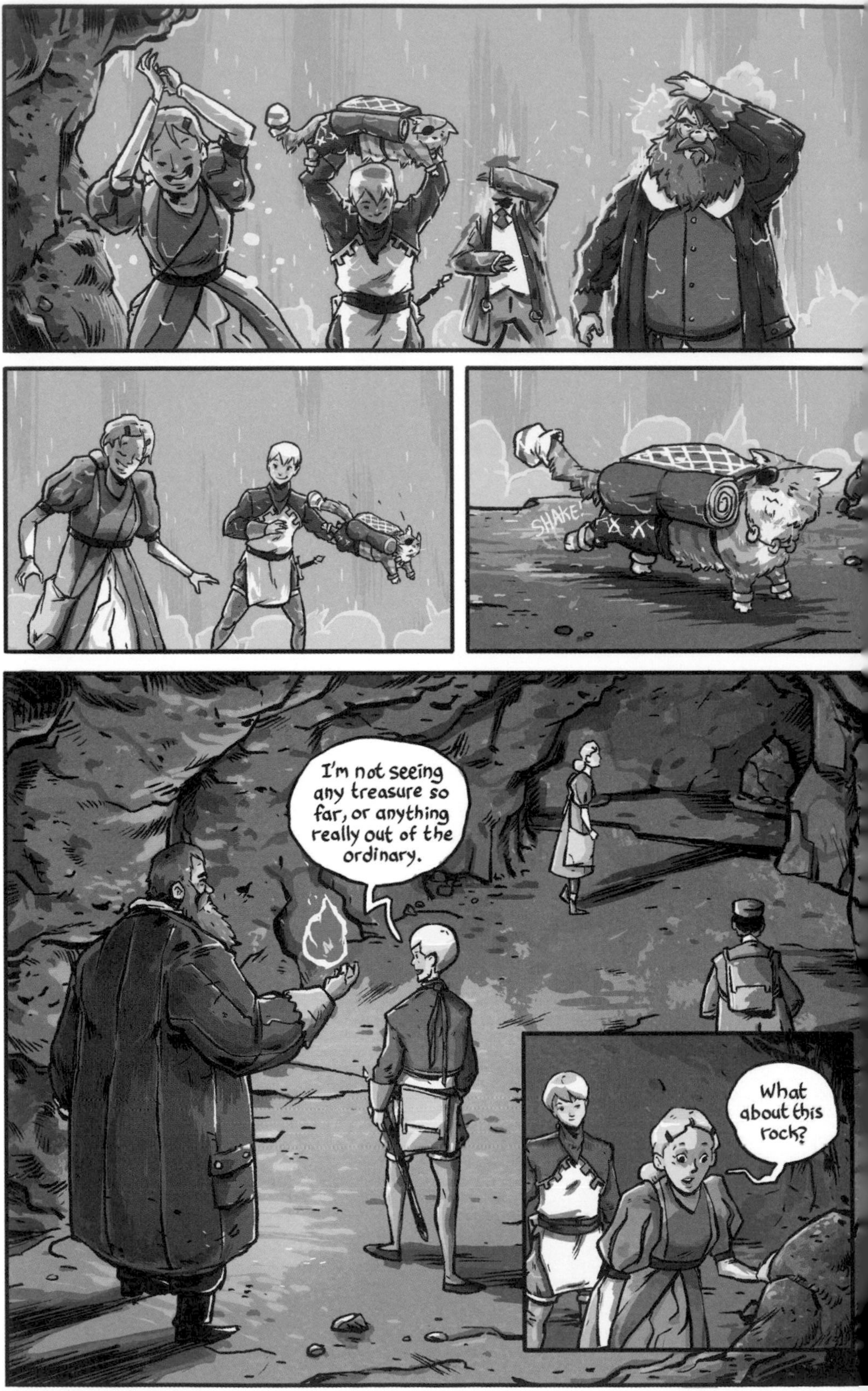
SHAKE!
I'm not seeing any treasure so far, or anything really out of the ordinary.
What about this rock?

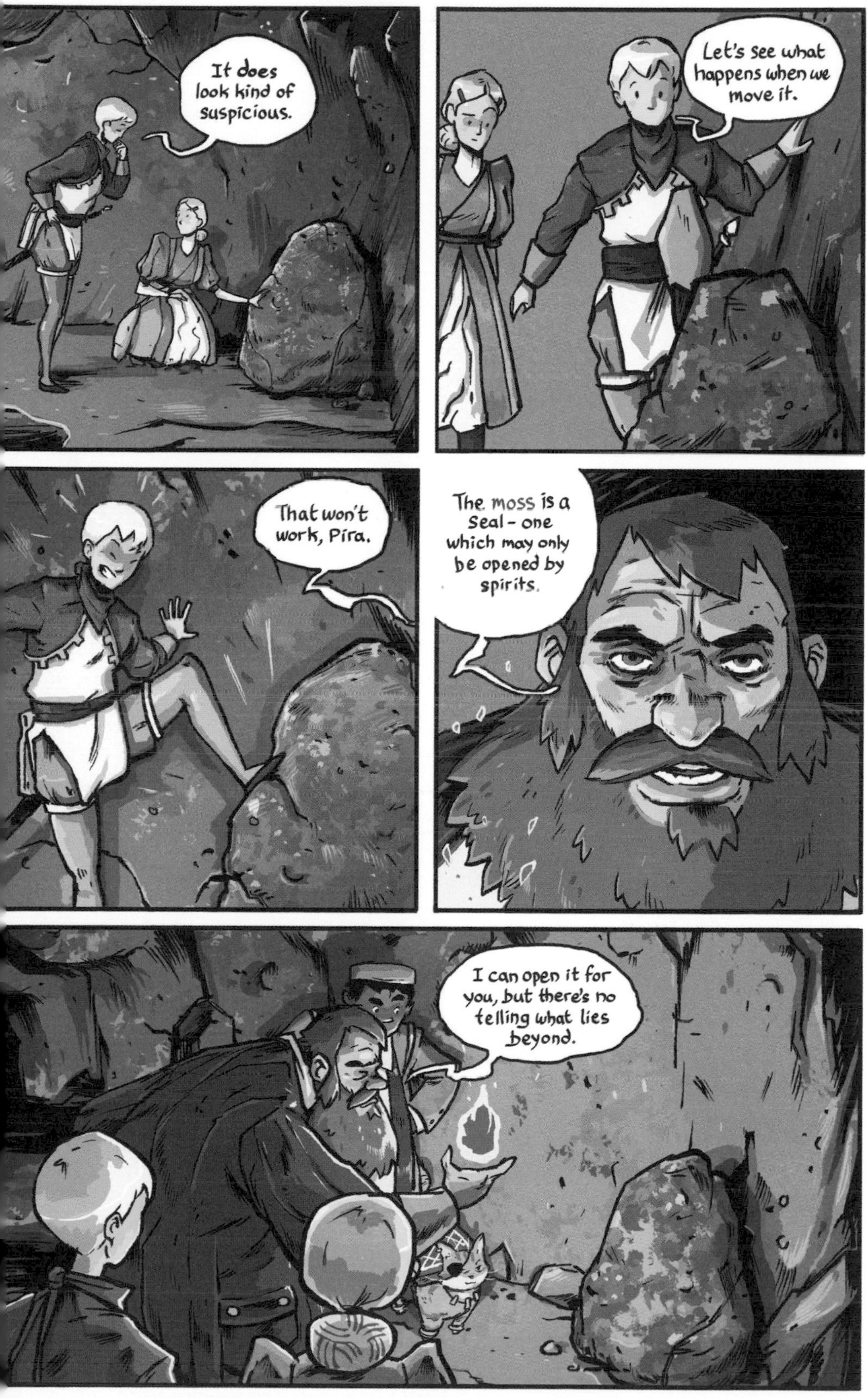
It does look kind of suspicious.
Let's see what happens when we move it.
That won't work, Pira.
The moss is a Seal - one which may only be opened by spirits.
I can open it for you, but there's no telling what lies beyond.

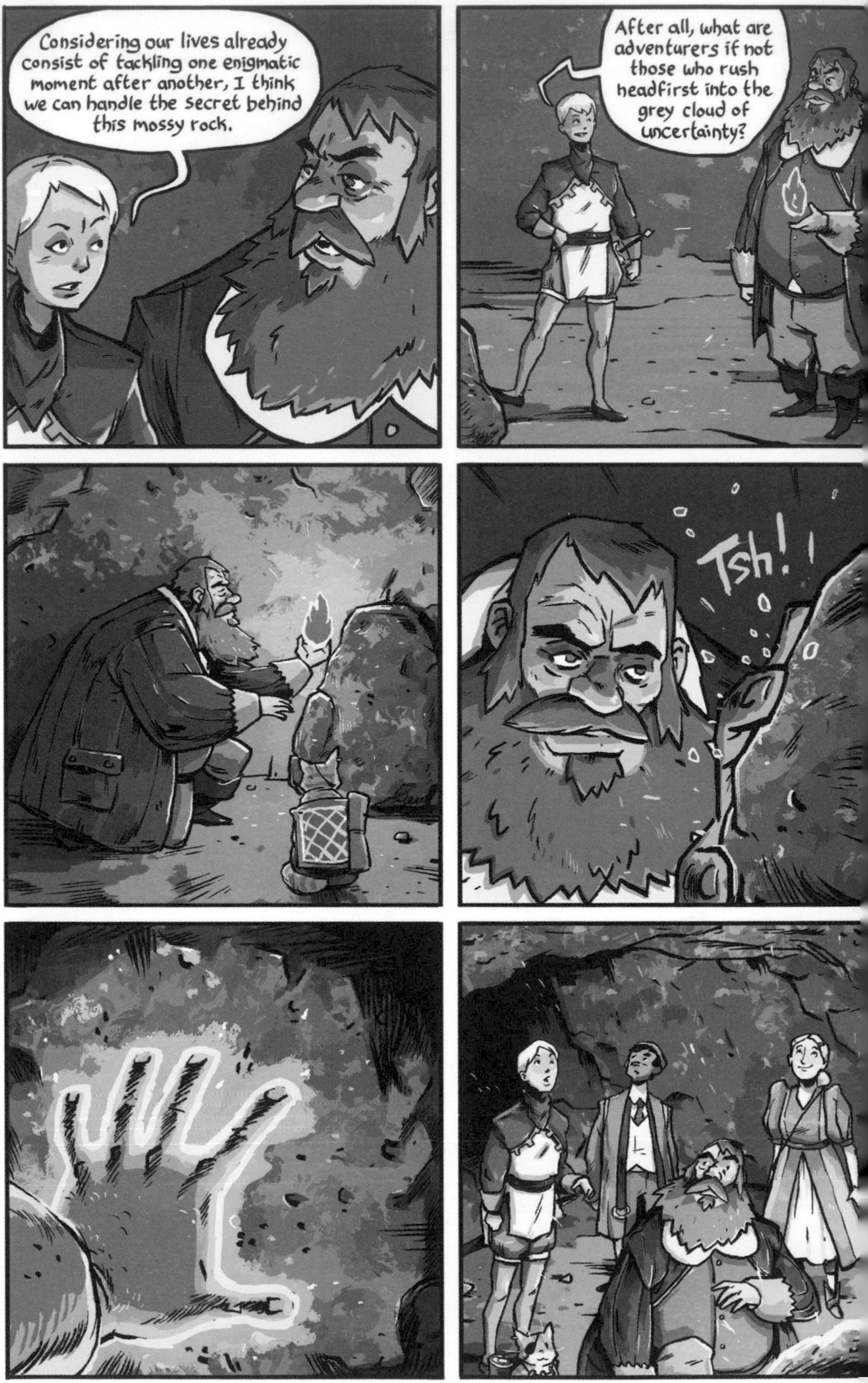
Considering our lives already consist of tackling one enigmatic moment after another, I think we can handle the secret behind this mossy rock.
After all, what are adventurers if not those who rush headfirst into the grey cloud of uncertainty?
Tsh!

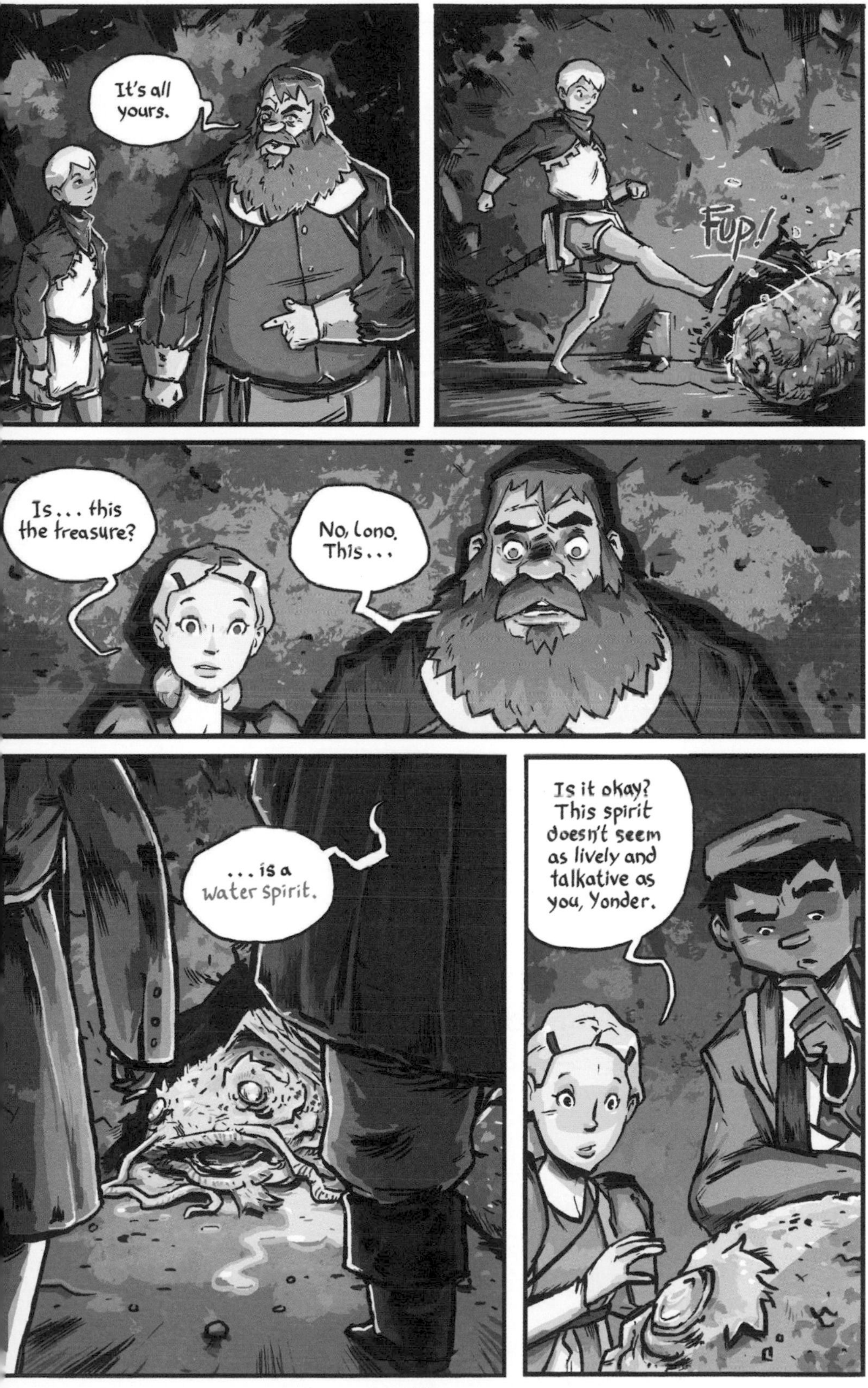
It's all yours.
Fup!
Is... this the treasure?
No, Lono. This...
...is a Water spirit.
Is it okay? This spirit doesn't seem as lively and talkative as you, Yonder.

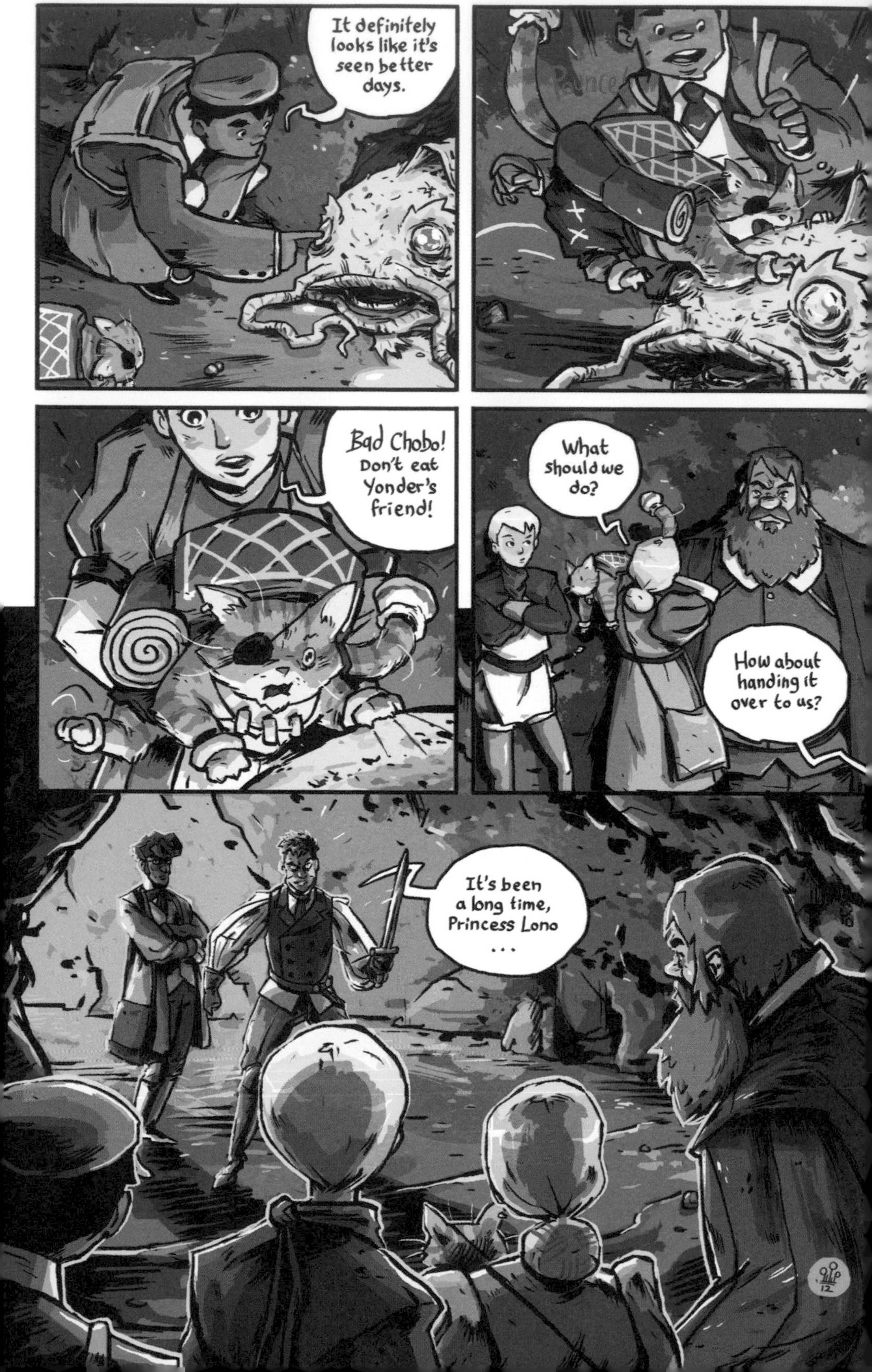
It definitely looks like it's seen better days.
Pounce!
Bad Chobo! Don't eat Yonder's friend!
What should we do?
How about handing it over to us?
It's been a long time, Princess Lono . . .

GOLIATH BEETLE

CREATURE | INSECT

One of the largest creatures in all of Spera.
Attempting to eat its larvae is a very bad idea.

Roll a die; if >4, take 10 points of damage.

Event locations and points of interest for your character to explore.

...ble quests and skill masters here.

Friendly and enemy creatures fill the landscape of Spera.

...gic | Determines the...

...alth & Magic | Denotes items or sk...

...andard Weapons | Weapons that off...

...eavy Weapons | Weapons that offer...

...ight Weapons | Weapons that offer li...

...egendary Weapons | Speci... ...pons that offer unique damage, stamina, and buffer stats.

Nature Element | Elemental classification for creatures, weapons and spells.

LONO

As much as I hate monsters, I think I know what **Yonder** means. Maybe some of the scary creatures we find are only heading out for groceries to feed their families, and then we come along and beat them up – or worse!

Cavern of the Water Spirit

CHAPTER TWO
Betrayal and the Fall

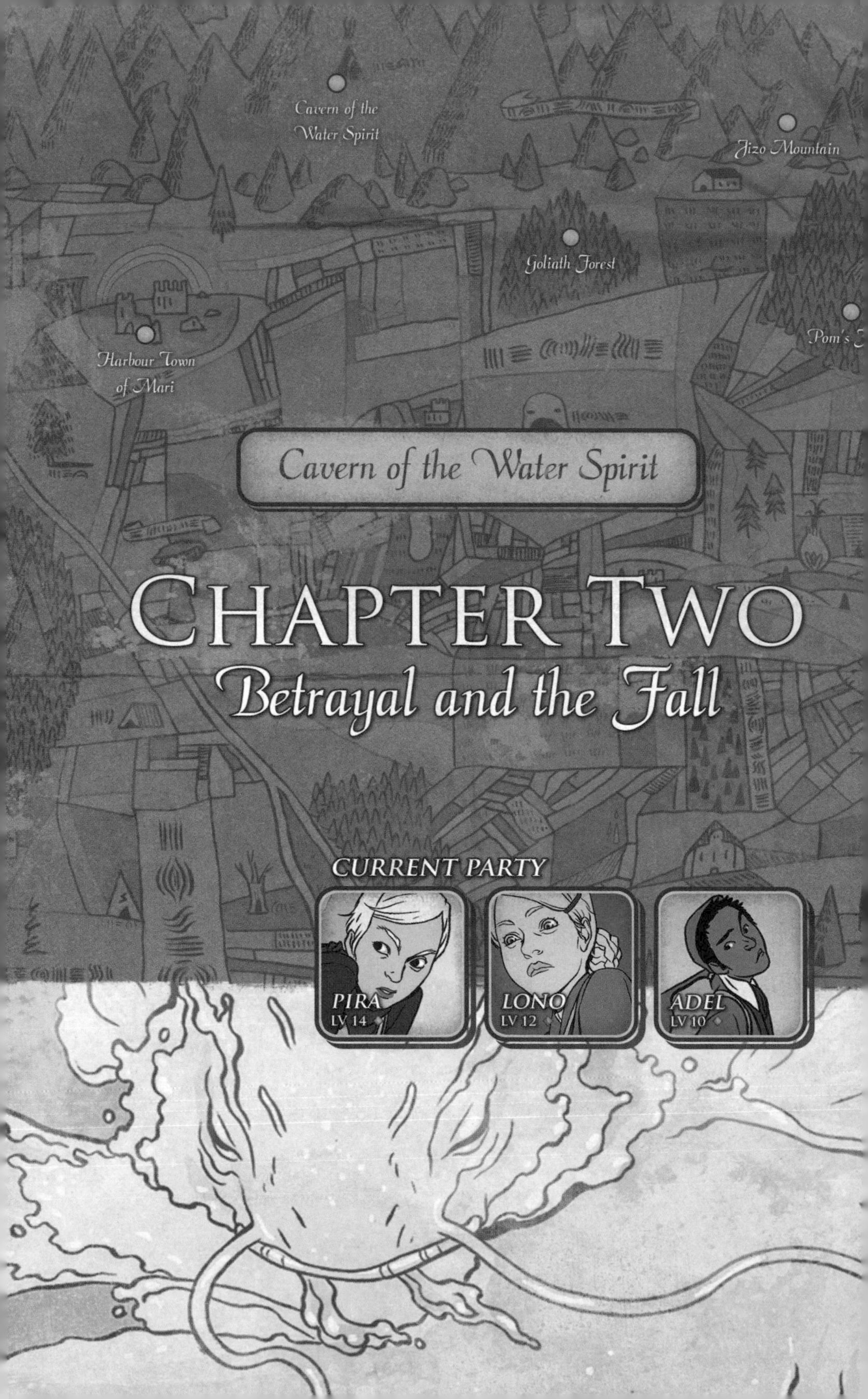
Cavern of the Water Spirit
Jizo Mountain
Goliath Forest
Harbour Town of Mari
CURRENT PARTY
PIRA LV 14
LONO LV 12
ADEL LV 10

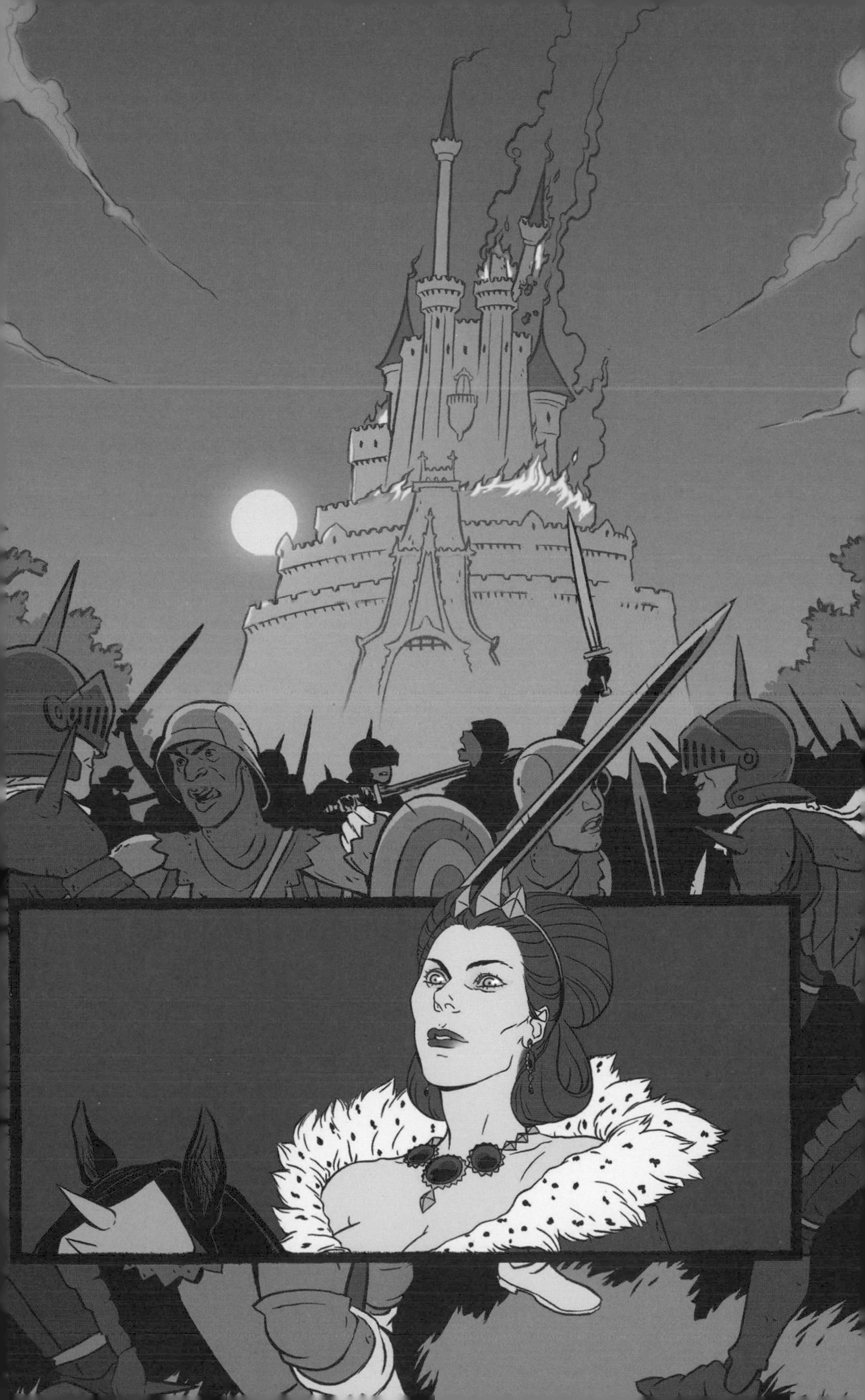

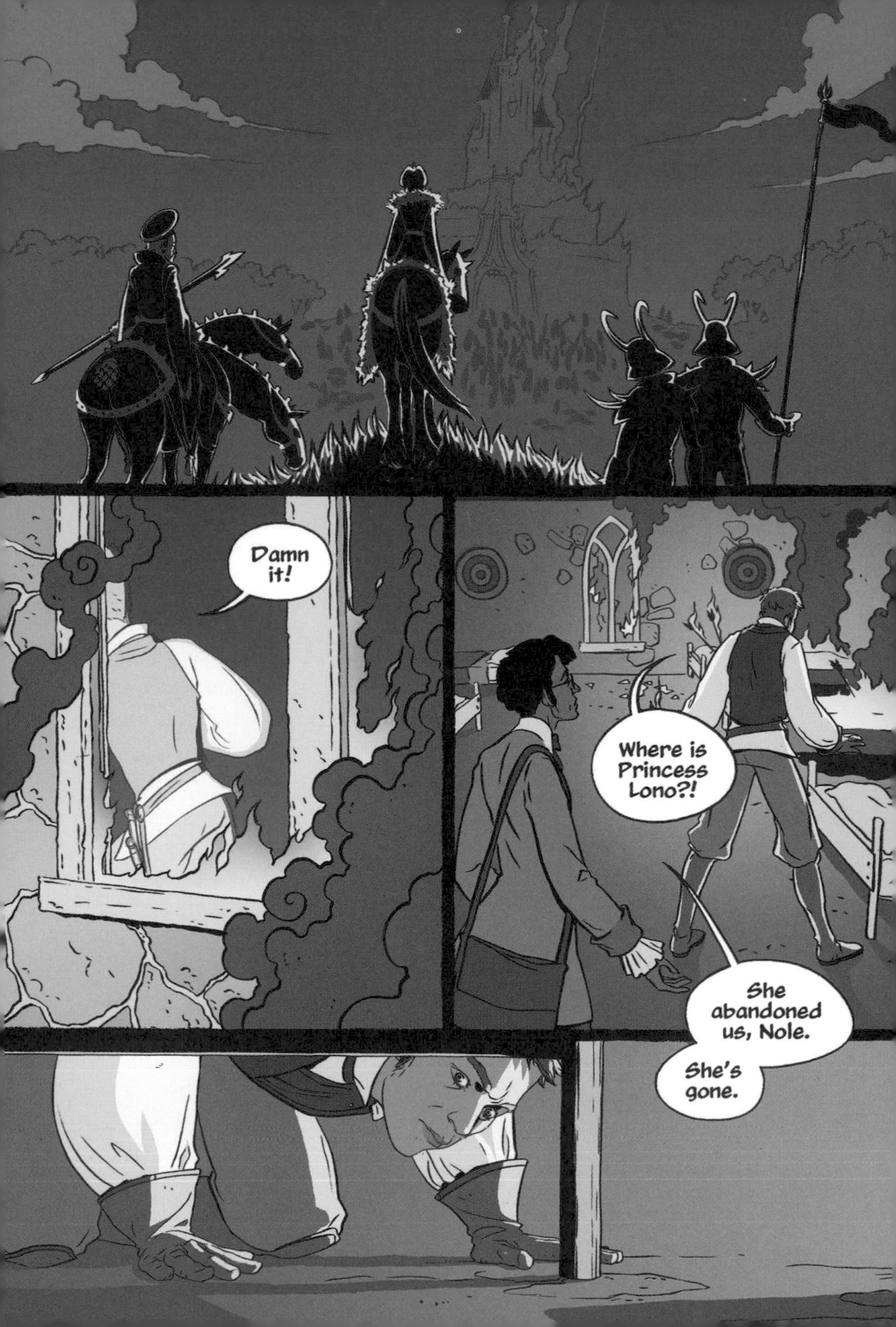
Damn it!
Where is Princess Lono?!
She abandoned us, Nole.
She's gone.

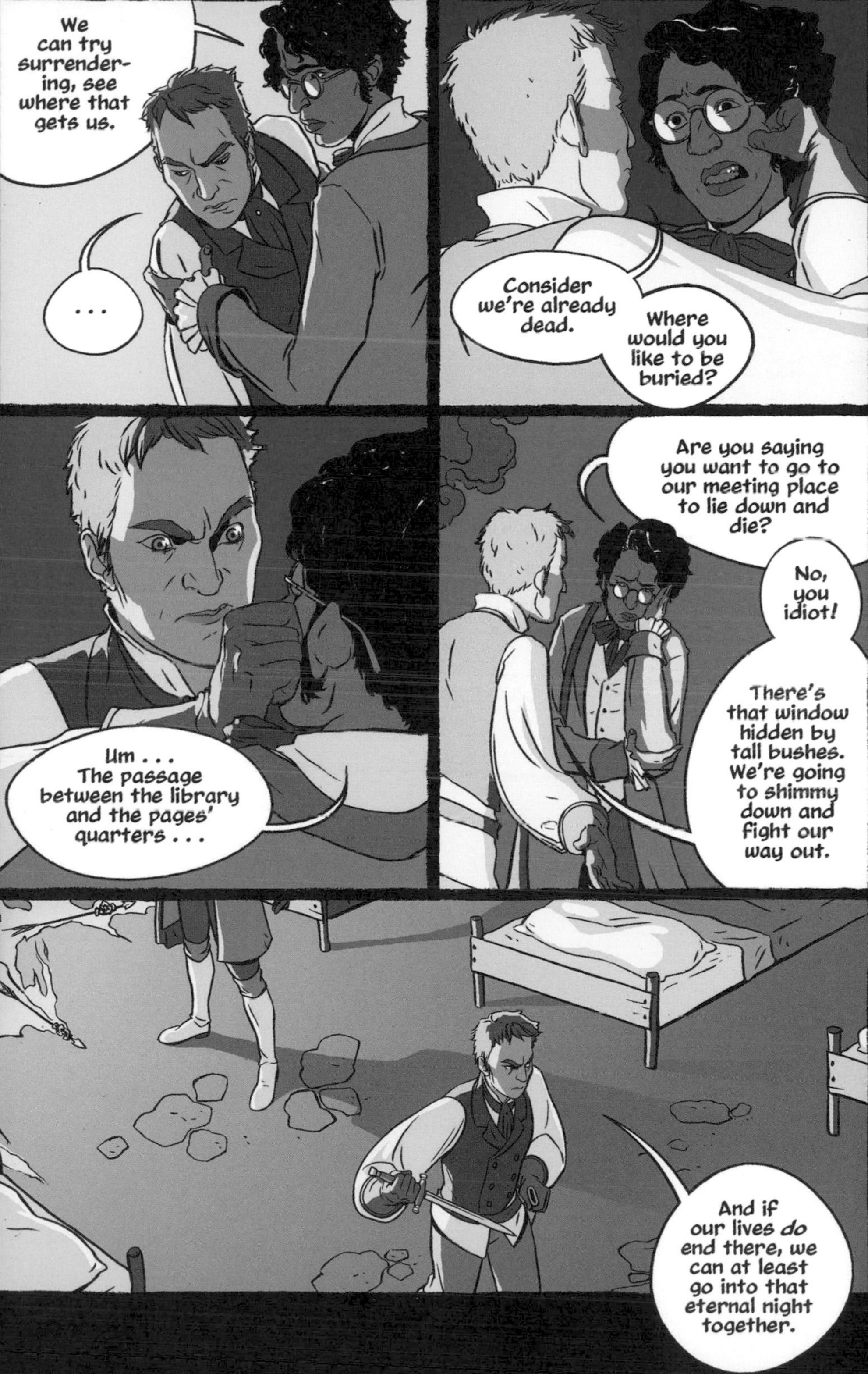
We can try surrendering, see where that gets us.
. . .
Consider we're already dead.
Where would you like to be buried?
Um . . . The passage between the library and the pages' quarters . . .
Are you saying you want to go to our meeting place to lie down and die?
No, you idiot!
There's that window hidden by tall bushes. We're going to shimmy down and fight our way out.
And if our lives *do* end there, we can at least go into that eternal night together.

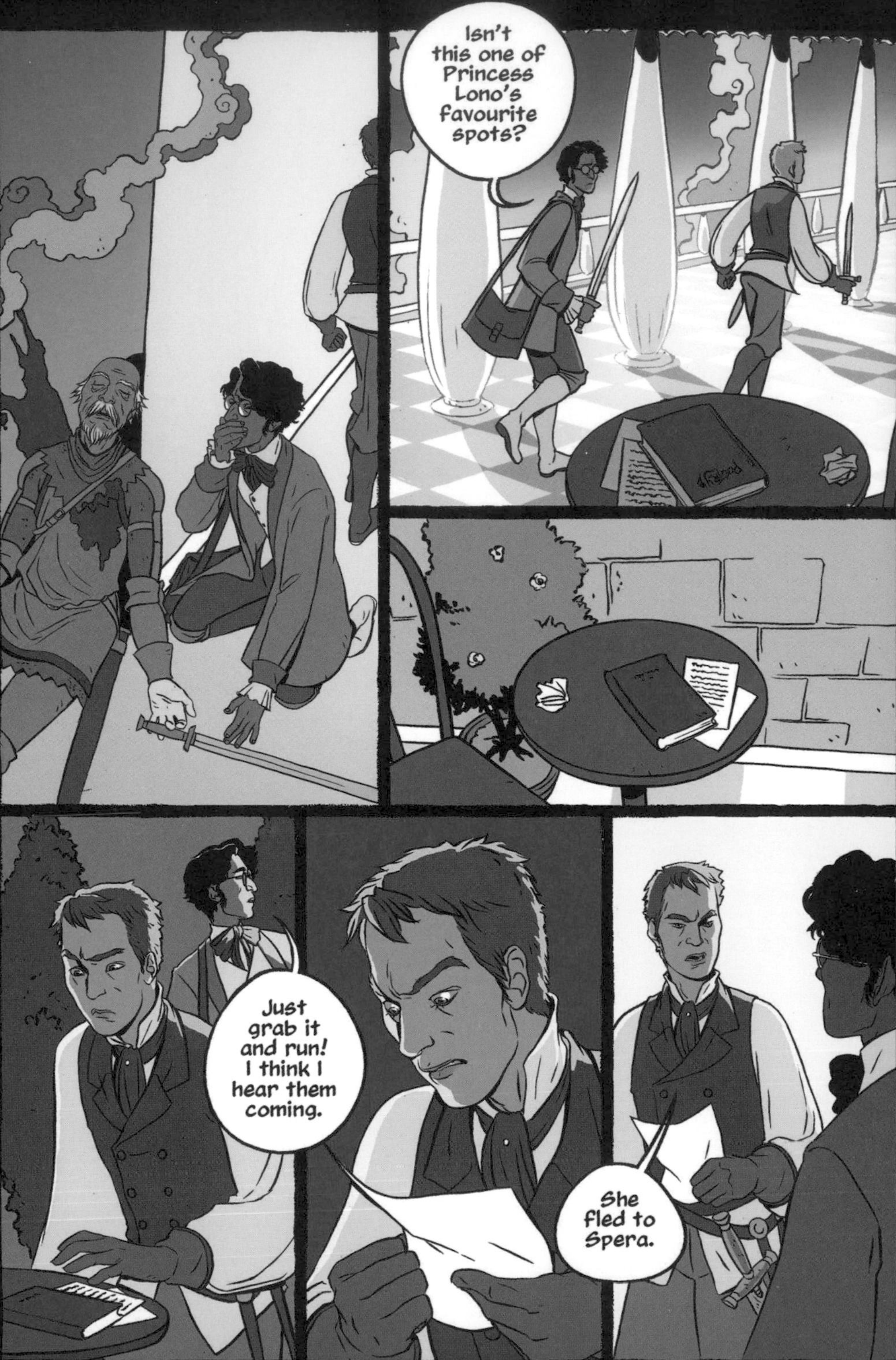
Isn't this one of Princess Lono's favourite spots?
Just grab it and run! I think I hear them coming.
She fled to Spera.

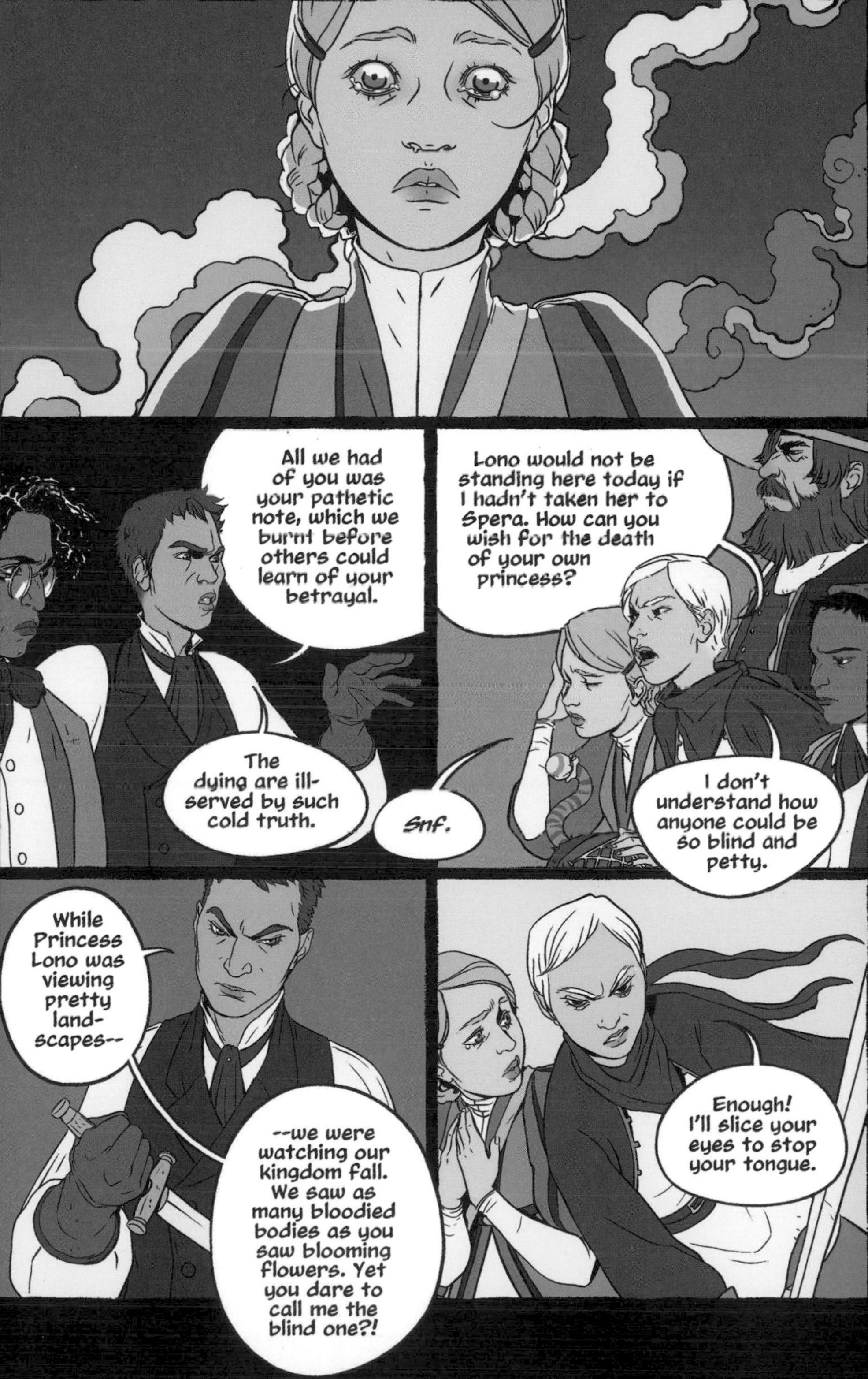
All we had of you was your pathetic note, which we burnt before others could learn of your betrayal.
The dying are ill-served by such cold truth.
Snf.
Lono would not be standing here today if I hadn't taken her to Spera. How can you wish for the death of your own princess?
I don't understand how anyone could be so blind and petty.
While Princess Lono was viewing pretty land-scapes--
--we were watching our kingdom fall. We saw as many bloodied bodies as you saw blooming flowers. Yet you dare to call me the blind one?!
Enough! I'll slice your eyes to stop your tongue.

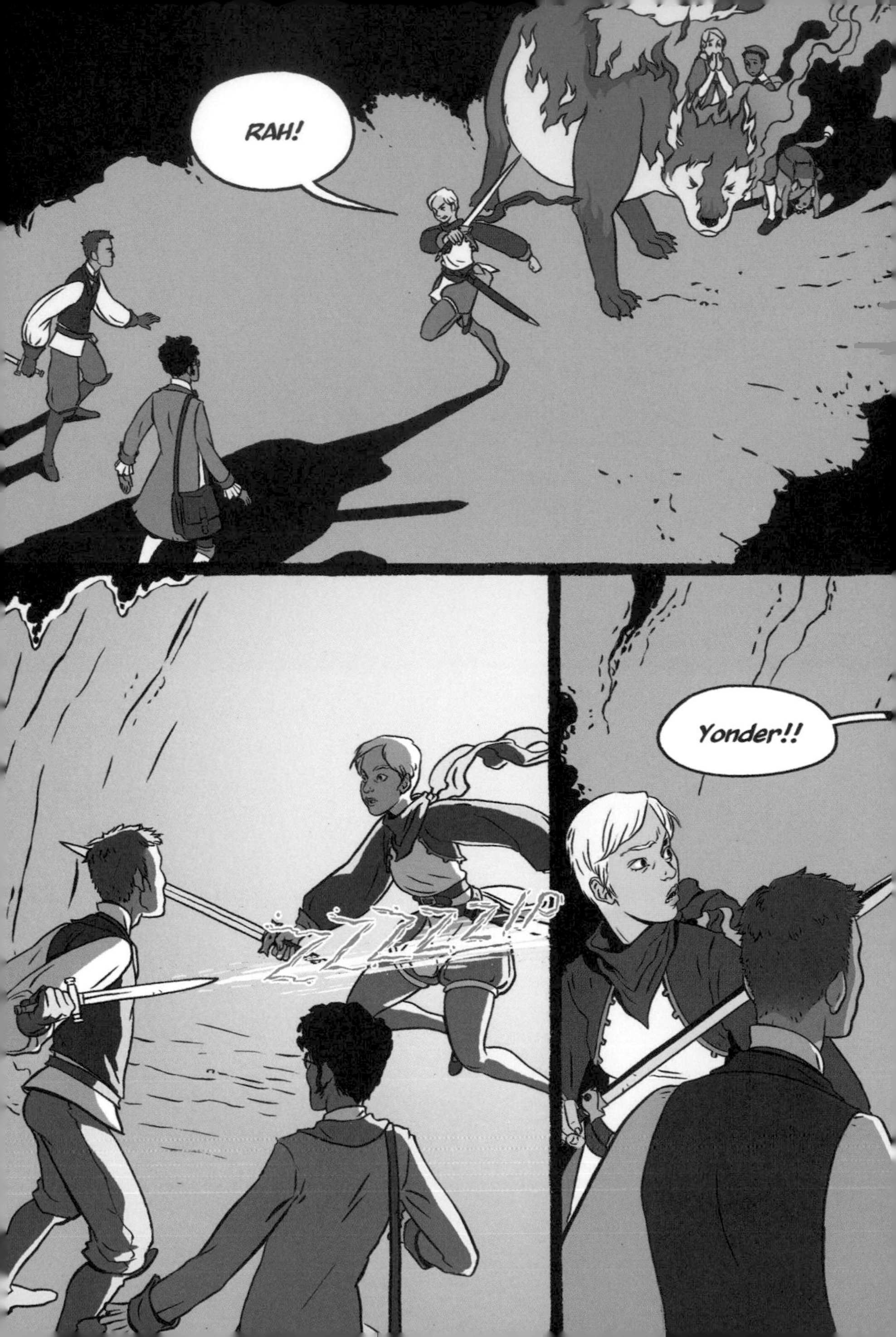
RAH!
ZZZZIP
Yonder!!

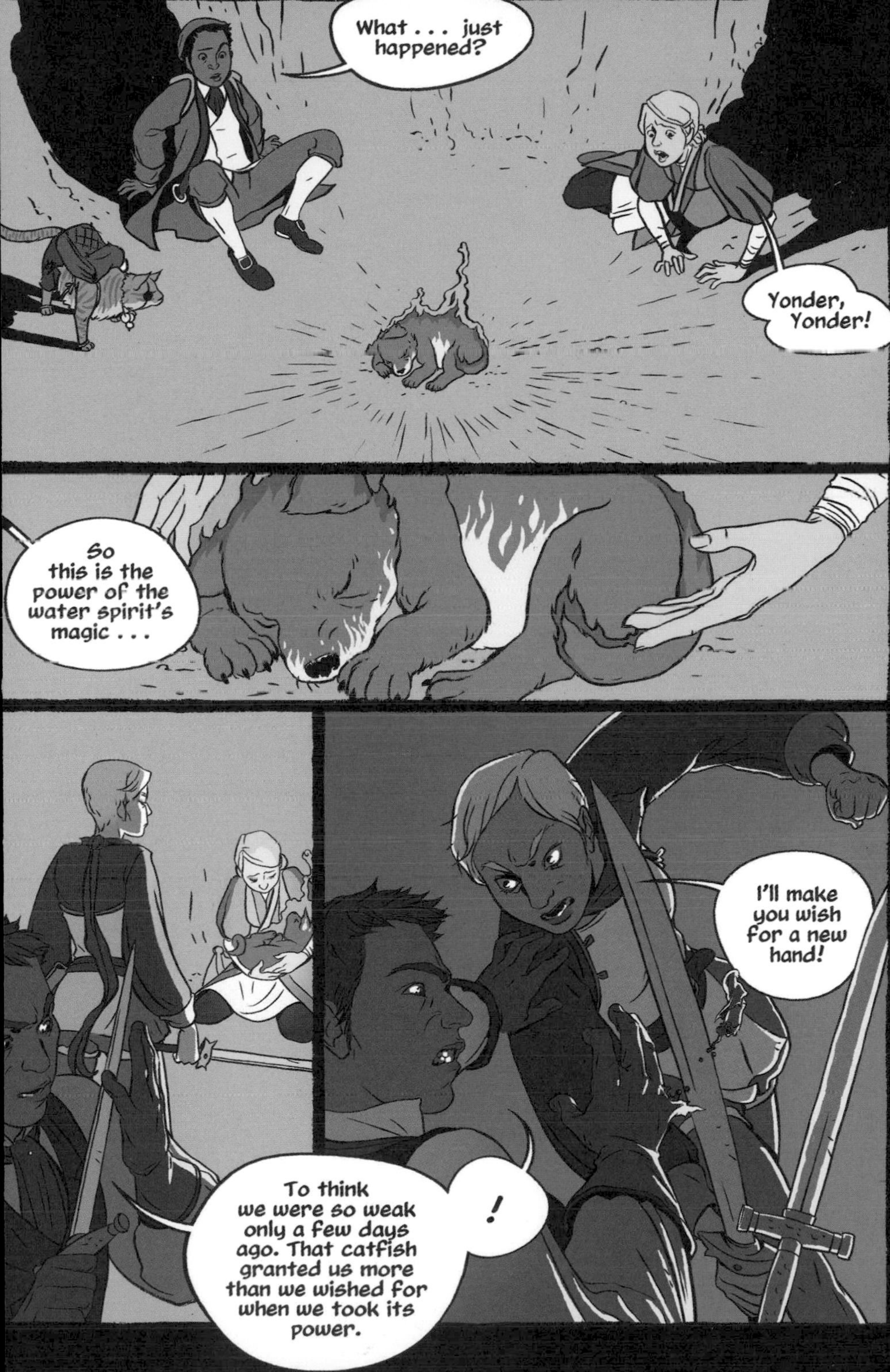
What . . . just happened?
Yonder, Yonder!
So this is the power of the water spirit's magic . . .
I'll make you wish for a new hand!
!
To think we were so weak only a few days ago. That catfish granted us more than we wished for when we took its power.

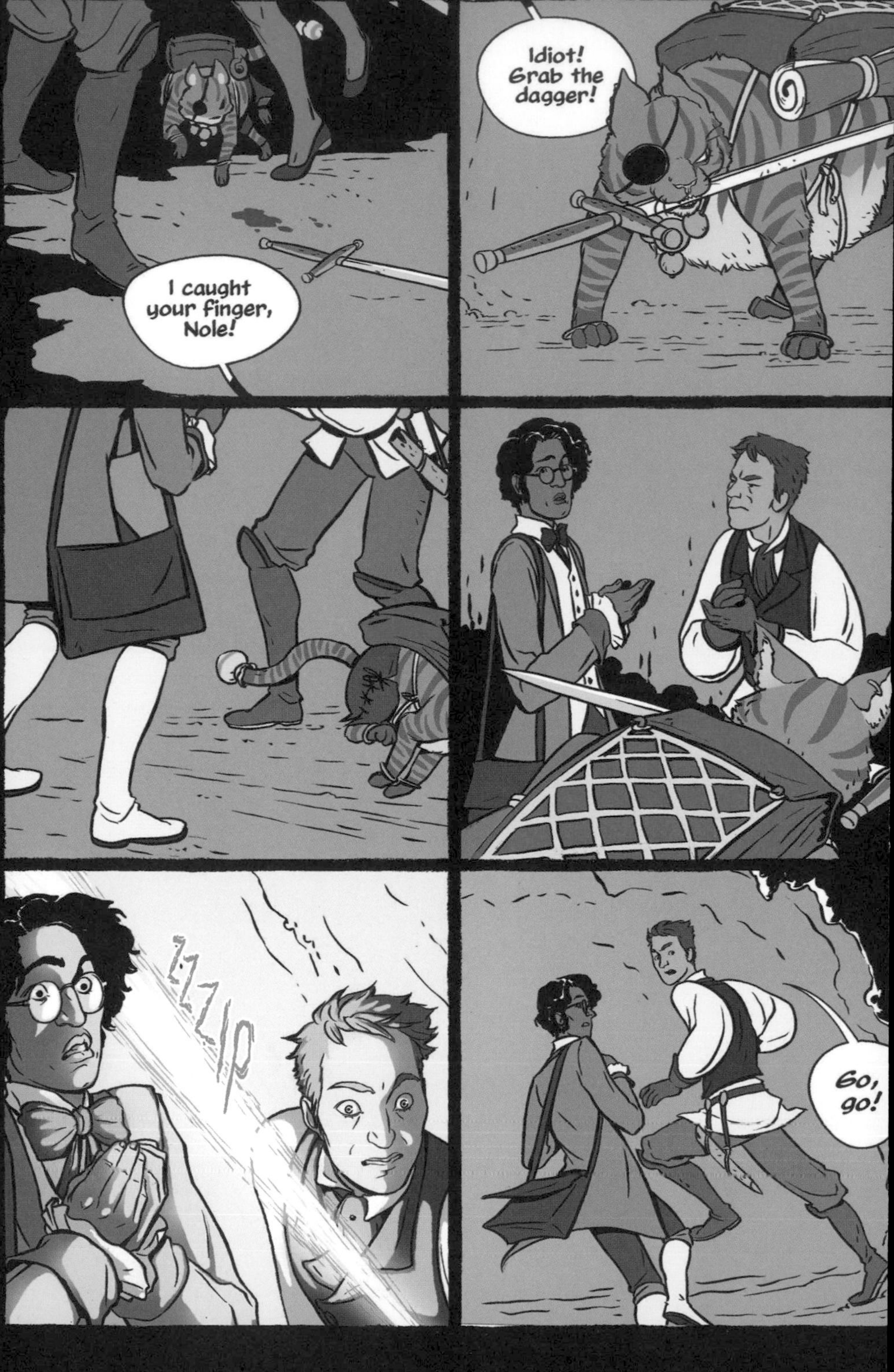
I caught your finger, Nole!
Idiot! Grab the dagger!
ZZZIP
Go, go!

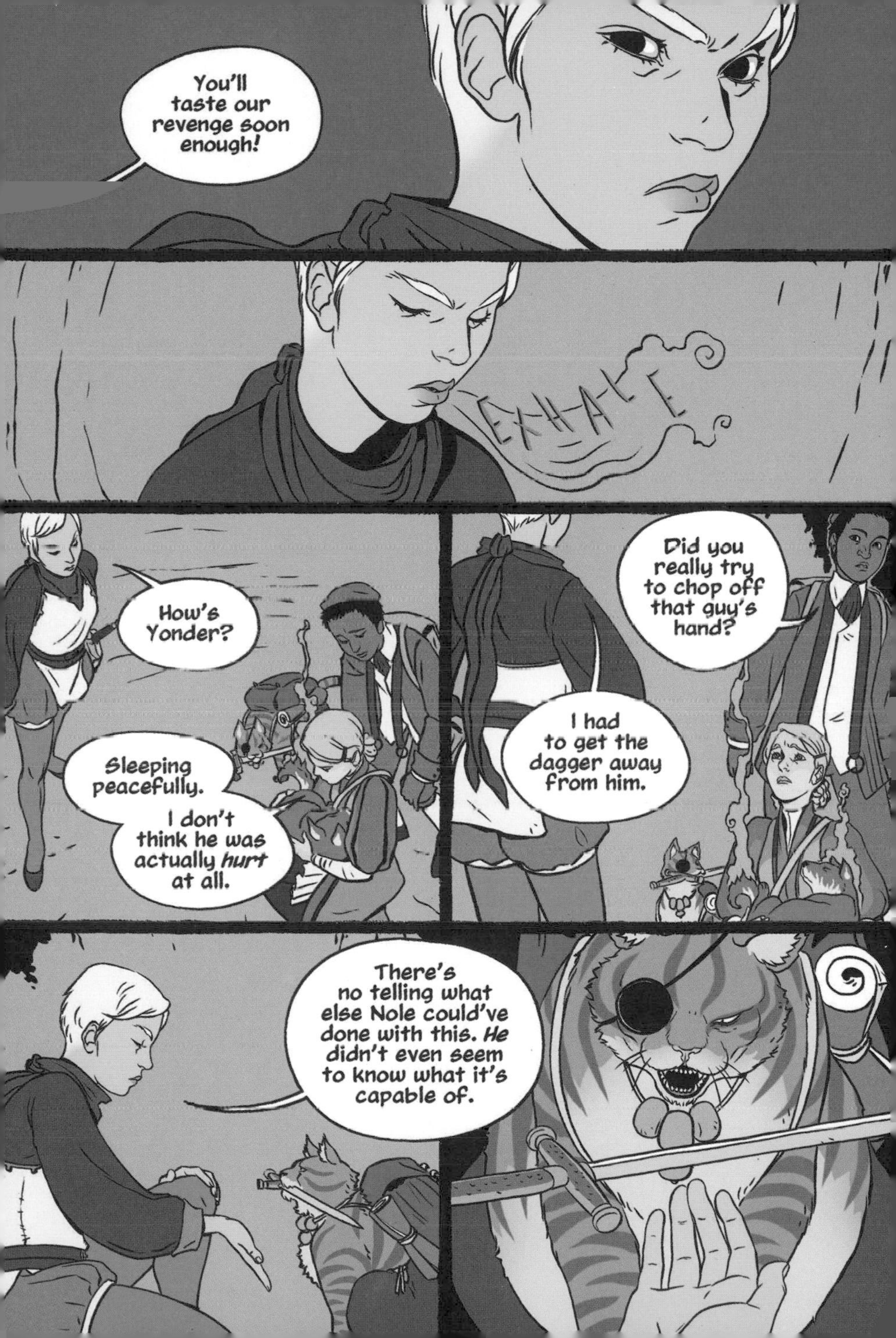
You'll taste our revenge soon enough!
EXHALE
How's Yonder?
Sleeping peacefully.
I don't think he was actually *hurt* at all.
Did you really try to chop off that guy's hand?
I had to get the dagger away from him.
There's no telling what else Nole could've done with this. *He* didn't even seem to know what it's capable of.

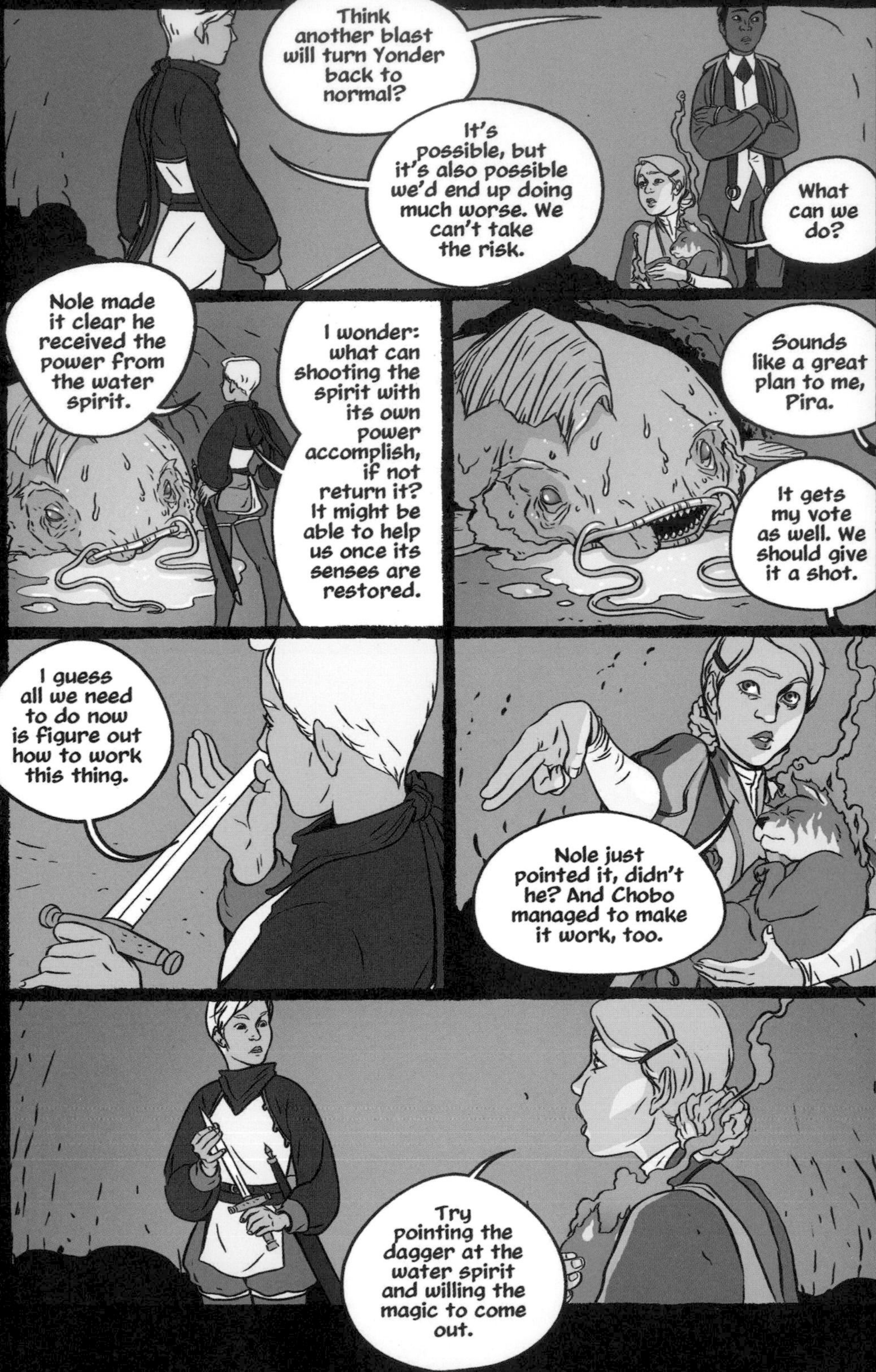

Think another blast will turn Yonder back to normal?
It's possible, but it's also possible we'd end up doing much worse. We can't take the risk.
What can we do?
Nole made it clear he received the power from the water spirit.
I wonder: what can shooting the spirit with its own power accomplish, if not return it? It might be able to help us once its senses are restored.
Sounds like a great plan to me, Pira.
It gets my vote as well. We should give it a shot.
I guess all we need to do now is figure out how to work this thing.
Nole just pointed it, didn't he? And Chobo managed to make it work, too.
Try pointing the dagger at the water spirit and willing the magic to come out.

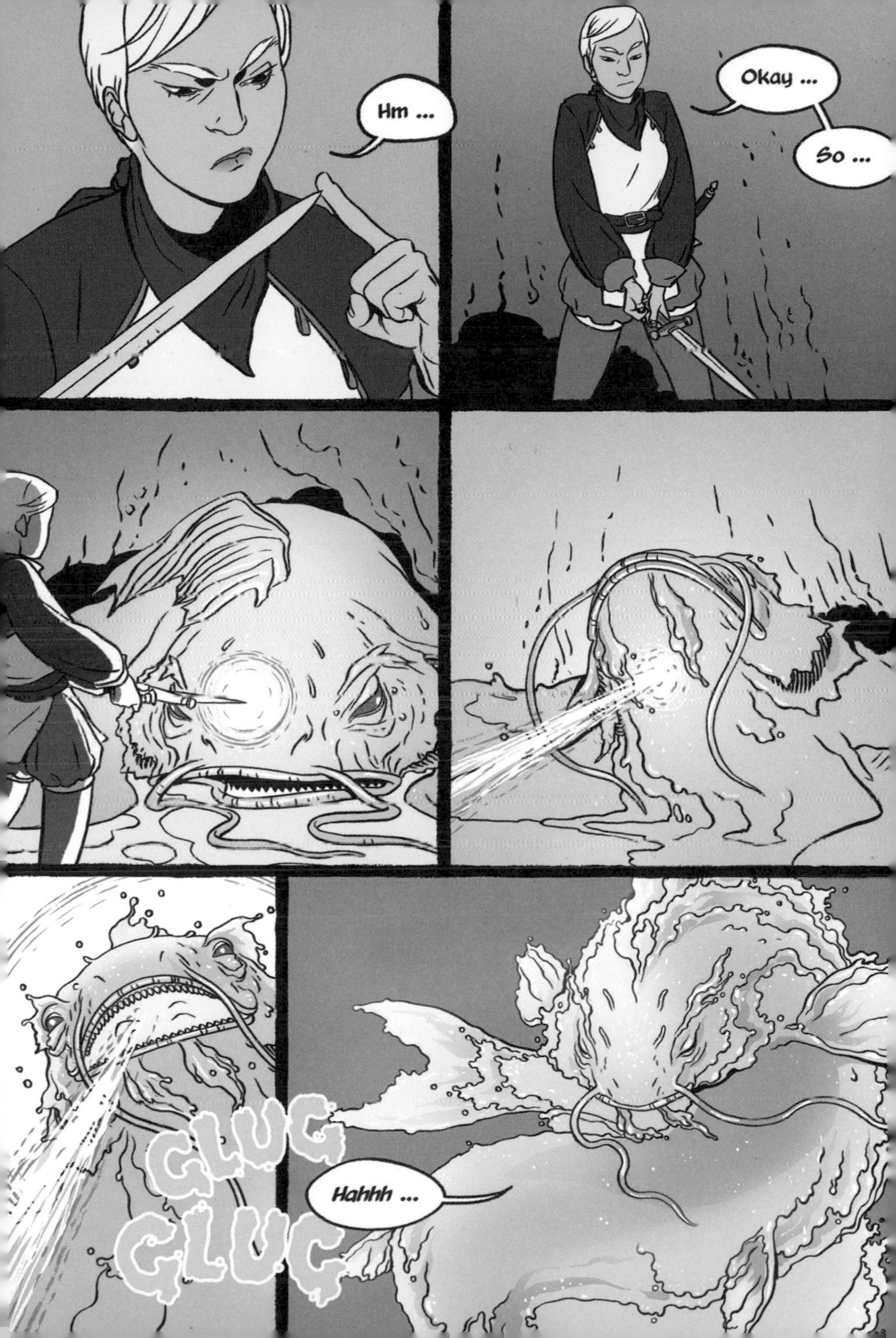
Hm ...
Okay ...
So ...
GLUG
GLUG
Hahhh ...

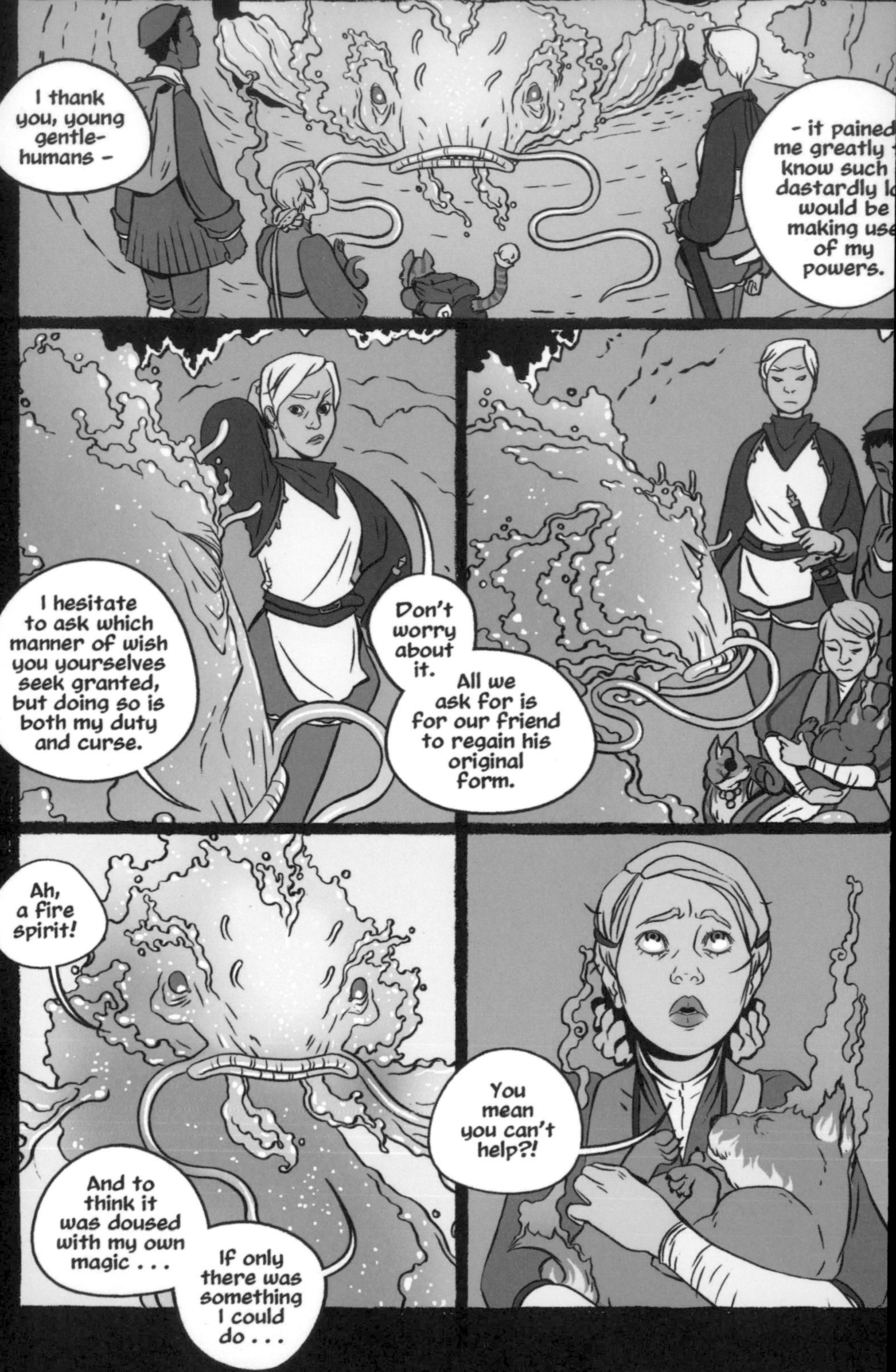
I thank you, young gentle-humans -
- it paine me greatly know such dastardly l would be making us of my powers.
I hesitate to ask which manner of wish you yourselves seek granted, but doing so is both my duty and curse.
Don't worry about it.
All we ask for is for our friend to regain his original form.
Ah, a fire spirit!
You mean you can't help?!
And to think it was doused with my own magic . . .
If only there was something I could do . . .

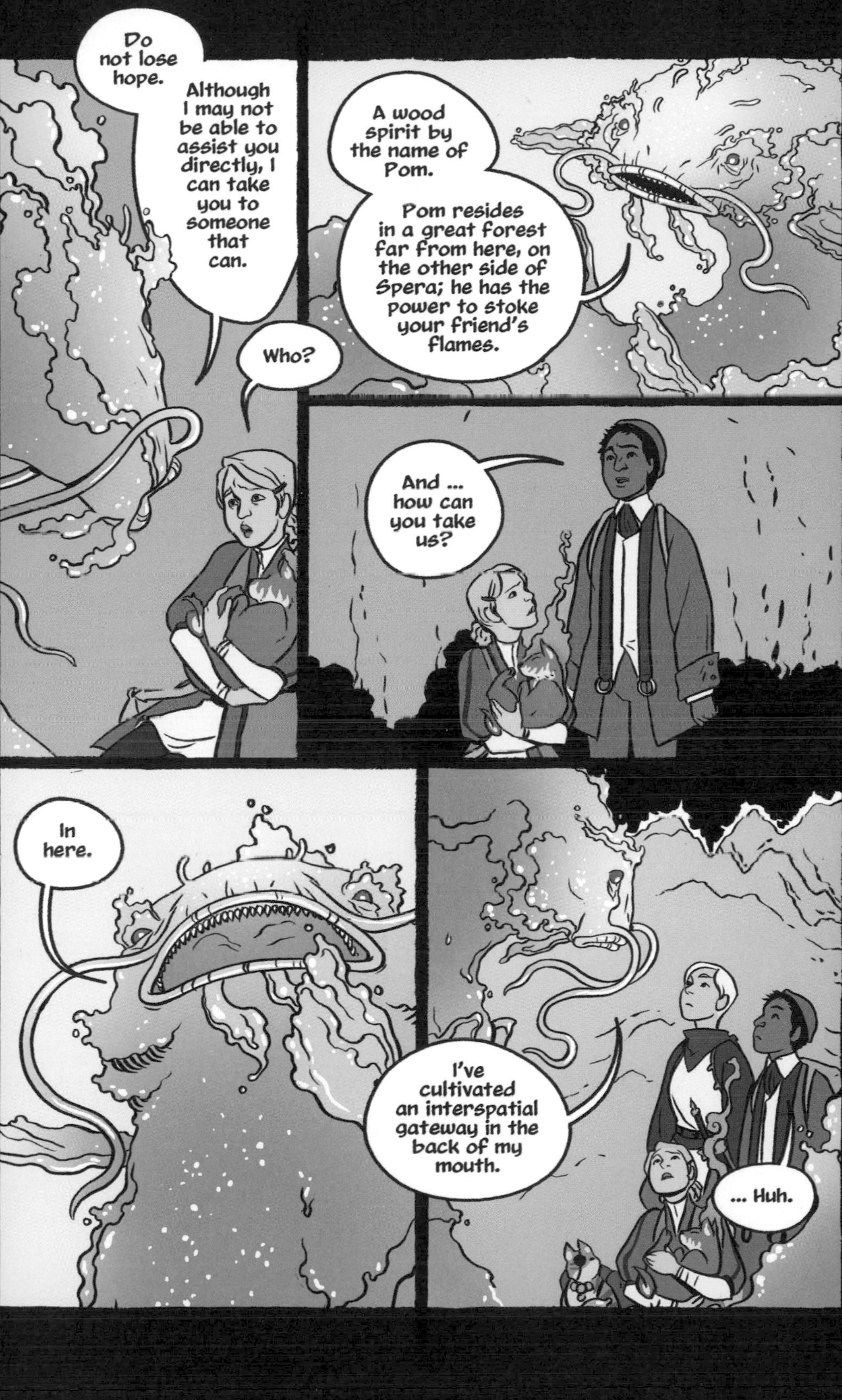
Do not lose hope.
Although I may not be able to assist you directly, I can take you to someone that can.
Who?
A wood spirit by the name of Pom.
Pom resides in a great forest far from here, on the other side of Spera; he has the power to stoke your friend's flames.
And ... how can you take us?
In here.
I've cultivated an interspatial gateway in the back of my mouth.
... Huh.

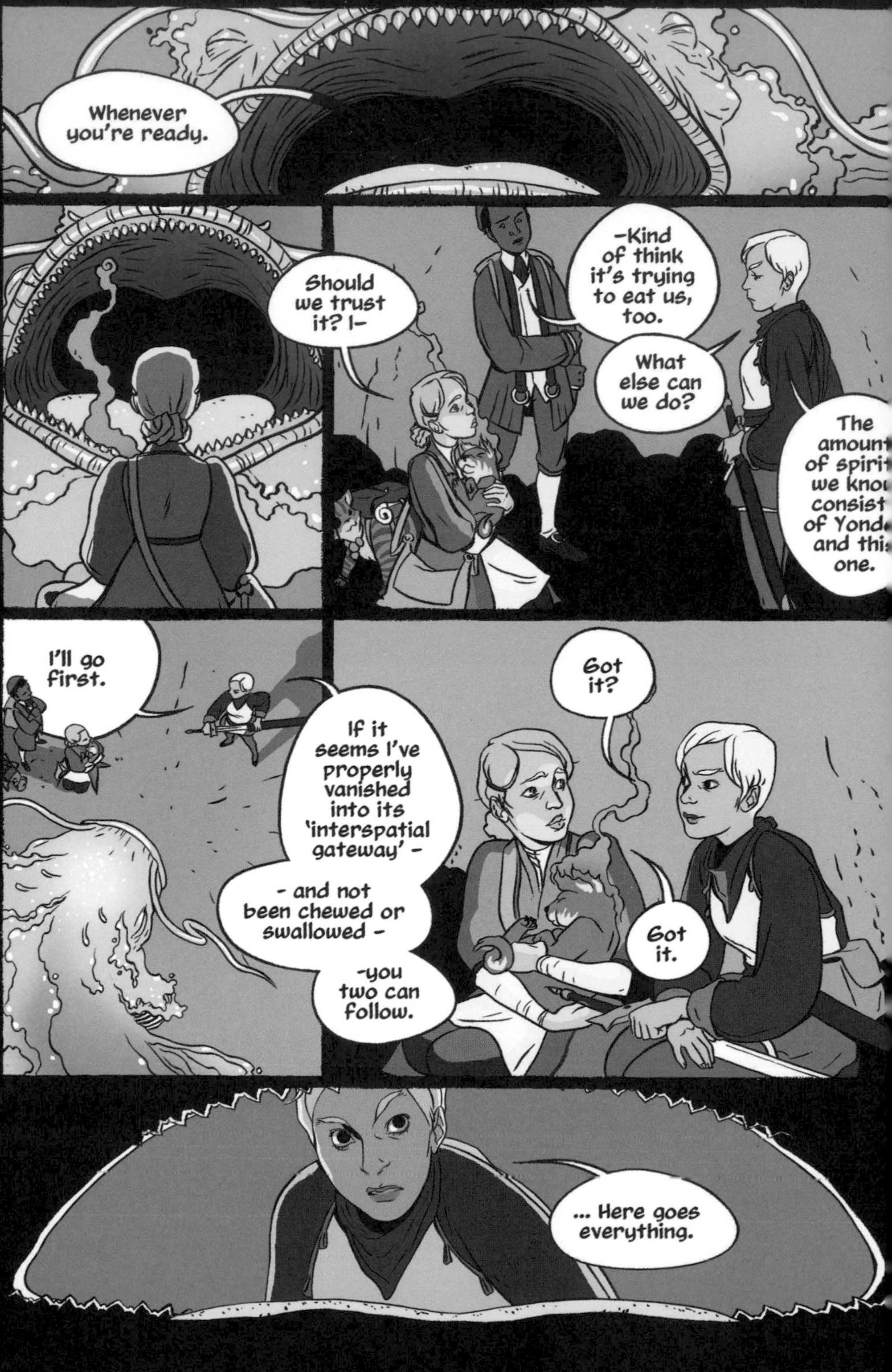
Whenever you're ready.
Should we trust it? I–
–Kind of think it's trying to eat us, too.
What else can we do?
The amount of spirit we know consists of Yond and this one.
I'll go first.
If it seems I've properly vanished into its 'interspatial gateway' –
– and not been chewed or swallowed –
–you two can follow.
Got it?
Got it.
... Here goes everything.

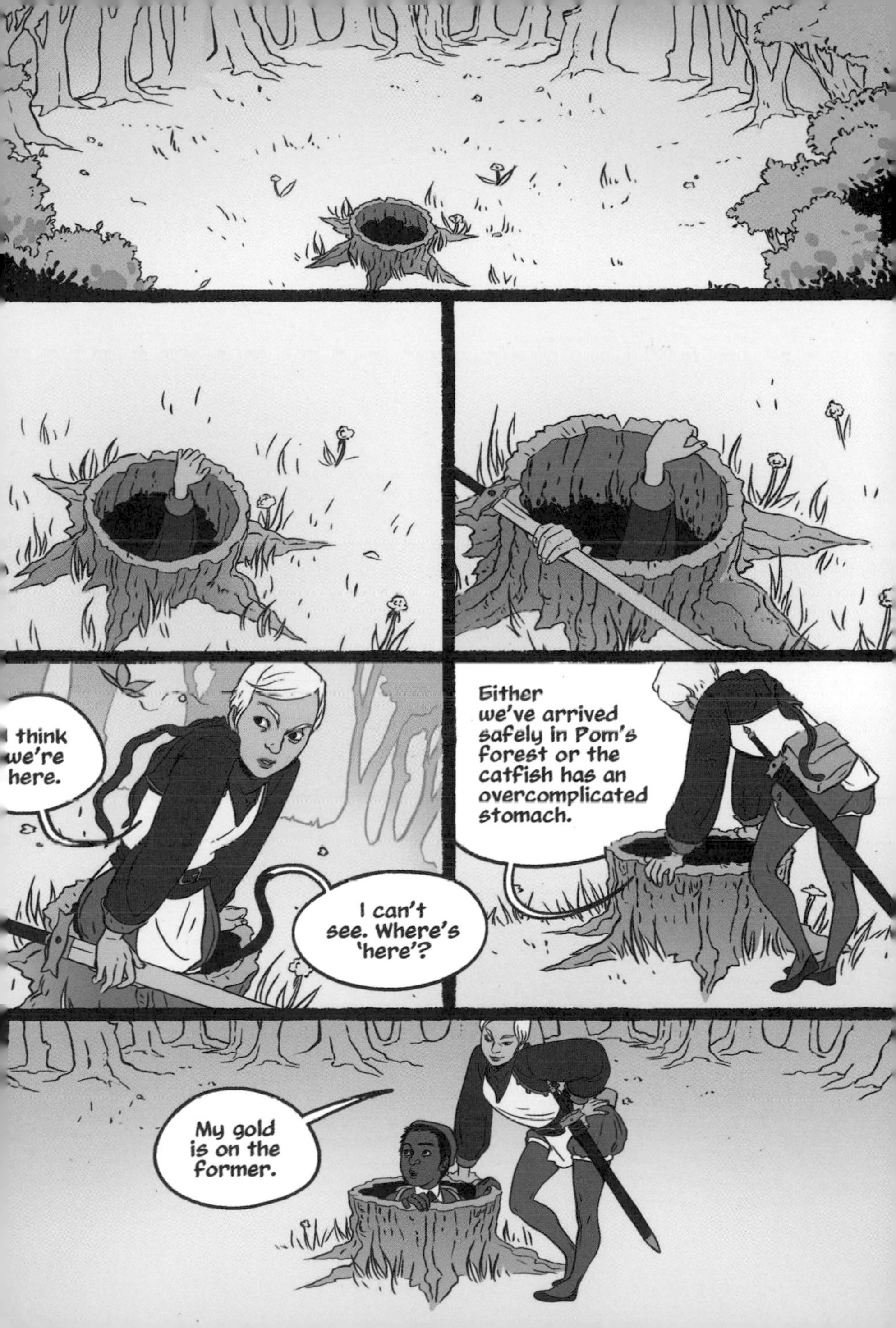

think we're here.
I can't see. Where's 'here'?
Either we've arrived safely in Pom's forest or the catfish has an overcomplicated stomach.
My gold is on the former.

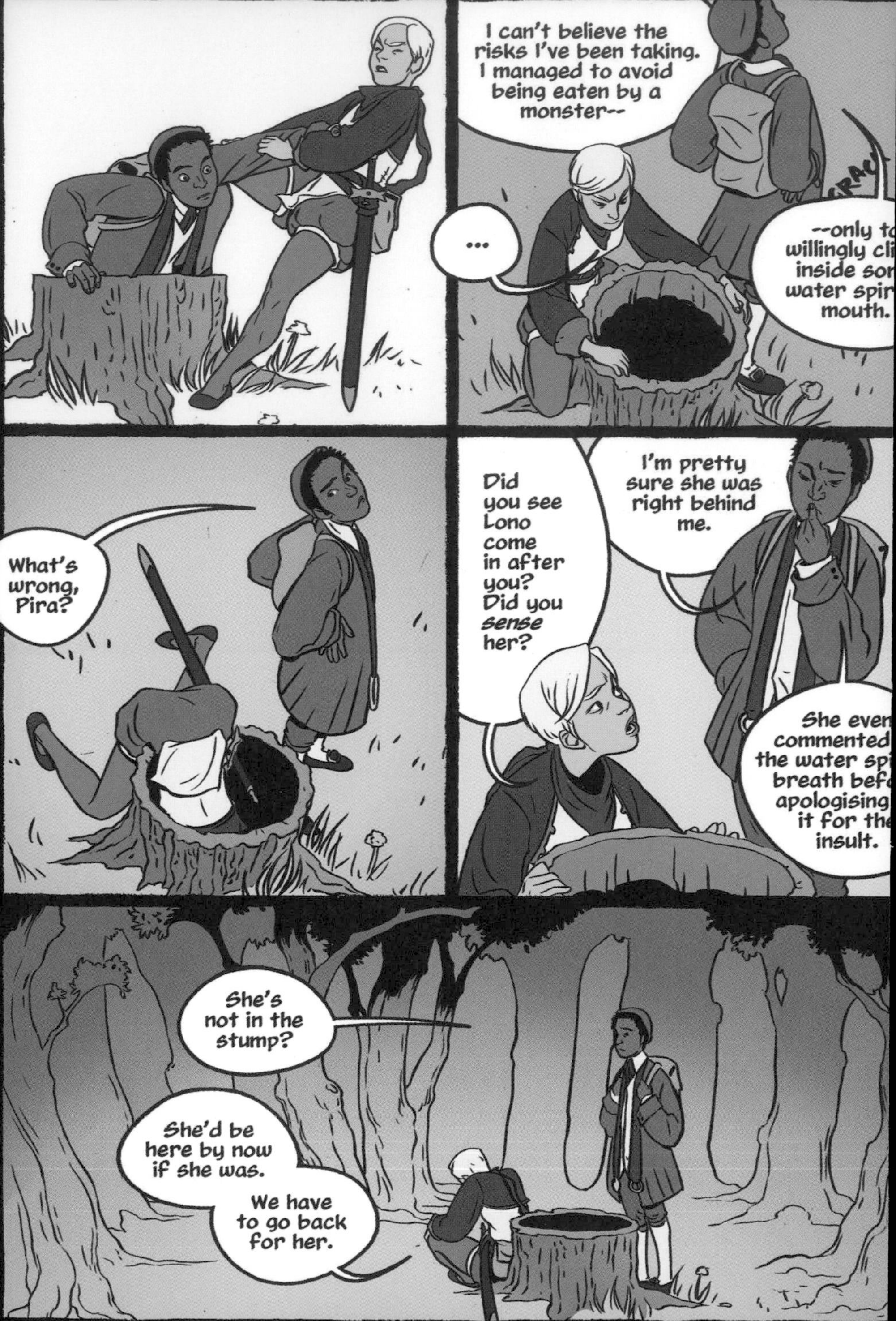

I can't believe the risks I've been taking. I managed to avoid being eaten by a monster--
...
--only t
willingly cl
inside so
water spir
mouth.
What's wrong, Pira?
Did you see Lono come in after you? Did you *sense* her?
I'm pretty sure she was right behind me.
She eve
commented
the water sp
breath bef
apologising
it for th
insult.
She's not in the stump?
She'd be here by now if she was.
We have to go back for her.

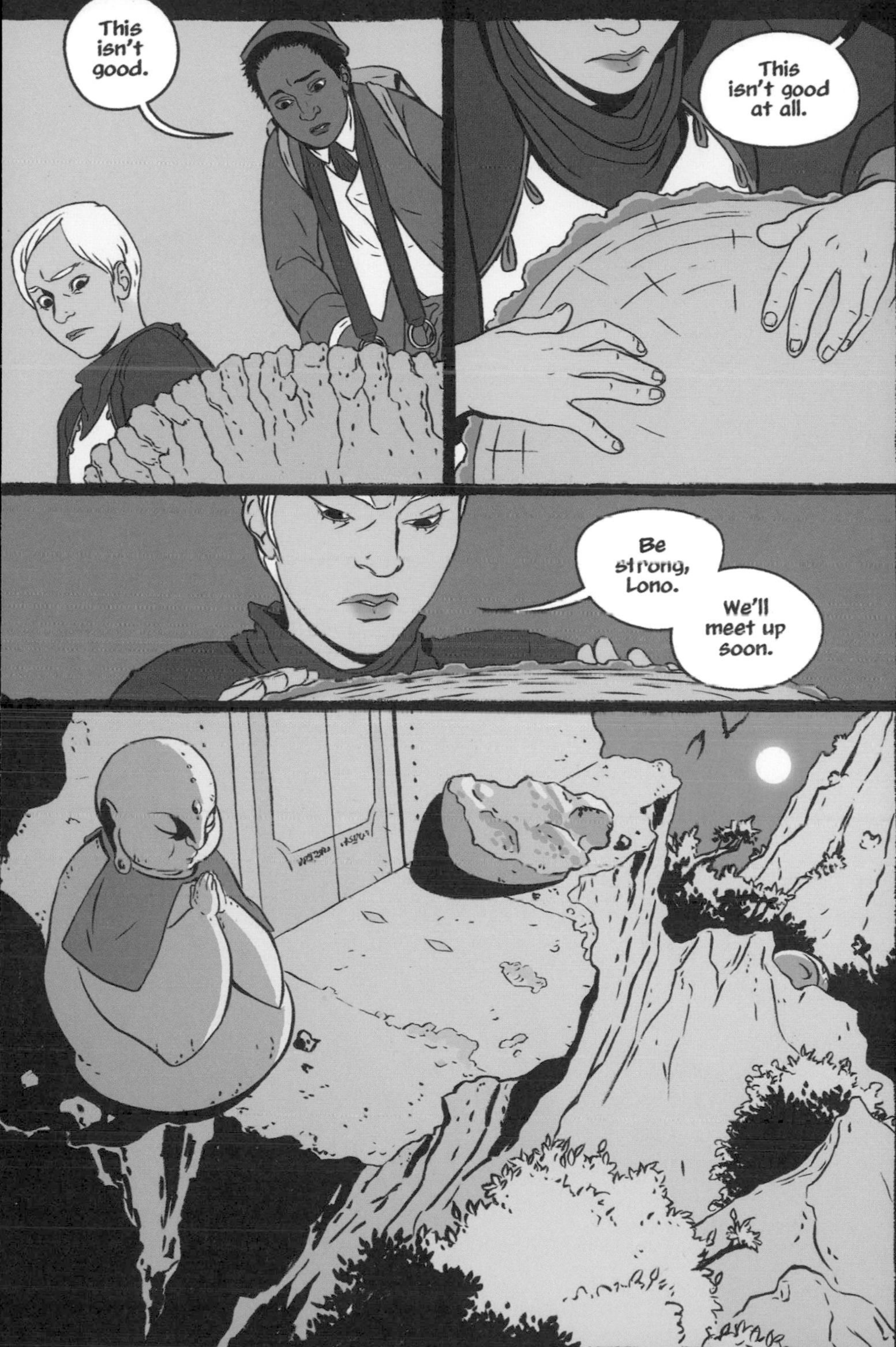
This isn't good.
This isn't good at all.
Be strong, Lono.
We'll meet up soon.

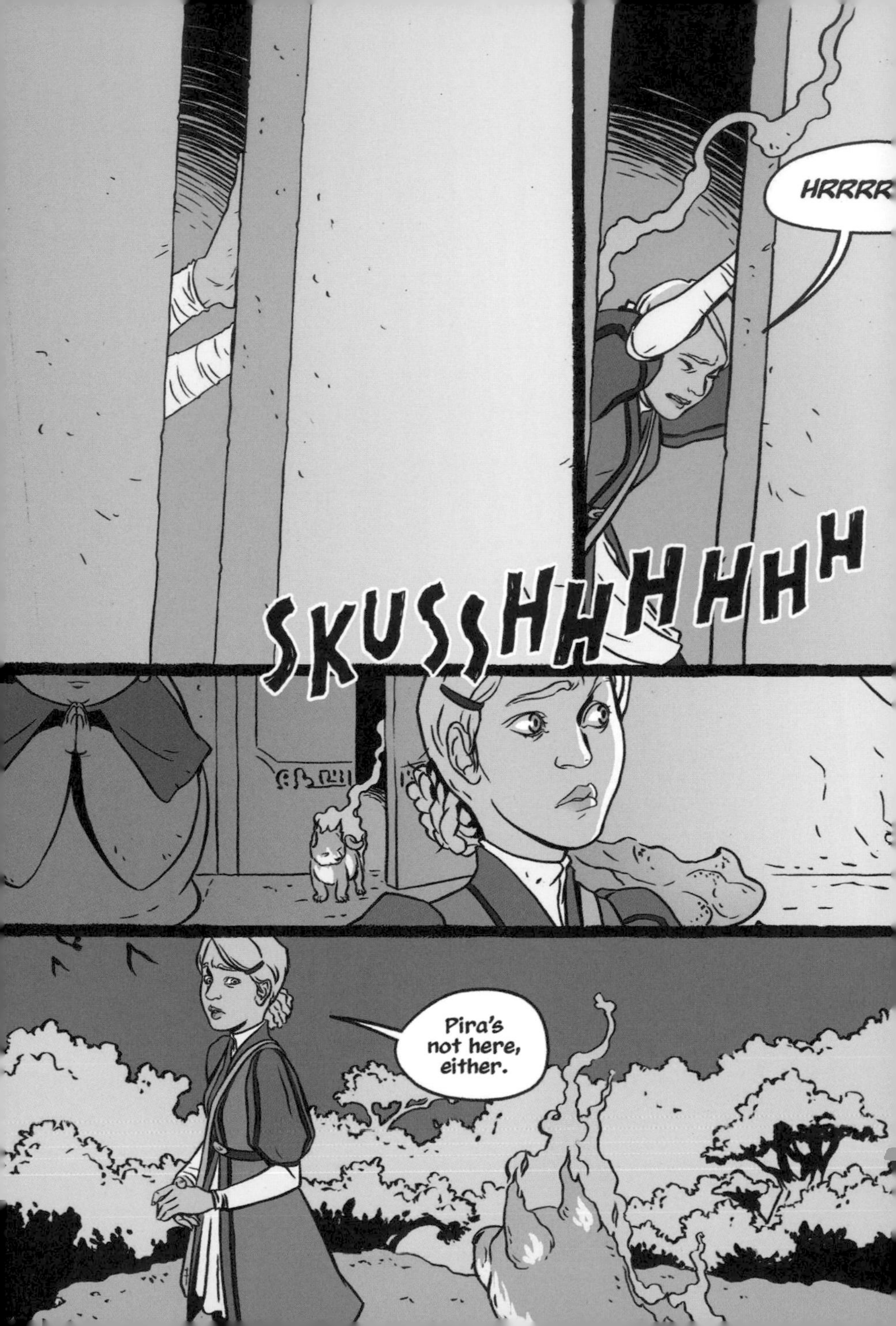
HRRRR
SKUSSHHHHHHH
Pira's not here, either.

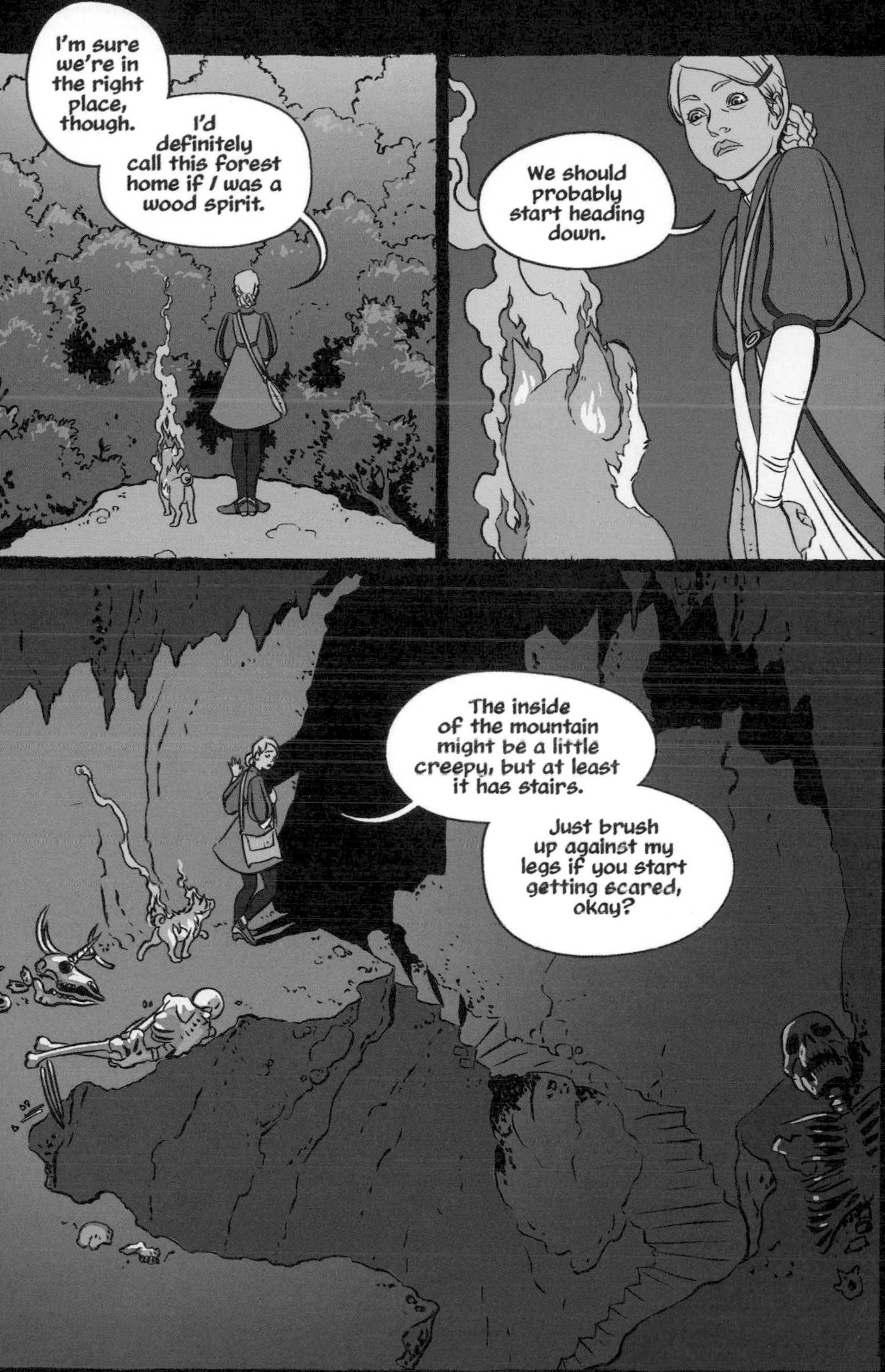

I'm sure we're in the right place, though.
I'd definitely call this forest home if I was a wood spirit.
We should probably start heading down.
The inside of the mountain might be a little creepy, but at least it has stairs.
Just brush up against my legs if you start getting scared, okay?

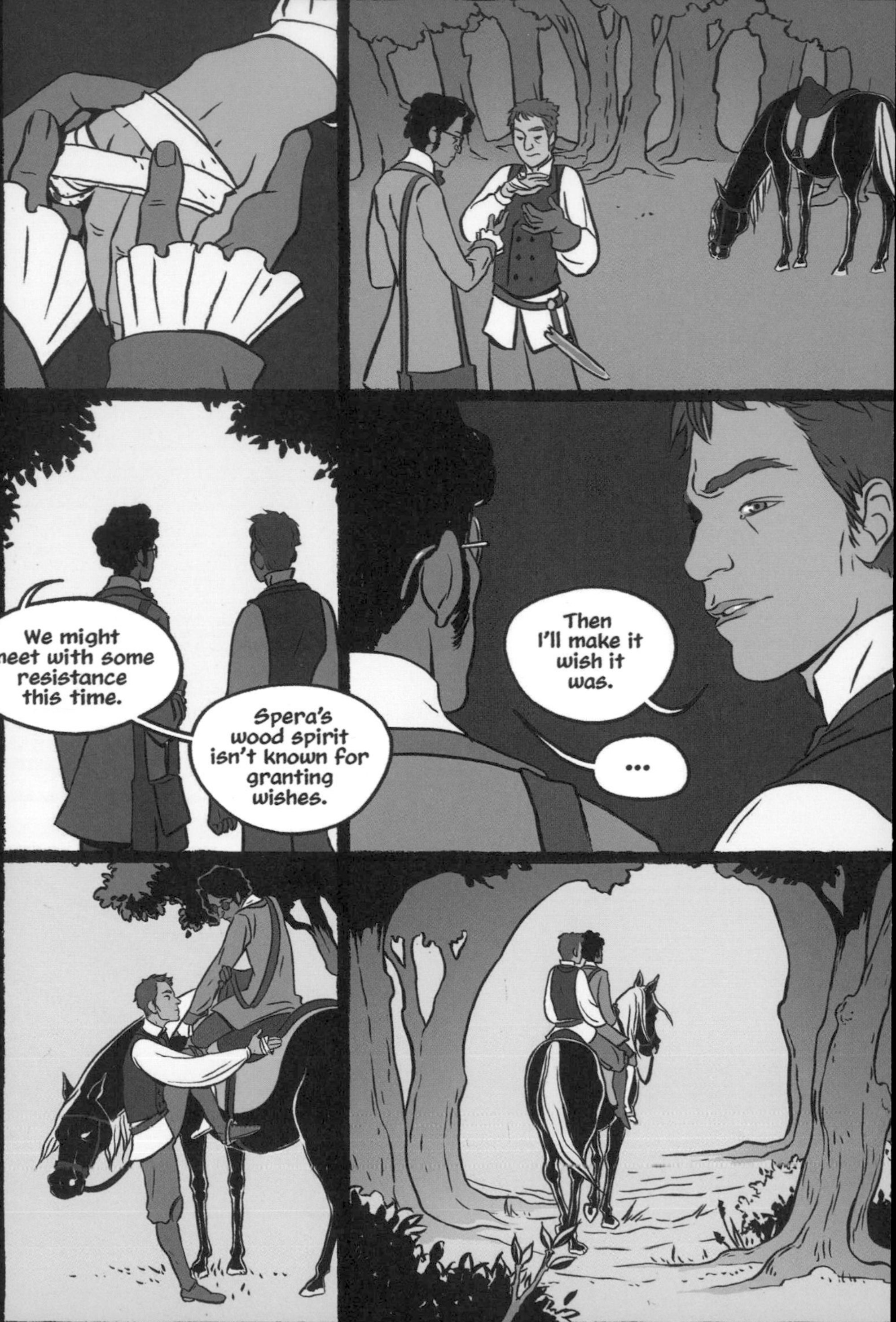
We might meet with some resistance this time.
Spera's wood spirit isn't known for granting wishes.
Then I'll make it wish it was.
...

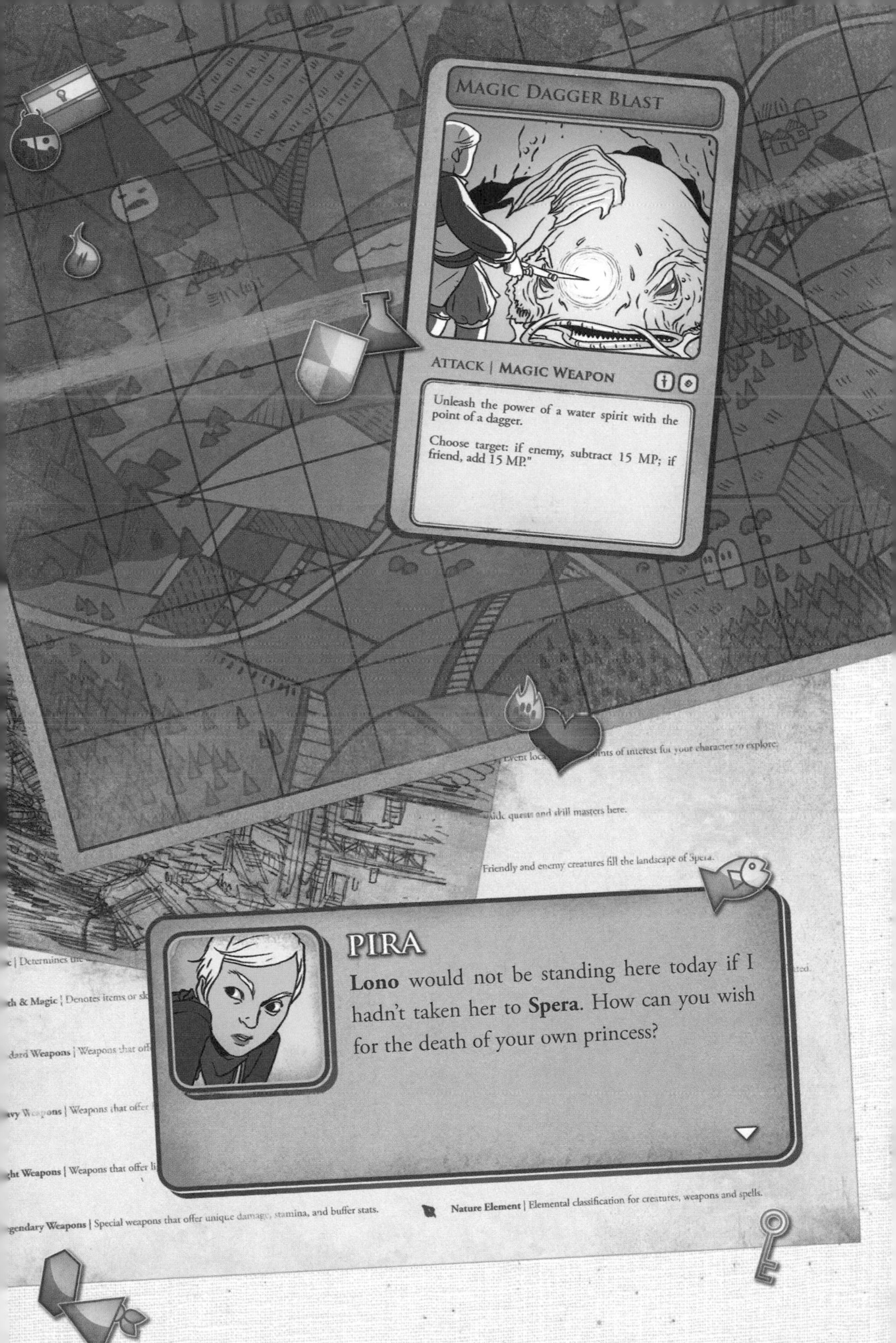
Magic Dagger Blast
Attack | Magic Weapon
Unleash the power of a water spirit with the point of a dagger.
Choose target: if enemy, subtract 15 MP; if friend, add 15 MP."
points of interest for your character to explore.
side quests and skill masters here.
Friendly and enemy creatures fill the landscape of Spera.
PIRA
Lono would not be standing here today if I hadn't taken her to Spera. How can you wish for the death of your own princess?
| Determines the
th & Magic | Denotes items or sk
dard Weapons | Weapons that off
avy Weapons | Weapons that offer
ght Weapons | Weapons that offer li
gendary Weapons | Special weapons that offer unique damage, stamina, and buffer stats.
Nature Element | Elemental classification for creatures, weapons and spells.

Chapter Three
A Piece of the Puzzle

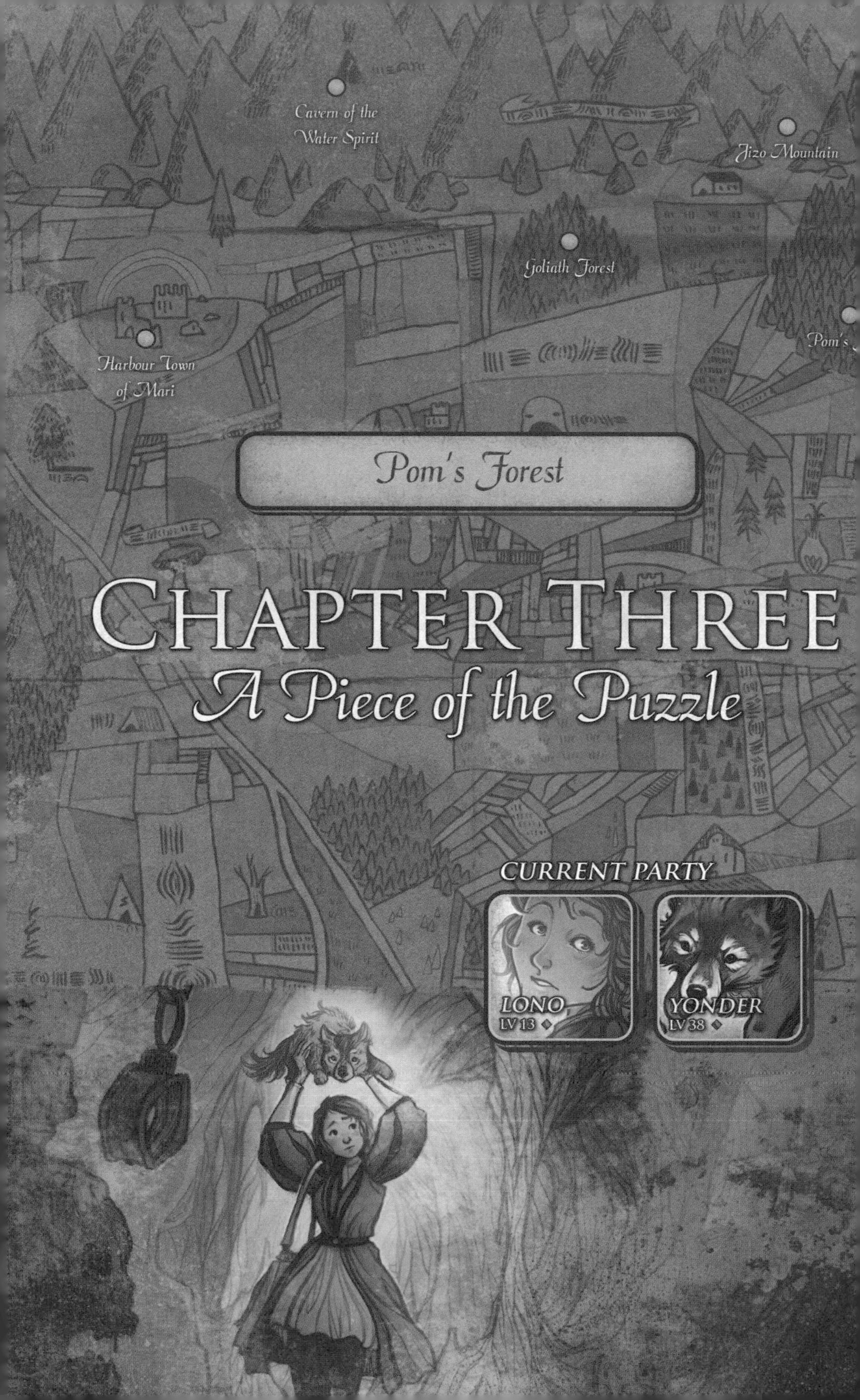
Cavern of the Water Spirit
Jizo Mountain
Goliath Forest
Pom's
Harbour Town of Mari
Pom's Forest
CURRENT PARTY
LONO
LV 13
YONDER
LV 38

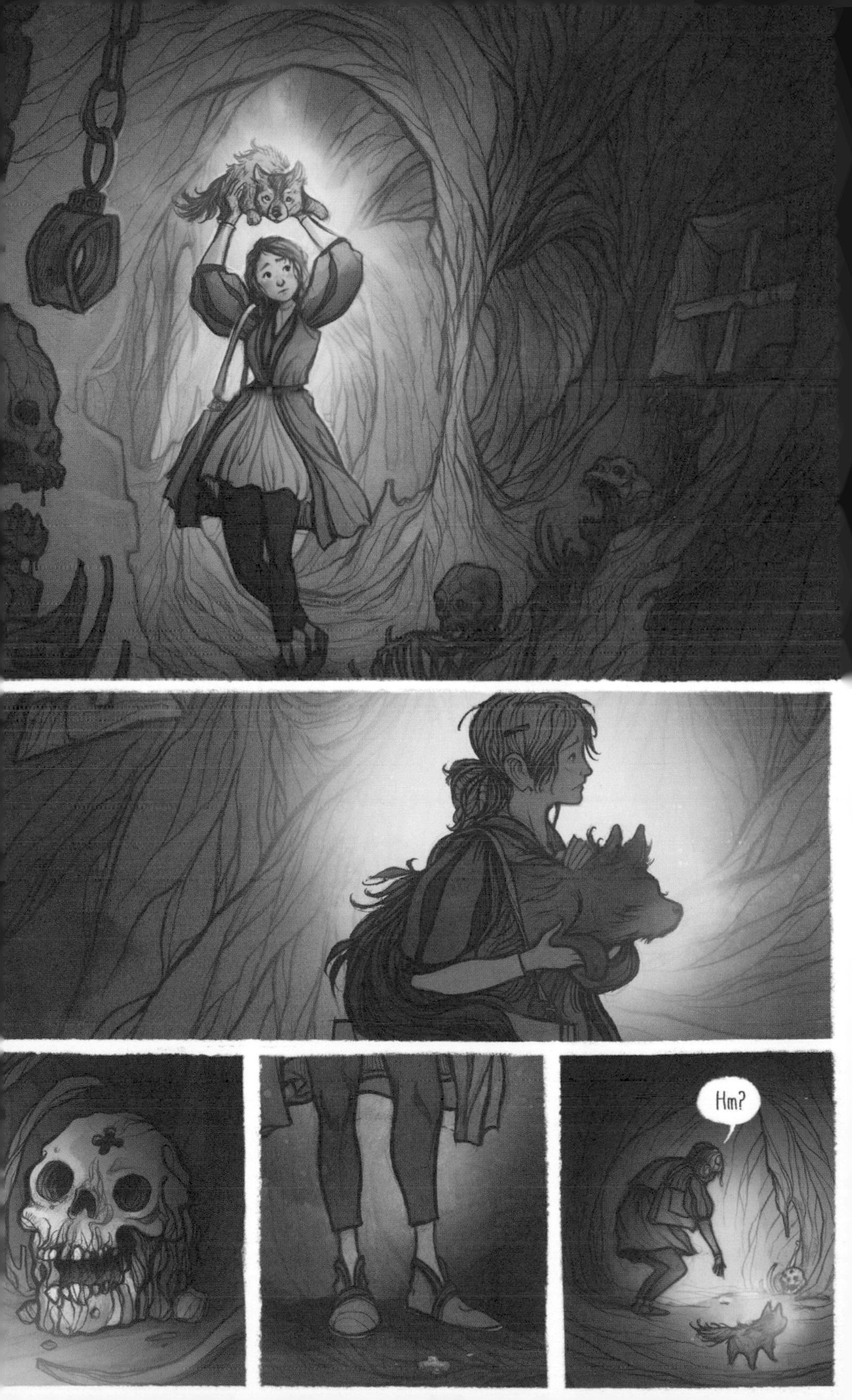
Hm?

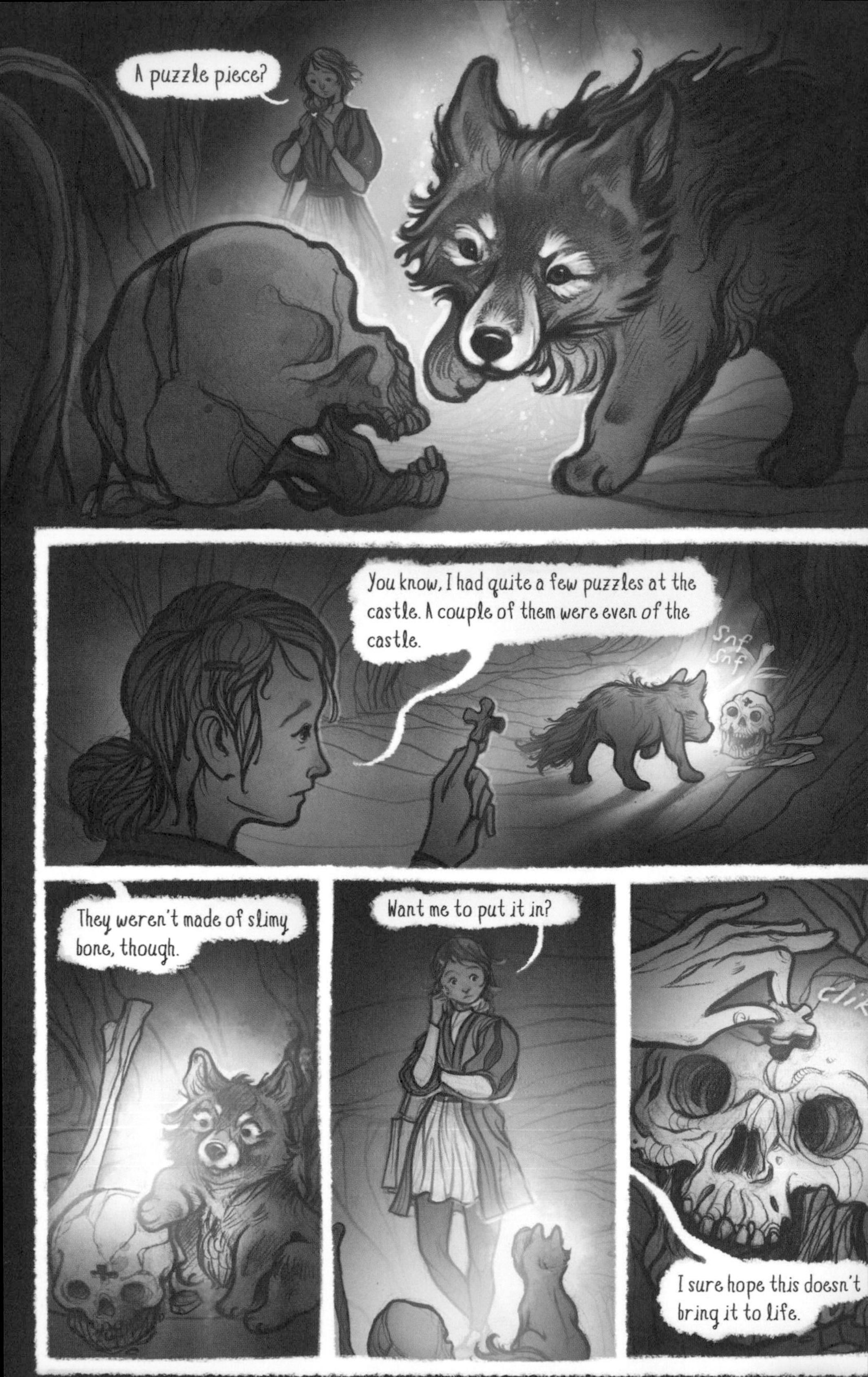
A puzzle piece?
You know, I had quite a few puzzles at the castle. A couple of them were even of the castle.
Snf Snf
They weren't made of slimy bone, though.
Want me to put it in?
I sure hope this doesn't bring it to life.

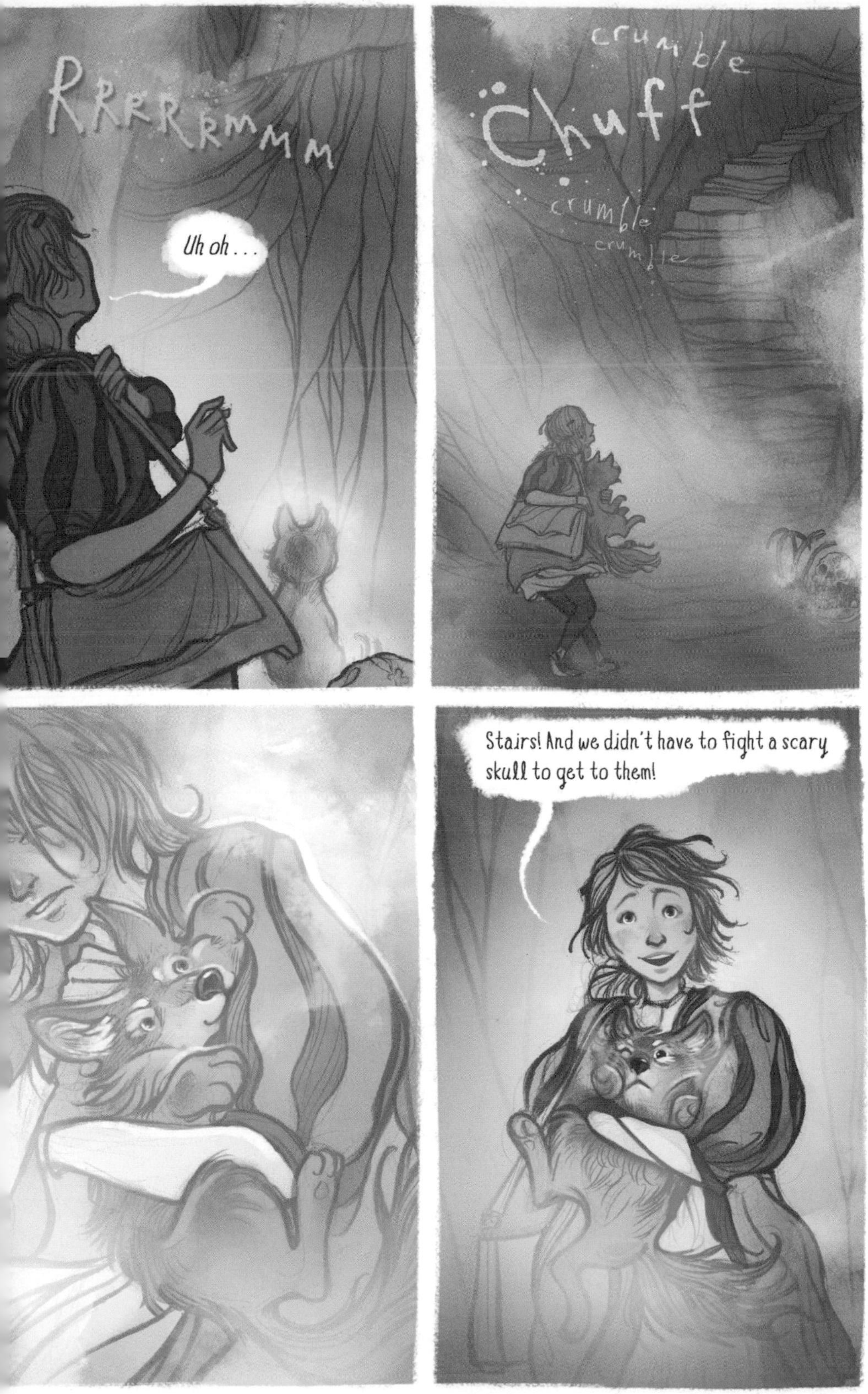
RRRRRRMMMM
Uh oh . . .
crumble
Chuff
crumble
crumble
Stairs! And we didn't have to fight a scary skull to get to them!

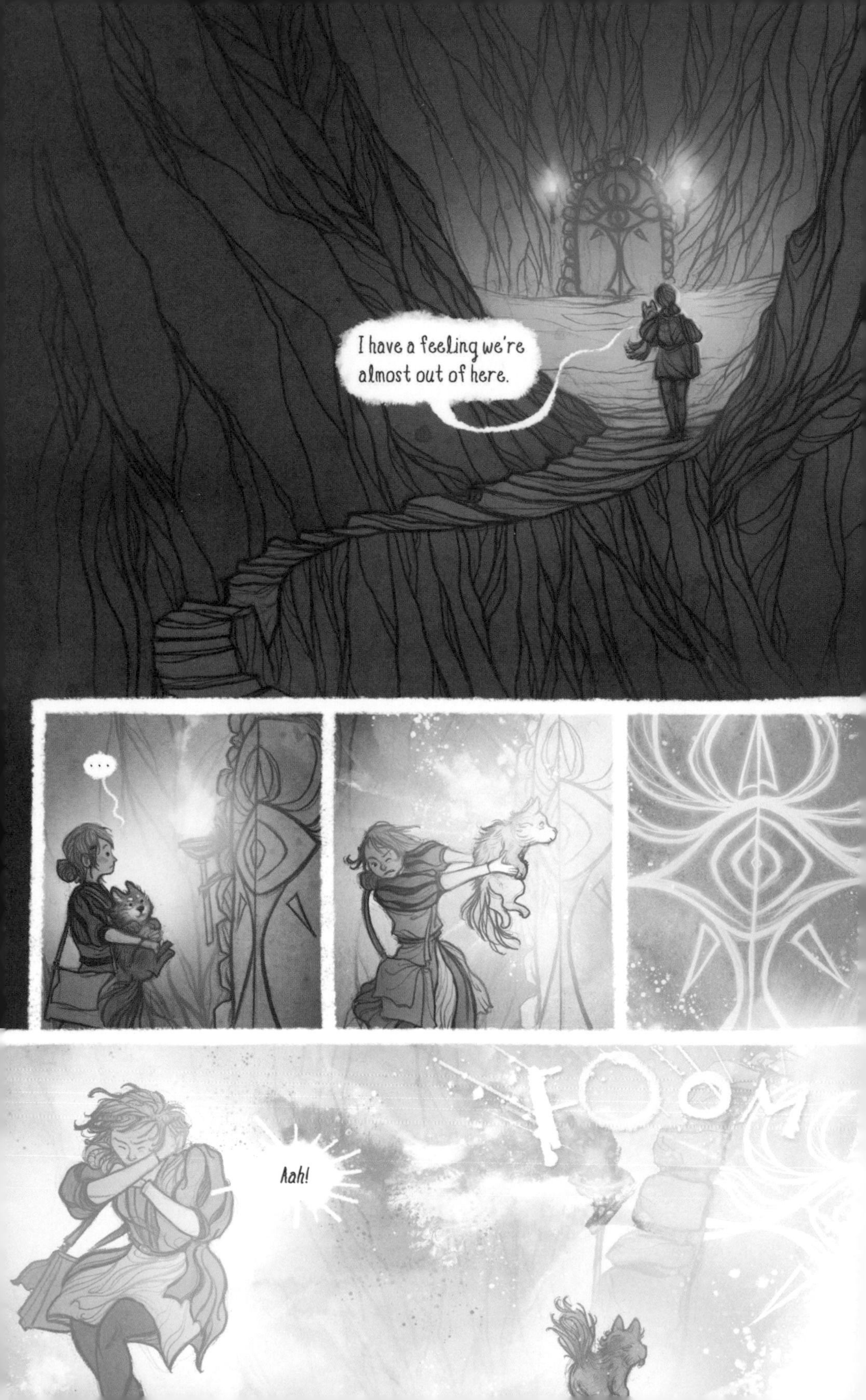
I have a feeling we're almost out of here.
...
Aah!
FOOM

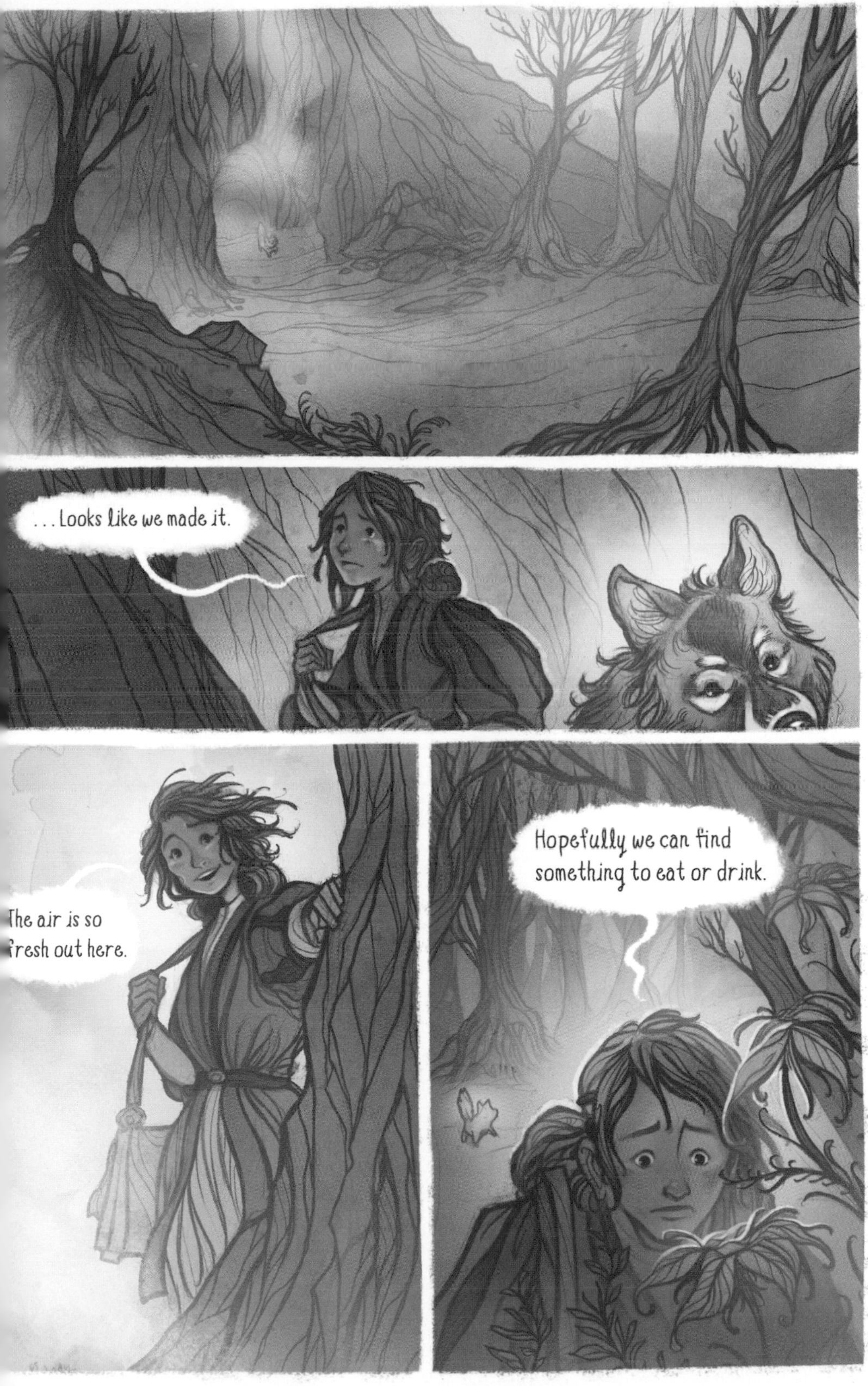

...Looks like we made it.
The air is so fresh out here.
Hopefully we can find something to eat or drink.

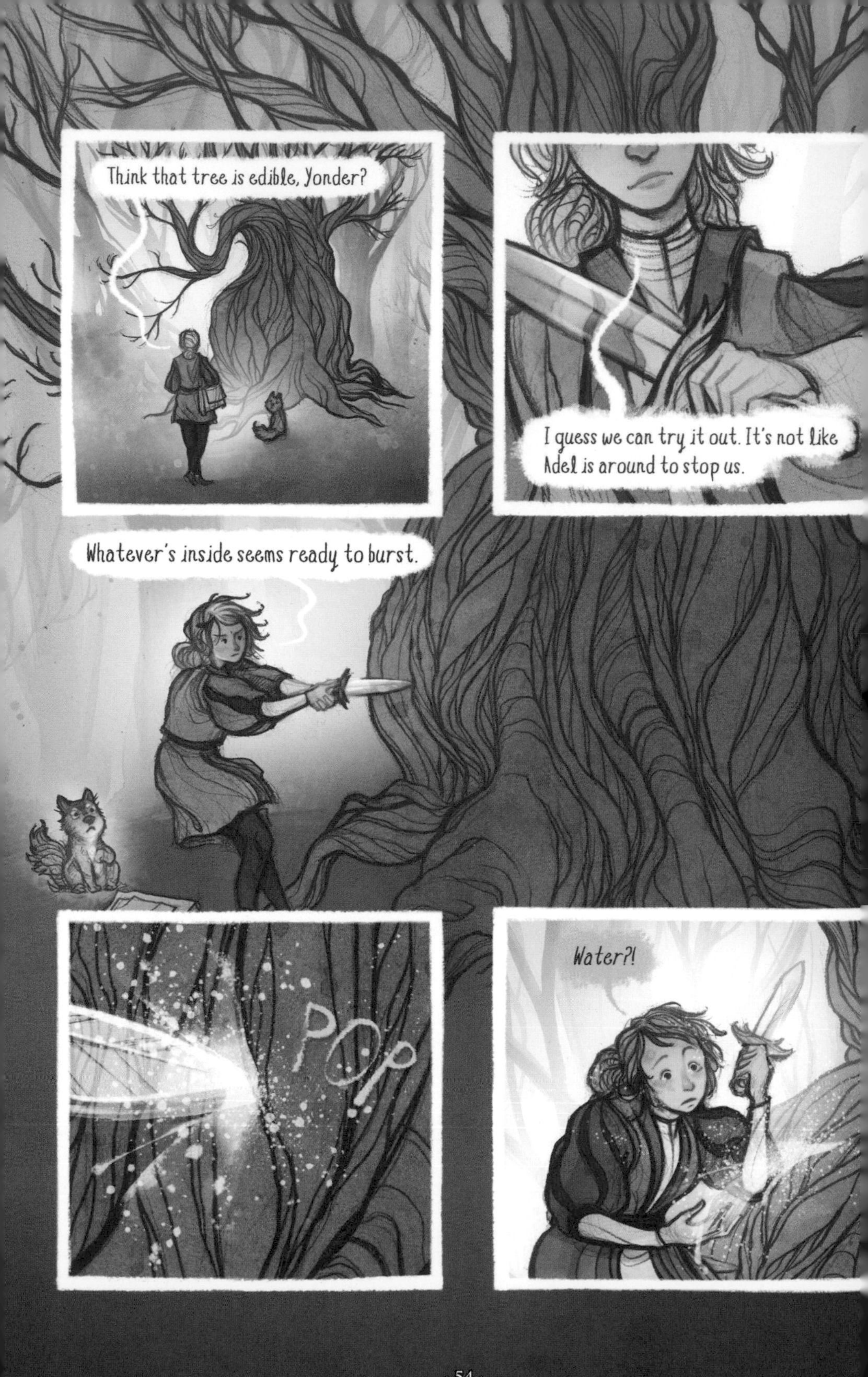
Think that tree is edible, Yonder?
I guess we can try it out. It's not like Adel is around to stop us.
Whatever's inside seems ready to burst.
POP
Water?!

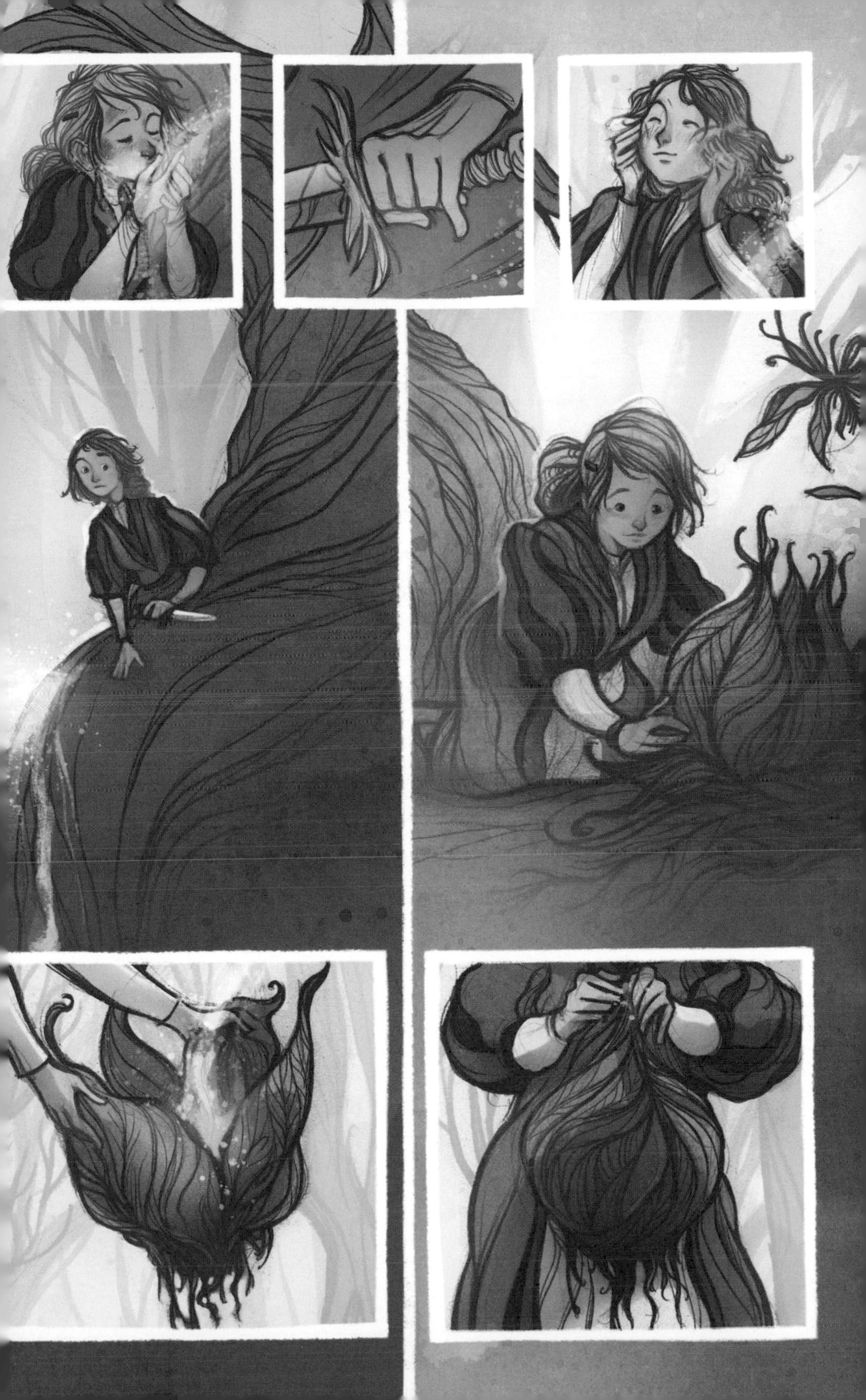

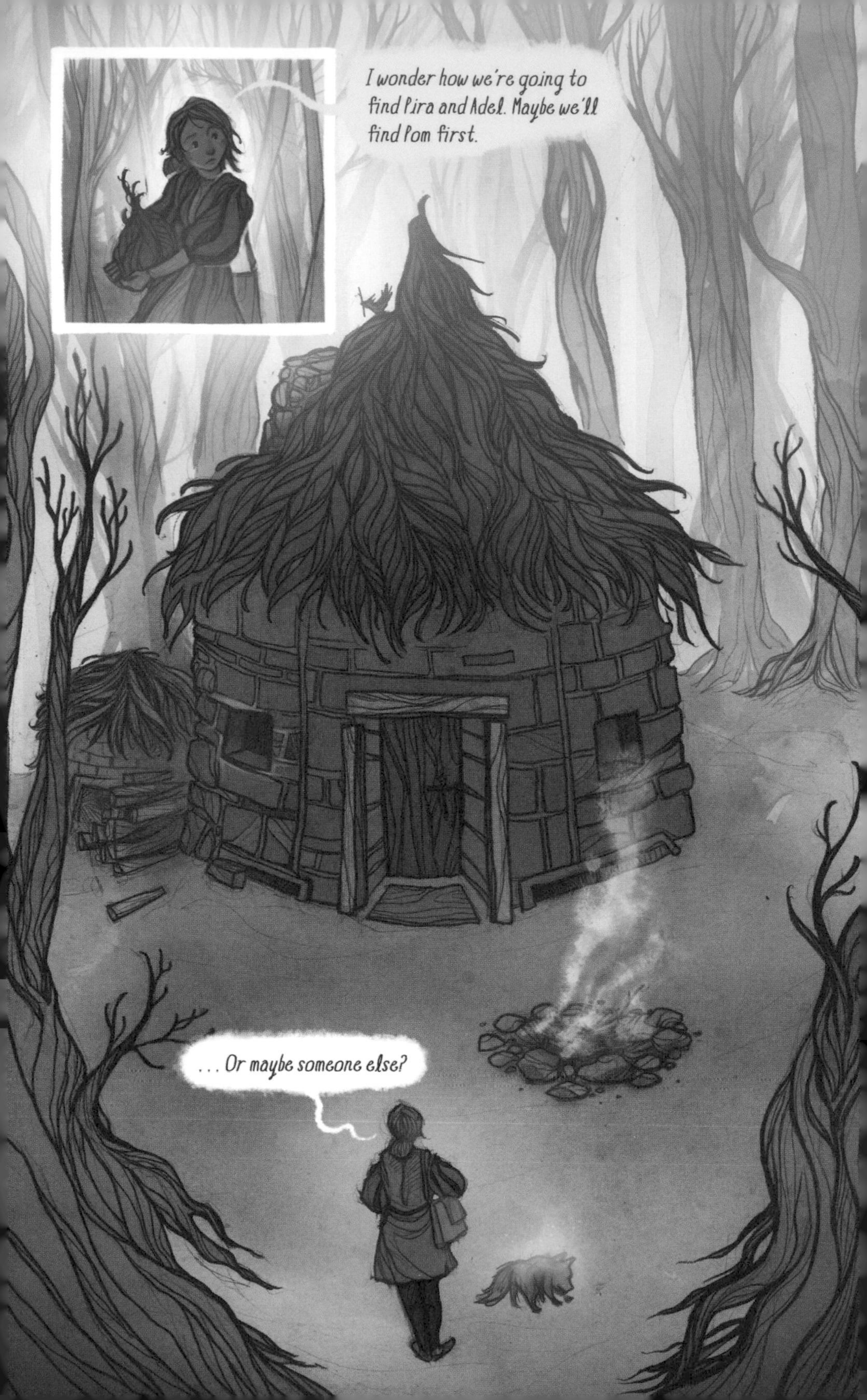

I wonder how we're going to find Pira and Adel. Maybe we'll find Pom first.
. . . Or maybe someone else?

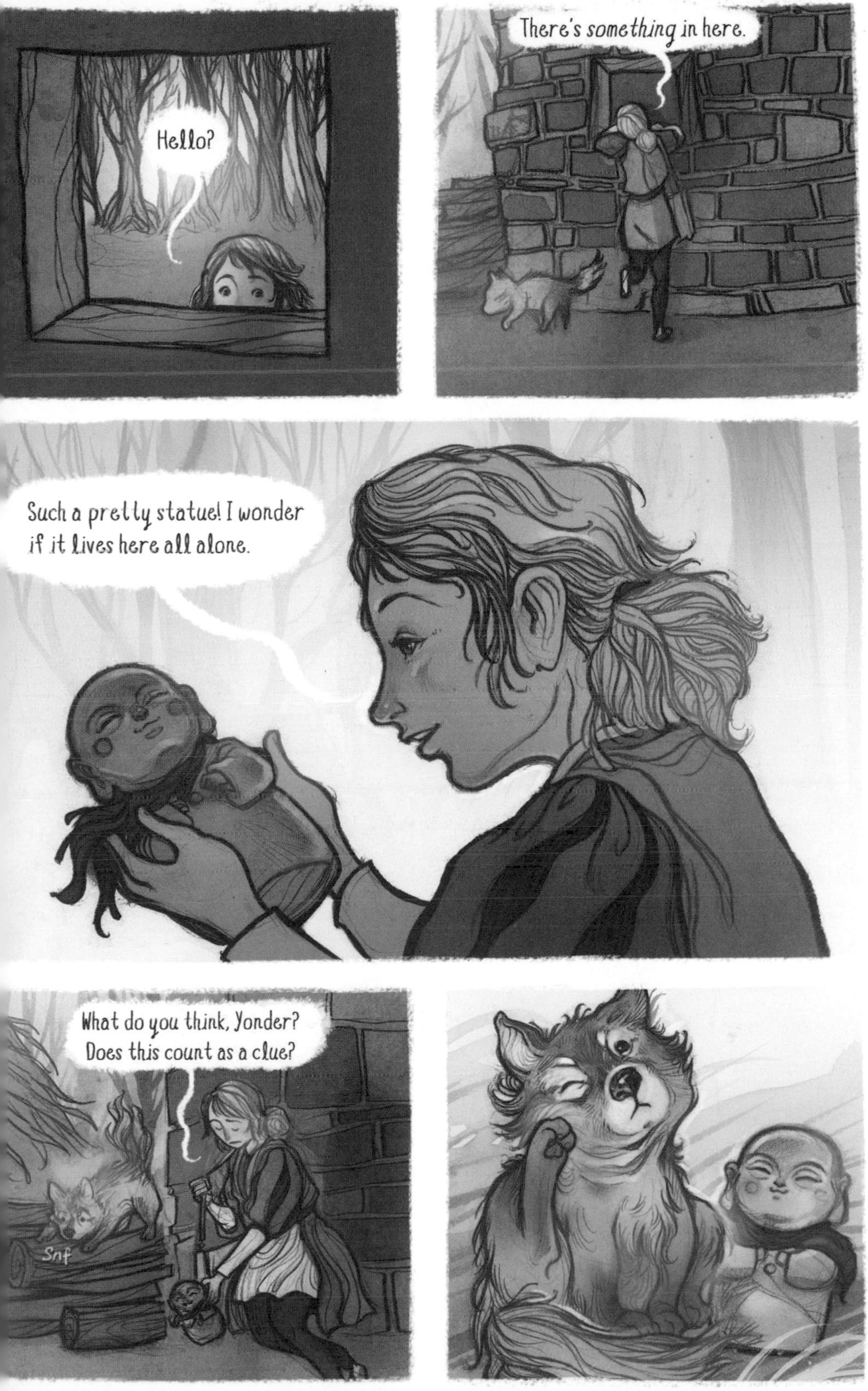
Hello?
There's something in here.
Such a pretty statue! I wonder if it lives here all alone.
What do you think, Yonder? Does this count as a clue?
Snf

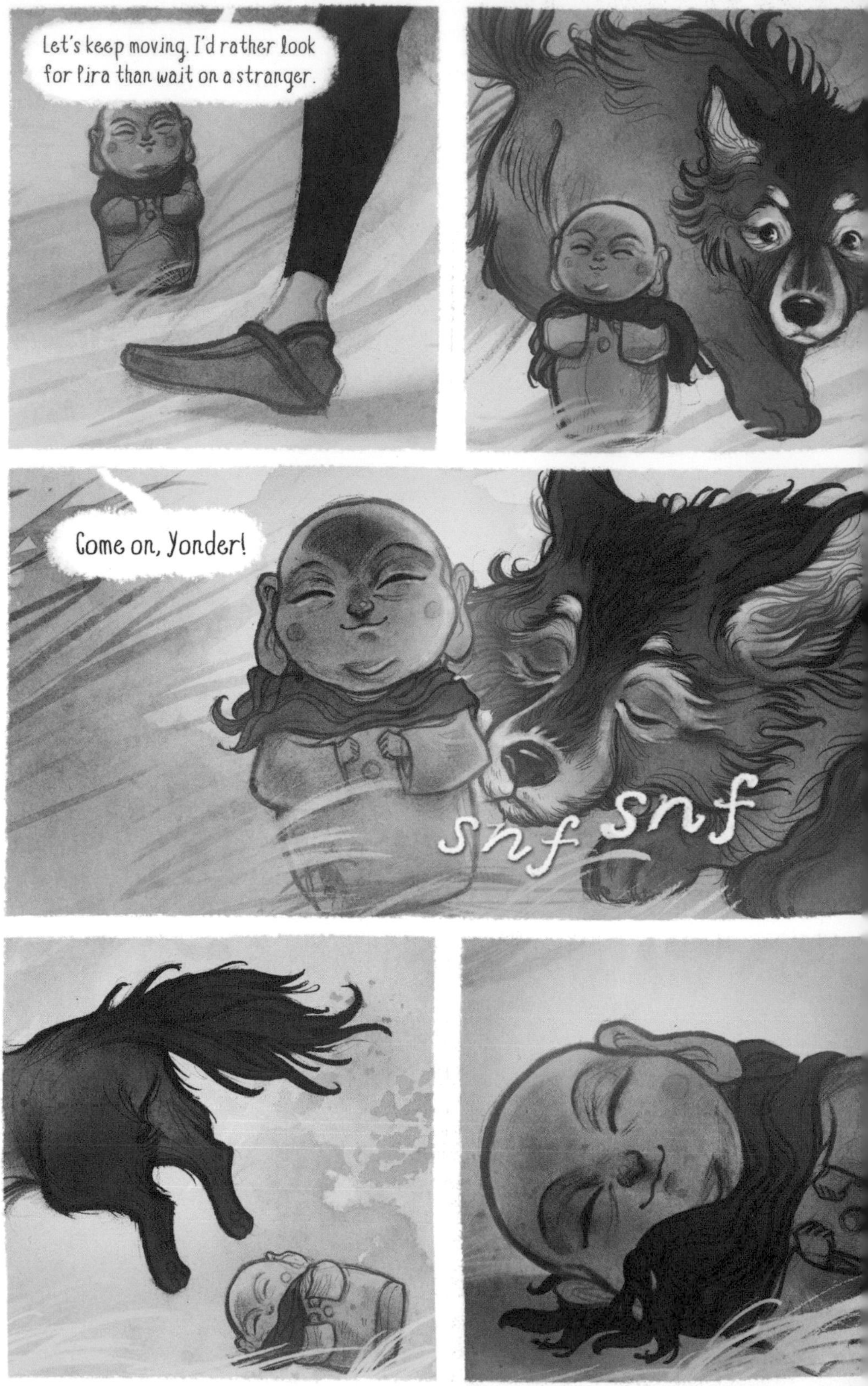
Let's keep moving. I'd rather look for Pira than wait on a stranger.
Come on, Yonder!
snf snf

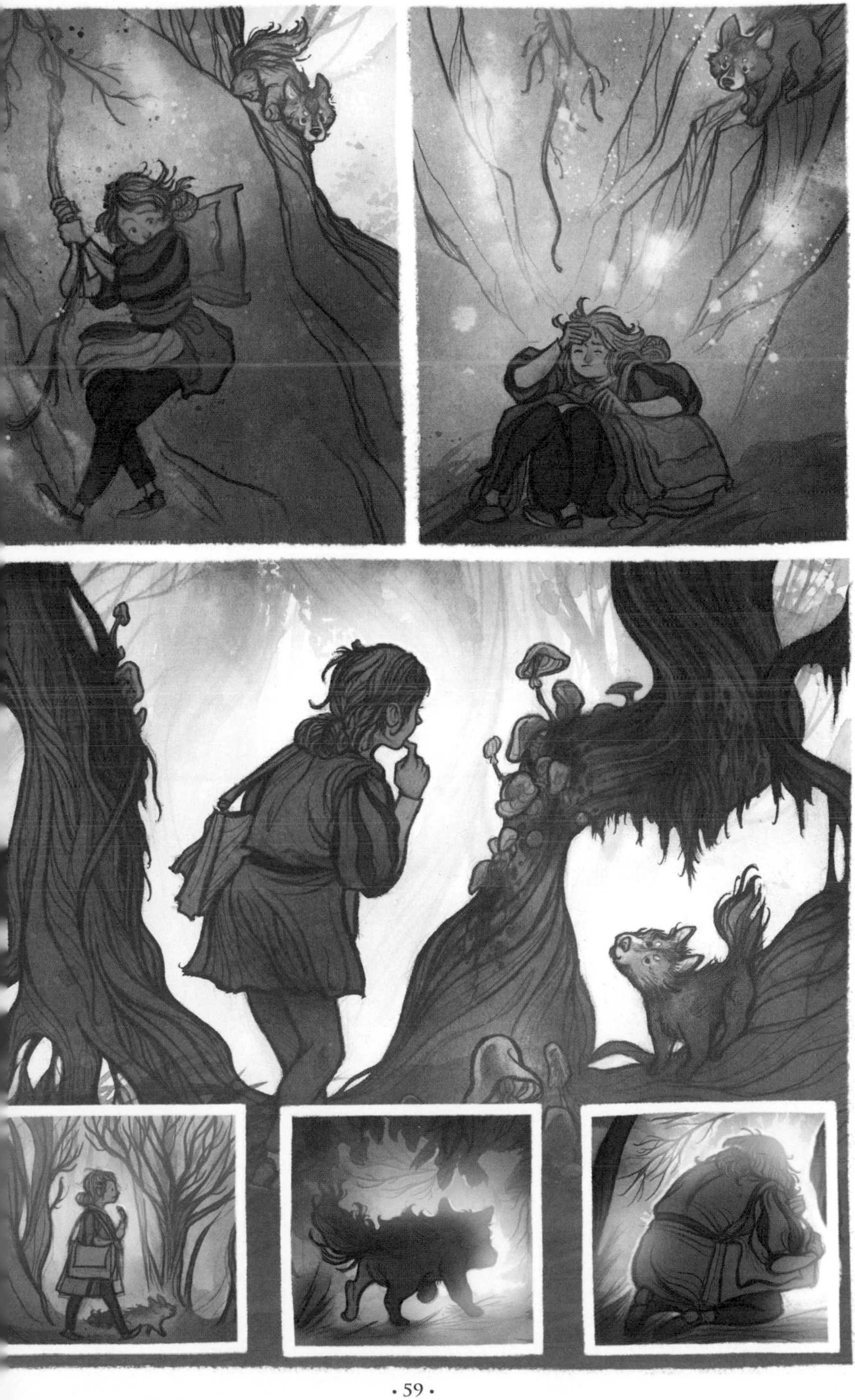

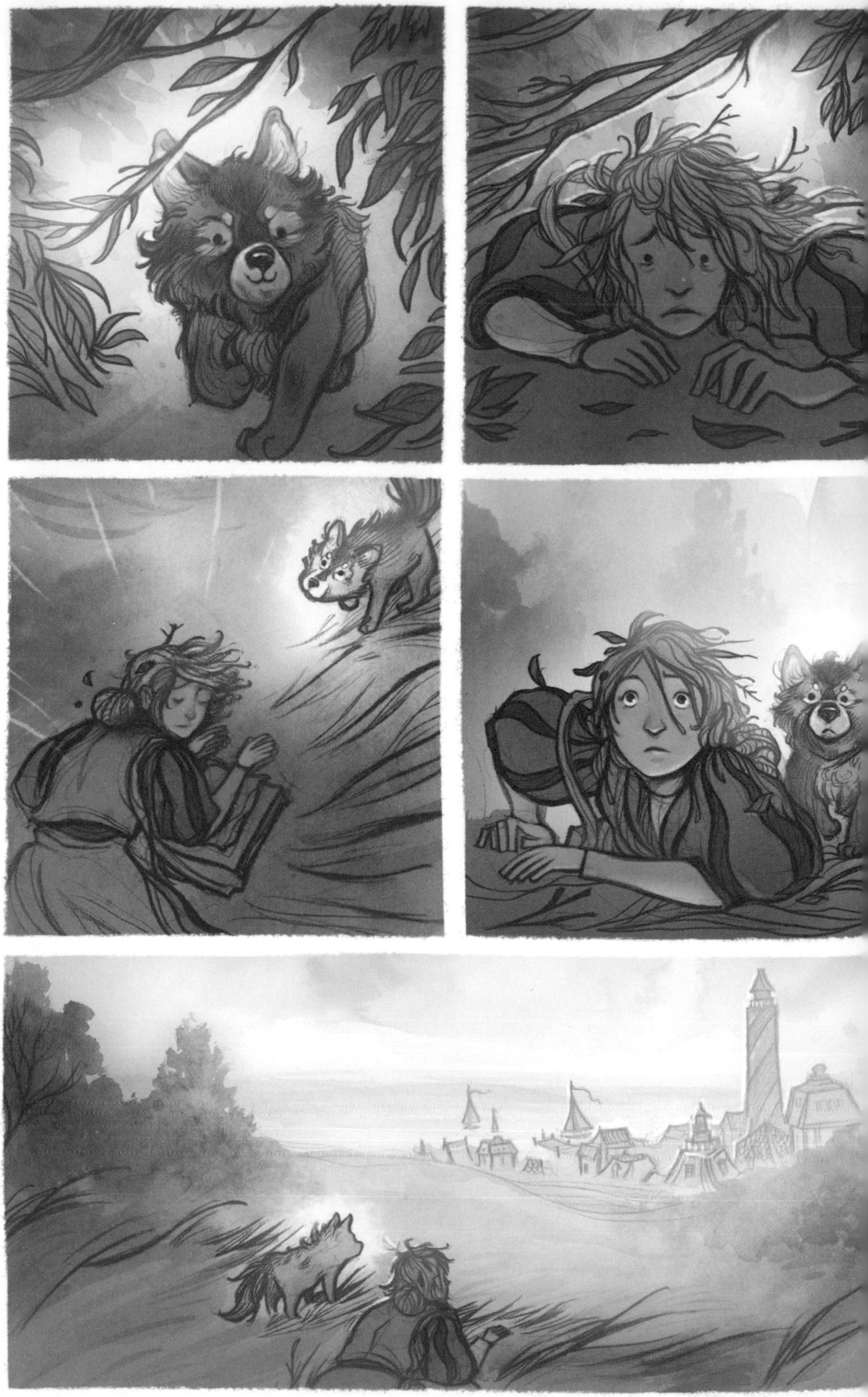

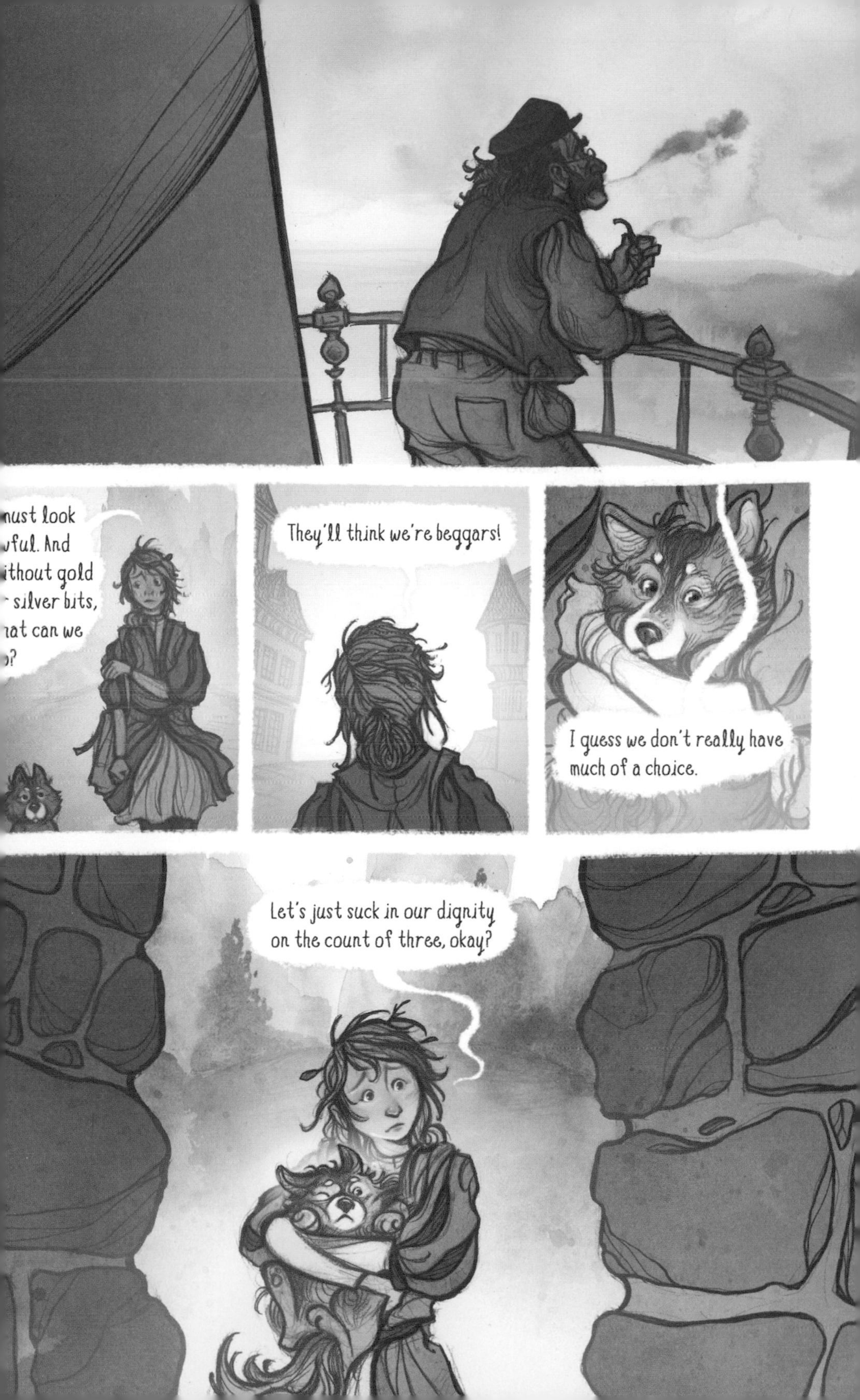

ust look ful. And ithout gold silver bits, at can we
They'll think we're beggars!
I guess we don't really have much of a choice.
Let's just suck in our dignity on the count of three, okay?

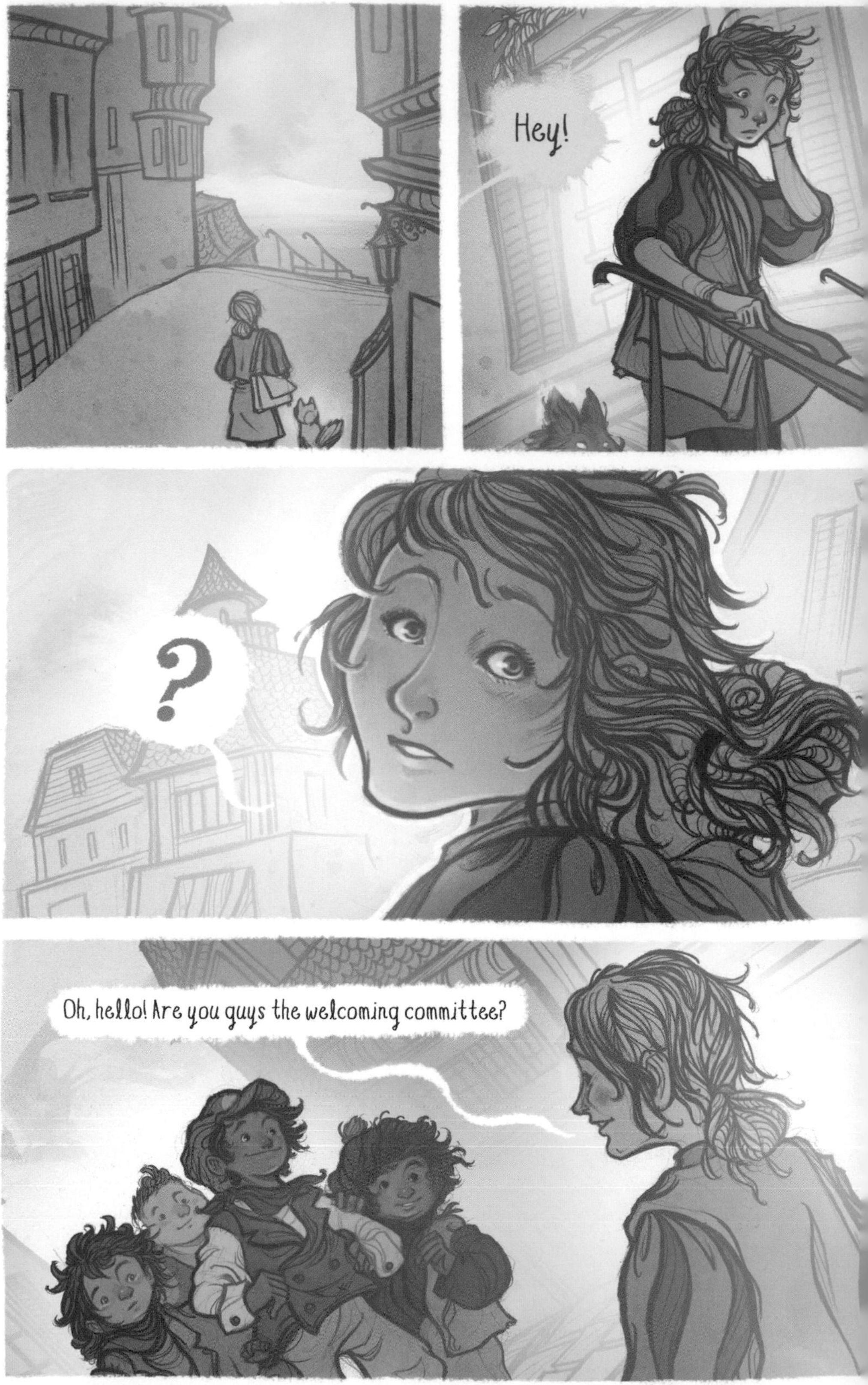
Hey!
?
Oh, hello! Are you guys the welcoming committee?

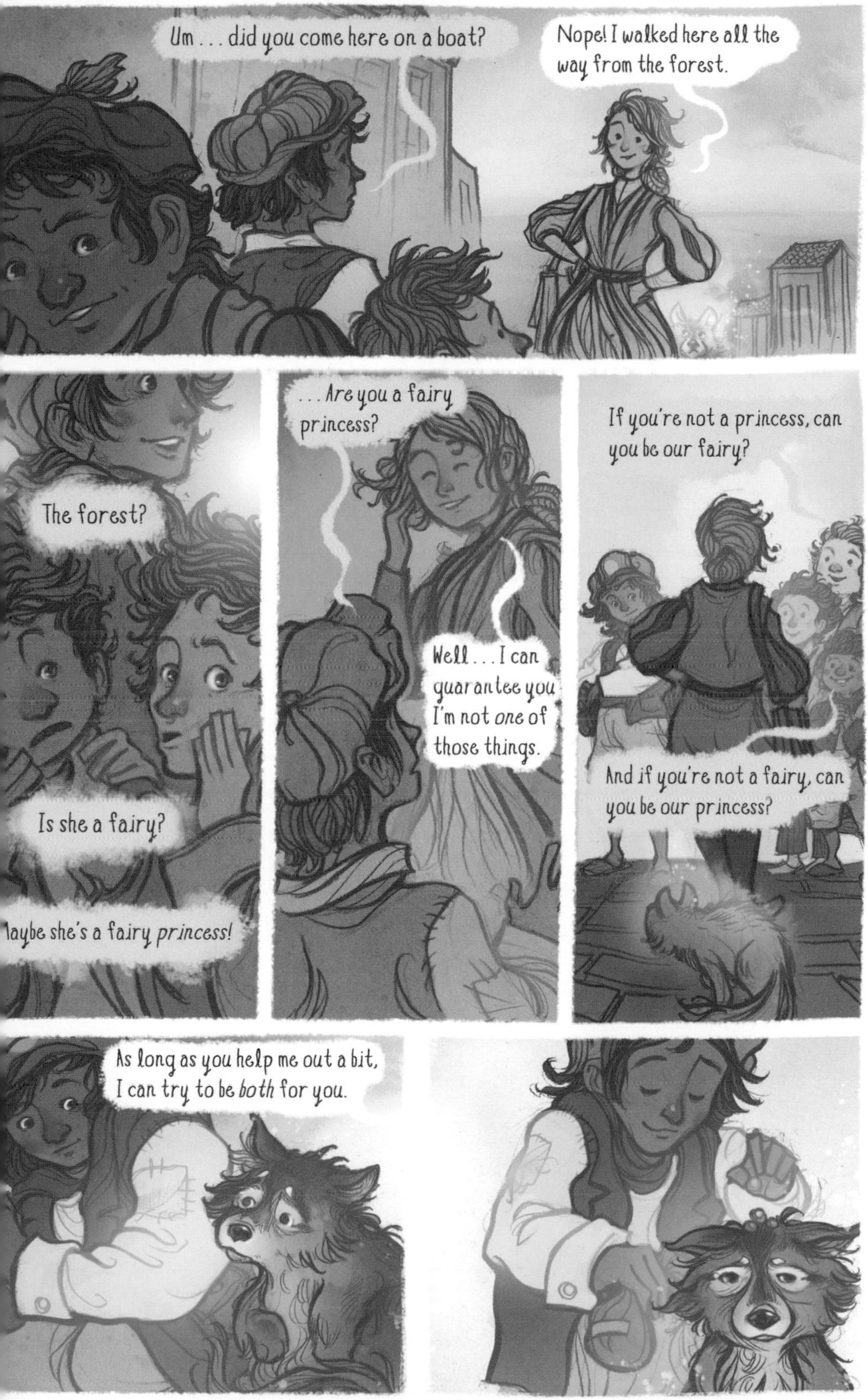
Um . . . did you come here on a boat?
Nope! I walked here all the way from the forest.
The forest?
Is she a fairy?
aybe she's a fairy *princess*!
. . . Are you a fairy princess?
Well . . . I can guarantee you I'm not *one* of those things.
If you're not a princess, can you be our fairy?
And if you're not a fairy, can you be our princess?
As long as you help me out a bit, I can try to be *both* for you.

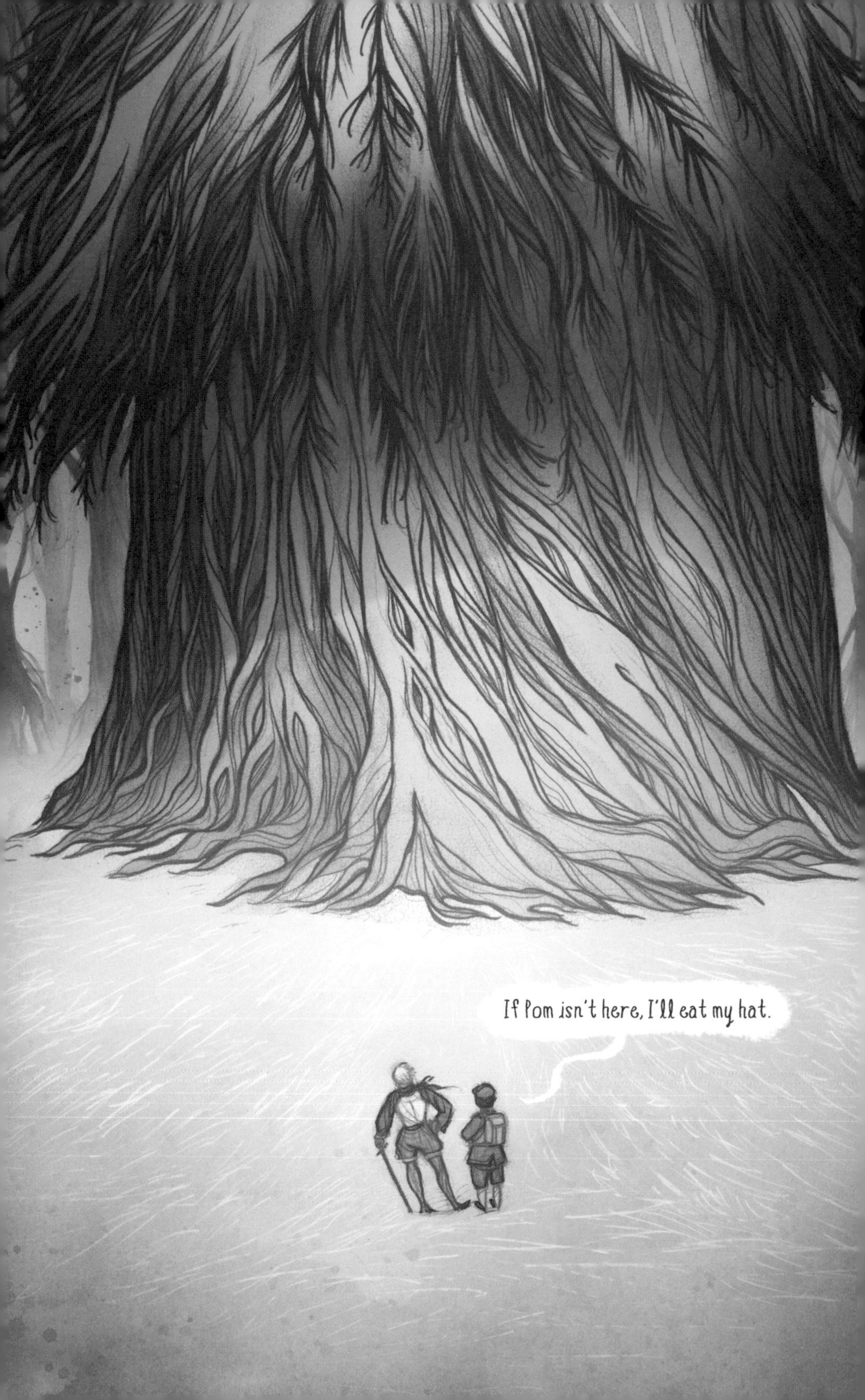
If Pom isn't here, I'll eat my hat.

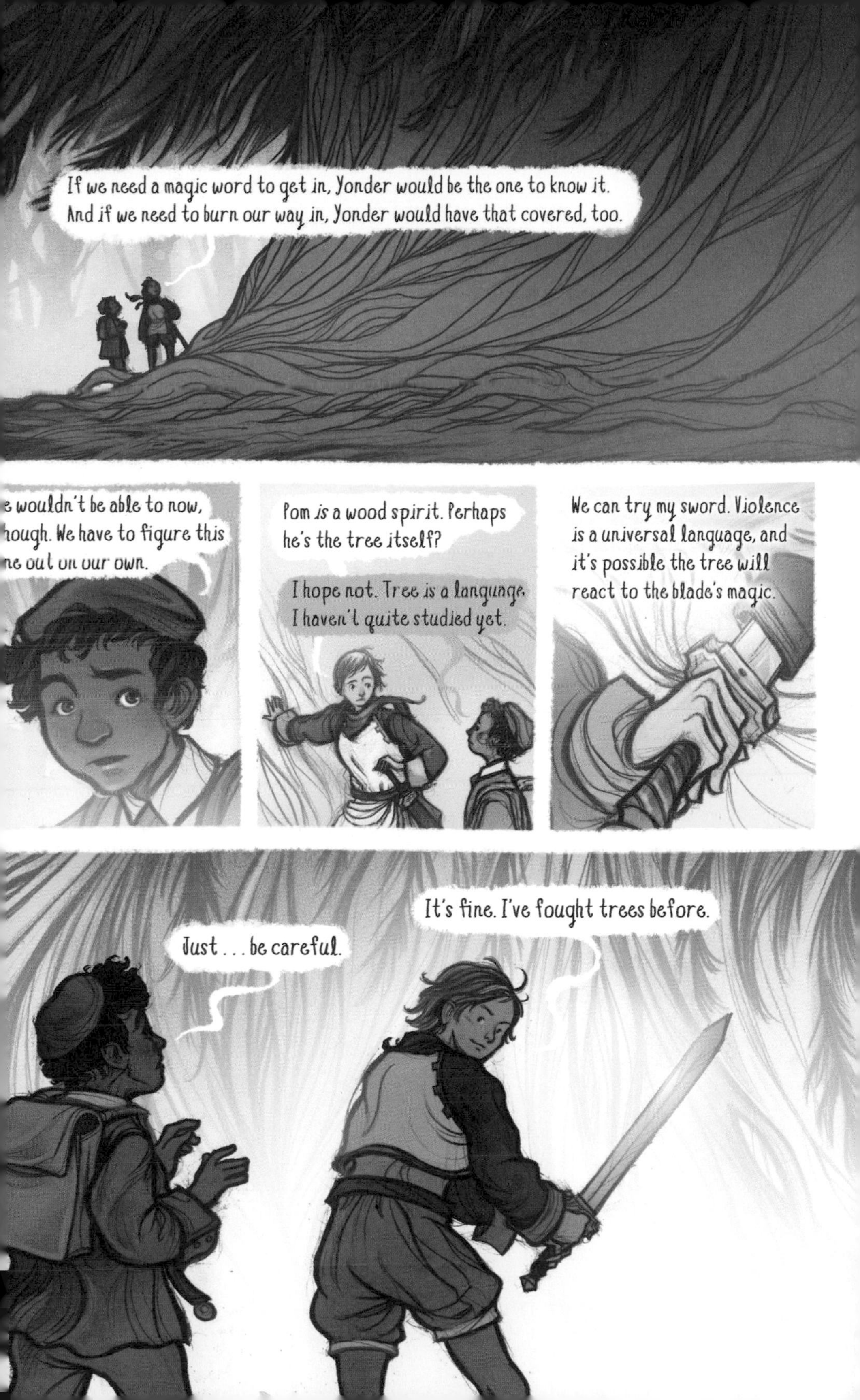
If we need a magic word to get in, Yonder would be the one to know it. And if we need to burn our way in, Yonder would have that covered, too.
e wouldn't be able to now, hough. We have to figure this ne out on our own.
Pom *is* a wood spirit. Perhaps he's the tree itself?
I hope not. Tree is a language I haven't quite studied yet.
We can try my sword. Violence is a universal language, and it's possible the tree will react to the blade's magic.
It's fine. I've fought trees before.
Just . . . be careful.

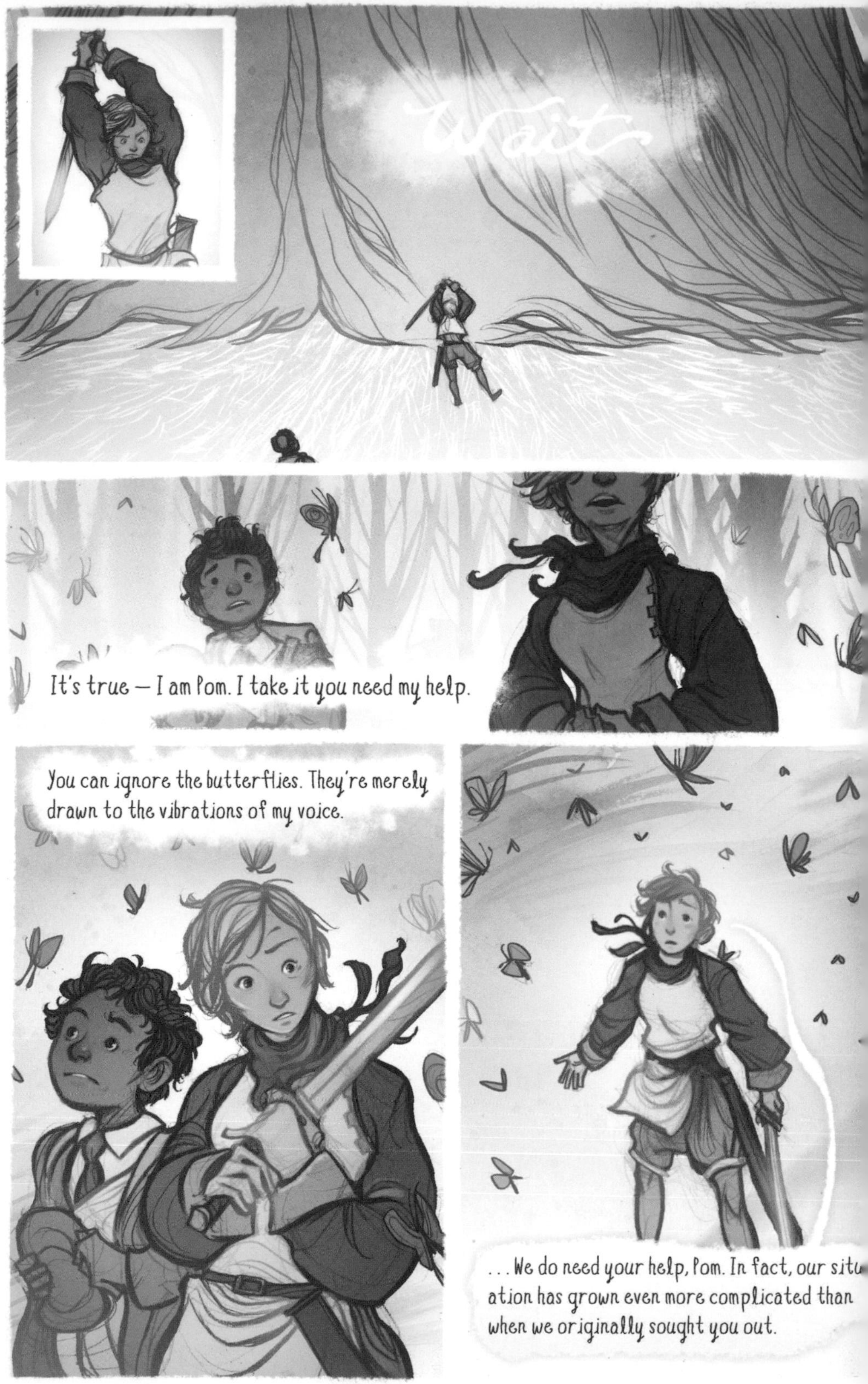
Wait
It's true — I am Pom. I take it you need my help.
You can ignore the butterflies. They're merely drawn to the vibrations of my voice.
. . . We do need your help, Pom. In fact, our situ ation has grown even more complicated than when we originally sought you out.

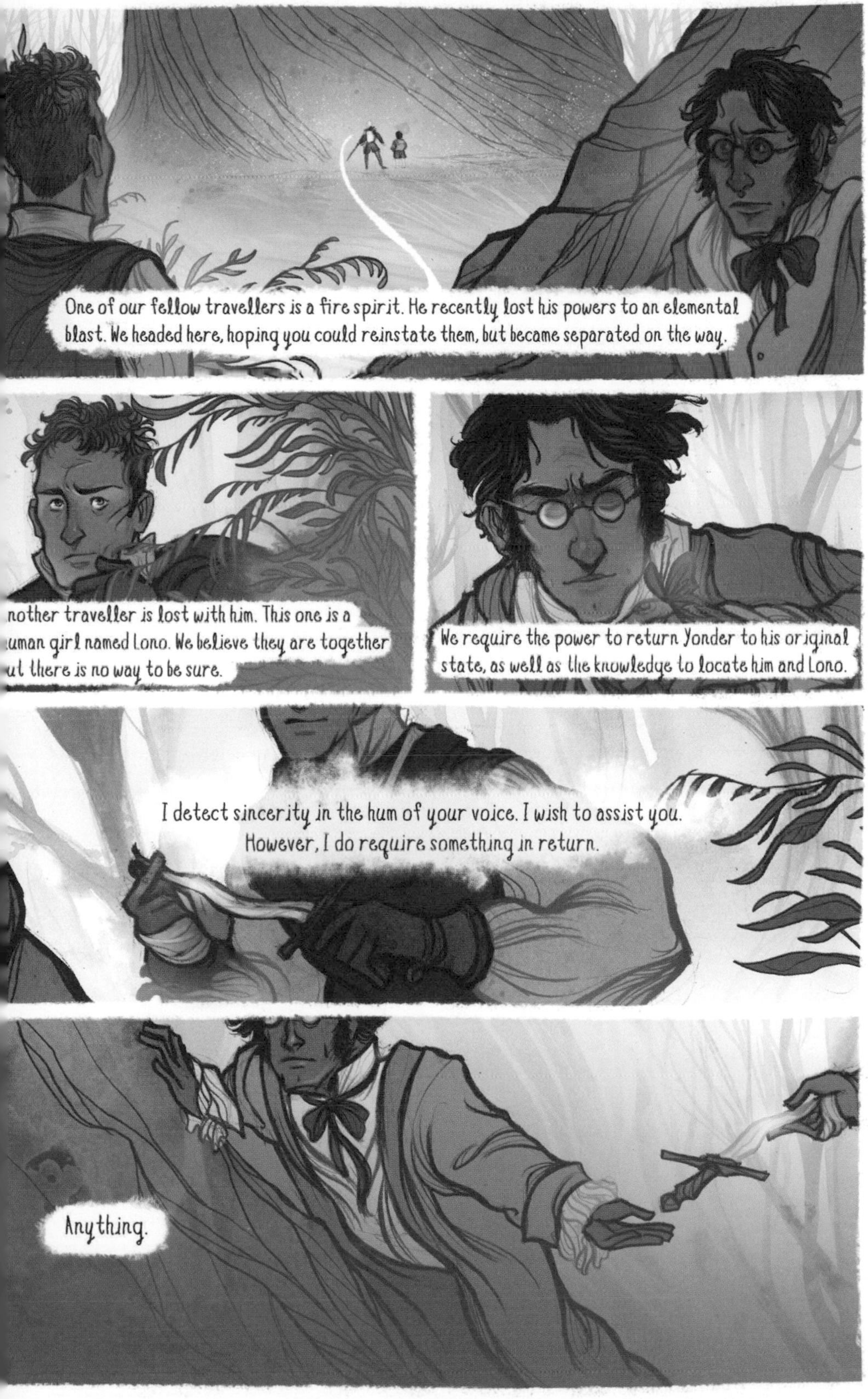
One of our fellow travellers is a fire spirit. He recently lost his powers to an elemental blast. We headed here, hoping you could reinstate them, but became separated on the way.
nother traveller is lost with him. This one is a uman girl named Lono. We believe they are together ut there is no way to be sure.
We require the power to return Yonder to his original state, as well as the knowledge to locate him and Lono.
I detect sincerity in the hum of your voice. I wish to assist you. However, I do require something in return.
Anything.

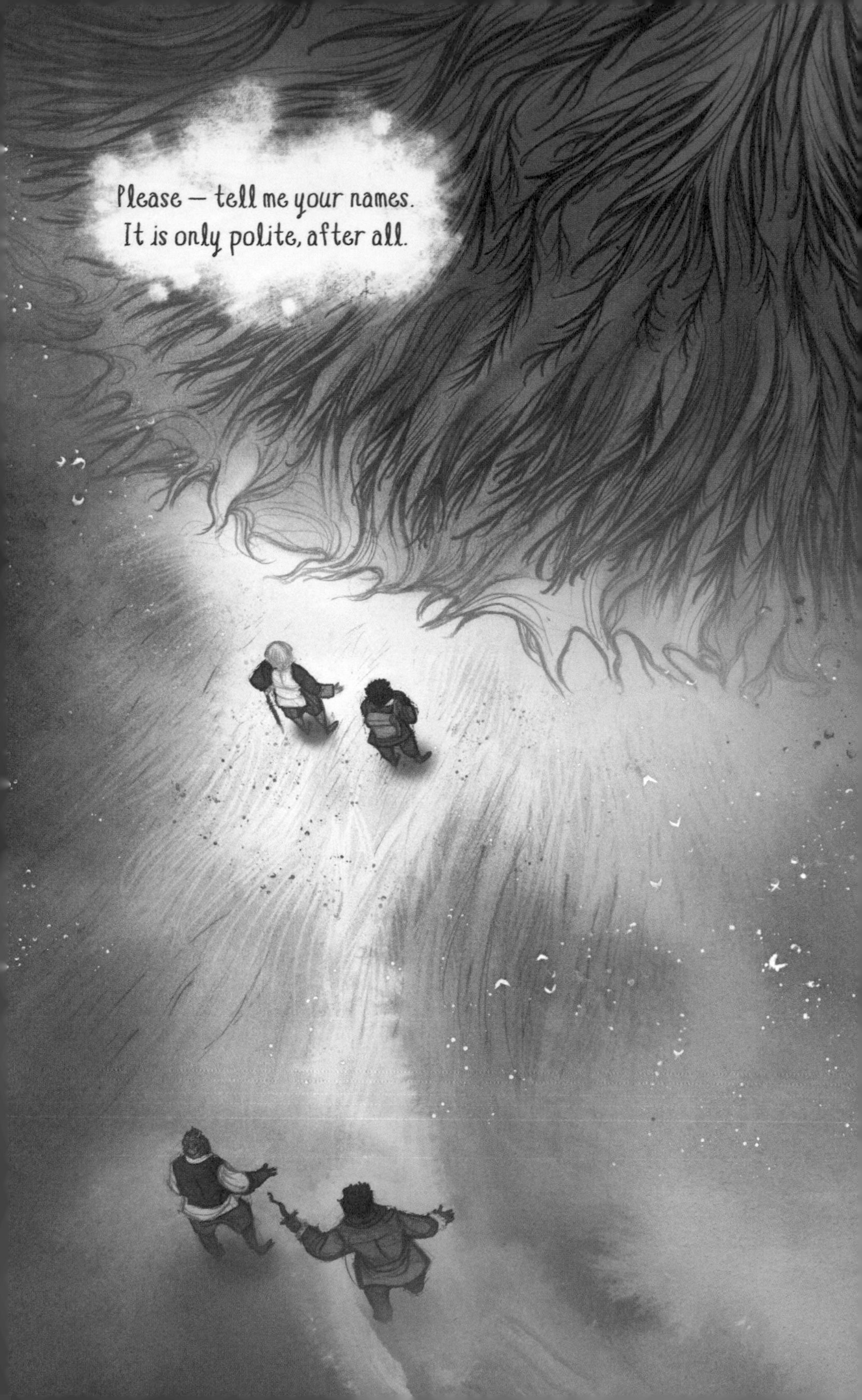
Please — tell me your names.
It is only polite, after all.

WATER ELIXIR

POTION | HEALTH & MAGIC

Fresh from a water tree, this natural elixir revitalises both body and spirit.

Restore 5 points to HP and MP and remove all status ailments from a single party member.

---

side quests and skill masters here.

Friendly and enemy creatures fill the landscape of Spera.

LONO

You know, I had quite a few puzzles at the castle. A couple of them were even of the castle. They weren't made of slimy bone, though.

| Determines the

& Magic | Denotes items or sk

ons | Weapons that off

vy W   t that offer

ht Weapons | W   ons that offer li

gendary Weapons | Special weapons that offer unique damage, stamina, and buffer stats.   **Nature Element** | Elemental classification for creatures, weapons and spells.

The Harbour Town of Mari

CHAPTER FOUR
The Vessel

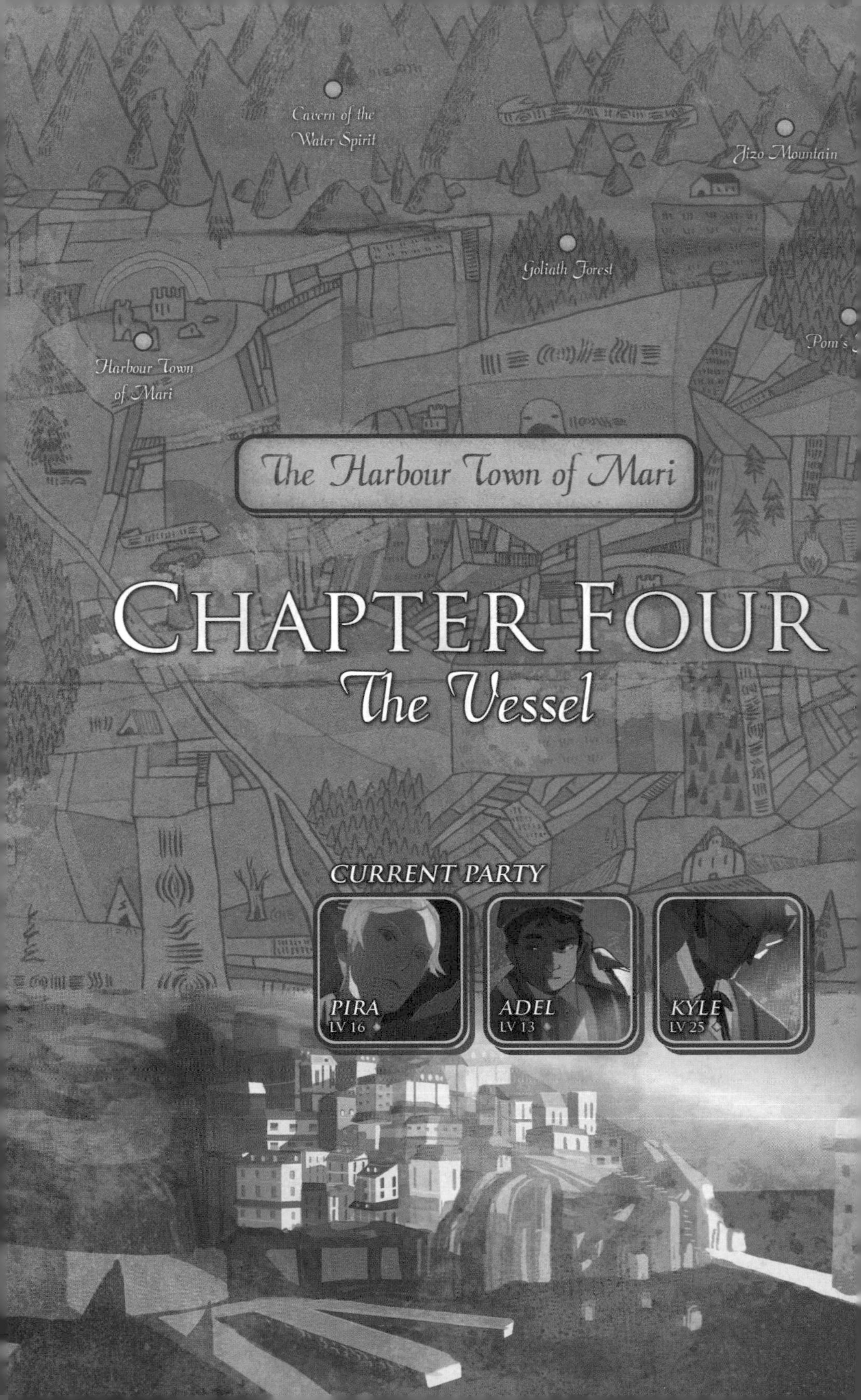

Cavern of the Water Spirit
Jizo Mountain
Goliath Forest
Harbour Town of Mari
Pom's
CURRENT PARTY
PIRA
LV 16
ADEL
LV 13
KYLE
LV 25

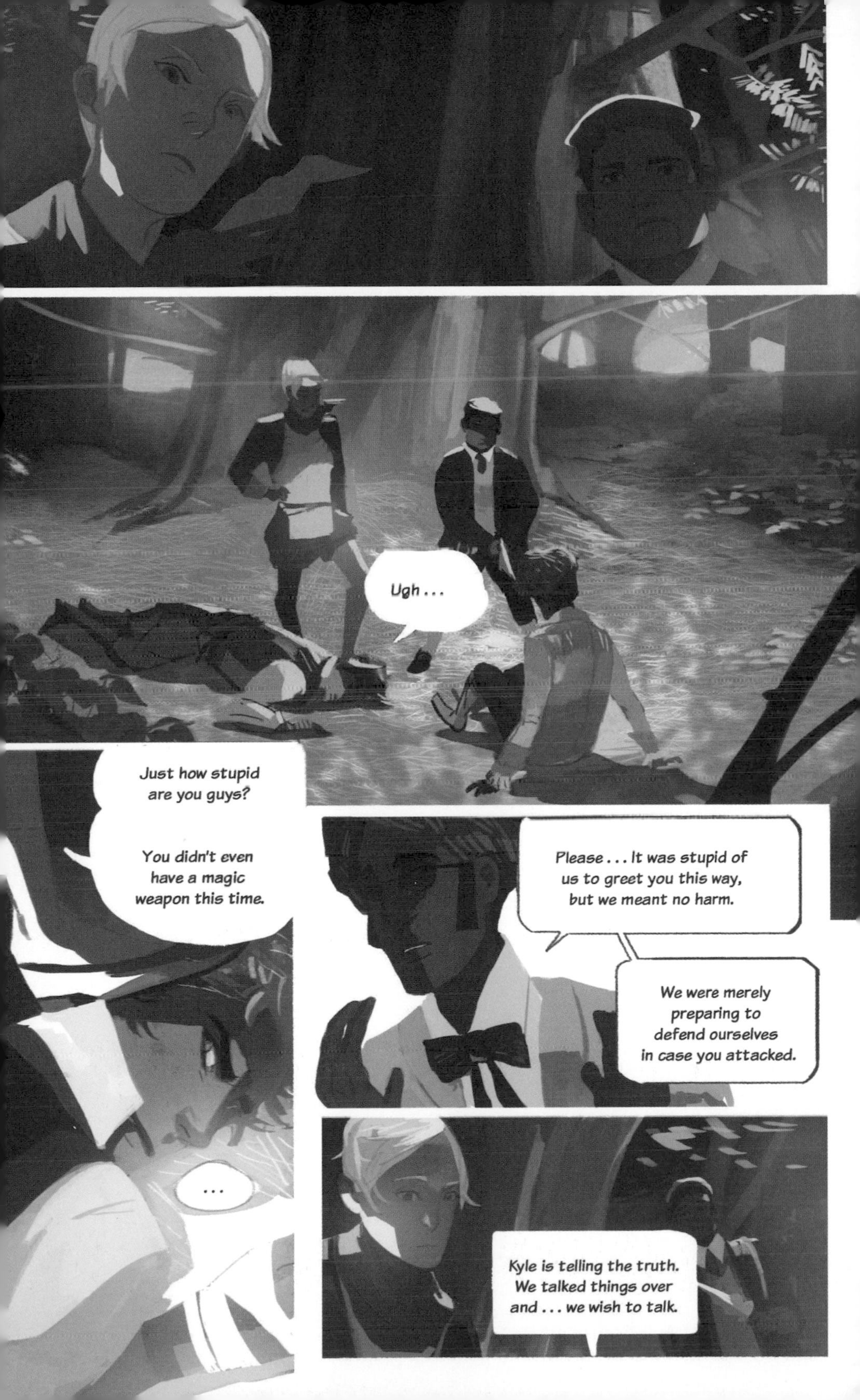
Ugh . . .
Just how stupid are you guys?
You didn't even have a magic weapon this time.
Please . . . It was stupid of us to greet you this way, but we meant no harm.
We were merely preparing to defend ourselves in case you attacked.
. . .
Kyle is telling the truth. We talked things over and . . . we wish to talk.

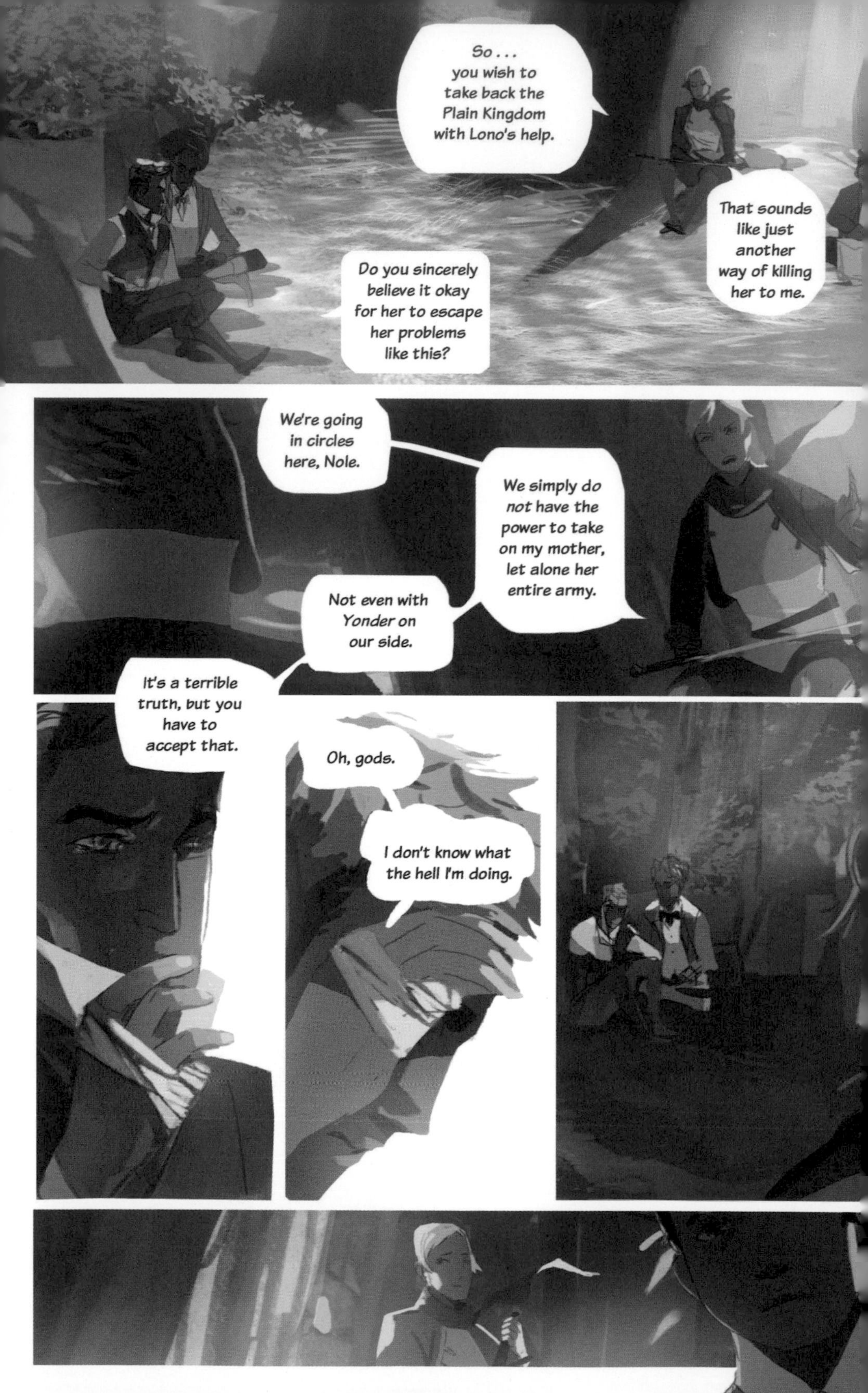
So . . .
you wish to take back the Plain Kingdom with Lono's help.
Do you sincerely believe it okay for her to escape her problems like this?
That sounds like just another way of killing her to me.
We're going in circles here, Nole.
We simply *do not* have the power to take on my mother, let alone her entire army.
Not even with *Yonder* on our side.
It's a terrible truth, but you have to accept that.
Oh, gods.
I don't know what the hell I'm doing.

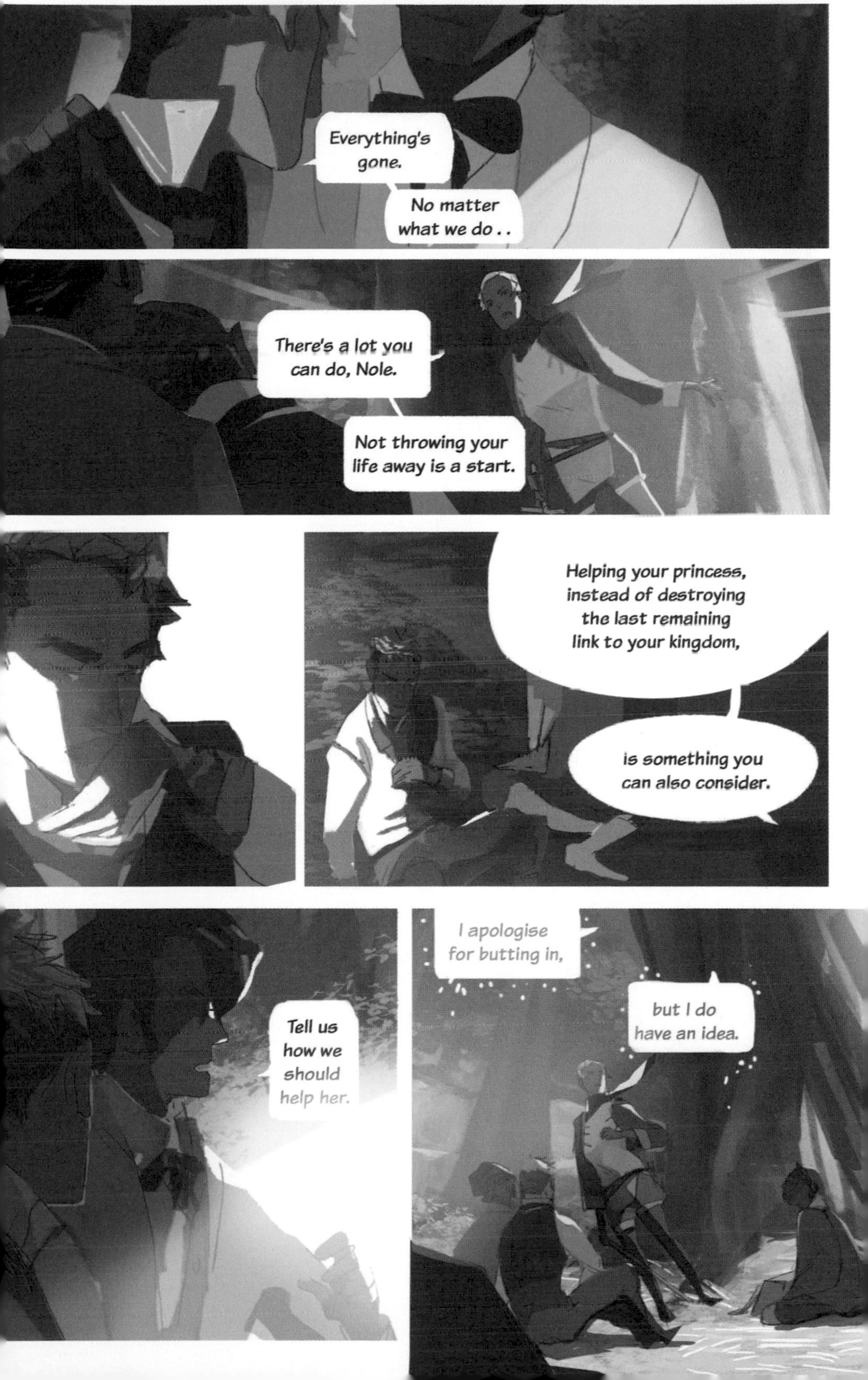
Everything's gone.
No matter what we do . .
There's a lot you can do, Nole.
Not throwing your life away is a start.
Helping your princess, instead of destroying the last remaining link to your kingdom,
is something you can also consider.
Tell us how we should help her.
I apologise for butting in,
but I do have an idea.

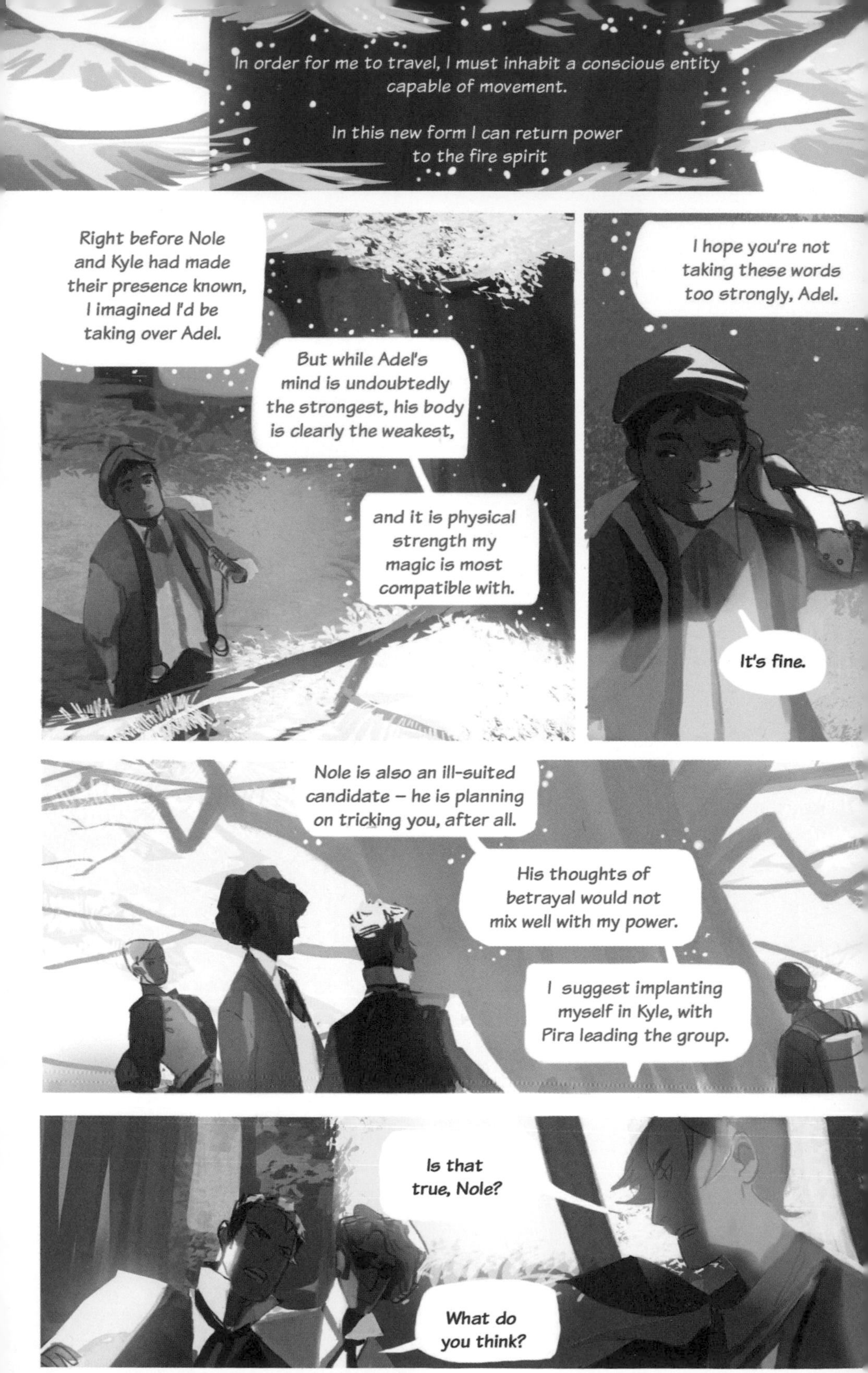
In order for me to travel, I must inhabit a conscious entity capable of movement.
In this new form I can return power to the fire spirit
Right before Nole and Kyle had made their presence known, I imagined I'd be taking over Adel.
But while Adel's mind is undoubtedly the strongest, his body is clearly the weakest,
and it is physical strength my magic is most compatible with.
I hope you're not taking these words too strongly, Adel.
It's fine.
Nole is also an ill-suited candidate – he is planning on tricking you, after all.
His thoughts of betrayal would not mix well with my power.
I suggest implanting myself in Kyle, with Pira leading the group.
Is that true, Nole?
What do you think?

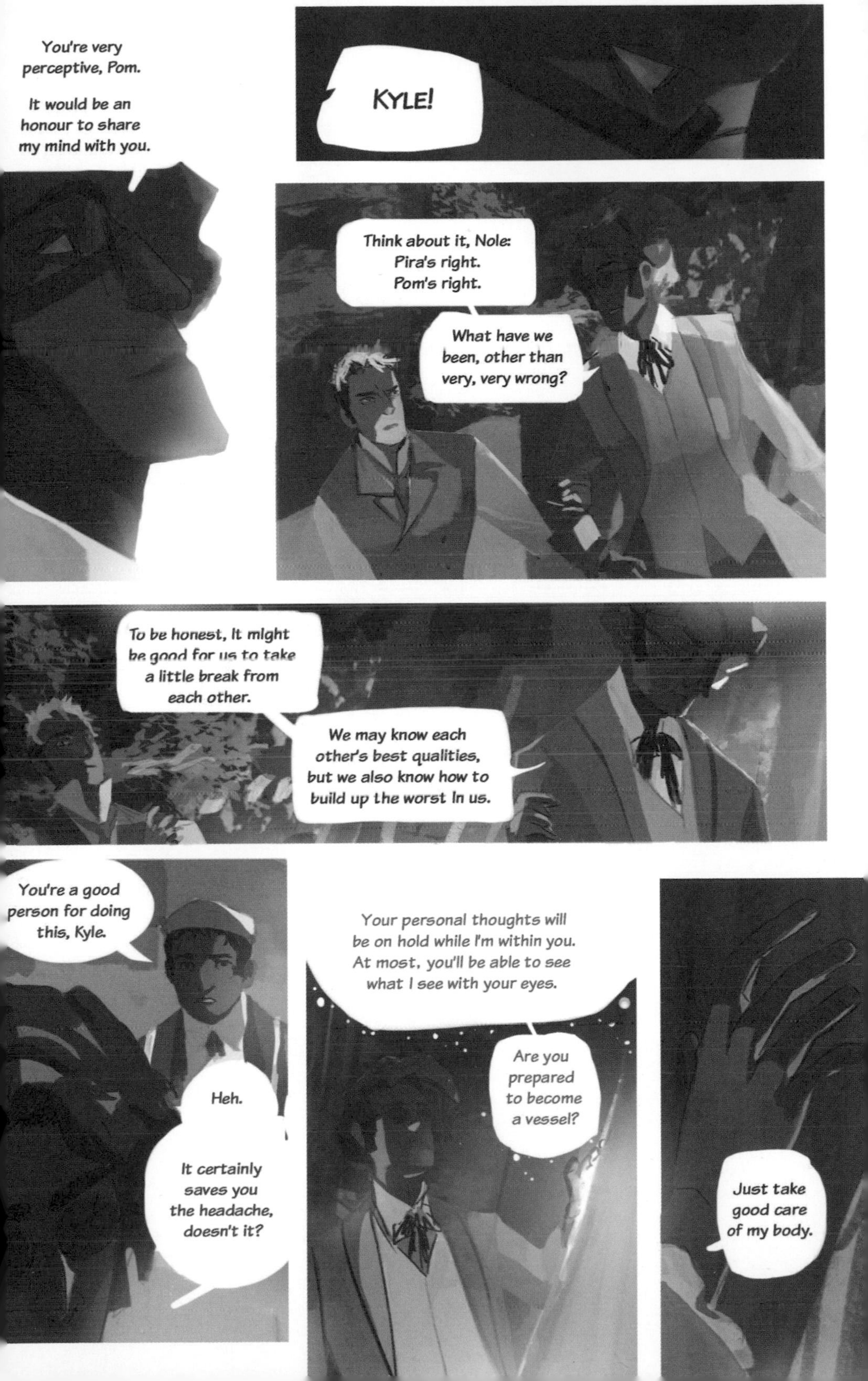
You're very perceptive, Pom.
It would be an honour to share my mind with you.
KYLE!
Think about it, Nole: Pira's right. Pom's right.
What have we been, other than very, very wrong?
To be honest, it might be good for us to take a little break from each other.
We may know each other's best qualities, but we also know how to build up the worst in us.
You're a good person for doing this, Kyle.
Heh.
It certainly saves you the headache, doesn't it?
Your personal thoughts will be on hold while I'm within you. At most, you'll be able to see what I see with your eyes.
Are you prepared to become a vessel?
Just take good care of my body.

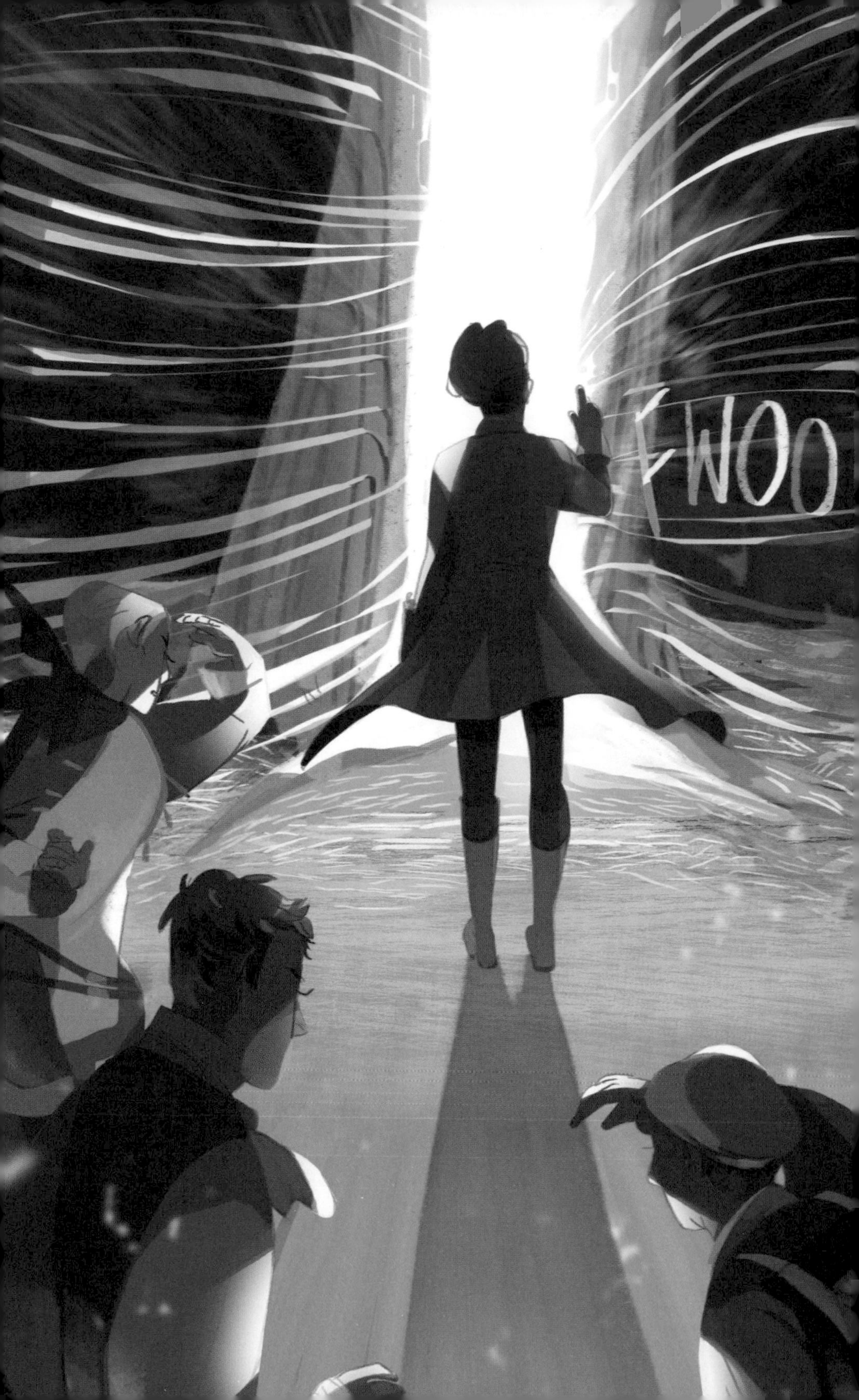
FWOO

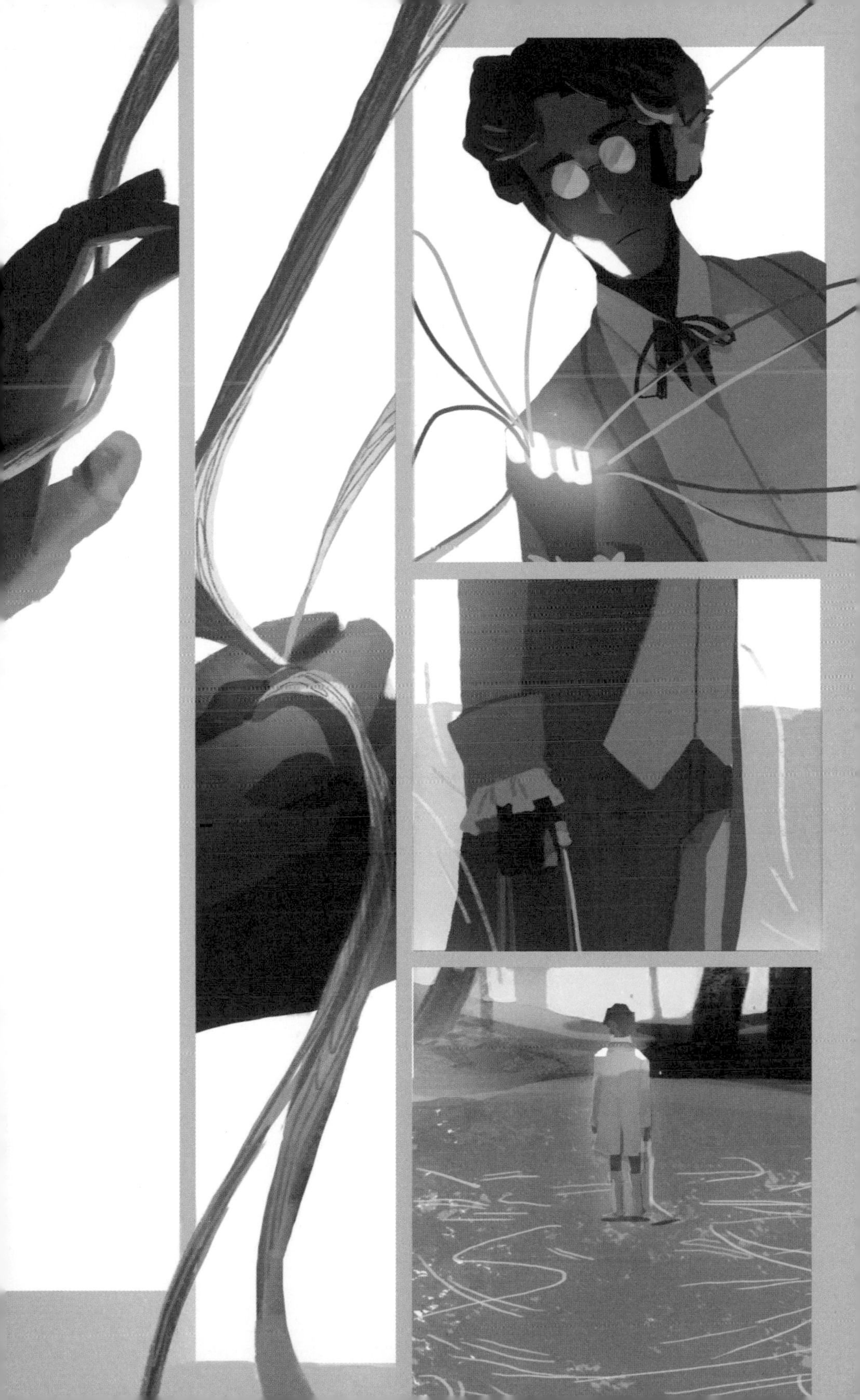

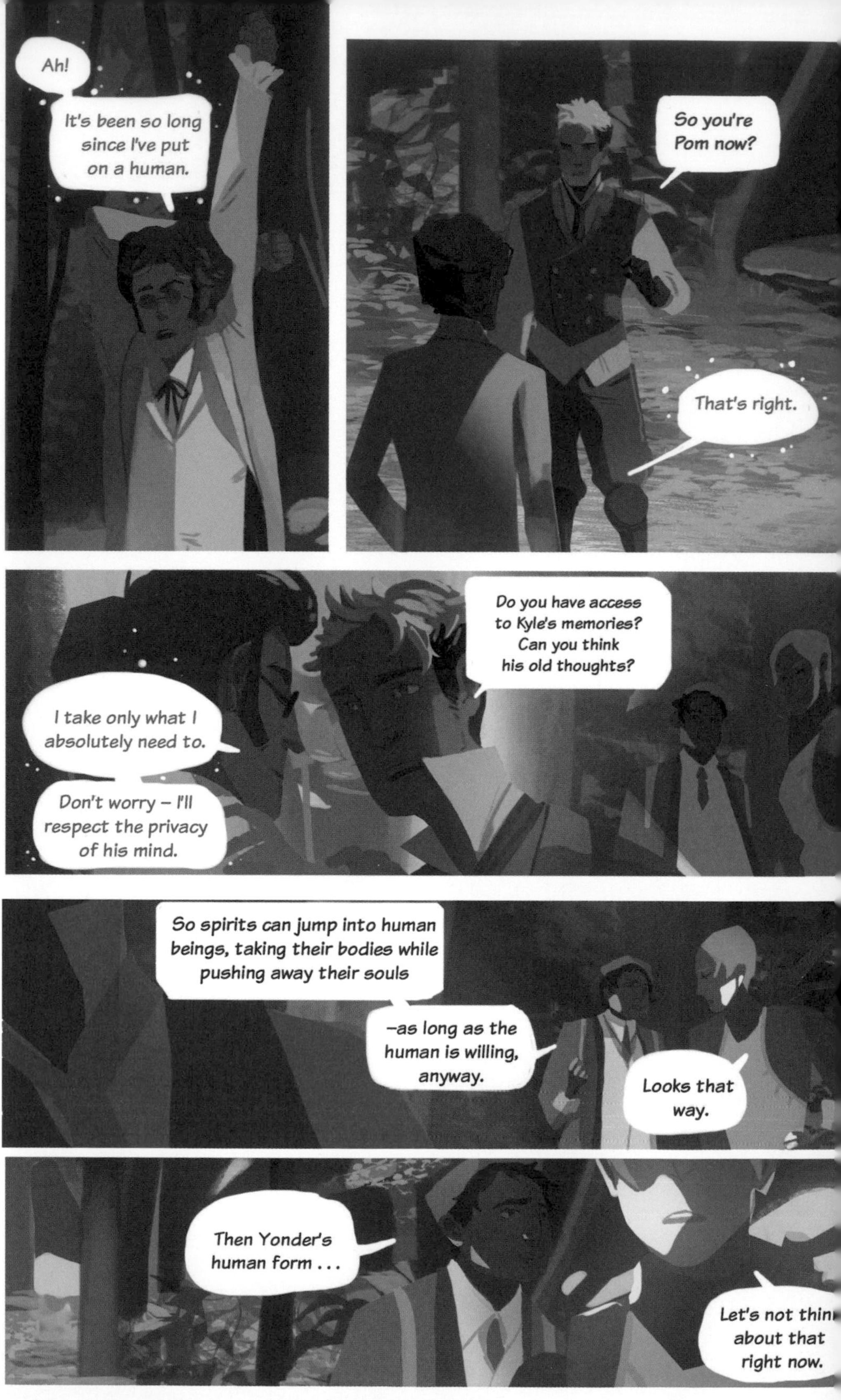
Ah!
It's been so long since I've put on a human.
So you're Pom now?
That's right.
Do you have access to Kyle's memories? Can you think his old thoughts?
I take only what I absolutely need to.
Don't worry – I'll respect the privacy of his mind.
So spirits can jump into human beings, taking their bodies while pushing away their souls
–as long as the human is willing, anyway.
Looks that way.
Then Yonder's human form . . .
Let's not thin about that right now.

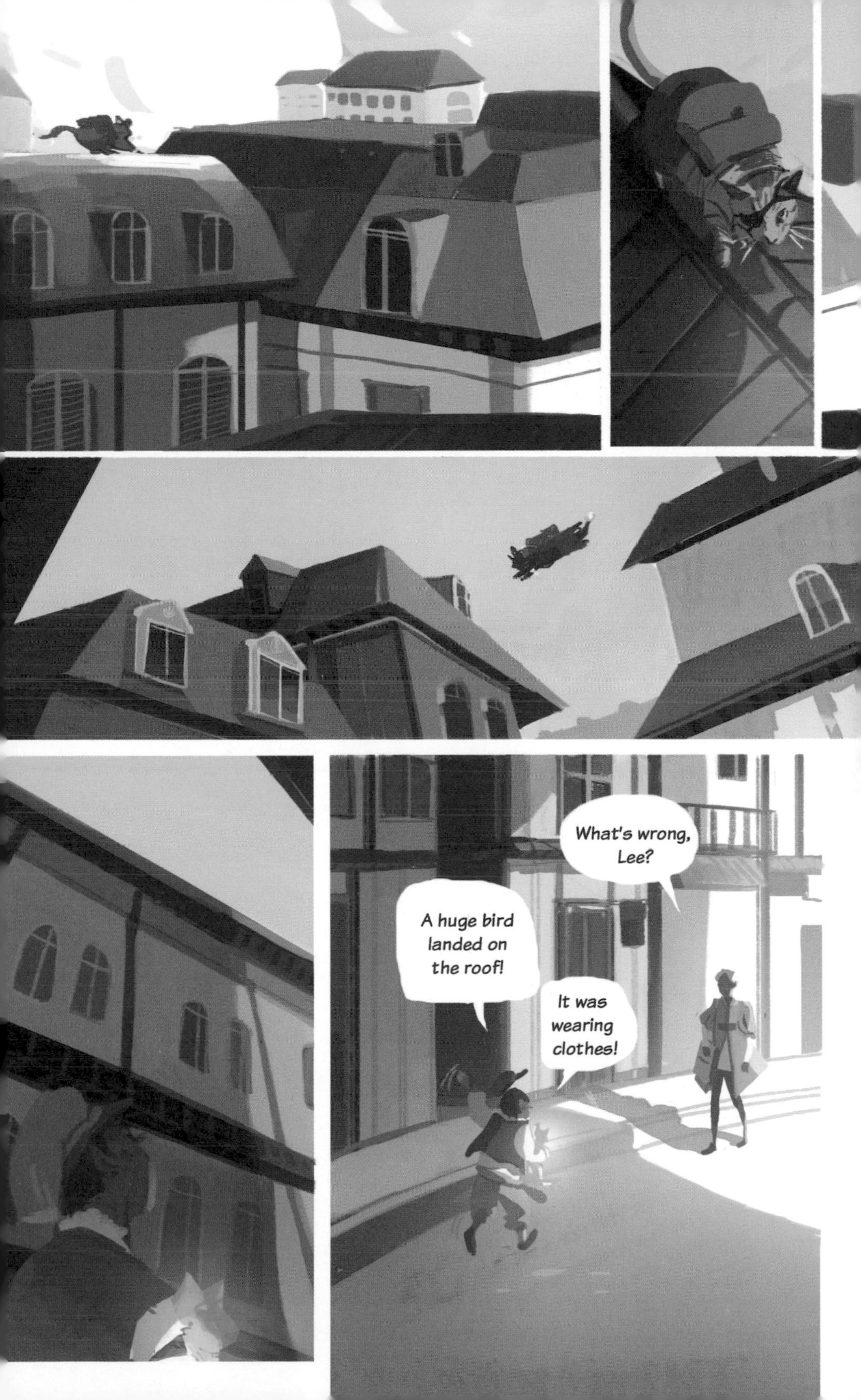
What's wrong, Lee?
A huge bird landed on the roof!
It was wearing clothes!

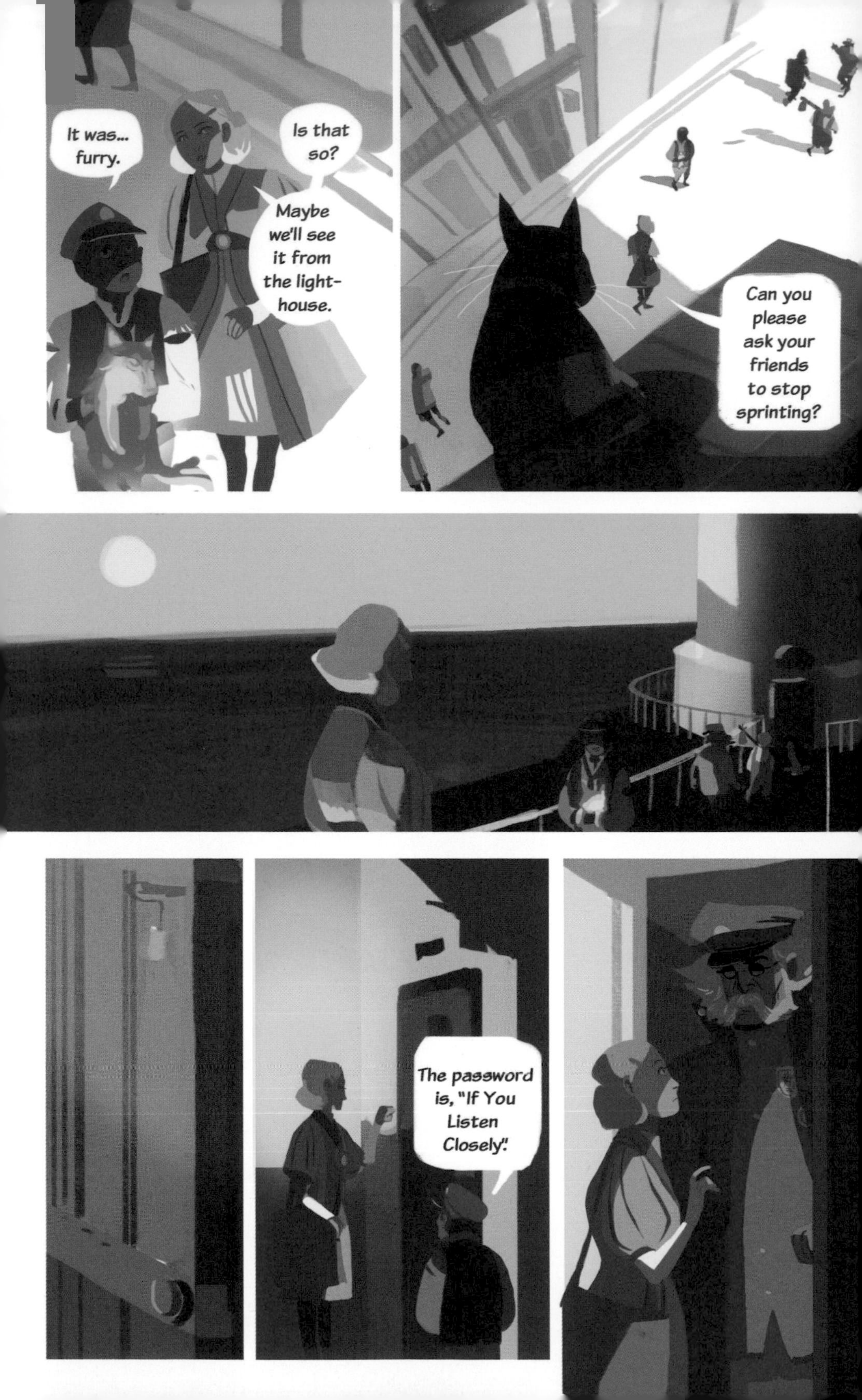
It was... furry.
Is that so?
Maybe we'll see it from the light-house.
Can you please ask your friends to stop sprinting?
The password is, "If You Listen Closely".

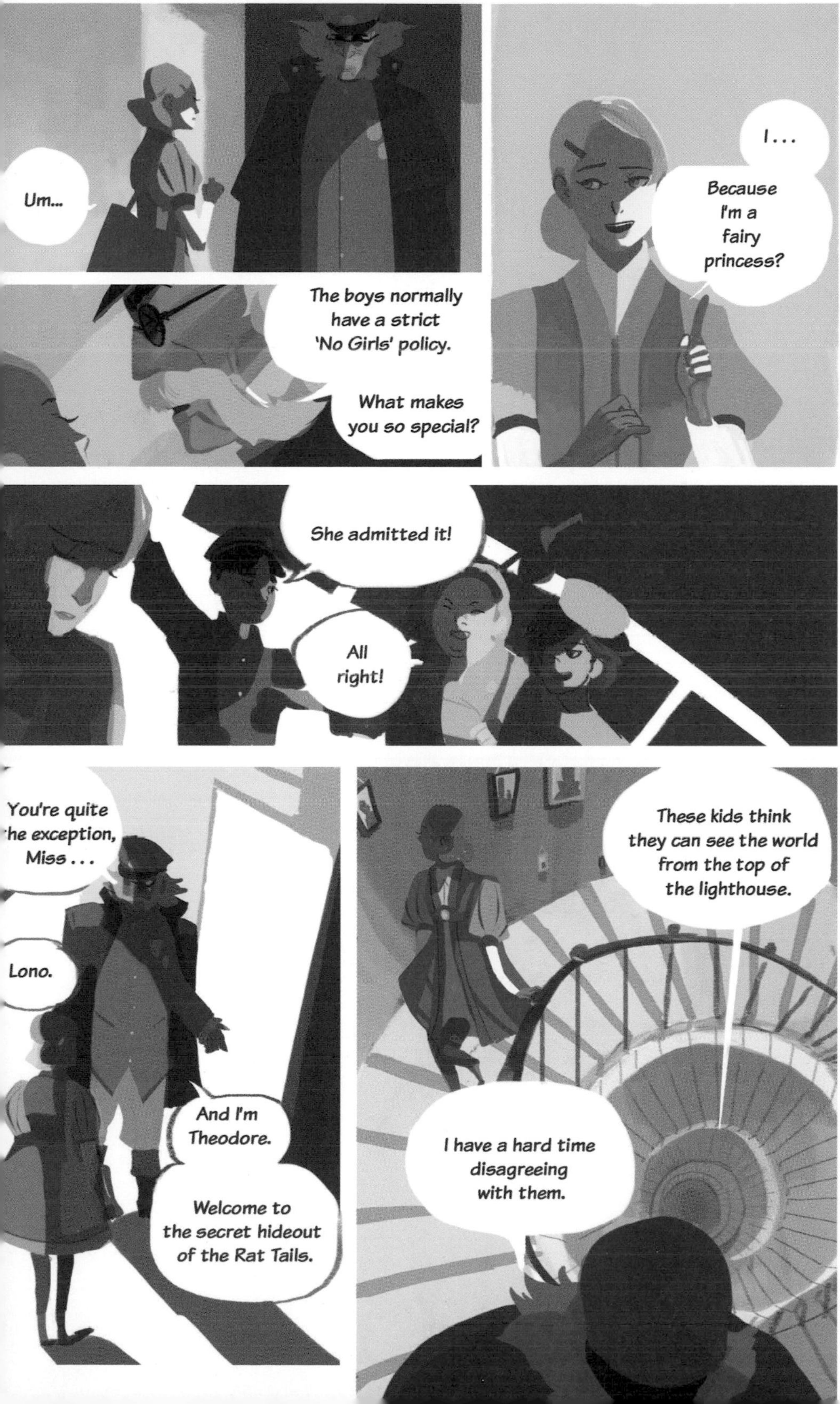
Um...
The boys normally have a strict 'No Girls' policy.
What makes you so special?
I . . .
Because I'm a fairy princess?
She admitted it!
All right!
You're quite the exception, Miss . . .
Lono.
And I'm Theodore.
Welcome to the secret hideout of the Rat Tails.
These kids think they can see the world from the top of the lighthouse.
I have a hard time disagreeing with them.

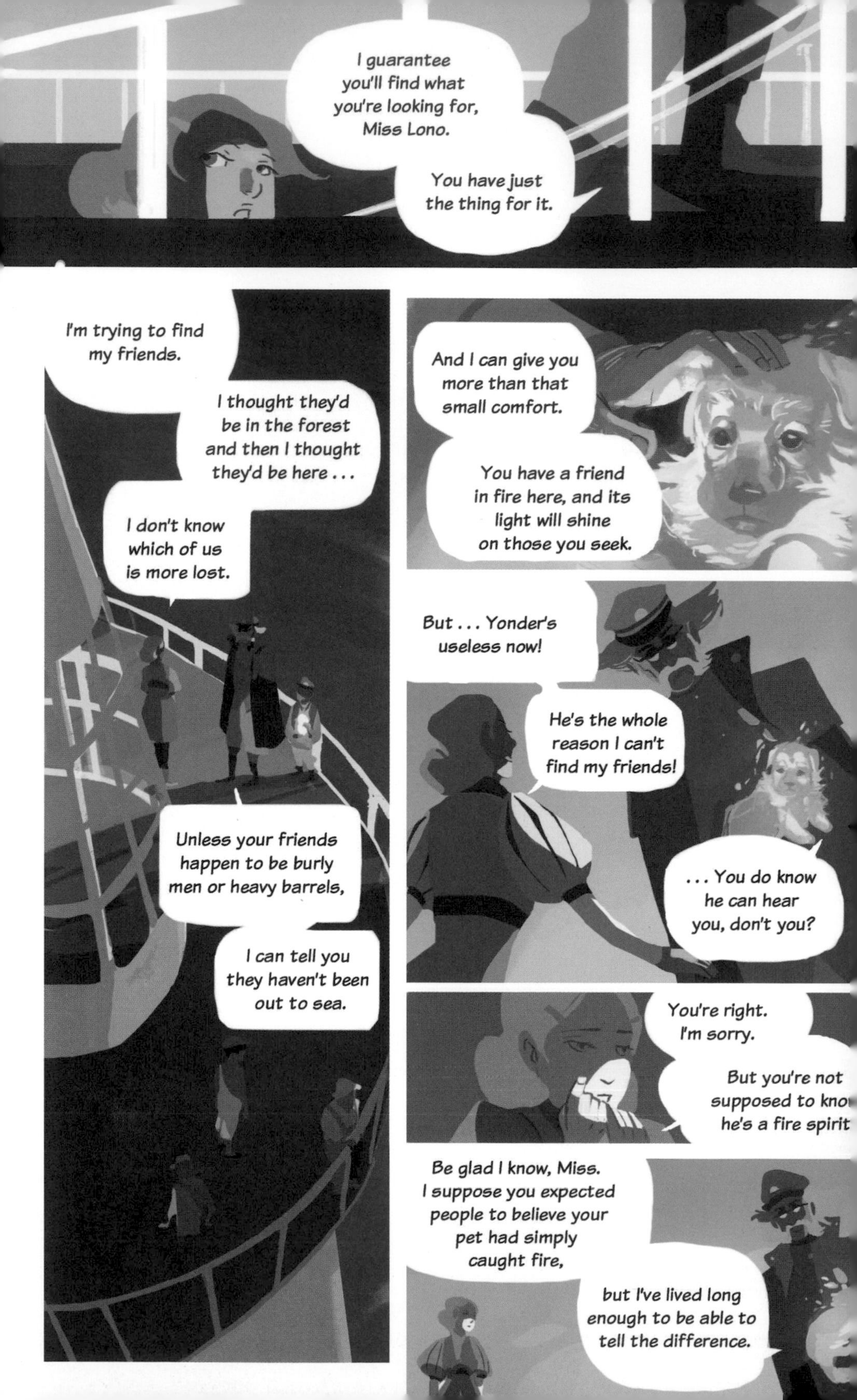
I guarantee you'll find what you're looking for, Miss Lono.
You have just the thing for it.
I'm trying to find my friends.
I thought they'd be in the forest and then I thought they'd be here . . .
I don't know which of us is more lost.
Unless your friends happen to be burly men or heavy barrels,
I can tell you they haven't been out to sea.
And I can give you more than that small comfort.
You have a friend in fire here, and its light will shine on those you seek.
But . . . Yonder's useless now!
He's the whole reason I can't find my friends!
. . . You do know he can hear you, don't you?
You're right. I'm sorry.
But you're not supposed to kno
he's a fire spirit
Be glad I know, Miss. I suppose you expected people to believe your pet had simply caught fire,
but I've lived long enough to be able to tell the difference.

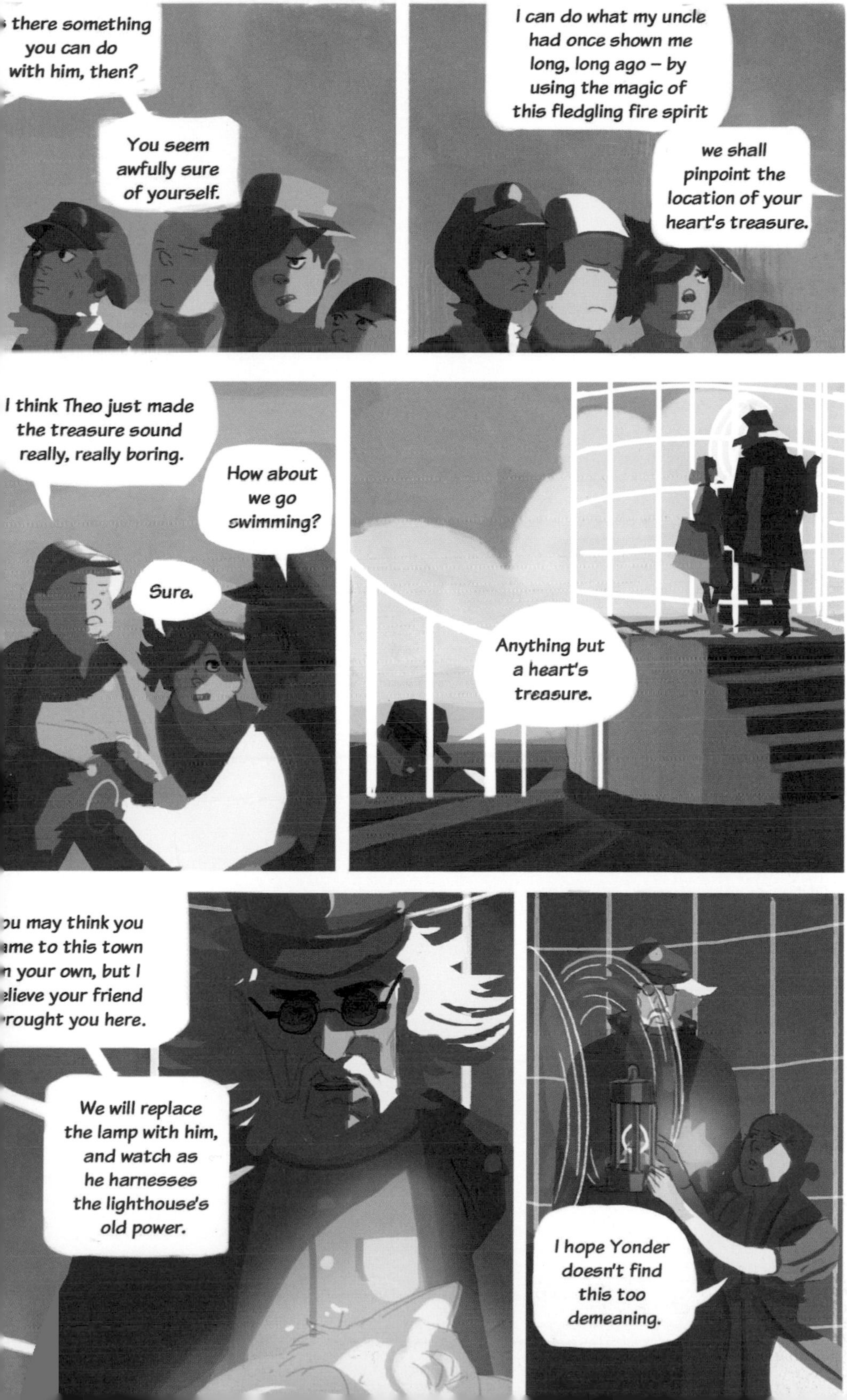
there something you can do with him, then?
You seem awfully sure of yourself.
I can do what my uncle had once shown me long, long ago – by using the magic of this fledgling fire spirit
we shall pinpoint the location of your heart's treasure.
I think Theo just made the treasure sound really, really boring.
How about we go swimming?
Sure.
Anything but a heart's treasure.
u may think you me to this town your own, but I lieve your friend rought you here.
We will replace the lamp with him, and watch as he harnesses the lighthouse's old power.
I hope Yonder doesn't find this too demeaning.

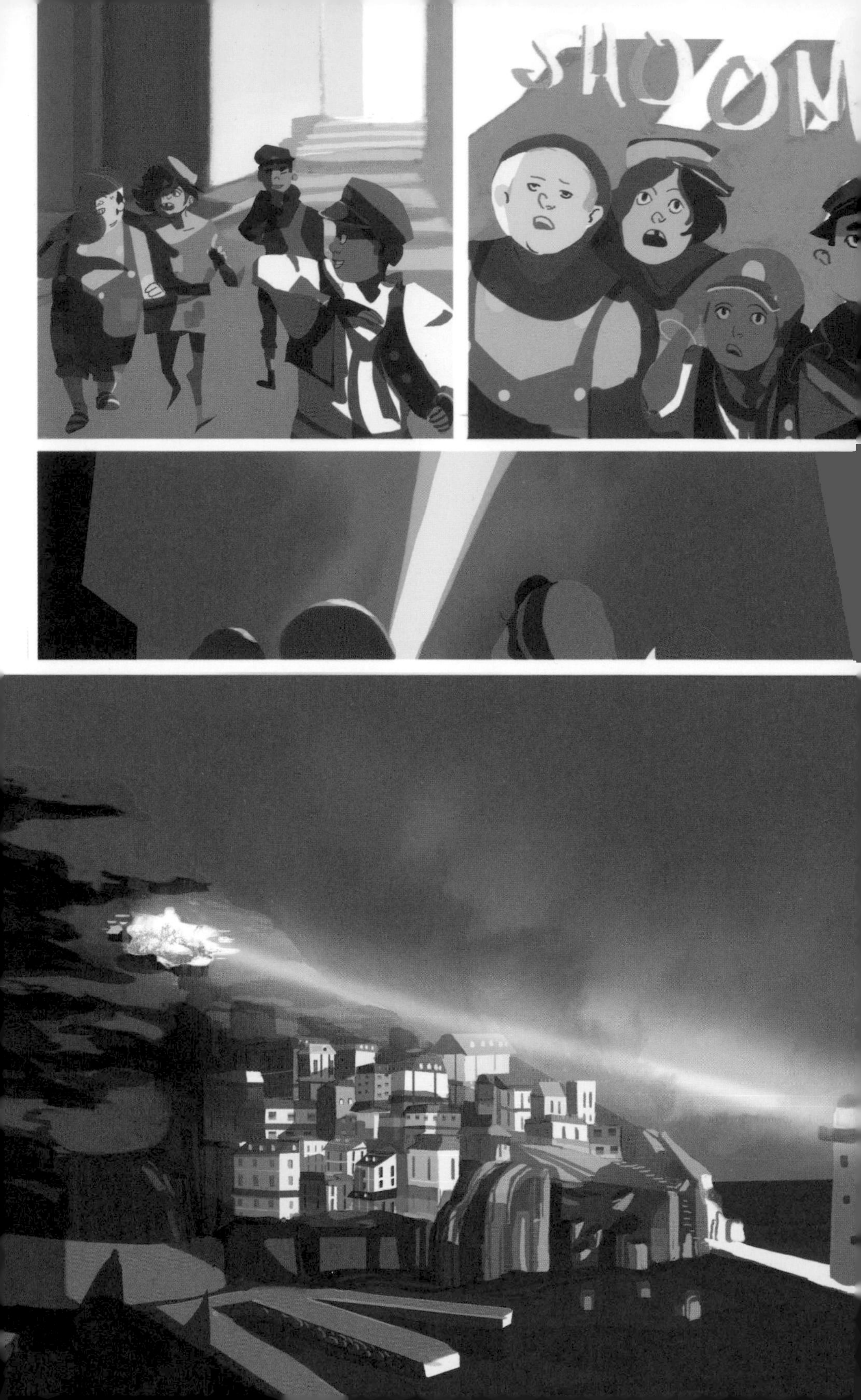
SHOOM

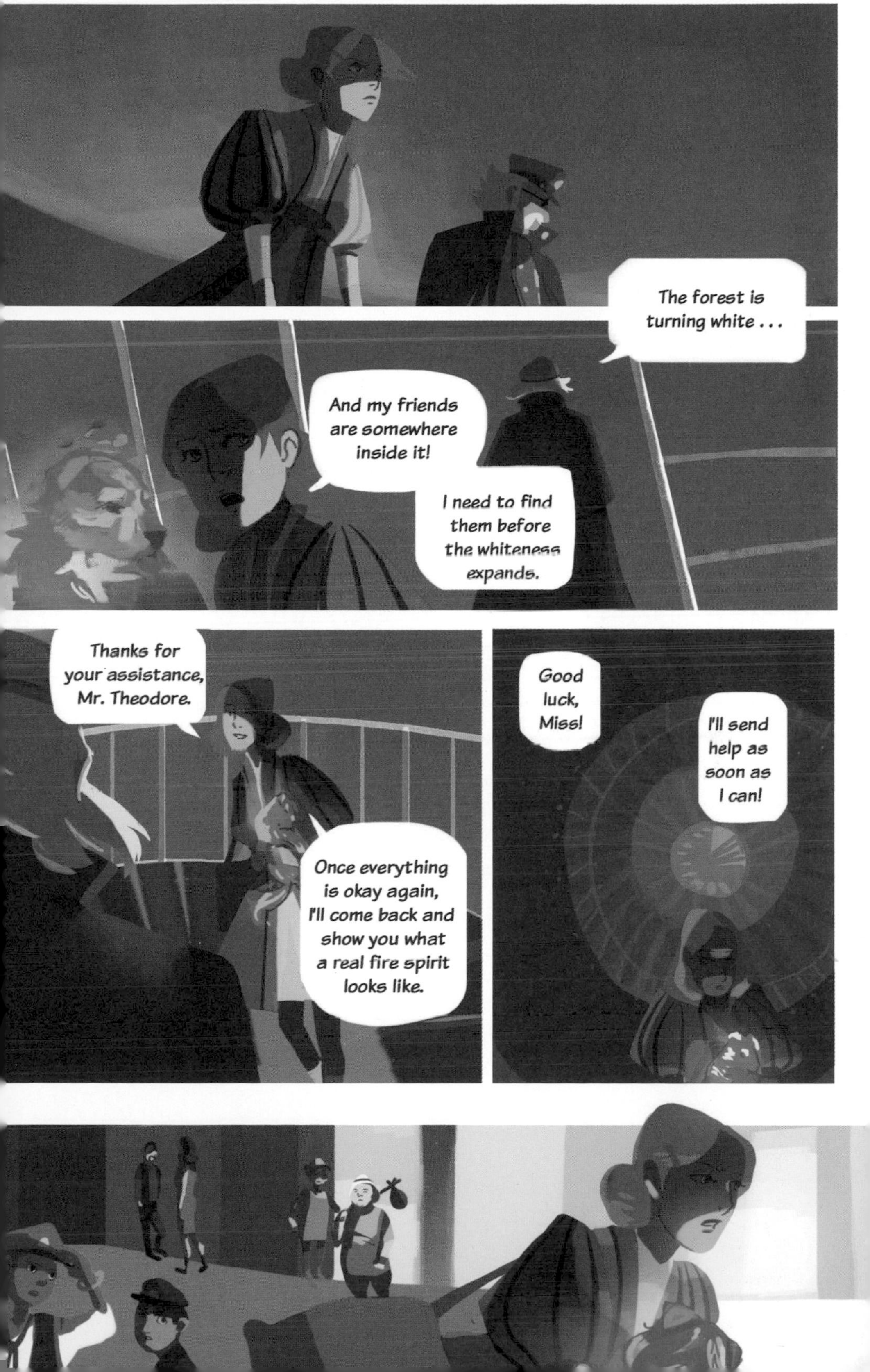
The forest is turning white . . .
And my friends are somewhere inside it!
I need to find them before the whiteness expands.
Thanks for your assistance, Mr. Theodore.
Once everything is okay again, I'll come back and show you what a real fire spirit looks like.
Good luck, Miss!
I'll send help as soon as I can!

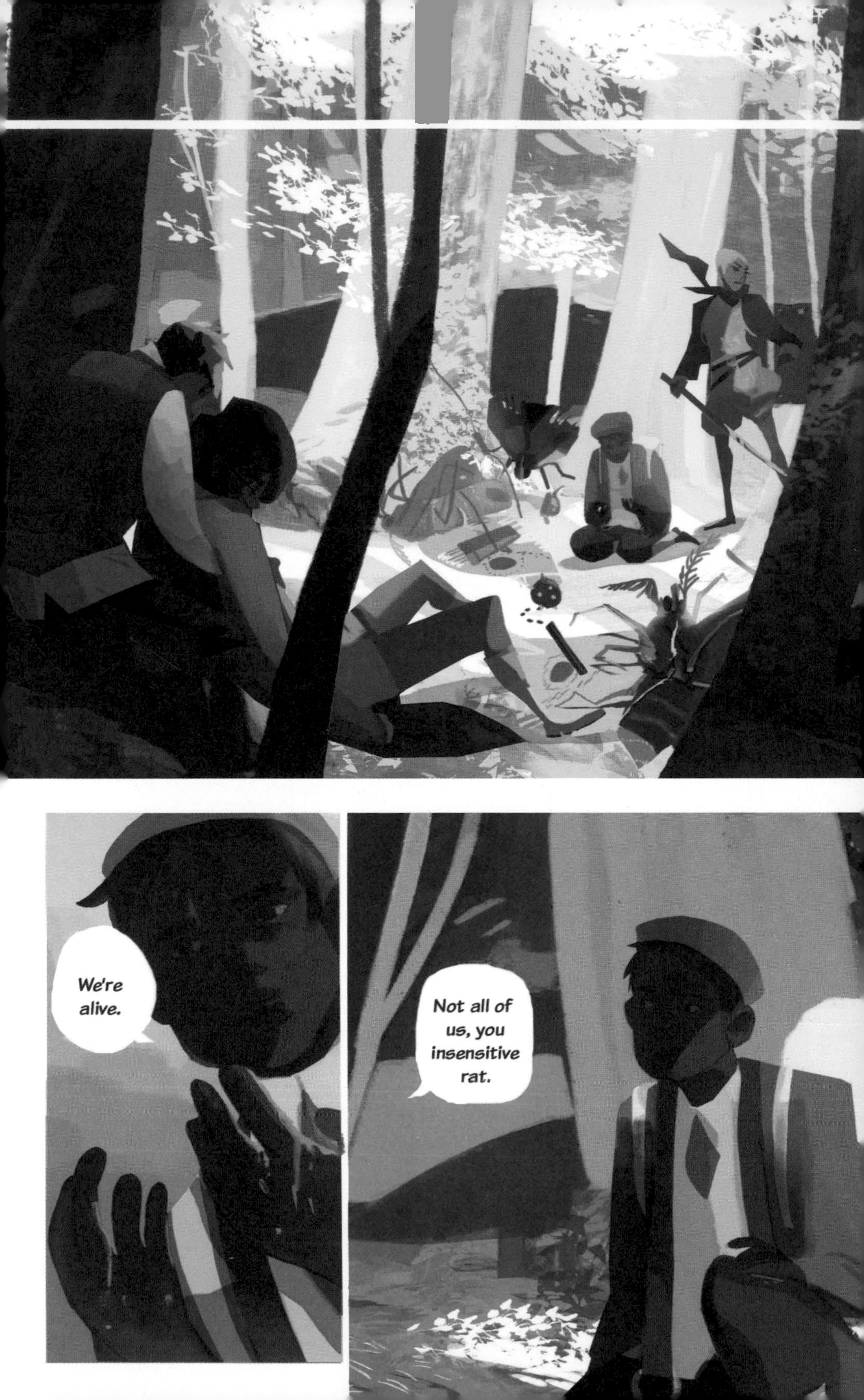
We're alive.
Not all of us, you insensitive rat.

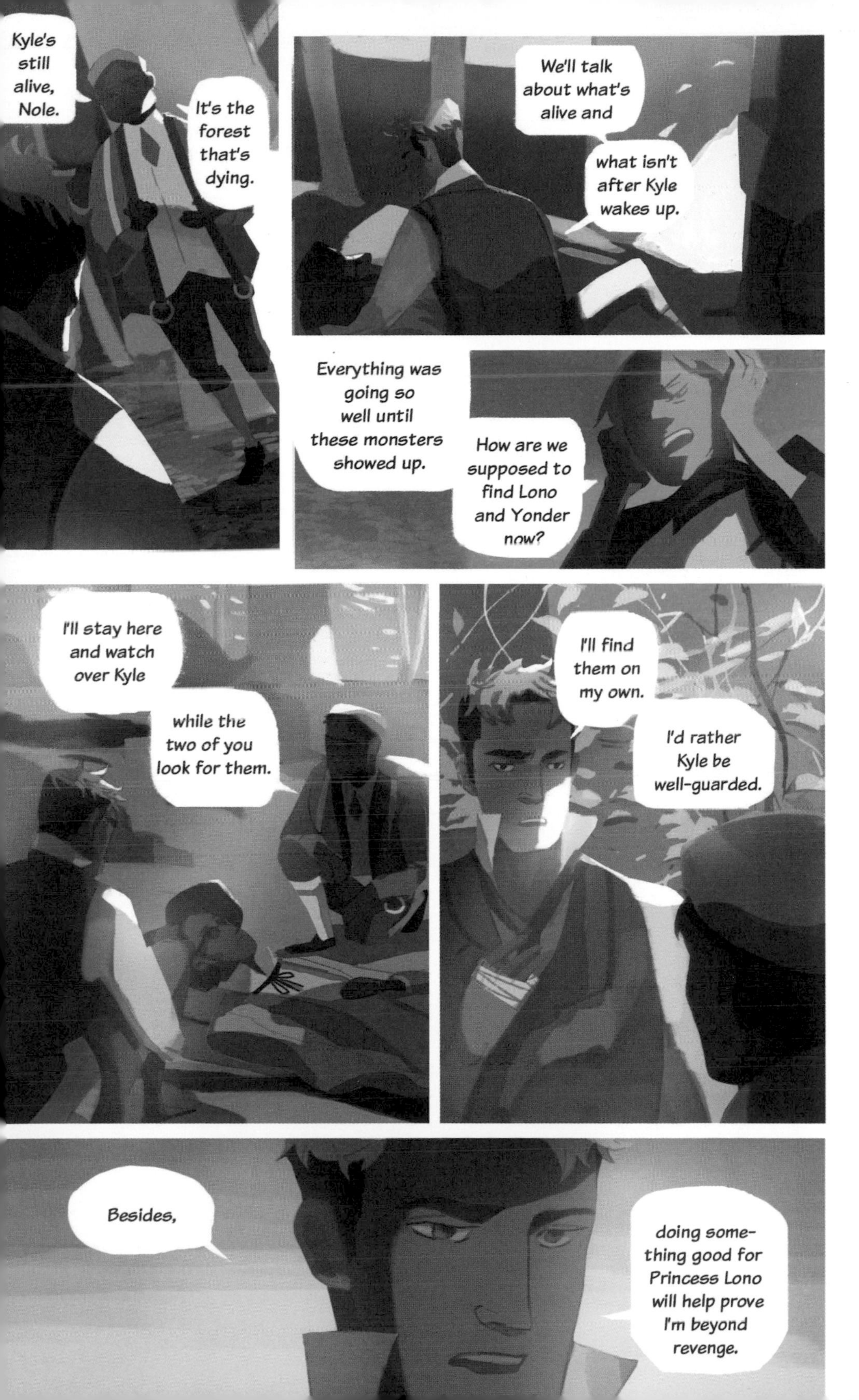
Kyle's still alive, Nole.
It's the forest that's dying.
We'll talk about what's alive and
what isn't after Kyle wakes up.
Everything was going so well until these monsters showed up.
How are we supposed to find Lono and Yonder now?
I'll stay here and watch over Kyle
while the two of you look for them.
I'll find them on my own.
I'd rather Kyle be well-guarded.
Besides,
doing some-thing good for Princess Lono will help prove I'm beyond revenge.

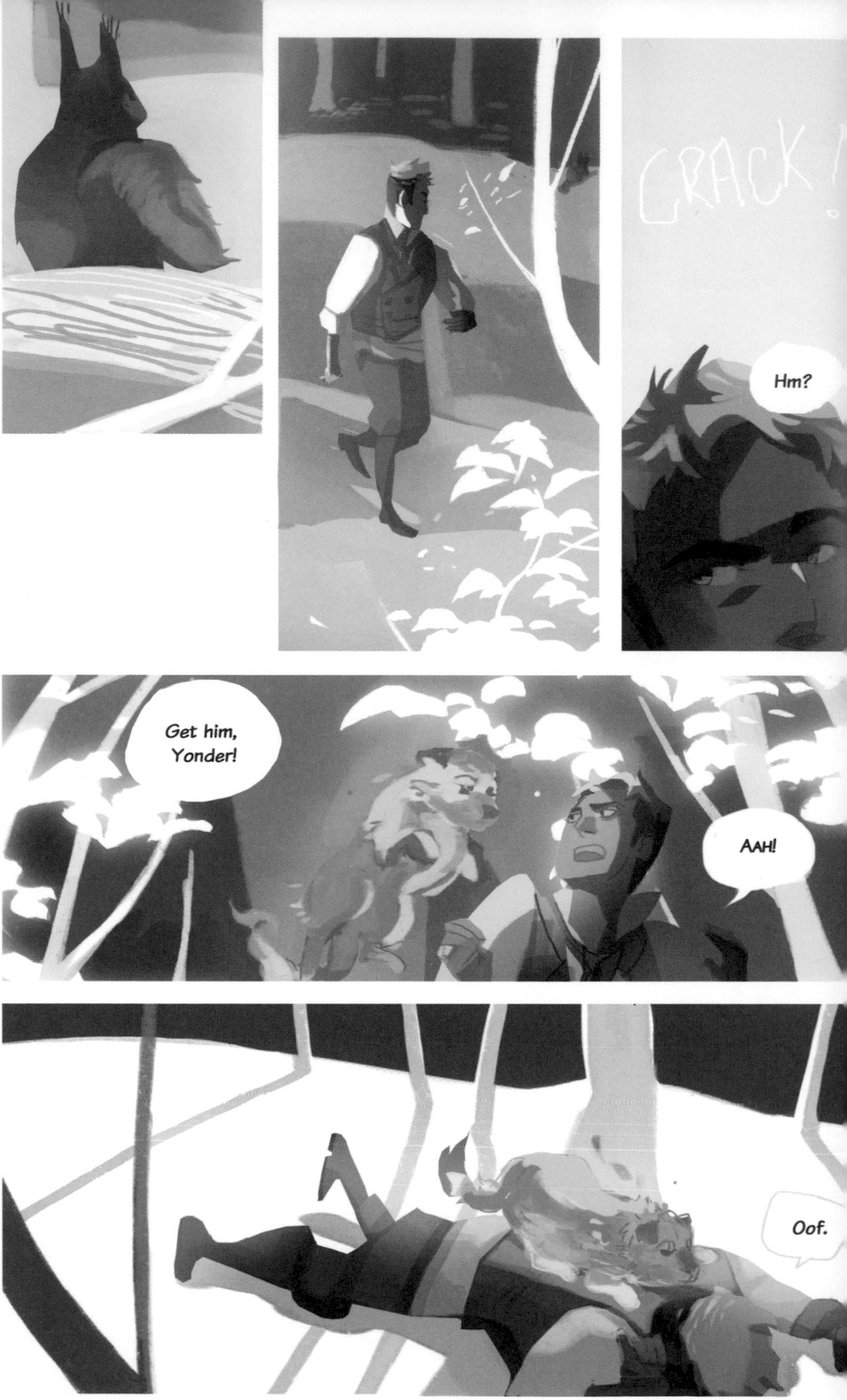
CRACK!
Hm?
Get him, Yonder!
AAH!
Oof.

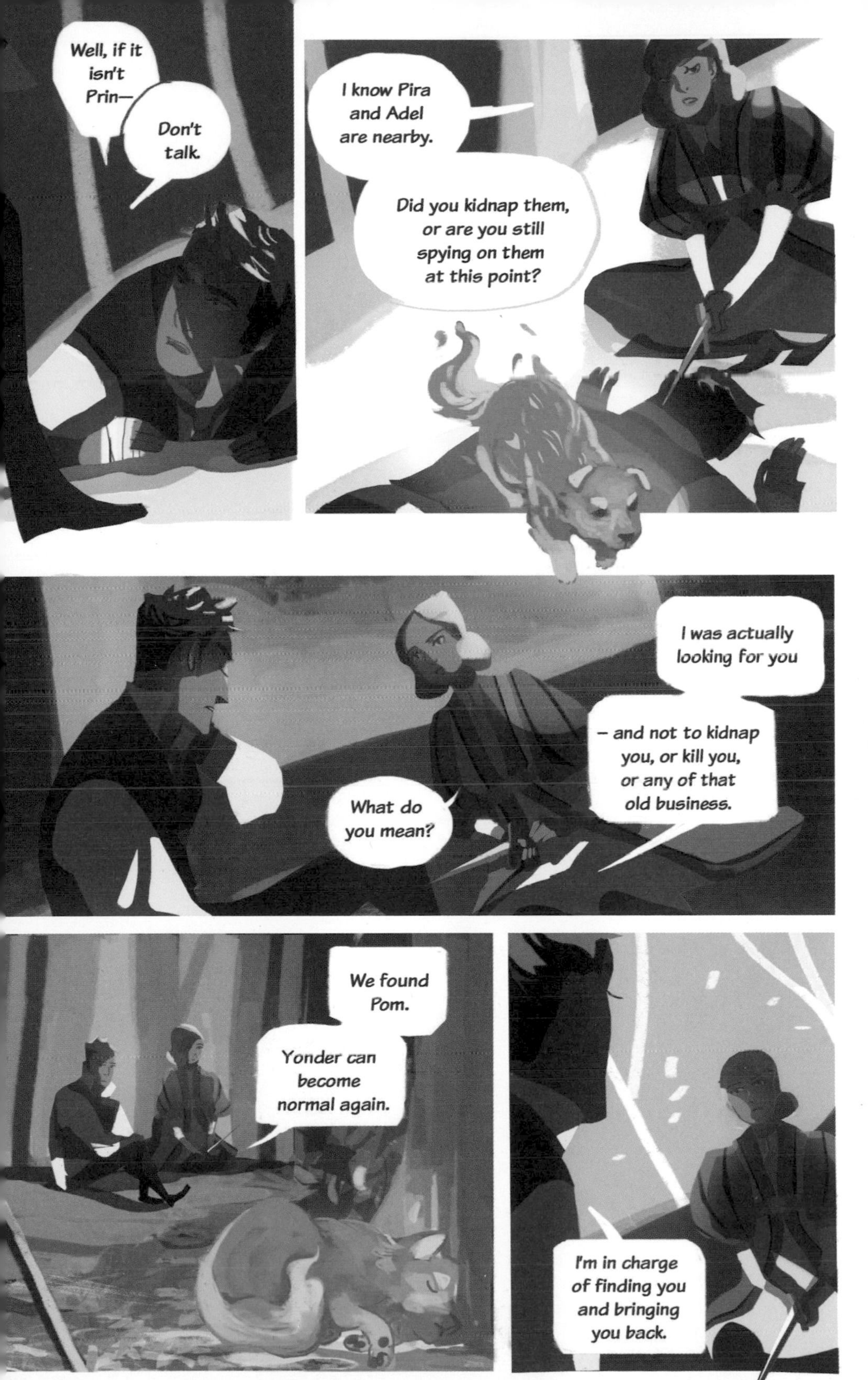
Well, if it isn't Prin—
Don't talk.
I know Pira and Adel are nearby.
Did you kidnap them, or are you still spying on them at this point?
I was actually looking for you
– and not to kidnap you, or kill you, or any of that old business.
What do you mean?
We found Pom.
Yonder can become normal again.
I'm in charge of finding you and bringing you back.

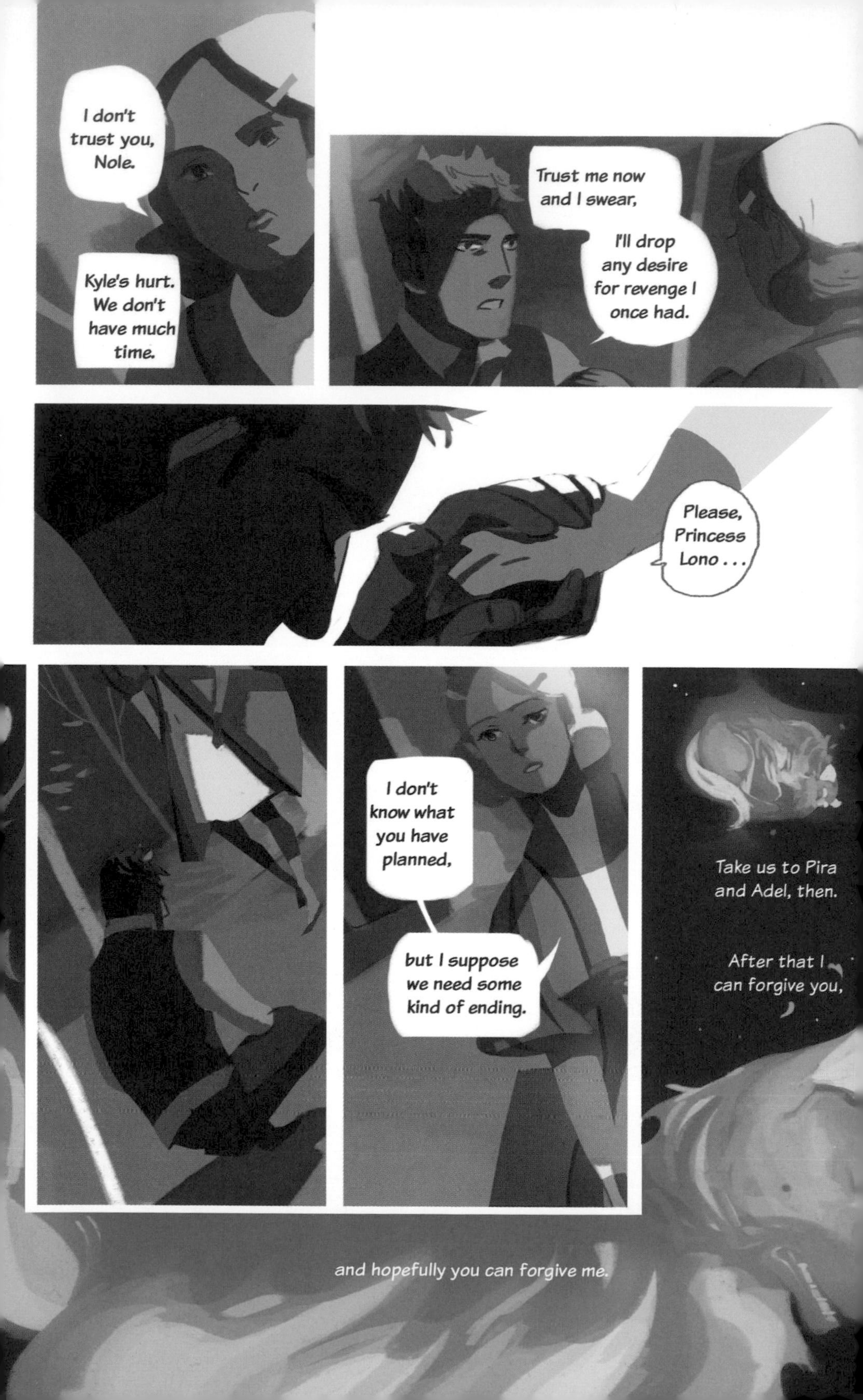
I don't trust you, Nole.
Kyle's hurt. We don't have much time.
Trust me now and I swear,
I'll drop any desire for revenge I once had.
Please, Princess Lono . . .
I don't know what you have planned,
but I suppose we need some kind of ending.
Take us to Pira and Adel, then.
After that I can forgive you,
and hopefully you can forgive me.

WARRIOR TABBY LEAP

MOVEMENT | JUMP

Even the fattest of cats can scale the greatest of heights.

Roll two dice to move instead of one.

Event locations and points of interest for your character to explore.

...ds, quests and skill monsters here.

...friendly and enemy creatures fill the landscape of Spera.

PIRA

Everything was going so well until these monsters showed up. How are we supposed to find **Lono** and **Yonder** now?

: | Determines the

h & Magic | Denotes items or sk

...dard Weapons | Weapons that off

...vy Weapons | Weapons that offer

...ght Weapons | Weapons that offer li

...gendary Weapons | Special weapons that offer unique damage, stamina, and buffer stats.

Nature Element | Elemental classification for creatures, weapons and spells.

CHAPTER FIVE
Whole Again

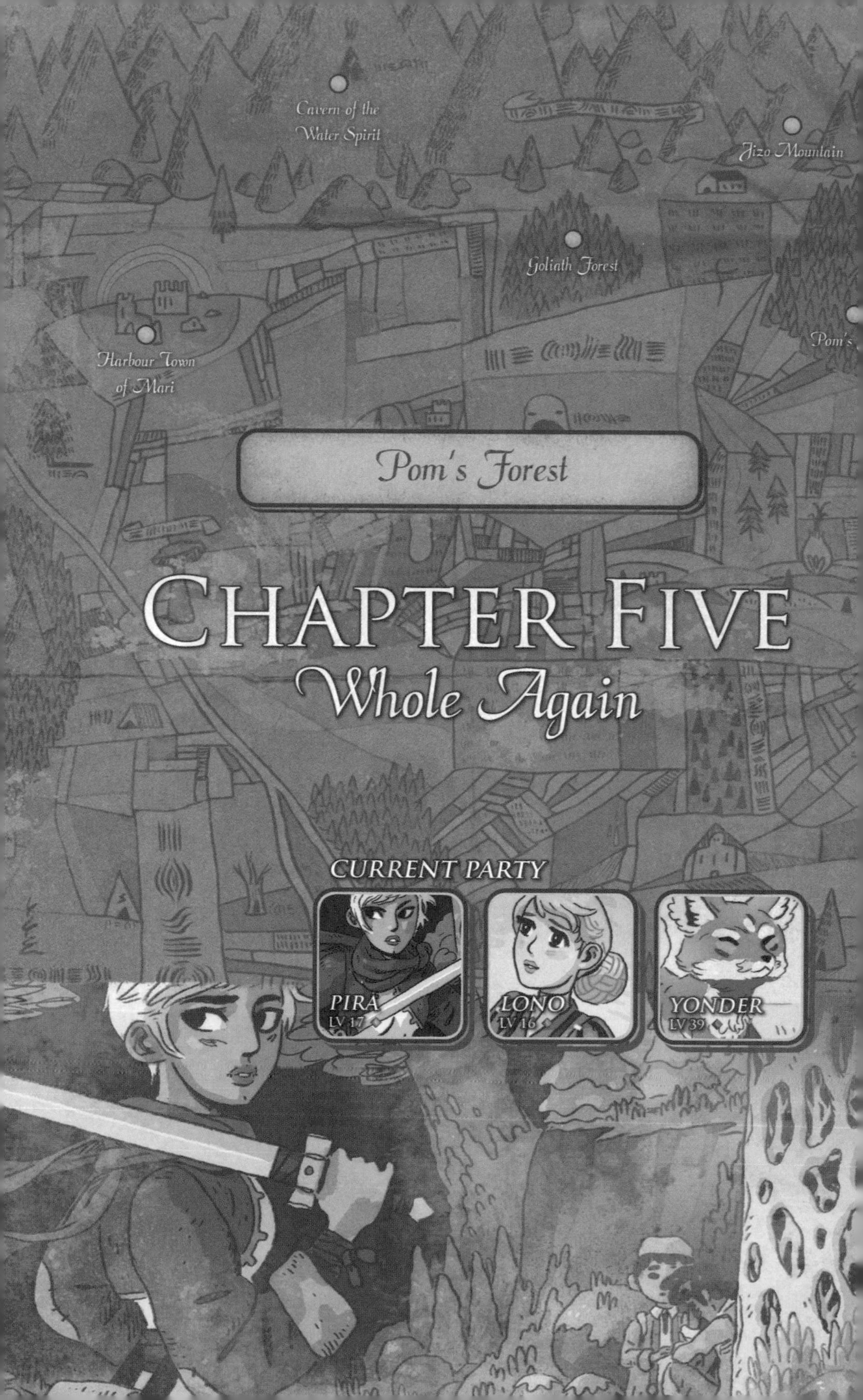
Cavern of the Water Spirit
Jizo Mountain
Goliath Forest
Harbour Town of Mari
Pom's
Pom's Forest
CURRENT PARTY
PIRA
LV 17
LONO
LV 16
YONDER
LV 39

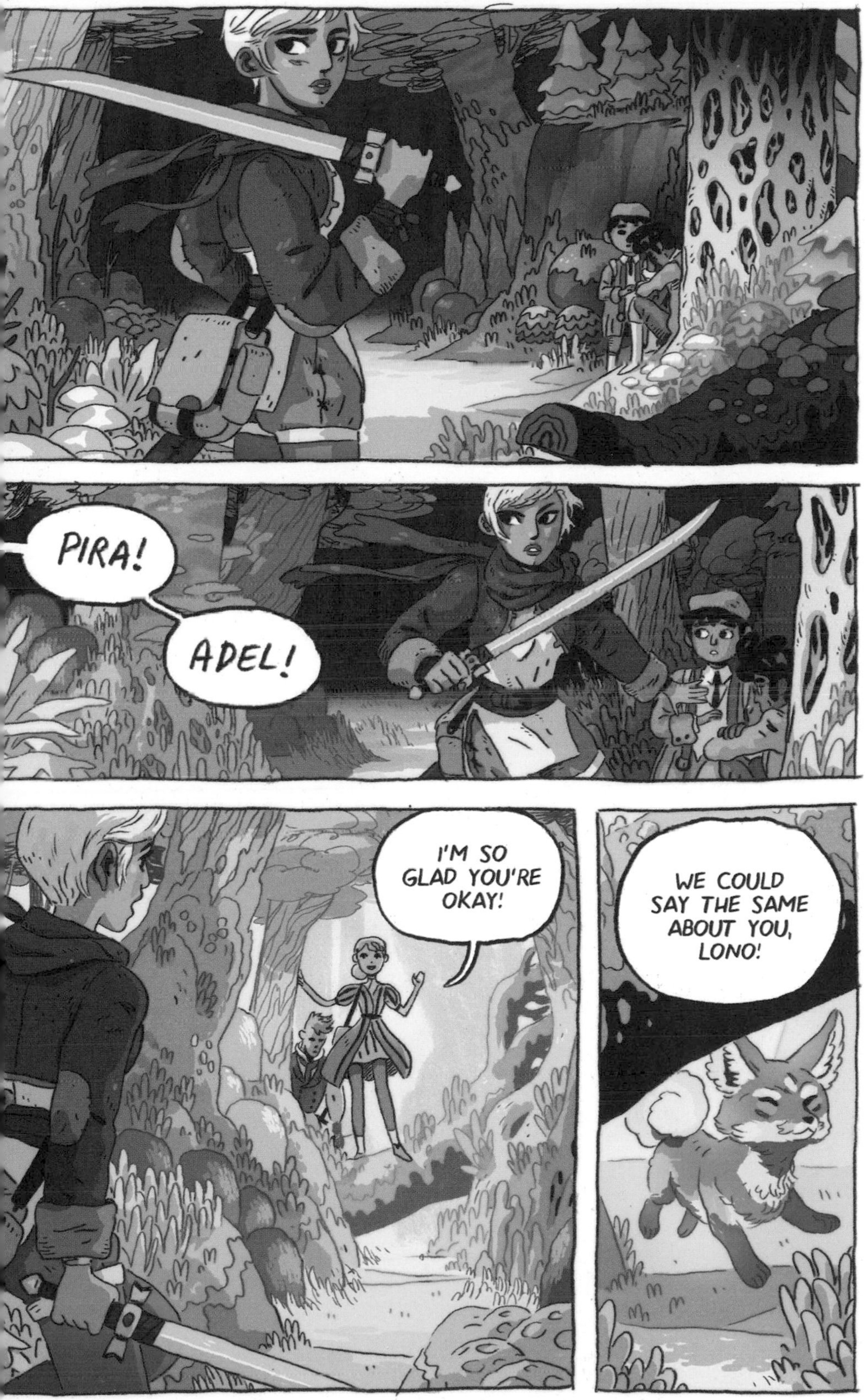
PIRA!
ADEL!
I'M SO GLAD YOU'RE OKAY!
WE COULD SAY THE SAME ABOUT YOU, LONO!

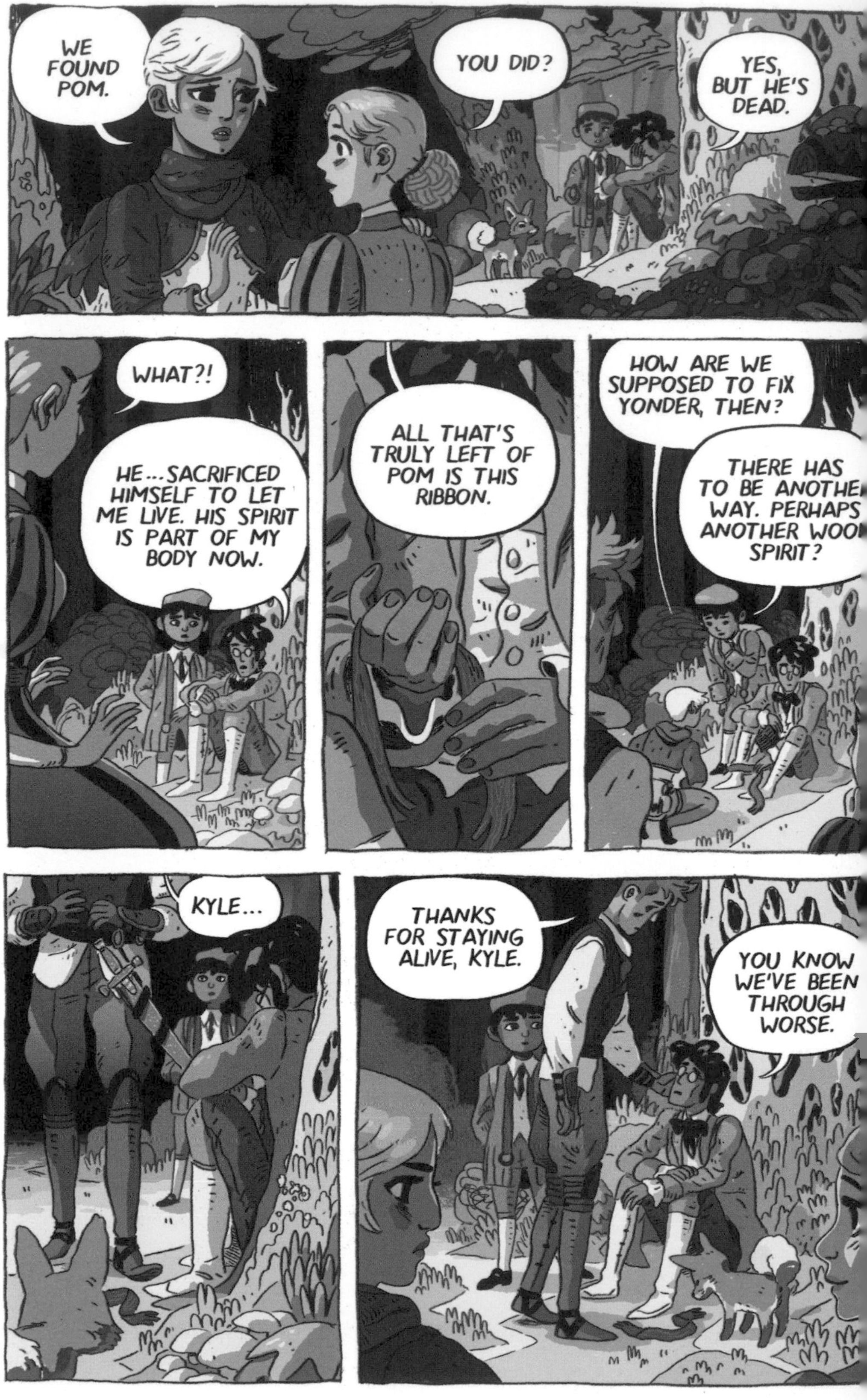
WE FOUND POM.
YOU DID?
YES, BUT HE'S DEAD.
WHAT?!
HE...SACRIFICED HIMSELF TO LET ME LIVE. HIS SPIRIT IS PART OF MY BODY NOW.
ALL THAT'S TRULY LEFT OF POM IS THIS RIBBON.
HOW ARE WE SUPPOSED TO FIX YONDER, THEN?
THERE HAS TO BE ANOTHE WAY. PERHAPS ANOTHER WOO SPIRIT?
KYLE...
THANKS FOR STAYING ALIVE, KYLE.
YOU KNOW WE'VE BEEN THROUGH WORSE.

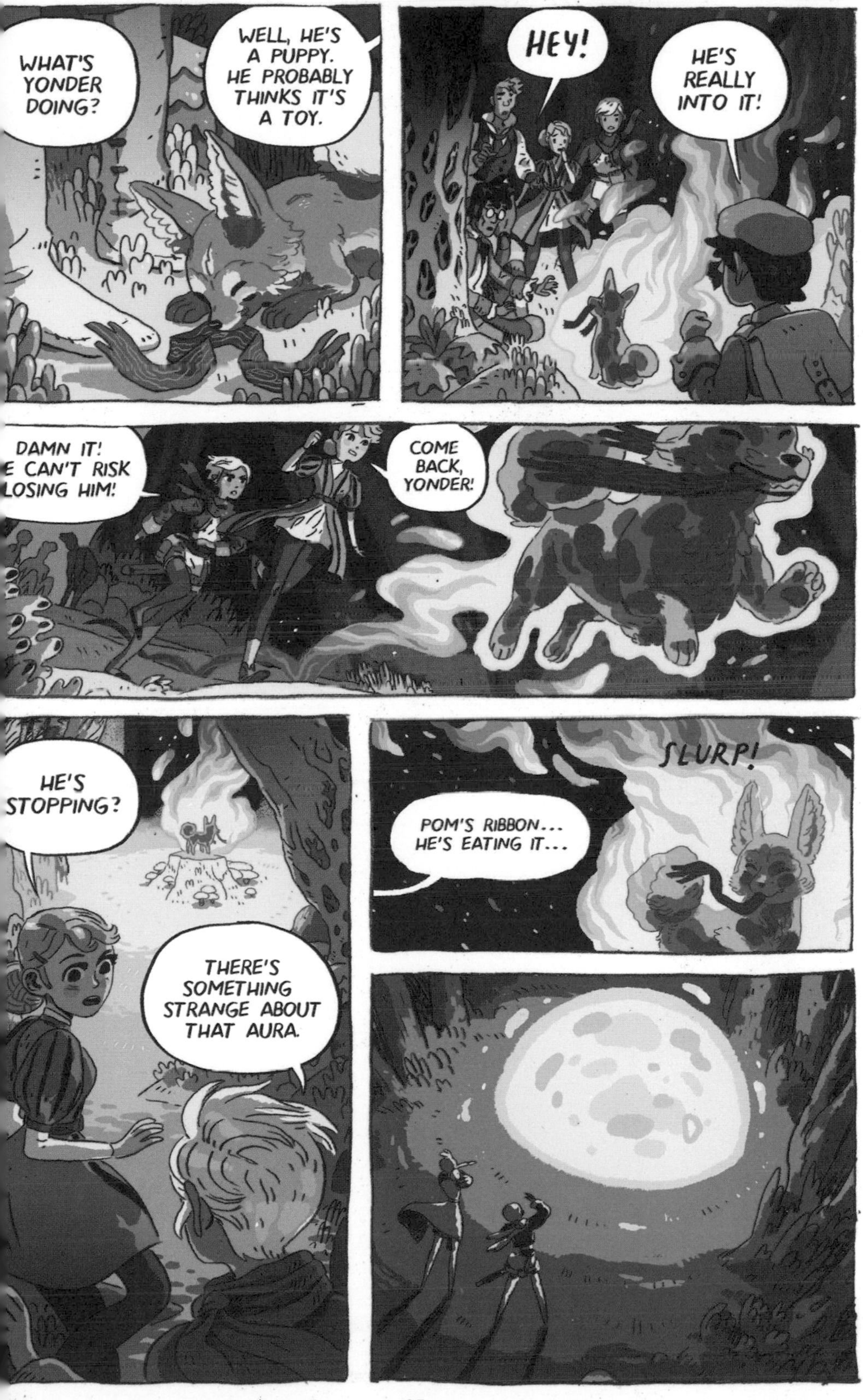

WHAT'S YONDER DOING?
WELL, HE'S A PUPPY. HE PROBABLY THINKS IT'S A TOY.
HEY!
HE'S REALLY INTO IT!
DAMN IT! E CAN'T RISK LOSING HIM!
COME BACK, YONDER!
HE'S STOPPING?
THERE'S SOMETHING STRANGE ABOUT THAT AURA.
SLURP!
POM'S RIBBON... HE'S EATING IT...

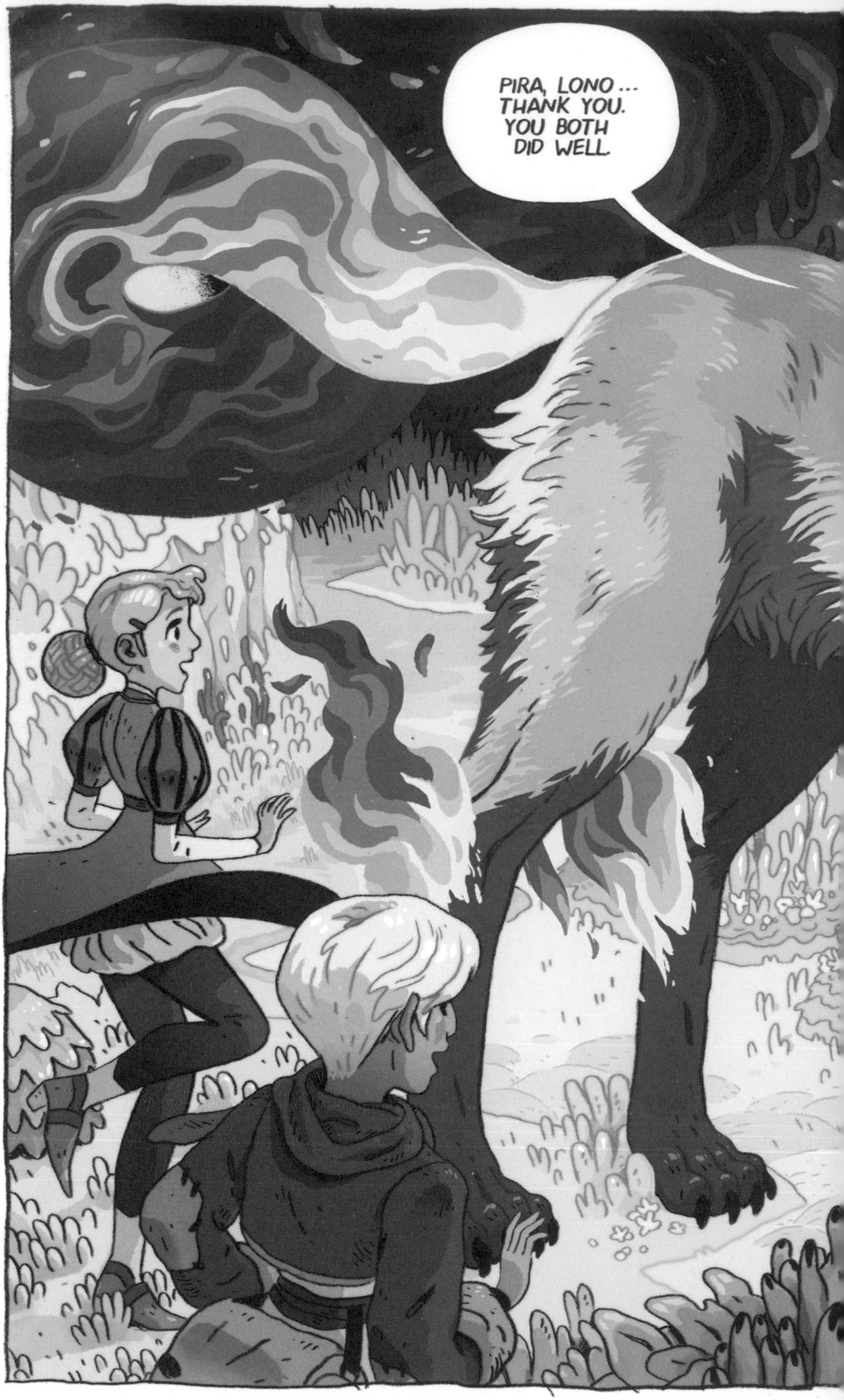
PIRA, LONO...
THANK YOU.
YOU BOTH
DID WELL.

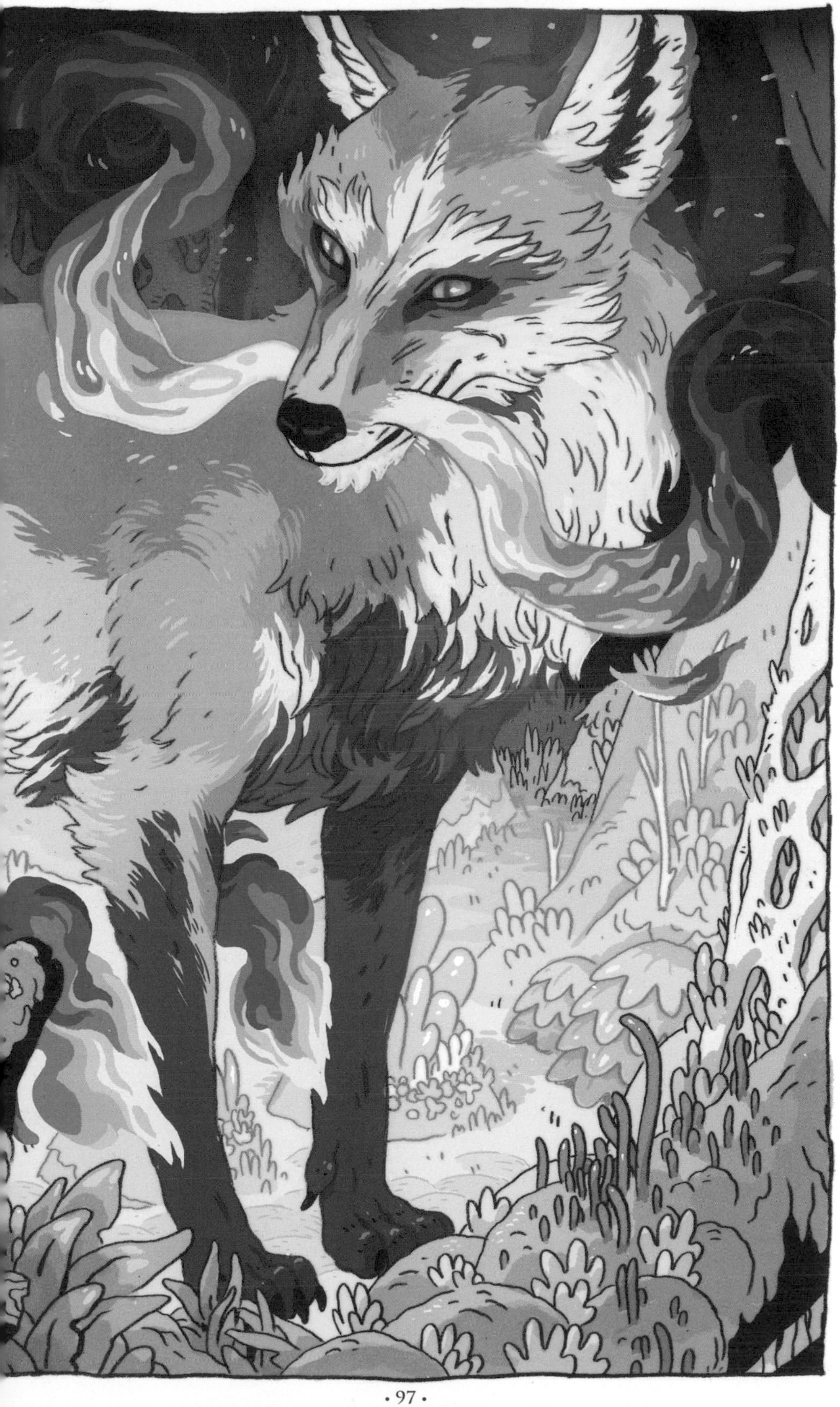

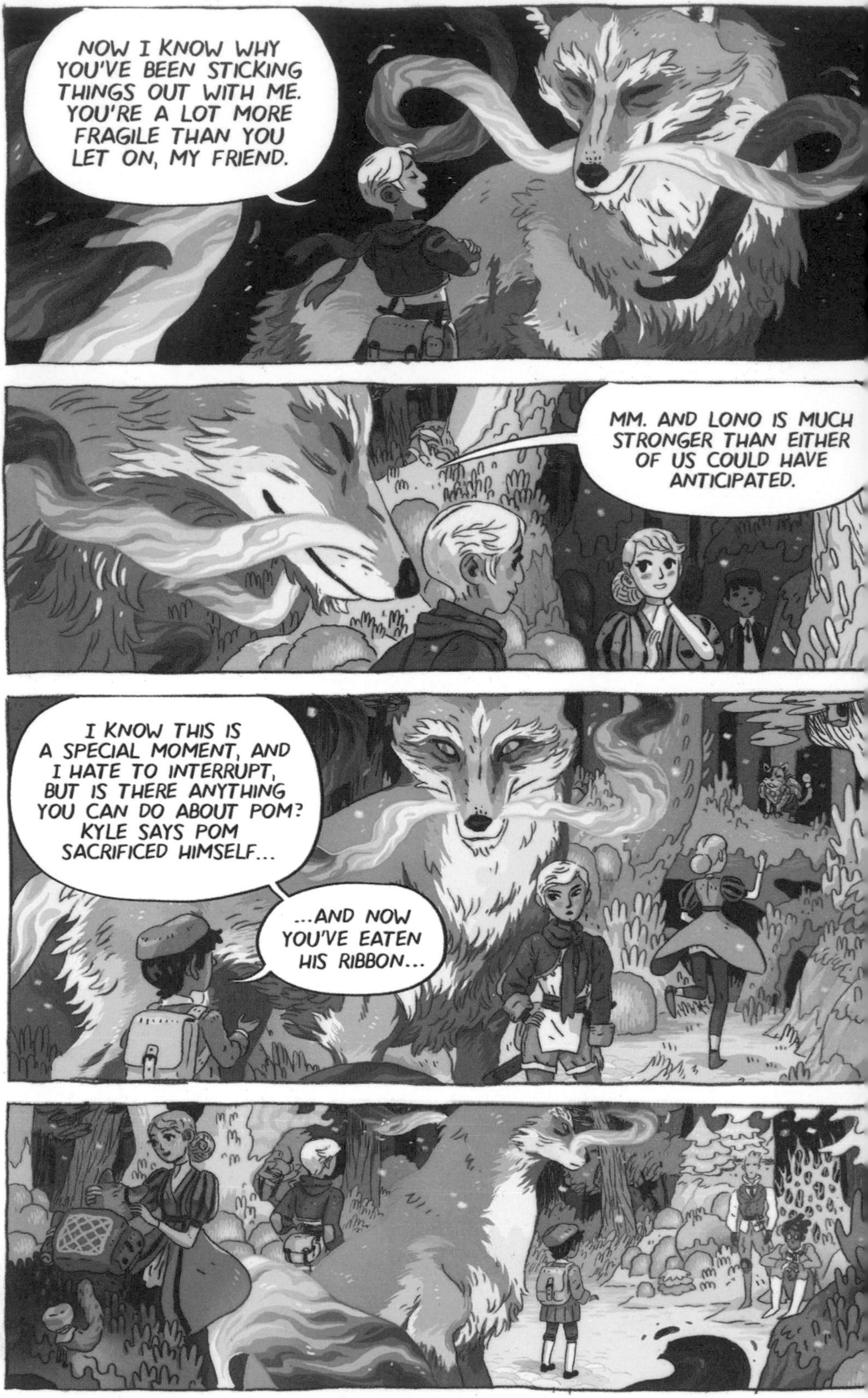
NOW I KNOW WHY YOU'VE BEEN STICKING THINGS OUT WITH ME. YOU'RE A LOT MORE FRAGILE THAN YOU LET ON, MY FRIEND.
MM. AND LONO IS MUCH STRONGER THAN EITHER OF US COULD HAVE ANTICIPATED.
I KNOW THIS IS A SPECIAL MOMENT, AND I HATE TO INTERRUPT, BUT IS THERE ANYTHING YOU CAN DO ABOUT POM? KYLE SAYS POM SACRIFICED HIMSELF...
...AND NOW YOU'VE EATEN HIS RIBBON...

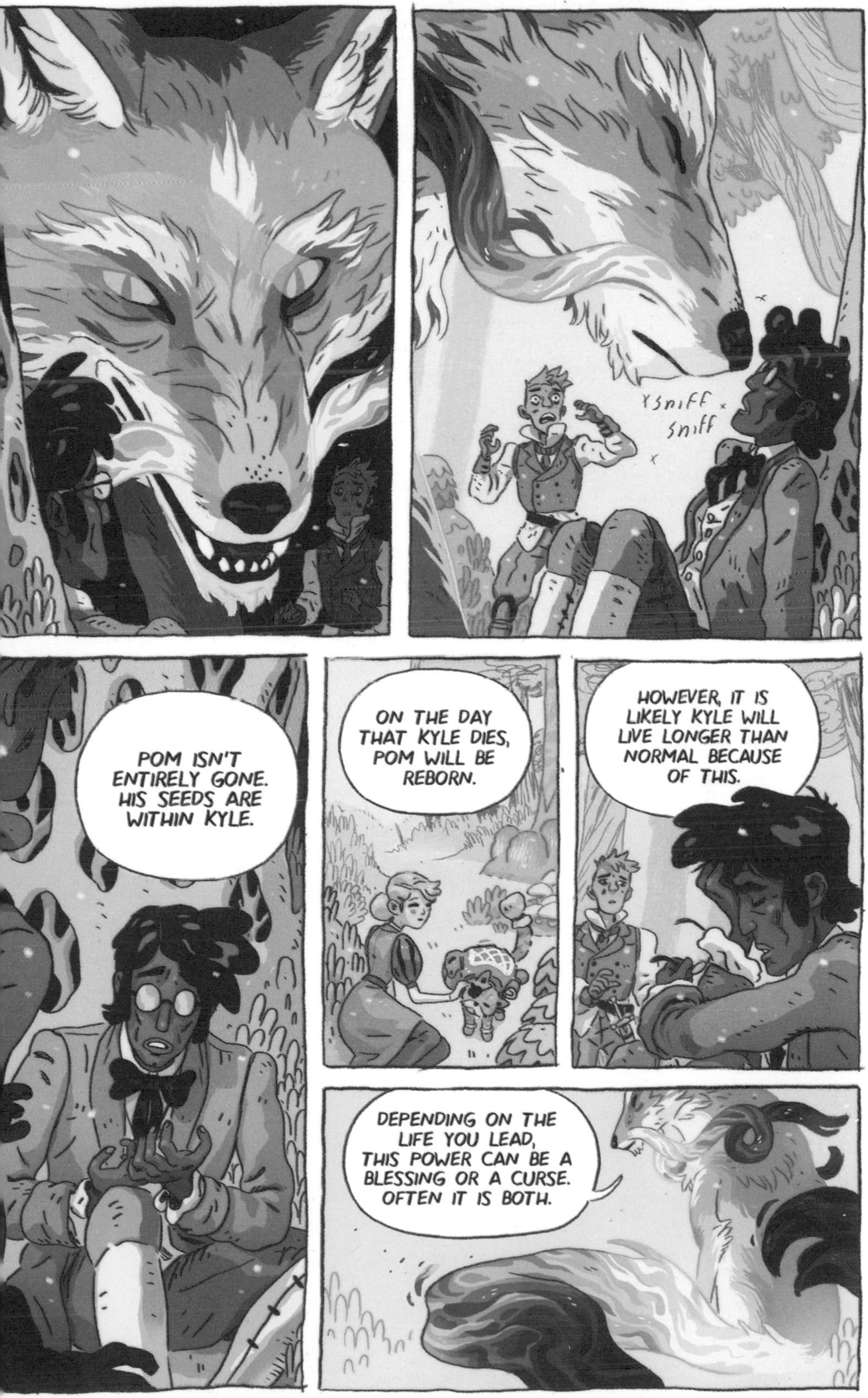

sniff
sniff
POM ISN'T ENTIRELY GONE. HIS SEEDS ARE WITHIN KYLE.
ON THE DAY THAT KYLE DIES, POM WILL BE REBORN.
HOWEVER, IT IS LIKELY KYLE WILL LIVE LONGER THAN NORMAL BECAUSE OF THIS.
DEPENDING ON THE LIFE YOU LEAD, THIS POWER CAN BE A BLESSING OR A CURSE. OFTEN IT IS BOTH.

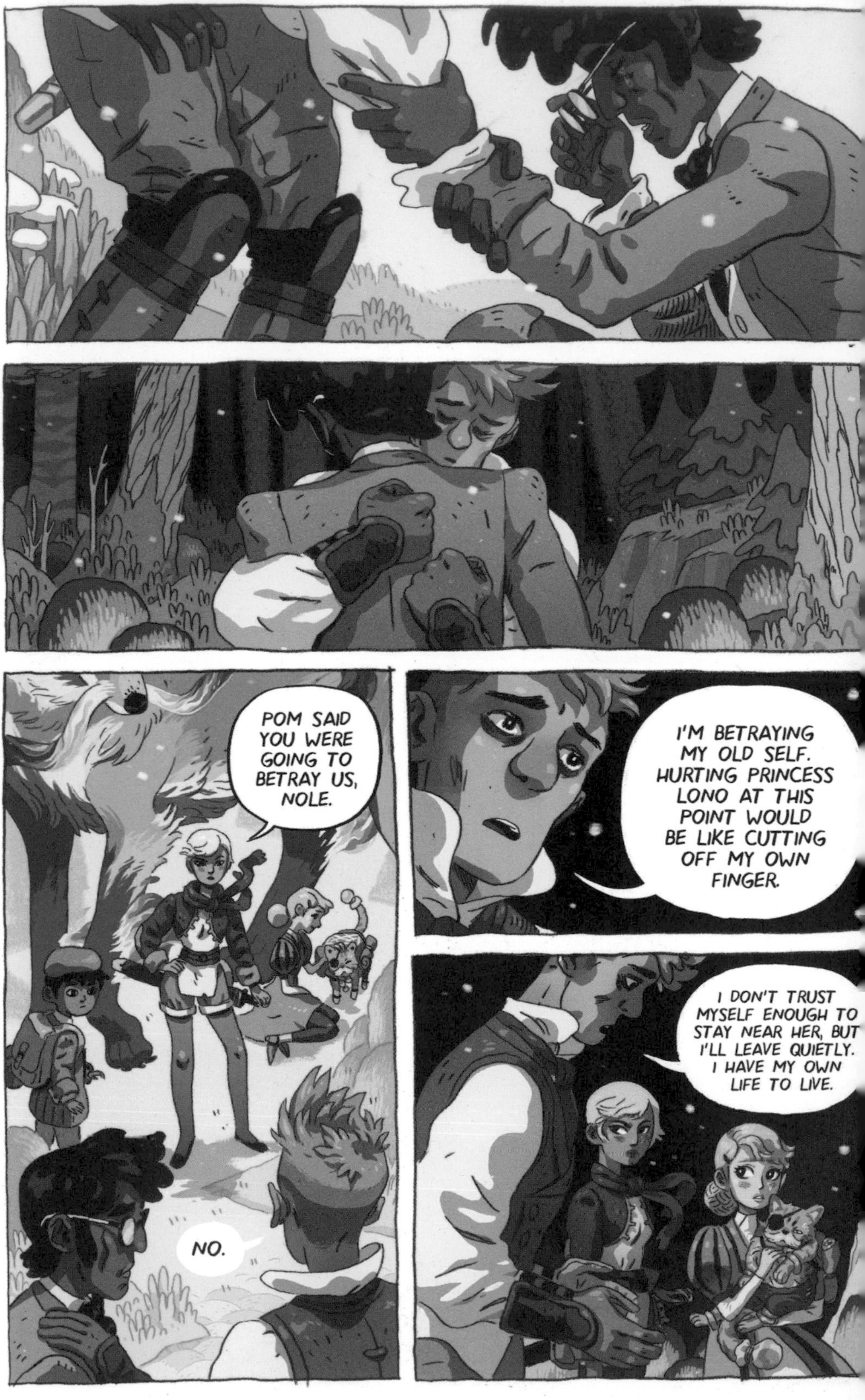
POM SAID YOU WERE GOING TO BETRAY US, NOLE.
NO.
I'M BETRAYING MY OLD SELF. HURTING PRINCESS LONO AT THIS POINT WOULD BE LIKE CUTTING OFF MY OWN FINGER.
I DON'T TRUST MYSELF ENOUGH TO STAY NEAR HER, BUT I'LL LEAVE QUIETLY. I HAVE MY OWN LIFE TO LIVE.

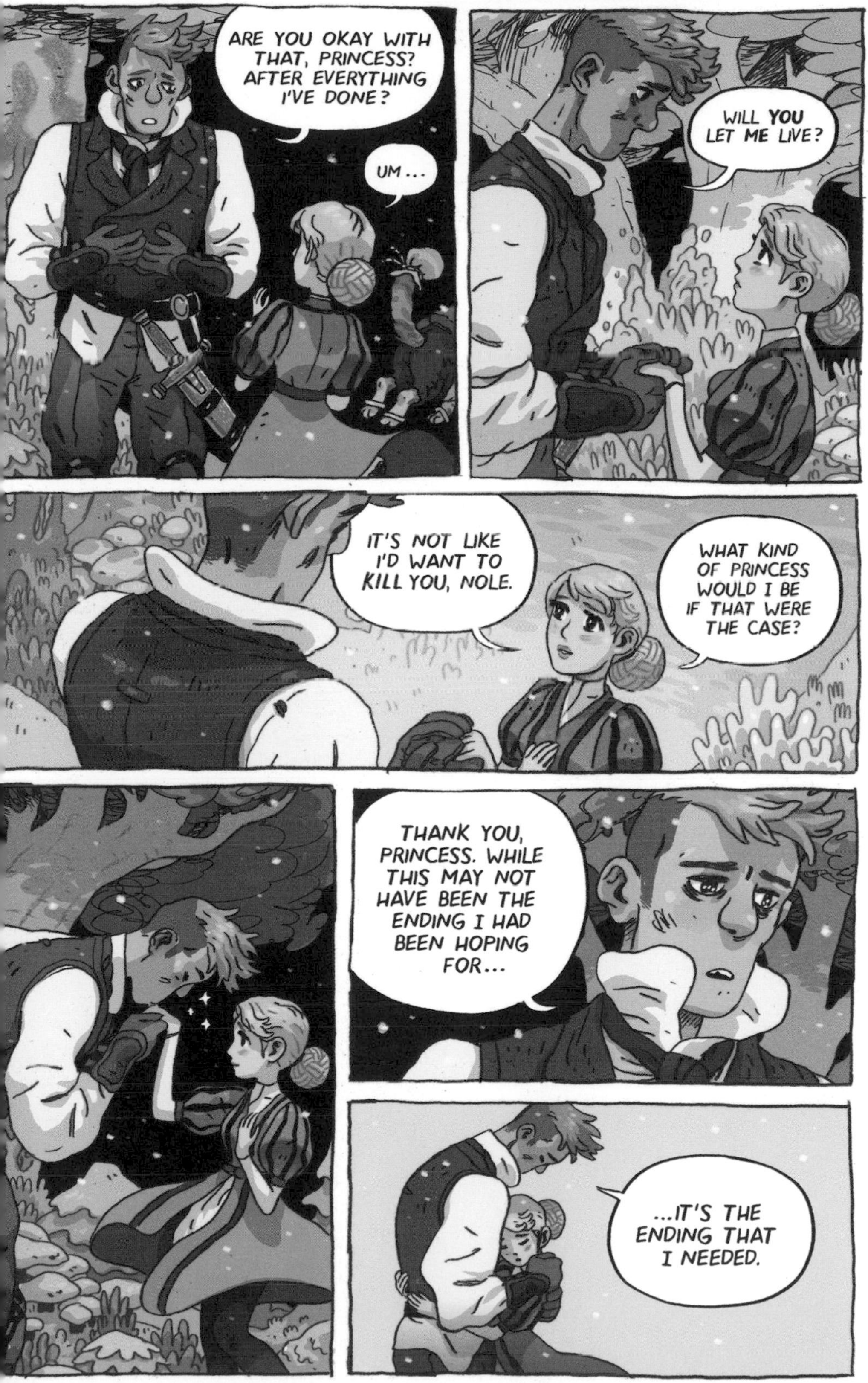
ARE YOU OKAY WITH THAT, PRINCESS? AFTER EVERYTHING I'VE DONE?
UM...
WILL YOU LET ME LIVE?
IT'S NOT LIKE I'D WANT TO KILL YOU, NOLE.
WHAT KIND OF PRINCESS WOULD I BE IF THAT WERE THE CASE?
THANK YOU, PRINCESS. WHILE THIS MAY NOT HAVE BEEN THE ENDING I HAD BEEN HOPING FOR...
...IT'S THE ENDING THAT I NEEDED.

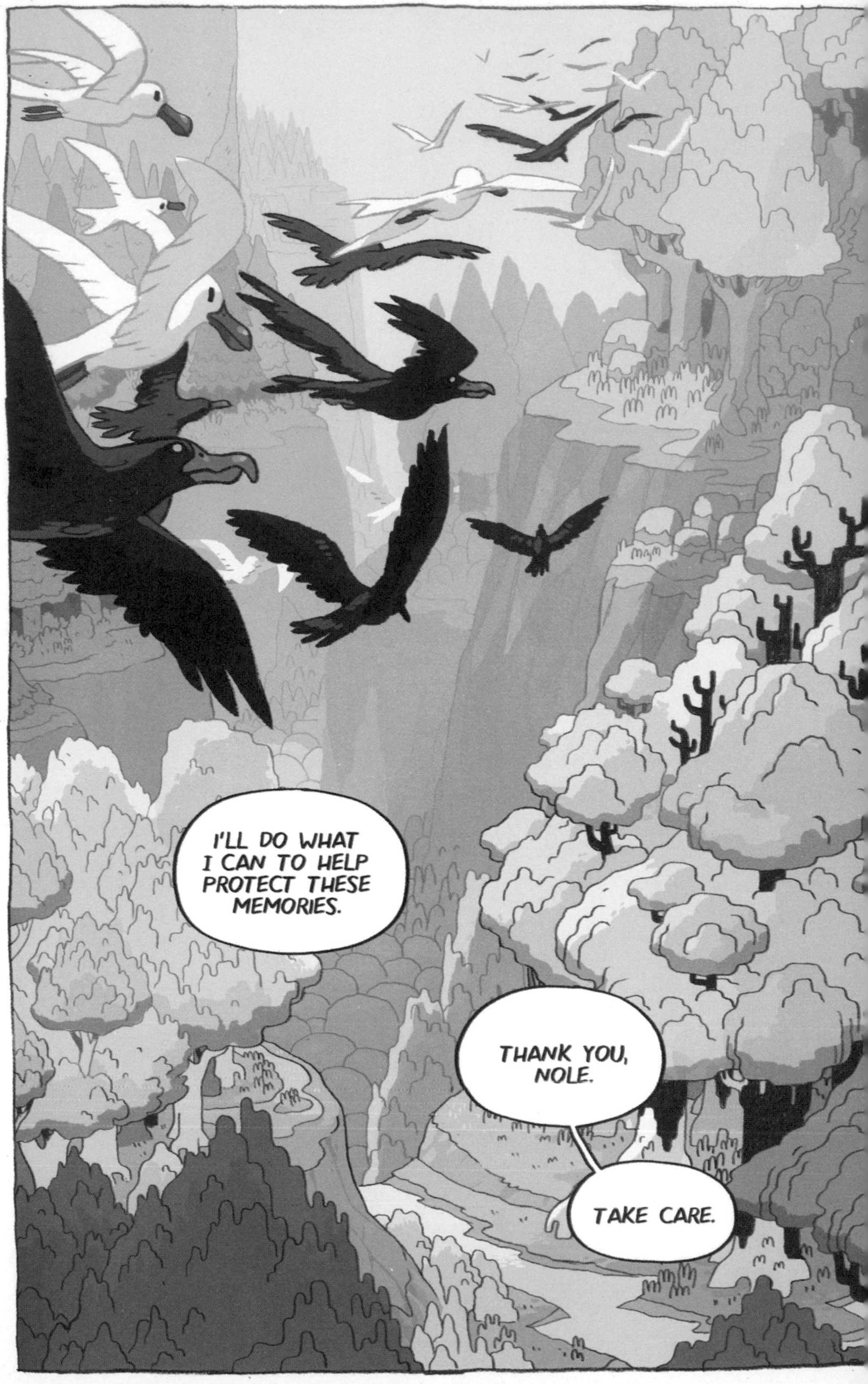
I'LL DO WHAT I CAN TO HELP PROTECT THESE MEMORIES.
THANK YOU, NOLE.
TAKE CARE.

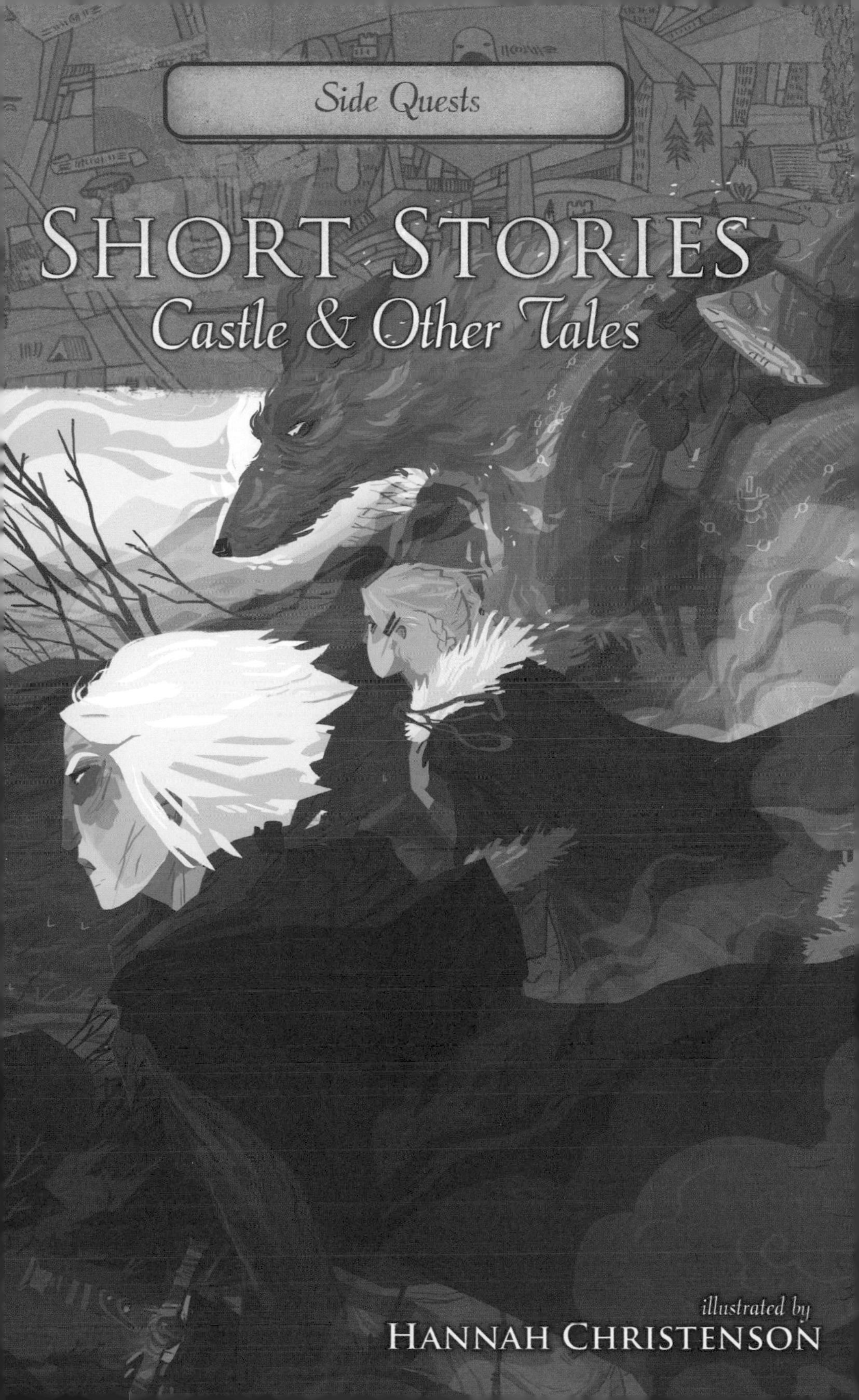
Side Quests
SHORT STORIES
Castle & Other Tales
illustrated by
HANNAH CHRISTENSON

TABLE of CONTENTS

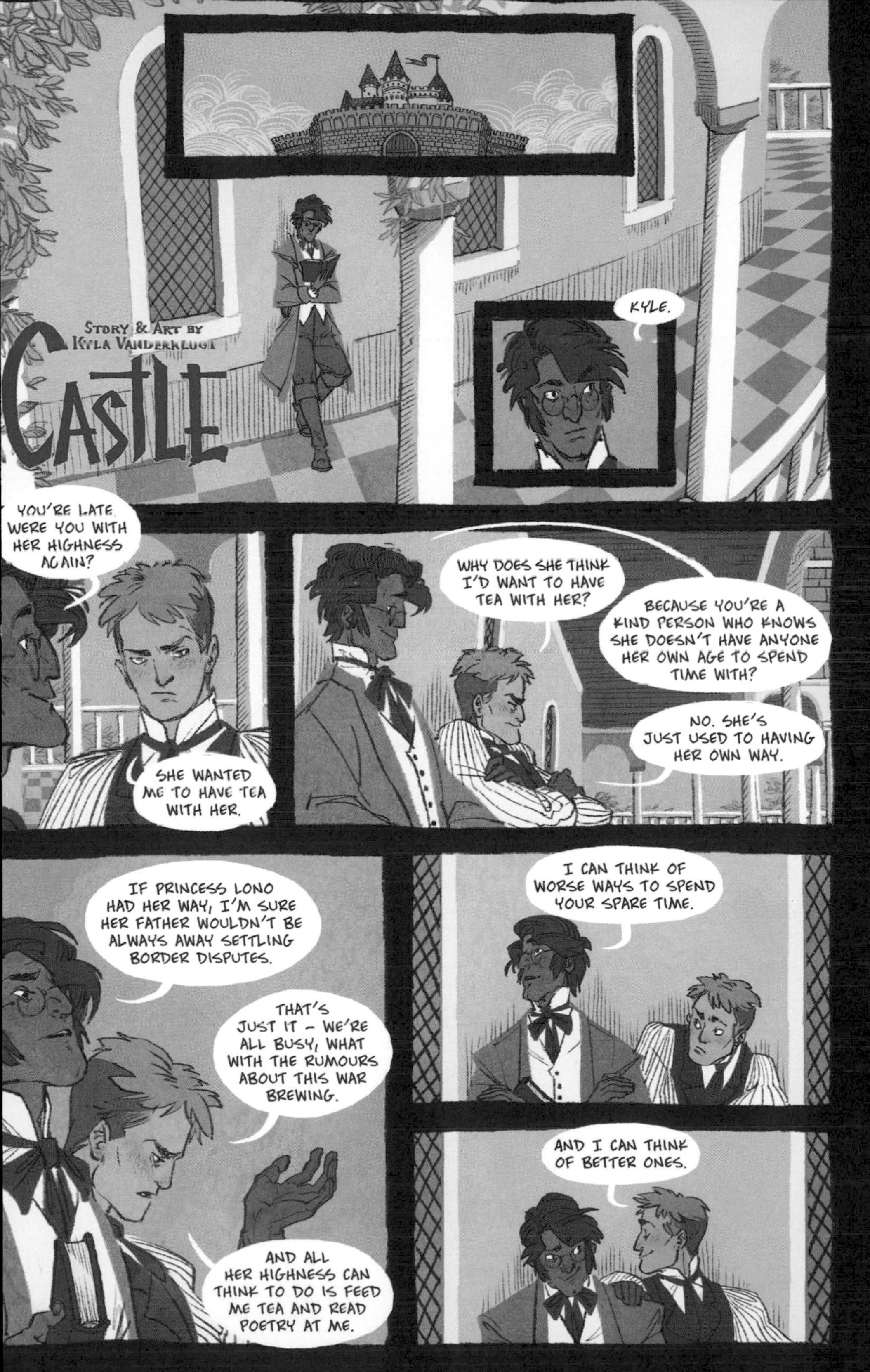
STORY & ART BY
KYLA VANDERKLUGT
CASTLE
KYLE.
YOU'RE LATE. WERE YOU WITH HER HIGHNESS AGAIN?
SHE WANTED ME TO HAVE TEA WITH HER.
WHY DOES SHE THINK I'D WANT TO HAVE TEA WITH HER?
BECAUSE YOU'RE A KIND PERSON WHO KNOWS SHE DOESN'T HAVE ANYONE HER OWN AGE TO SPEND TIME WITH?
NO. SHE'S JUST USED TO HAVING HER OWN WAY.
IF PRINCESS LONO HAD HER WAY, I'M SURE HER FATHER WOULDN'T BE ALWAYS AWAY SETTLING BORDER DISPUTES.
THAT'S JUST IT – WE'RE ALL BUSY, WHAT WITH THE RUMOURS ABOUT THIS WAR BREWING.
AND ALL HER HIGHNESS CAN THINK TO DO IS FEED ME TEA AND READ POETRY AT ME.
I CAN THINK OF WORSE WAYS TO SPEND YOUR SPARE TIME.
AND I CAN THINK OF BETTER ONES.

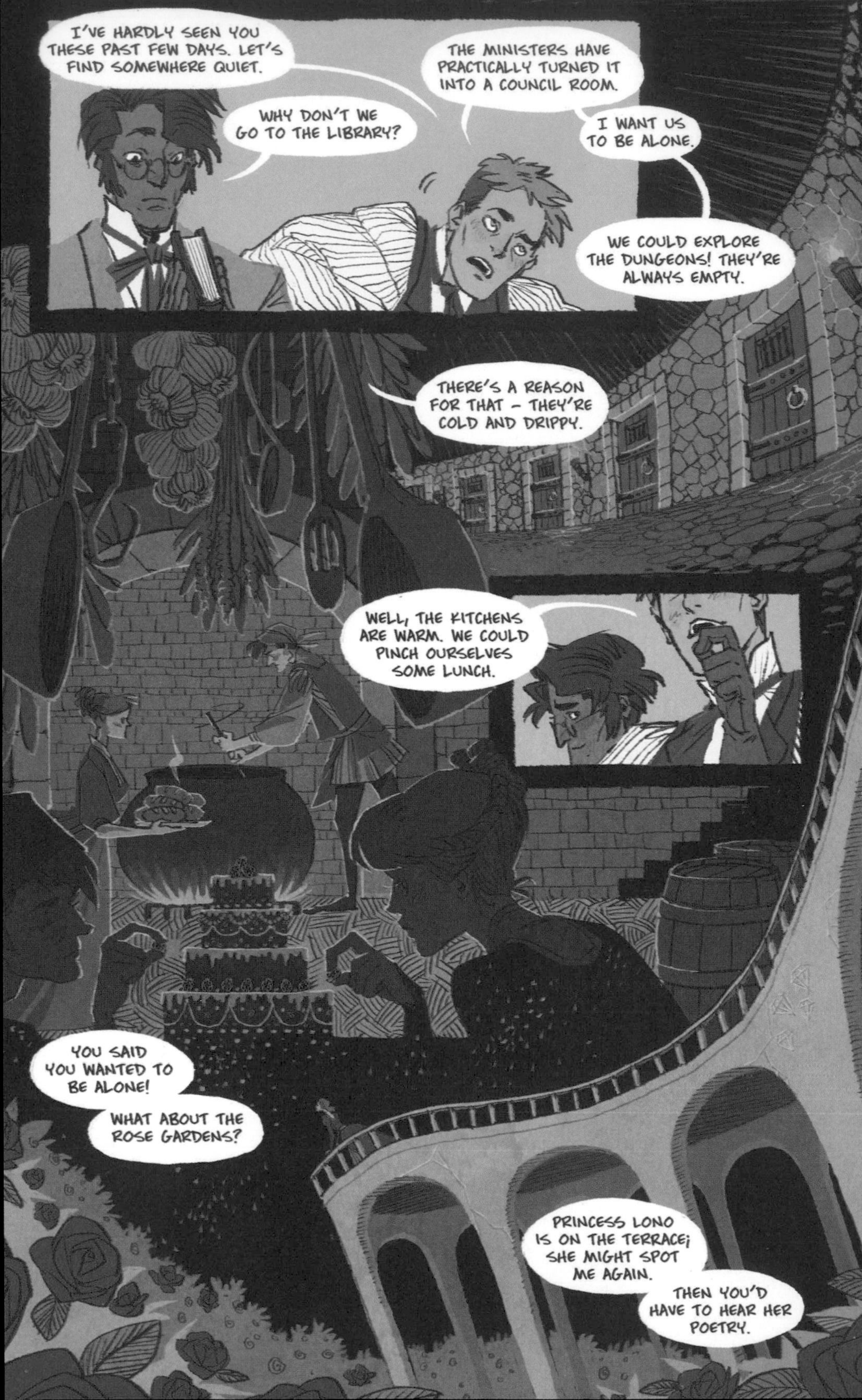
I'VE HARDLY SEEN YOU THESE PAST FEW DAYS. LET'S FIND SOMEWHERE QUIET.
WHY DON'T WE GO TO THE LIBRARY?
THE MINISTERS HAVE PRACTICALLY TURNED IT INTO A COUNCIL ROOM.
I WANT US TO BE ALONE.
WE COULD EXPLORE THE DUNGEONS! THEY'RE ALWAYS EMPTY.
THERE'S A REASON FOR THAT - THEY'RE COLD AND DRIPPY.
WELL, THE KITCHENS ARE WARM. WE COULD PINCH OURSELVES SOME LUNCH.
YOU SAID YOU WANTED TO BE ALONE!
WHAT ABOUT THE ROSE GARDENS?
PRINCESS LONO IS ON THE TERRACE; SHE MIGHT SPOT ME AGAIN.
THEN YOU'D HAVE TO HEAR HER POETRY.

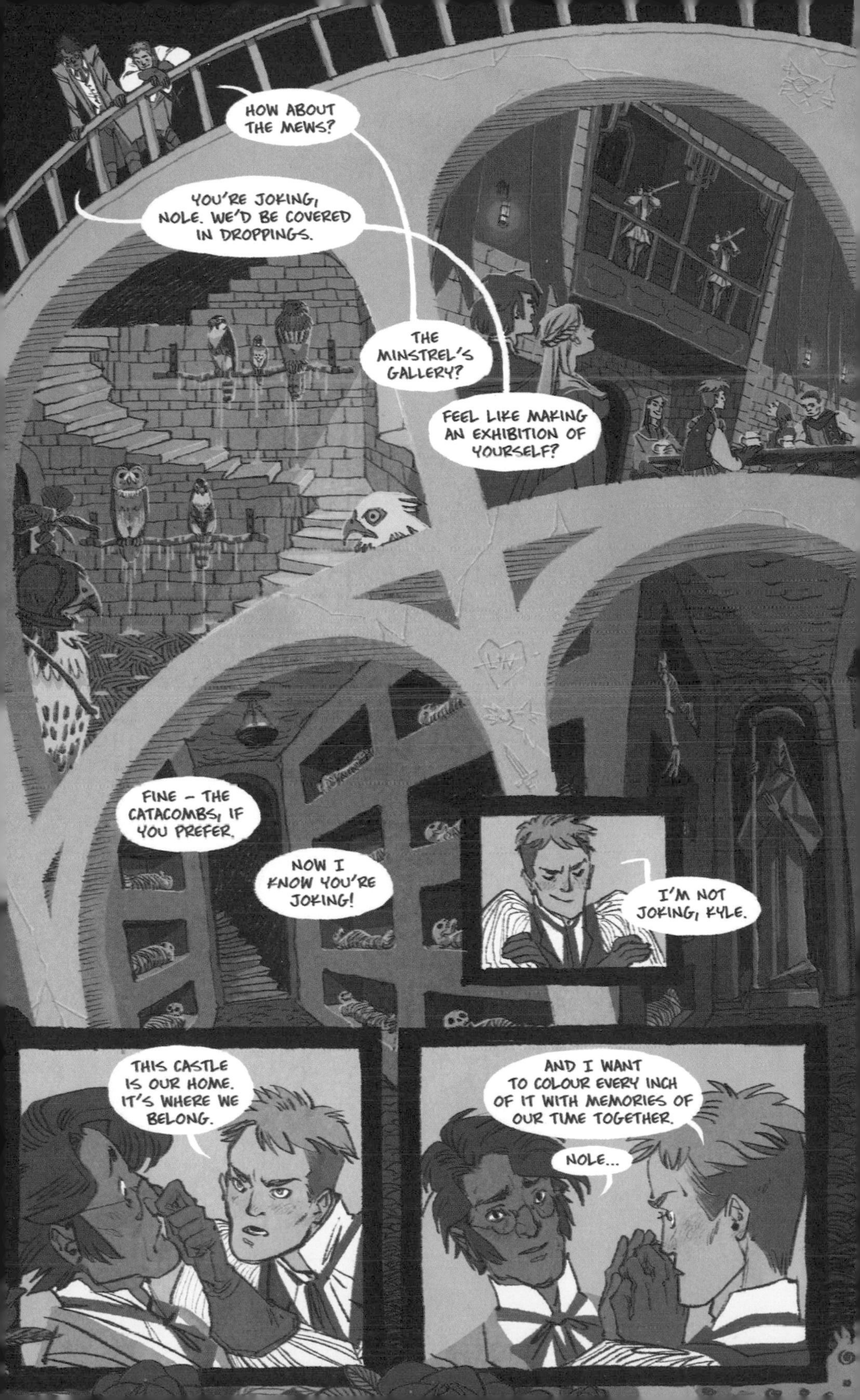
HOW ABOUT THE MEWS?
YOU'RE JOKING, NOLE. WE'D BE COVERED IN DROPPINGS.
THE MINSTREL'S GALLERY?
FEEL LIKE MAKING AN EXHIBITION OF YOURSELF?
FINE – THE CATACOMBS, IF YOU PREFER.
NOW I KNOW YOU'RE JOKING!
I'M NOT JOKING, KYLE.
THIS CASTLE IS OUR HOME. IT'S WHERE WE BELONG.
AND I WANT TO COLOUR EVERY INCH OF IT WITH MEMORIES OF OUR TIME TOGETHER.
NOLE...

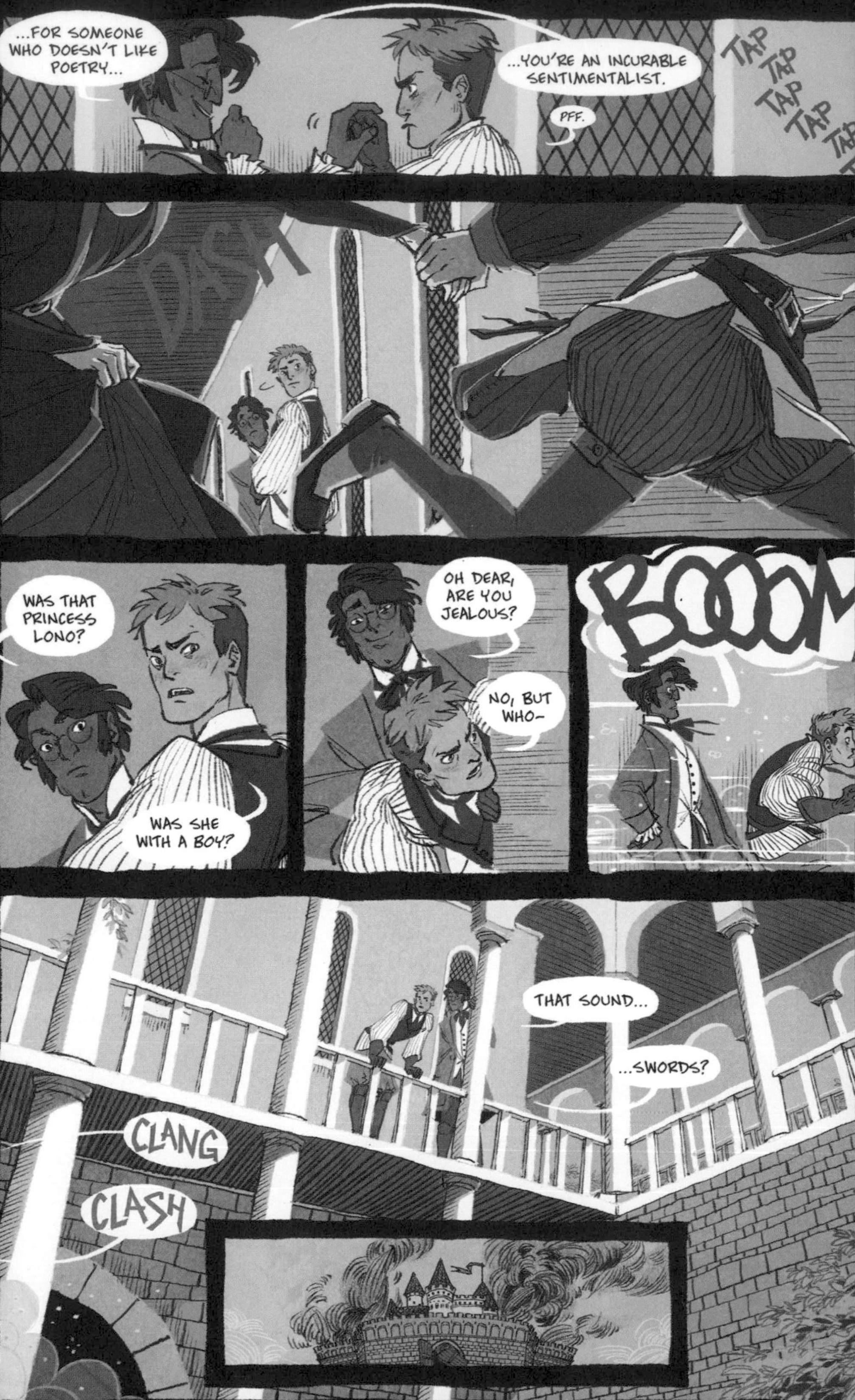
...FOR SOMEONE WHO DOESN'T LIKE POETRY...
...YOU'RE AN INCURABLE SENTIMENTALIST.
PFF.
TAP TAP TAP TAP TAP
DASH
WAS THAT PRINCESS LONO?
WAS SHE WITH A BOY?
OH DEAR, ARE YOU JEALOUS?
NO, BUT WHO-
BOOOM
THAT SOUND...
...SWORDS?
CLANG
CLASH

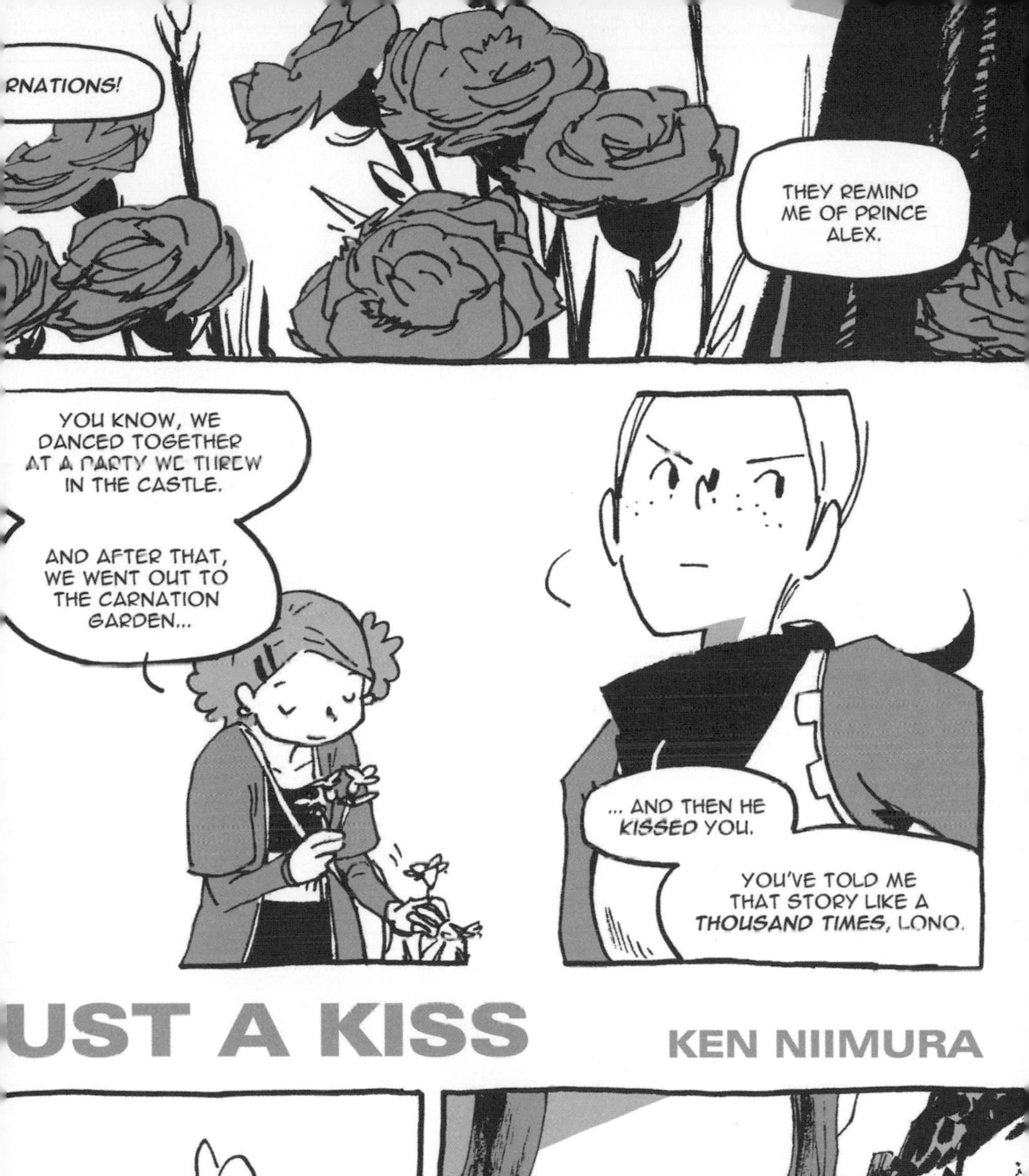
RNATIONS!
THEY REMIND ME OF PRINCE ALEX.
YOU KNOW, WE DANCED TOGETHER AT A PARTY WE THREW IN THE CASTLE.
AND AFTER THAT, WE WENT OUT TO THE CARNATION GARDEN...
... AND THEN HE KISSED YOU.
YOU'VE TOLD ME THAT STORY LIKE A THOUSAND TIMES, LONO.

UST A KISS

KEN NIIMURA

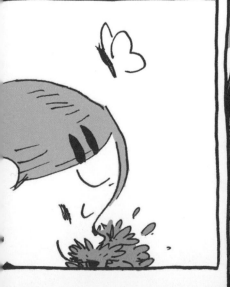

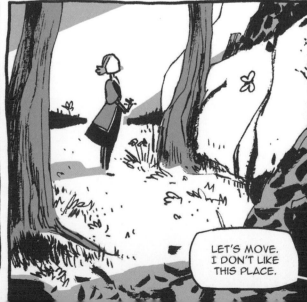

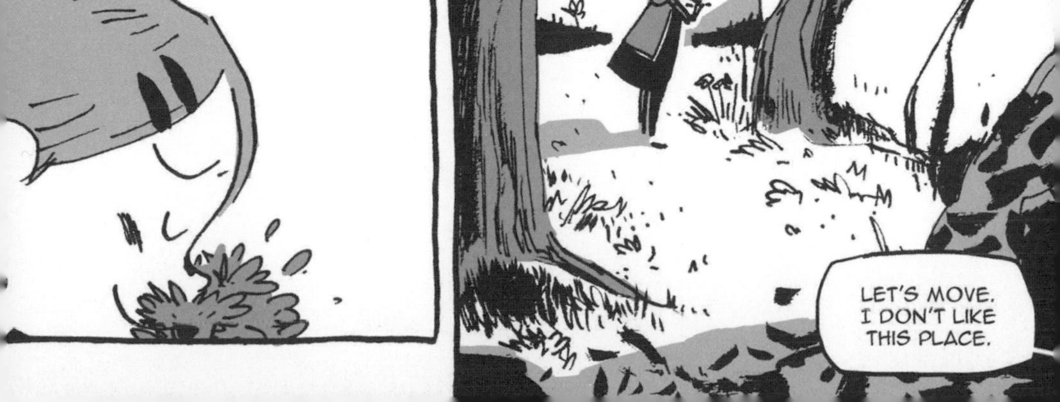
LET'S MOVE. I DON'T LIKE THIS PLACE.

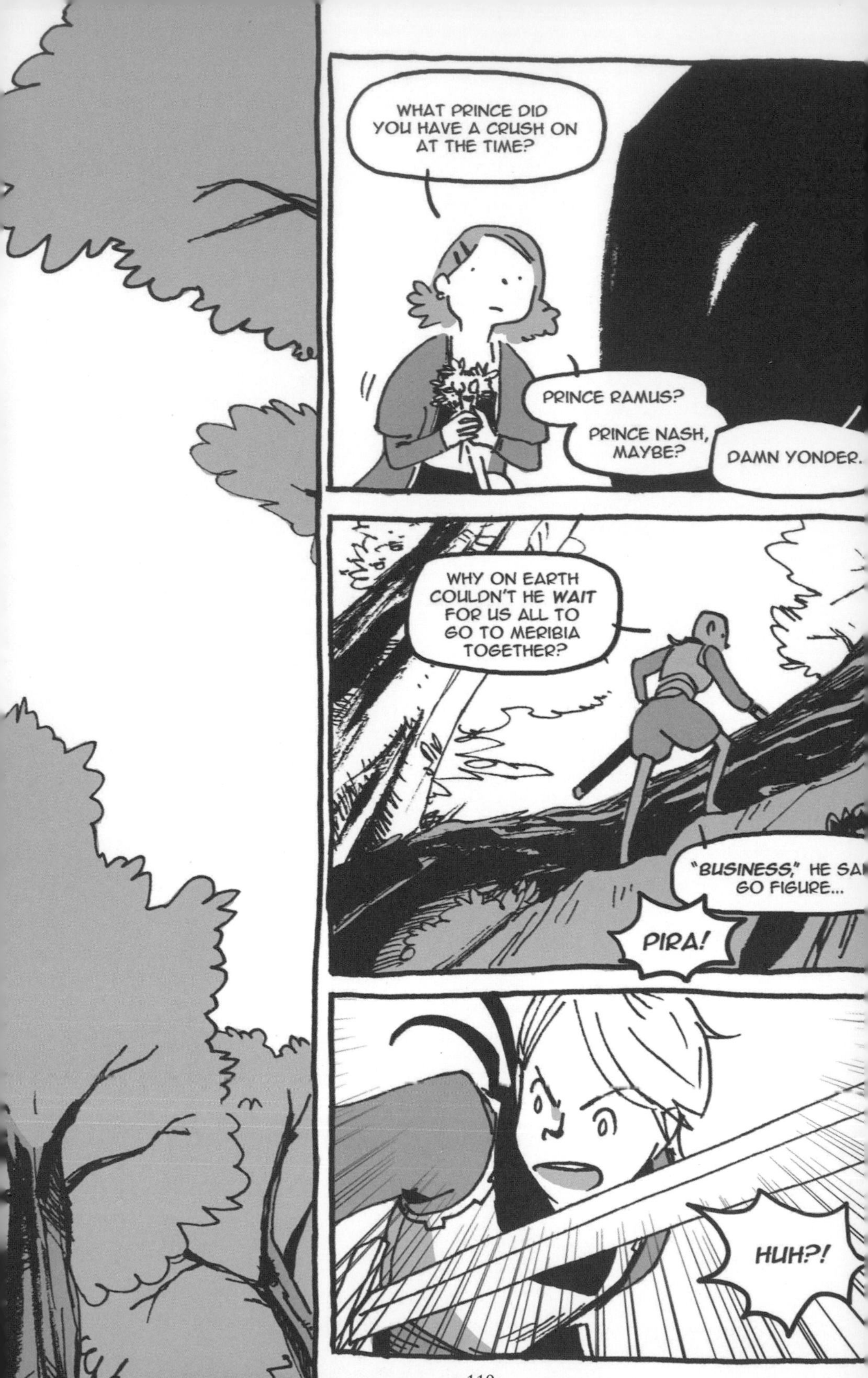
WHAT PRINCE DID YOU HAVE A CRUSH ON AT THE TIME?
PRINCE RAMUS?
PRINCE NASH, MAYBE?
DAMN YONDER.
WHY ON EARTH COULDN'T HE WAIT FOR US ALL TO GO TO MERIBIA TOGETHER?
"BUSINESS," HE SA
GO FIGURE...
PIRA!
HUH?!

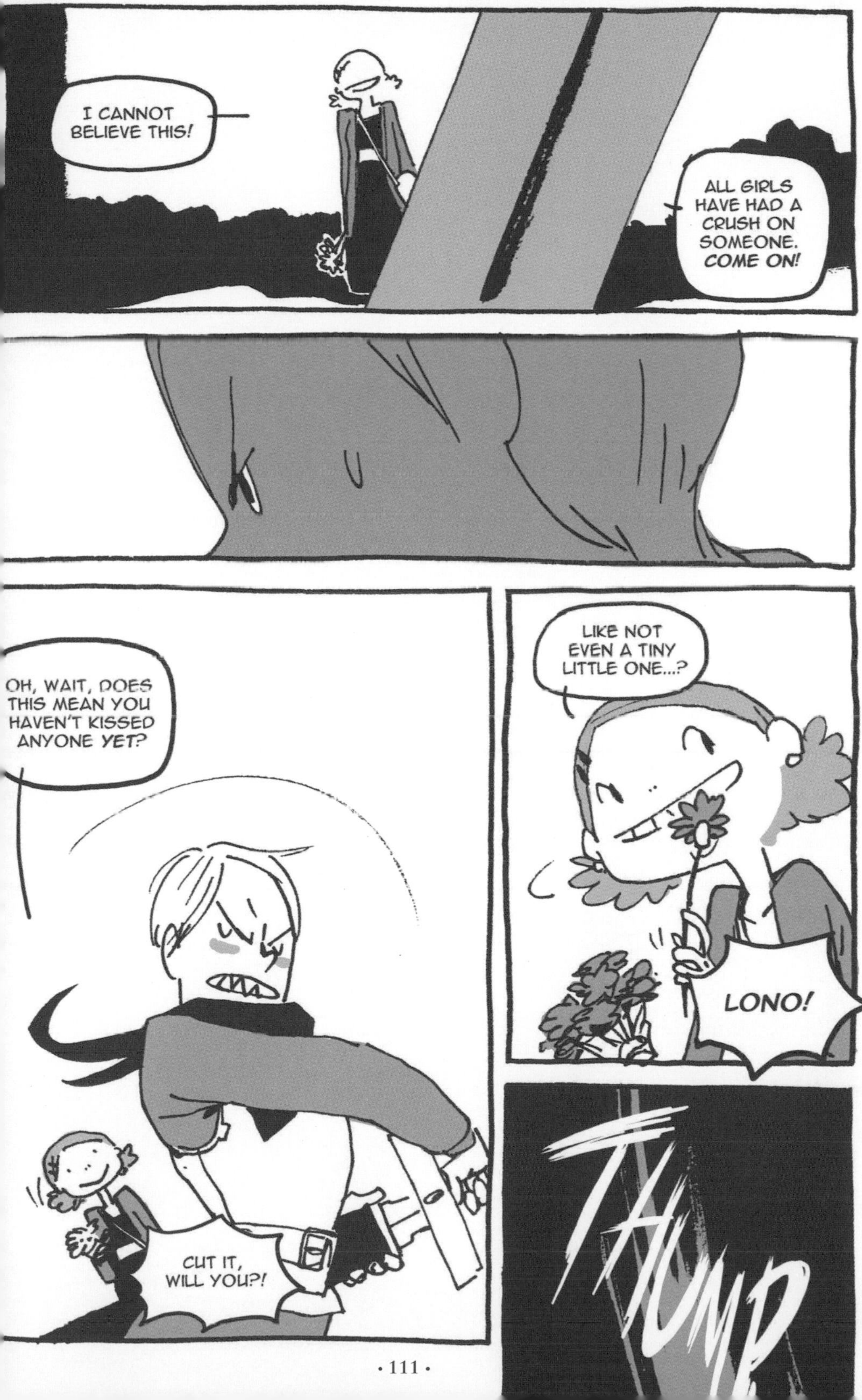

I CANNOT BELIEVE THIS!
ALL GIRLS HAVE HAD A CRUSH ON SOMEONE. COME ON!
OH, WAIT, DOES THIS MEAN YOU HAVEN'T KISSED ANYONE YET?
CUT IT, WILL YOU?!
LIKE NOT EVEN A TINY LITTLE ONE...?
LONO!
THUMP

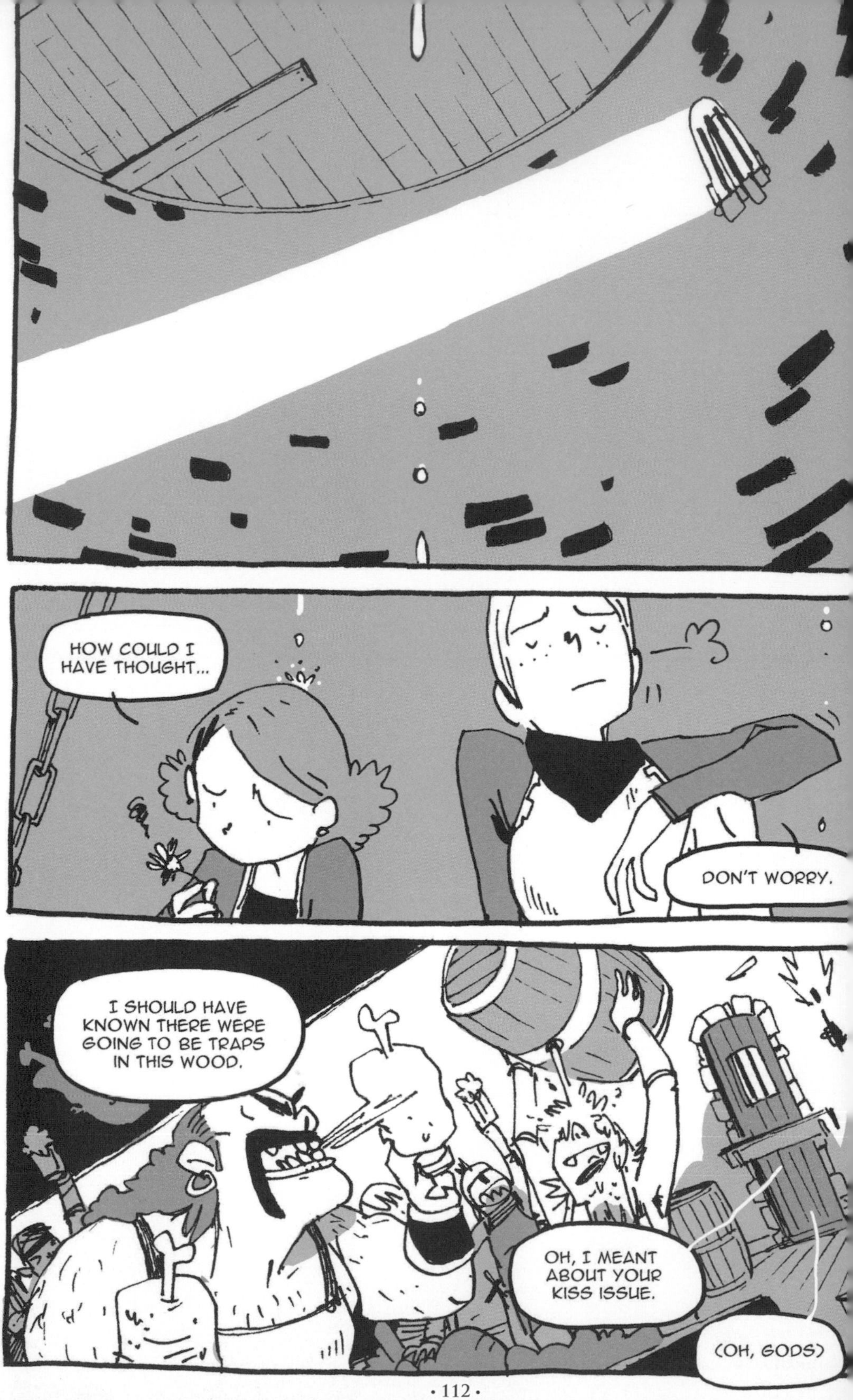
HOW COULD I HAVE THOUGHT...
DON'T WORRY.
I SHOULD HAVE KNOWN THERE WERE GOING TO BE TRAPS IN THIS WOOD.
OH, I MEANT ABOUT YOUR KISS ISSUE.
(OH, GODS)

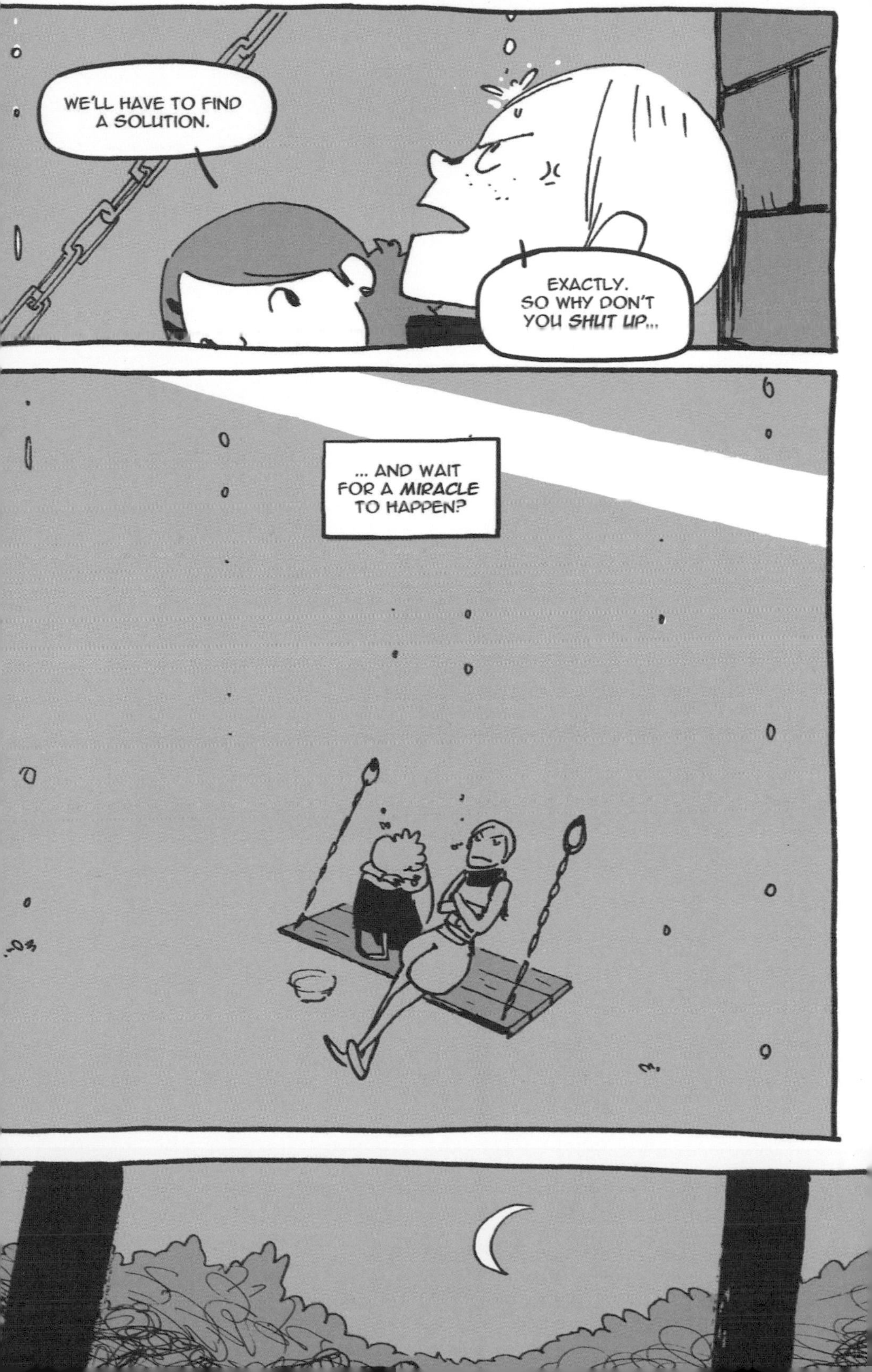
WE'LL HAVE TO FIND A SOLUTION.
EXACTLY. SO WHY DON'T YOU SHUT UP...
... AND WAIT FOR A MIRACLE TO HAPPEN?

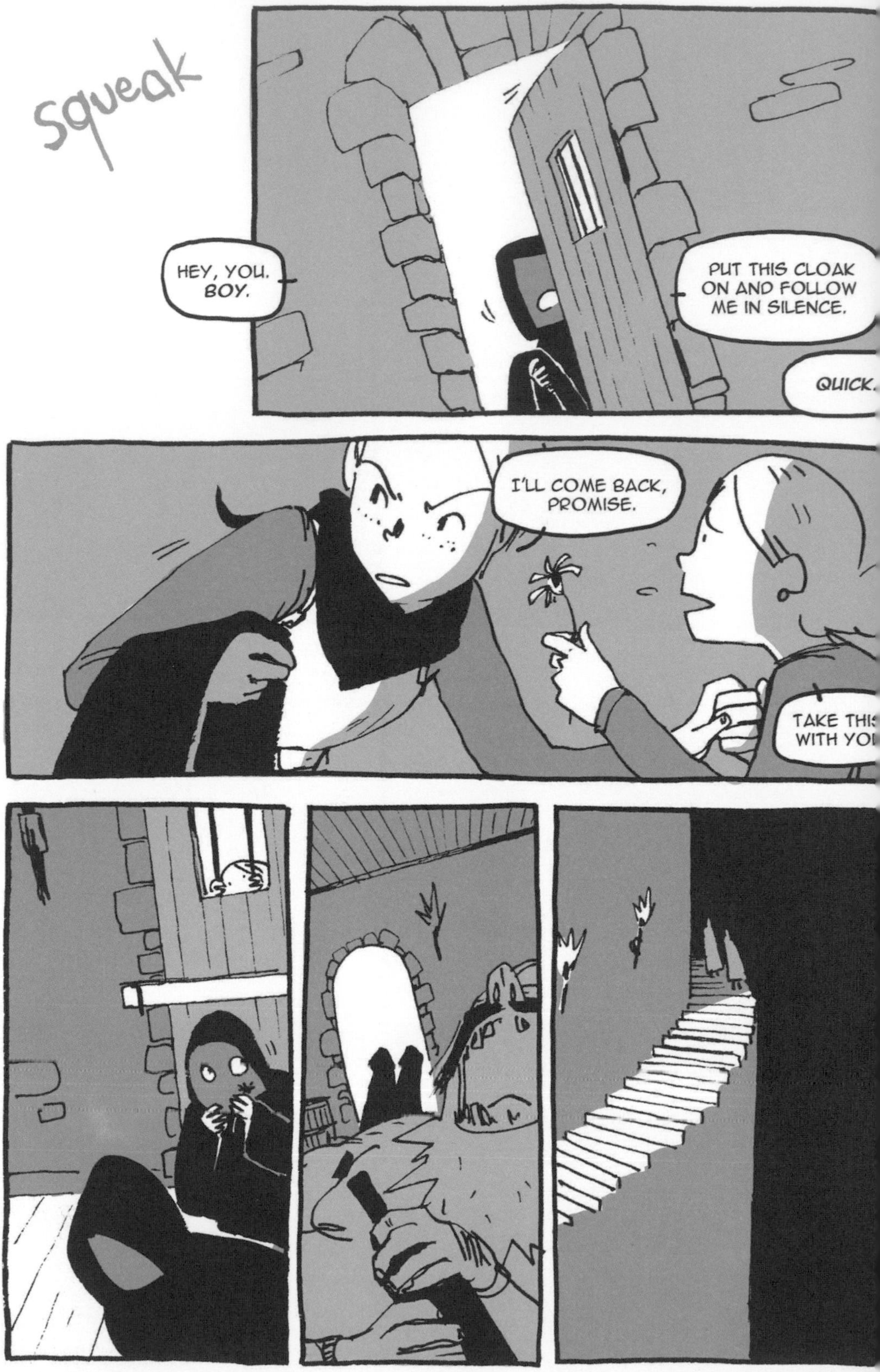

squeak
HEY, YOU. BOY.
PUT THIS CLOAK ON AND FOLLOW ME IN SILENCE.
QUICK.
I'LL COME BACK, PROMISE.
TAKE THIS WITH YO

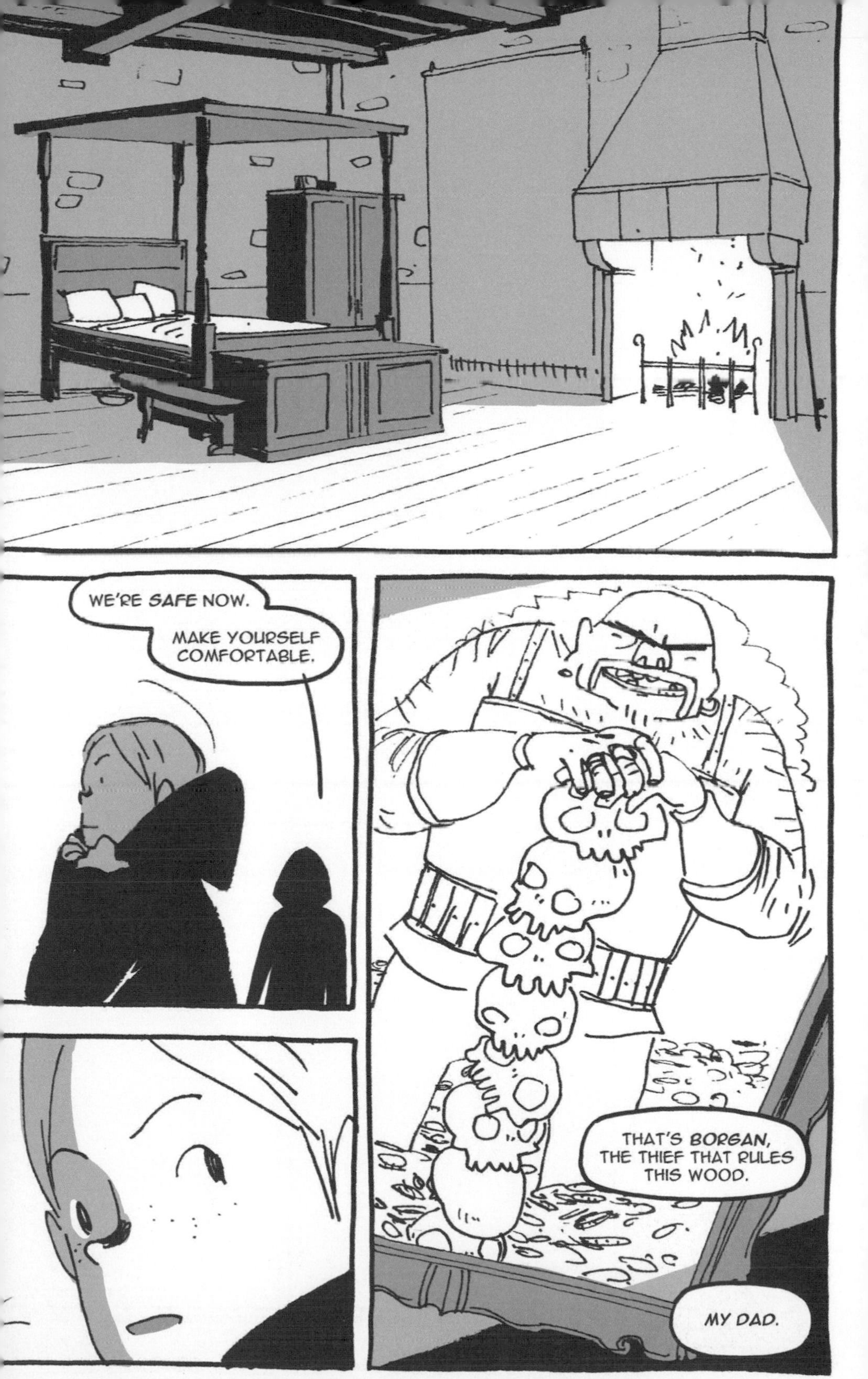
WE'RE SAFE NOW.
MAKE YOURSELF COMFORTABLE.
THAT'S BORGAN, THE THIEF THAT RULES THIS WOOD.
MY DAD.

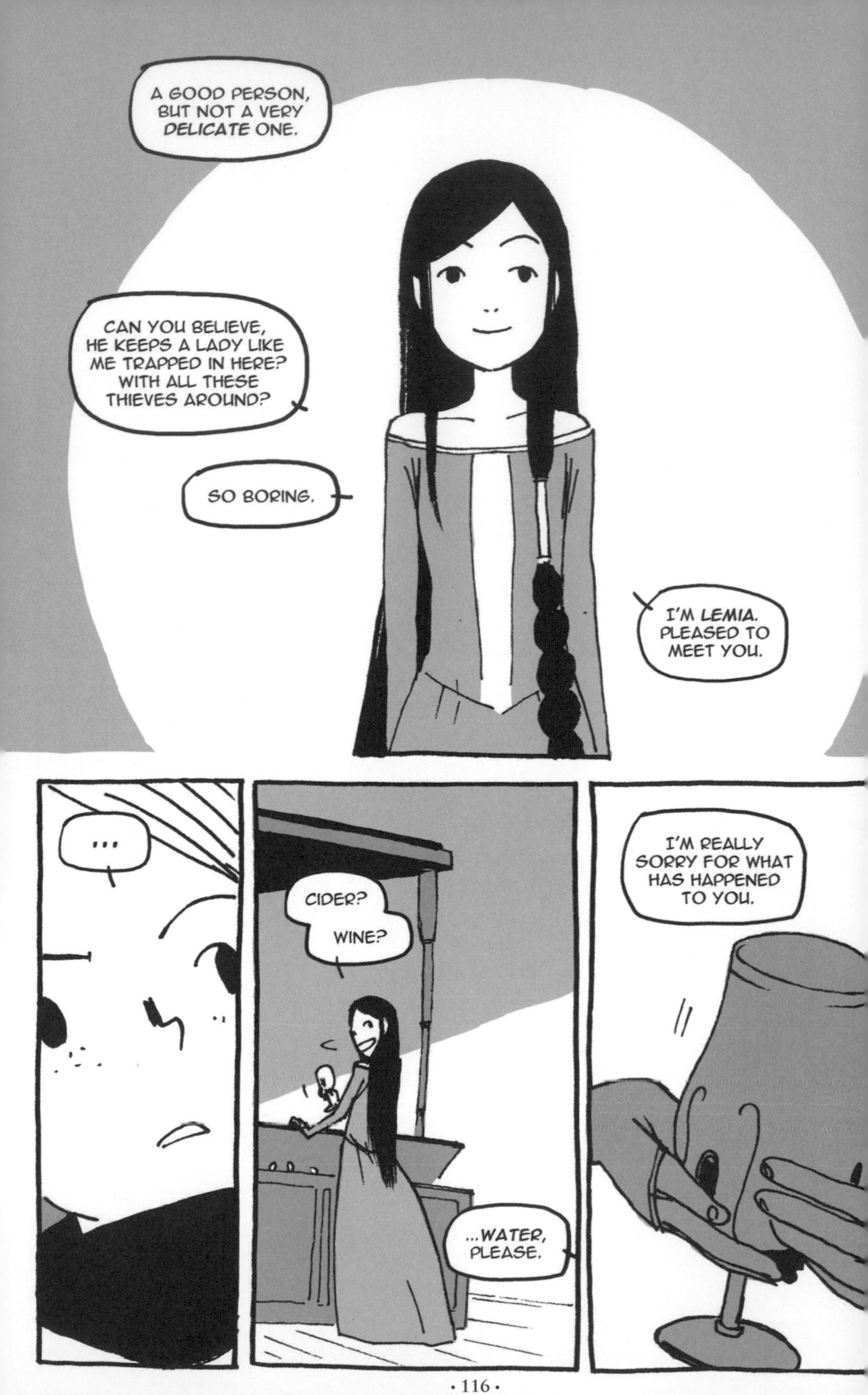
A GOOD PERSON, BUT NOT A VERY DELICATE ONE.
CAN YOU BELIEVE, HE KEEPS A LADY LIKE ME TRAPPED IN HERE? WITH ALL THESE THIEVES AROUND?
SO BORING.
I'M LEMIA. PLEASED TO MEET YOU.
...
CIDER?
WINE?
...WATER, PLEASE.
I'M REALLY SORRY FOR WHAT HAS HAPPENED TO YOU.

I'VE BROUGHT YOU HERE BECAUSE YOU'RE IN TERRIBLE DANGER.

I'VE HEARD MY DAD TALKING TO HIS THUGS...

...YOU'LL BE EXECUTED THIS VERY MORNING.

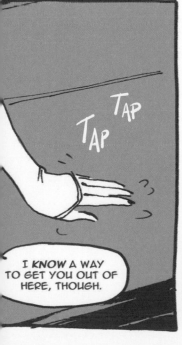

TAP TAP

I KNOW A WAY TO GET YOU OUT OF HERE, THOUGH.

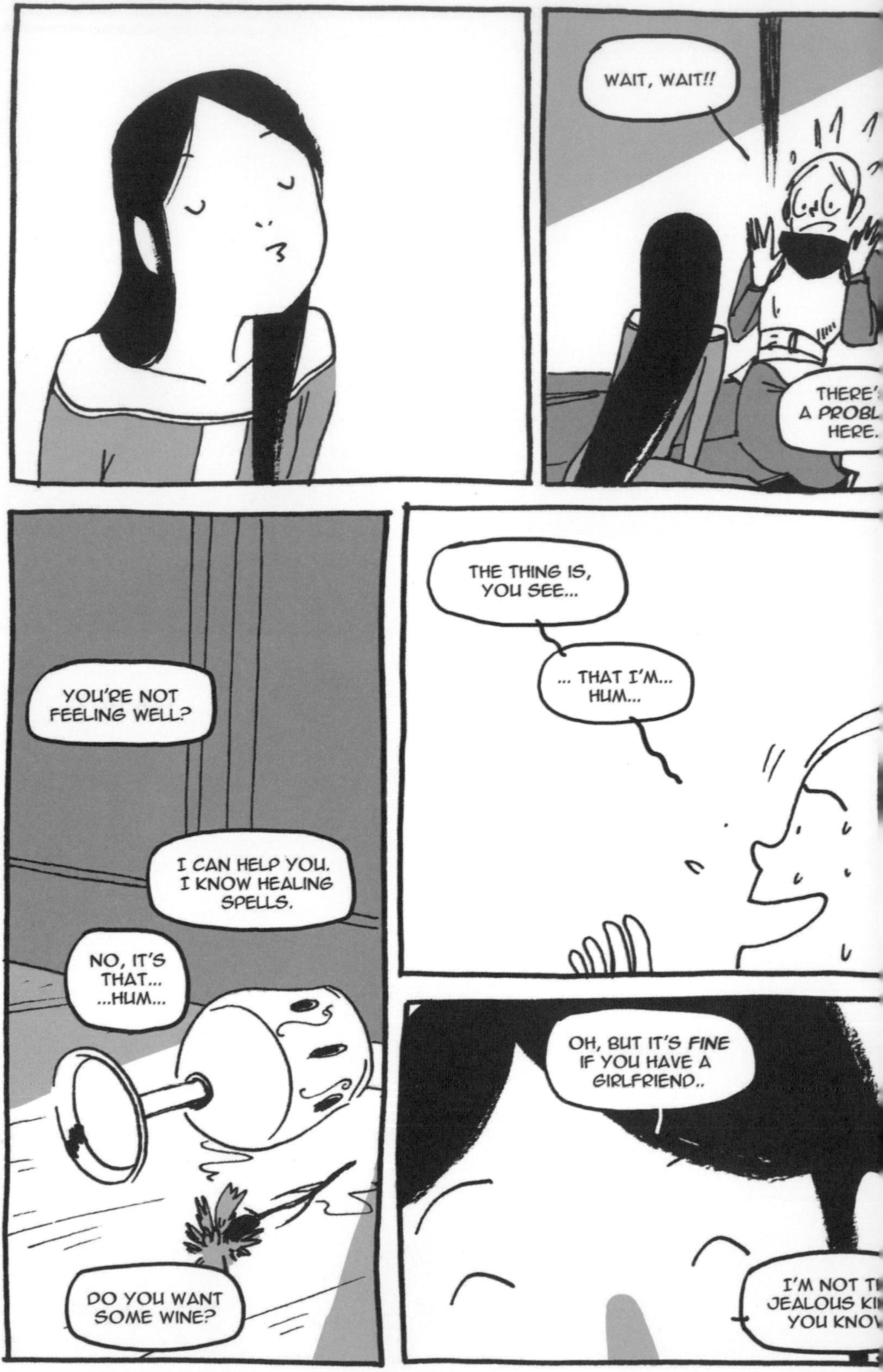
WAIT, WAIT!!
THERE'S A PROBL HERE.
YOU'RE NOT FEELING WELL?
I CAN HELP YOU. I KNOW HEALING SPELLS.
NO, IT'S THAT... ...HUM...
DO YOU WANT SOME WINE?
THE THING IS, YOU SEE...
... THAT I'M... HUM...
OH, BUT IT'S FINE IF YOU HAVE A GIRLFRIEND..
I'M NOT T JEALOUS KI YOU KNOW

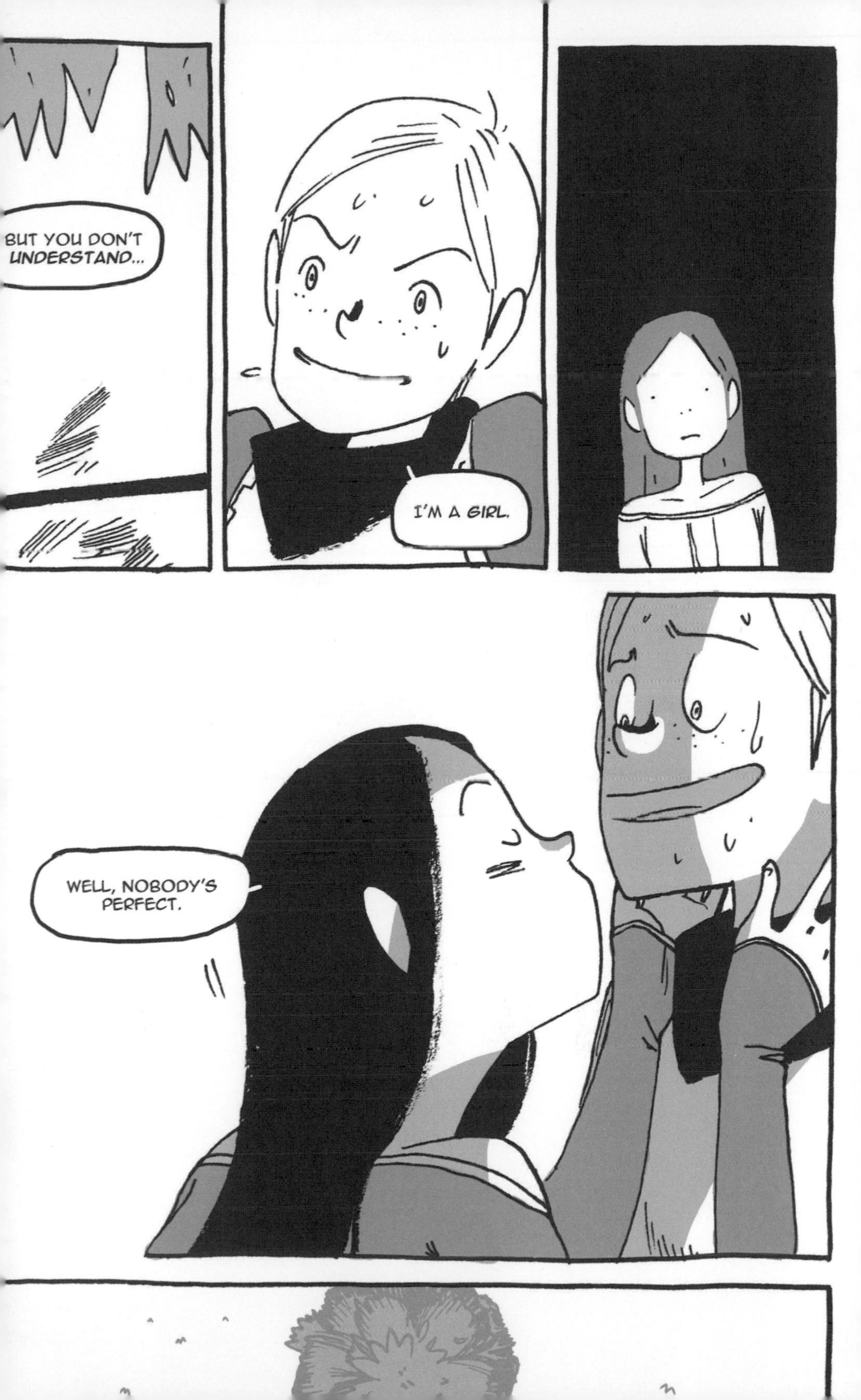
BUT YOU DON'T UNDERSTAND...
I'M A GIRL.
WELL, NOBODY'S PERFECT.

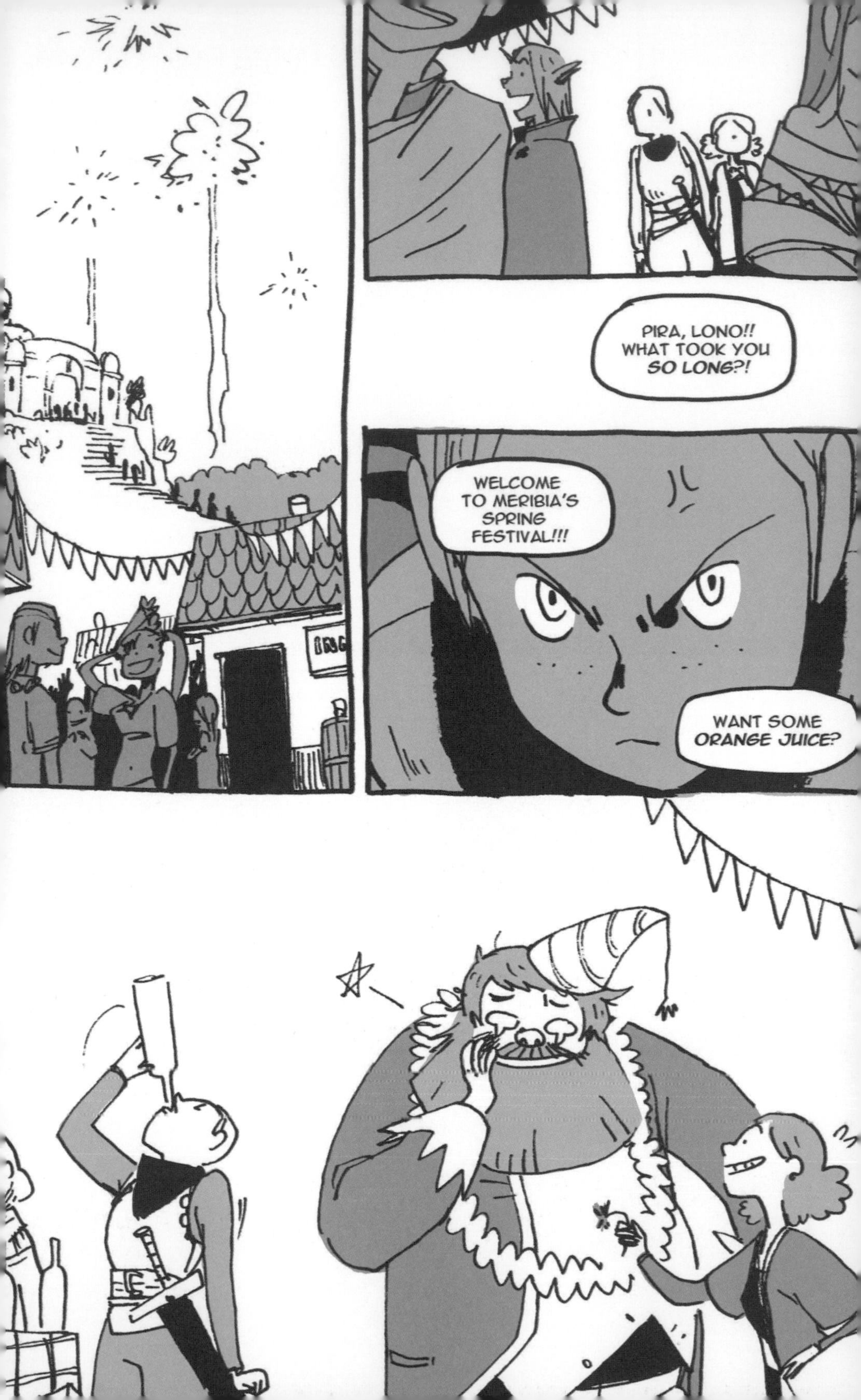
PIRA, LONO!!
WHAT TOOK YOU
SO LONG?!
WELCOME
TO MERIBIA'S
SPRING
FESTIVAL!!!
WANT SOME
ORANGE JUICE?

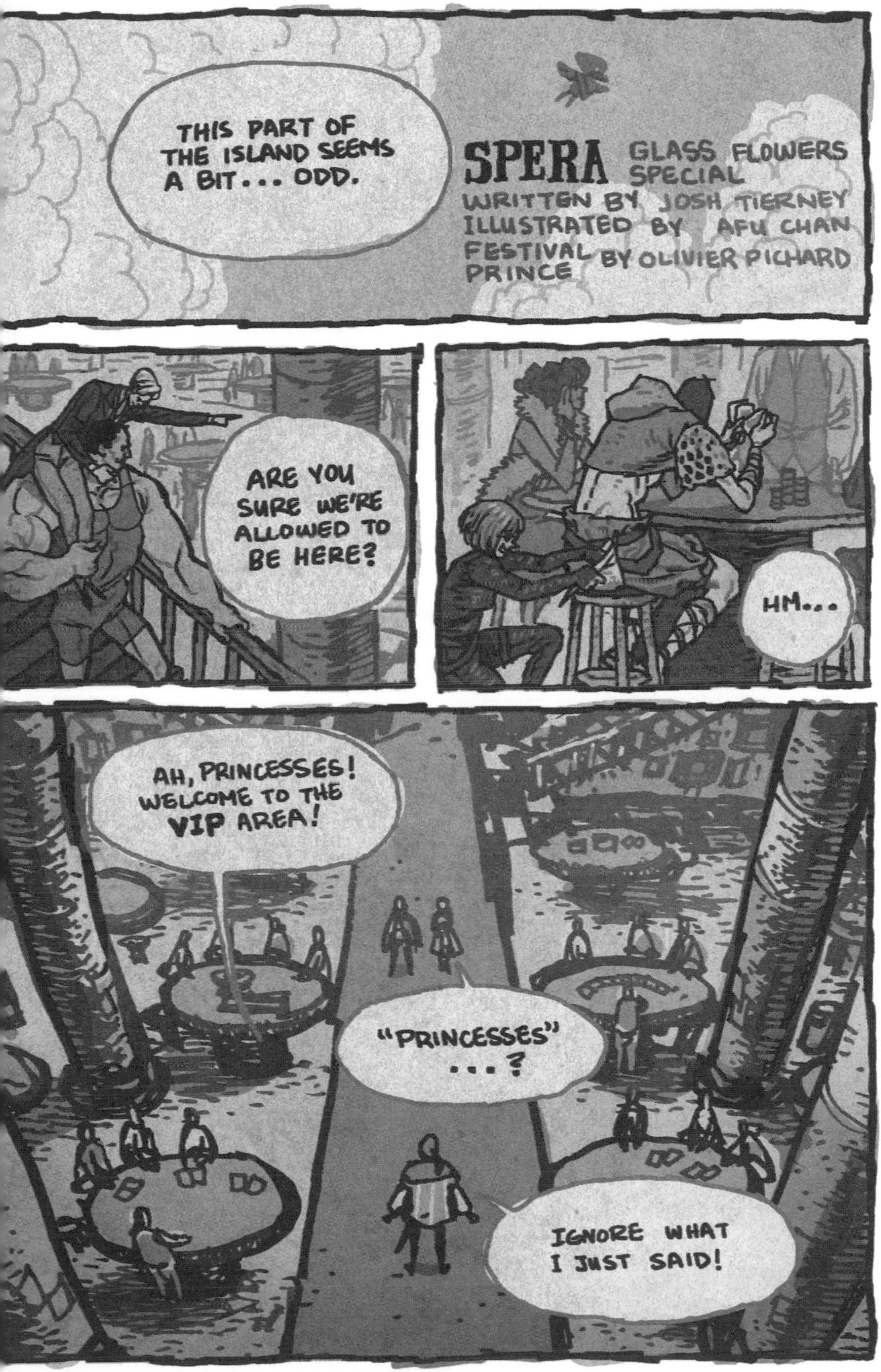
THIS PART OF THE ISLAND SEEMS A BIT... ODD.
SPERA GLASS FLOWERS SPECIAL
WRITTEN BY JOSH TIERNEY
ILLUSTRATED BY AFU CHAN
FESTIVAL PRINCE BY OLIVIER PICHARD
ARE YOU SURE WE'RE ALLOWED TO BE HERE?
HM...
AH, PRINCESSES! WELCOME TO THE VIP AREA!
"PRINCESSES" ...?
IGNORE WHAT I JUST SAID!

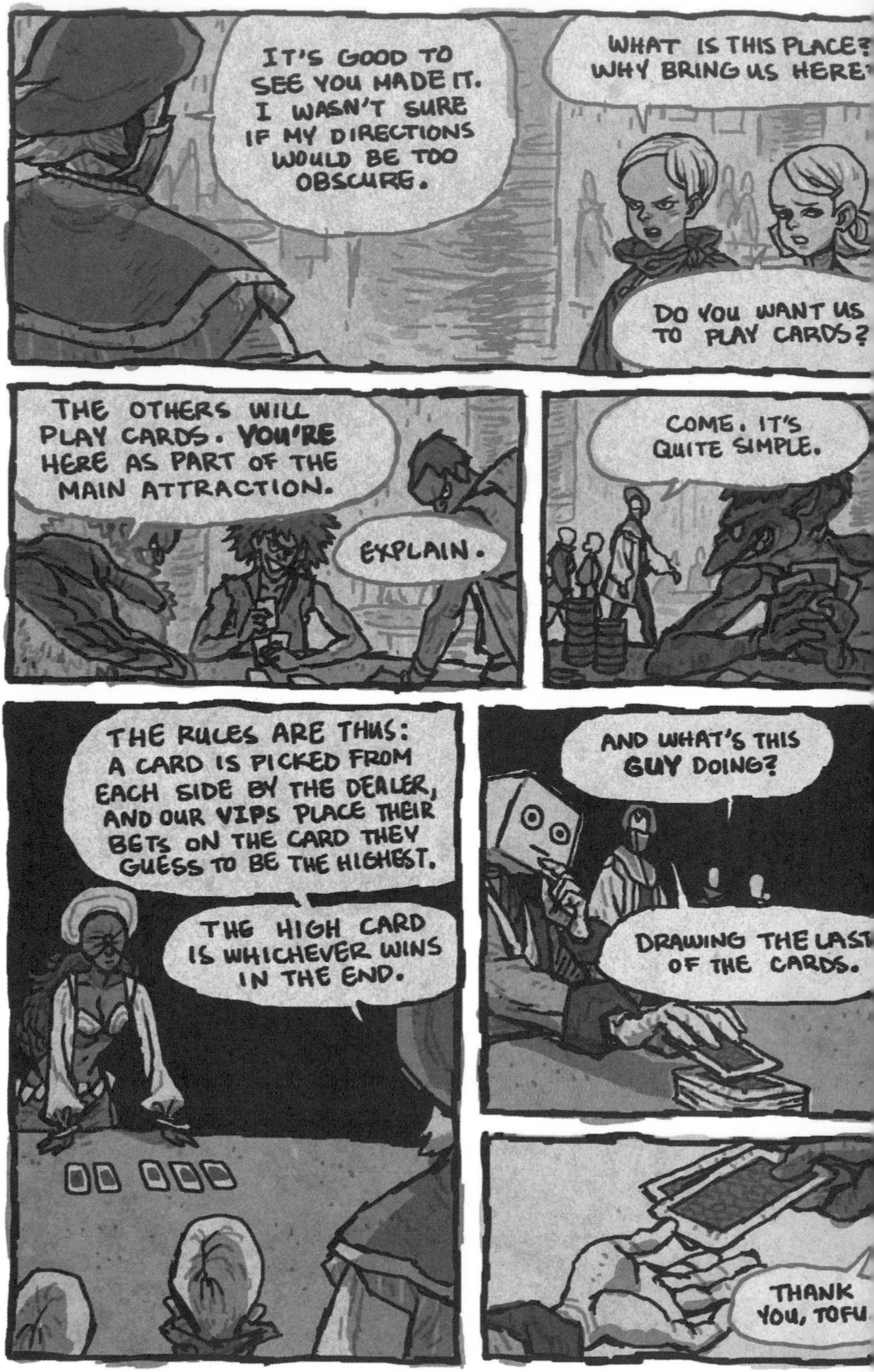
IT'S GOOD TO SEE YOU MADE IT. I WASN'T SURE IF MY DIRECTIONS WOULD BE TOO OBSCURE.
WHAT IS THIS PLACE? WHY BRING US HERE?
DO YOU WANT US TO PLAY CARDS?
THE OTHERS WILL PLAY CARDS. YOU'RE HERE AS PART OF THE MAIN ATTRACTION.
EXPLAIN.
COME. IT'S QUITE SIMPLE.
THE RULES ARE THUS: A CARD IS PICKED FROM EACH SIDE BY THE DEALER, AND OUR VIPS PLACE THEIR BETS ON THE CARD THEY GUESS TO BE THE HIGHEST.
THE HIGH CARD IS WHICHEVER WINS IN THE END.
AND WHAT'S THIS GUY DOING?
DRAWING THE LAST OF THE CARDS.
THANK YOU, TOFU.

FTLP LRDT LRM PLNT   PIRA LONO CHBO YNDR

MILA WILL SELECT A CARD FROM EACH SIDE. THEY WILL THEN FACE EACH OTHER IN THE ARENA.

SOME OF THESE CARDS LOOK AWFULLY FAMILIAR.

OF COURSE. THIS ONE'S YOU. I'M SURE PIRA UNDERSTANDS BY NOW.

LONO

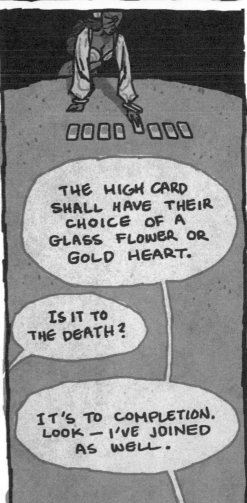

THE HIGH CARD SHALL HAVE THEIR CHOICE OF A GLASS FLOWER OR GOLD HEART.

IS IT TO THE DEATH?

IT'S TO COMPLETION. LOOK — I'VE JOINED AS WELL.

SO WE'RE HERE FOR A CONTEST BATTLE?

THAT'S RIGHT! YOU GOT IT!

WHAT DO YOU THINK, LONO?

I LIKE THE SOUND OF THE GLASS FLOWER. I'D BE WILLING TO BATTLE FOR IT.

OKAY — WE'RE IN!

TRULY! NOW LET'S HOPE YOU'RE SELECTED.

MILA?

THE GODS HAVE GUIDED MY HANDS. THE CARDS HAVE BEEN CHOSEN.

AND?

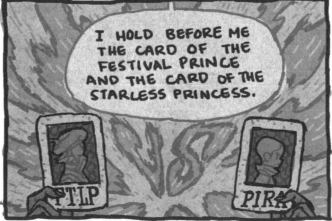

I HOLD BEFORE ME THE CARD OF THE FESTIVAL PRINCE AND THE CARD OF THE STARLESS PRINCESS.

TTLP

PIRA

THESE TWO SHALL BE TOSSED INTO THE ARENA IMMEDIATELY.

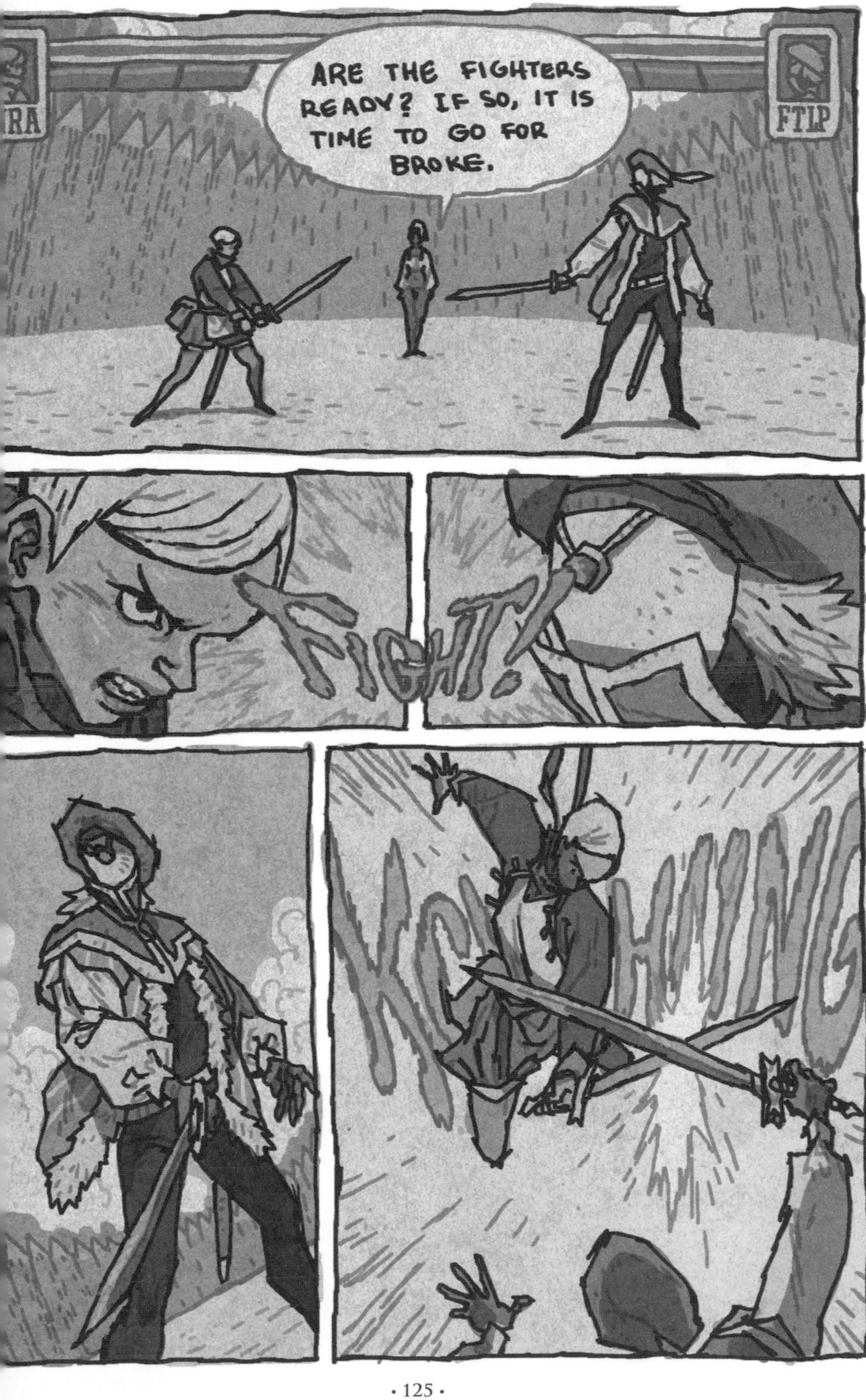
RA
FTLP
ARE THE FIGHTERS READY? IF SO, IT IS TIME TO GO FOR BROKE.
FIGHT!

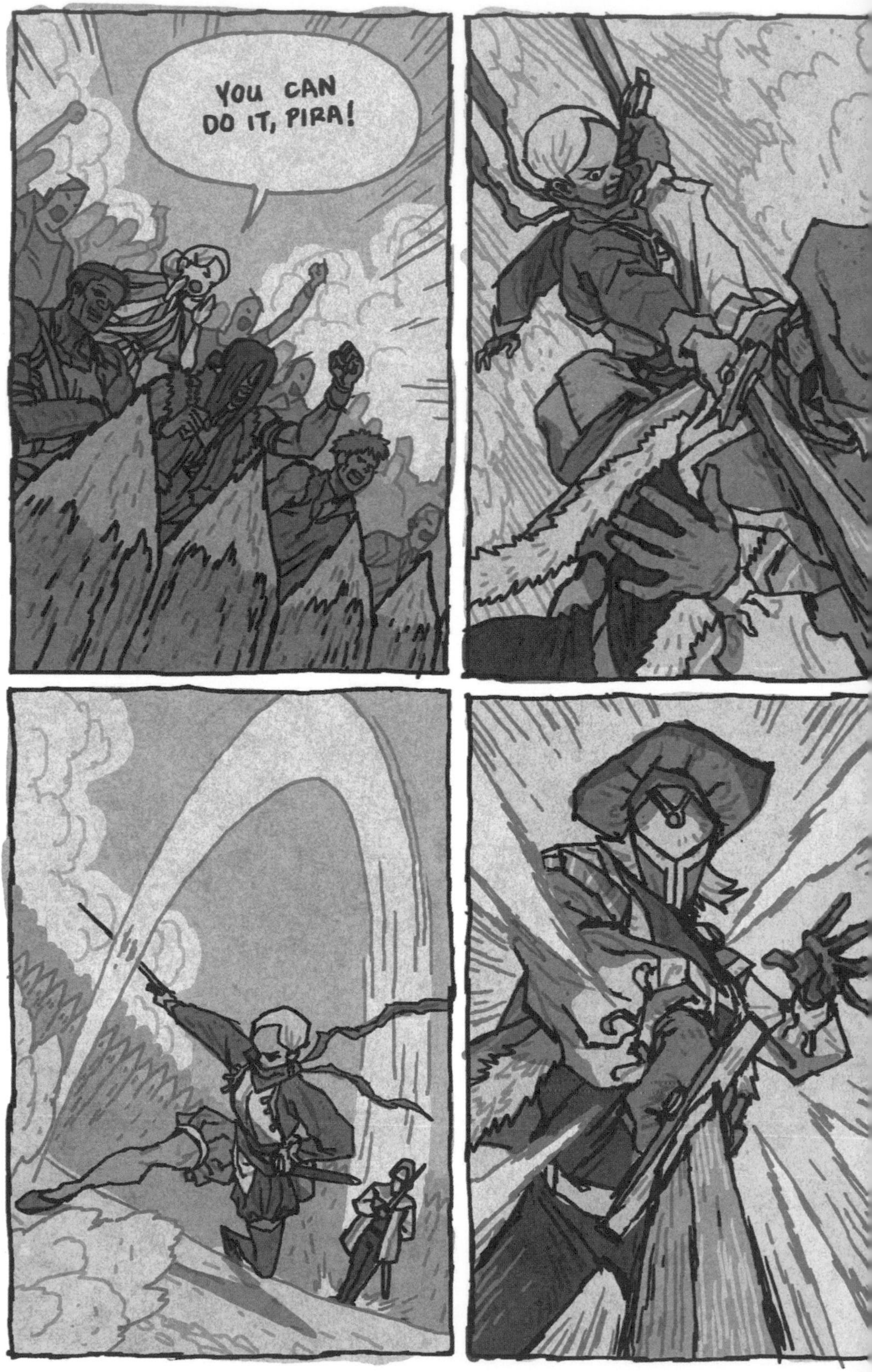
YOU CAN DO IT, PIRA!

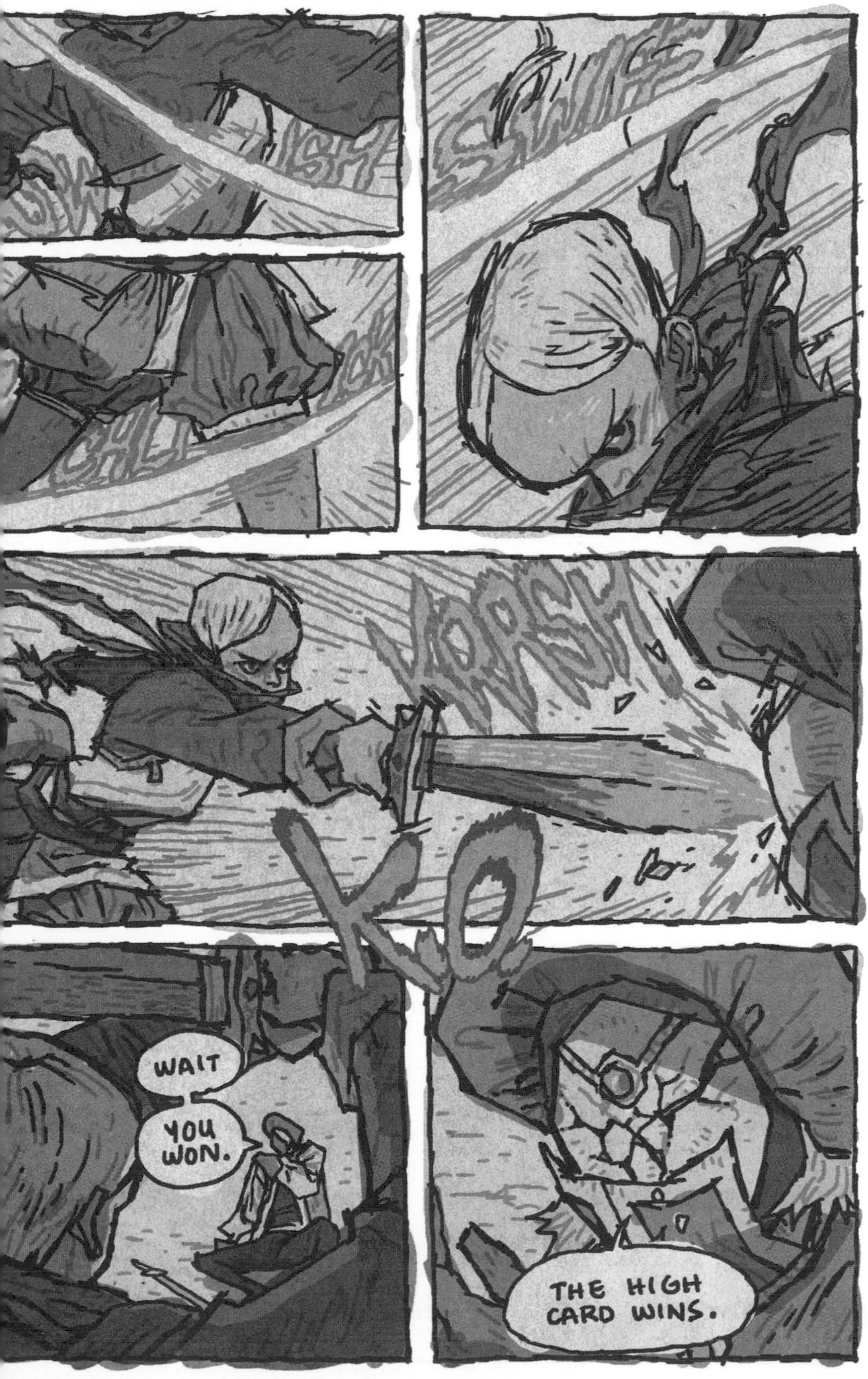
SWISH
SHLK
SHWISH
VORSH
KO
WAIT
YOU WON.
THE HIGH CARD WINS.

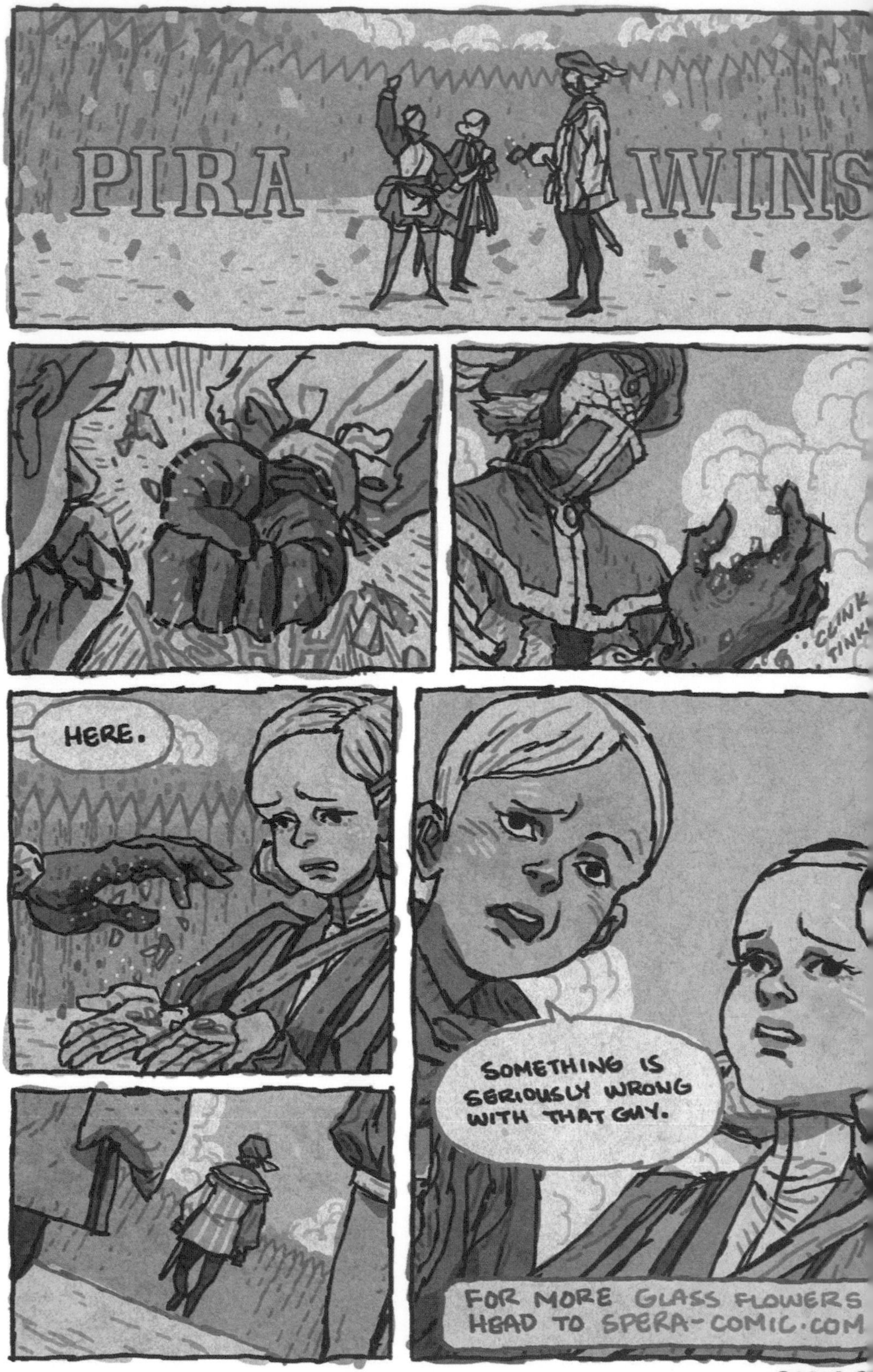
PIRA WINS
CLINK
TINK
HERE.
SOMETHING IS SERIOUSLY WRONG WITH THAT GUY.
FOR MORE GLASS FLOWERS HEAD TO SPERA-COMIC.COM

GAME O

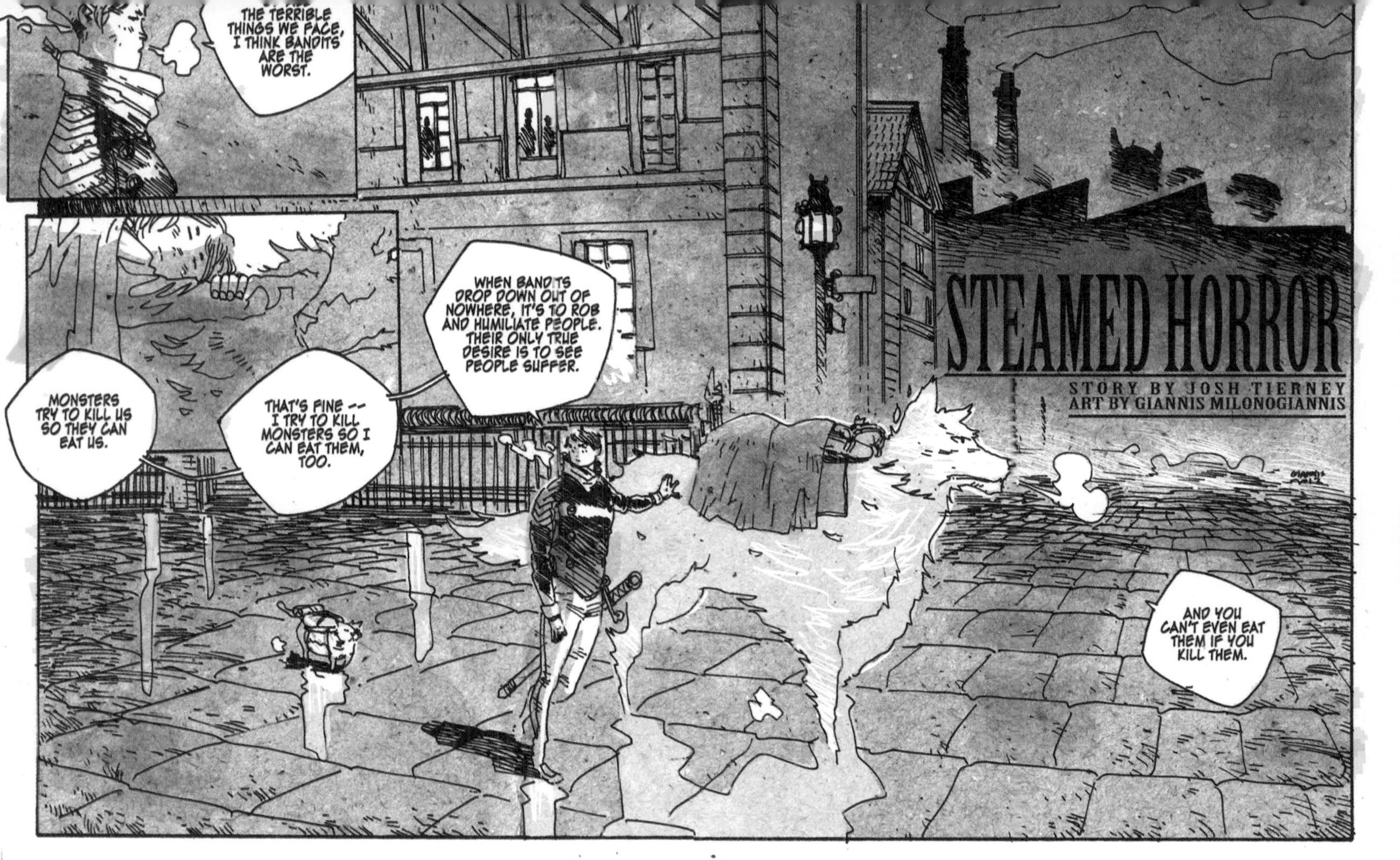
STEAMED HORROR
STORY BY JOSH TIERNEY
ART BY GIANNIS MILONOGIANNIS
THE TERRIBLE THINGS WE FACE, I THINK BANDITS ARE THE WORST.
WHEN BANDITS DROP DOWN OUT OF NOWHERE, IT'S TO ROB AND HUMILIATE PEOPLE. THEIR ONLY TRUE DESIRE IS TO SEE PEOPLE SUFFER.
MONSTERS TRY TO KILL US SO THEY CAN EAT US.
THAT'S FINE -- I TRY TO KILL MONSTERS SO I CAN EAT THEM, TOO.
AND YOU CAN'T EVEN EAT THEM IF YOU KILL THEM.

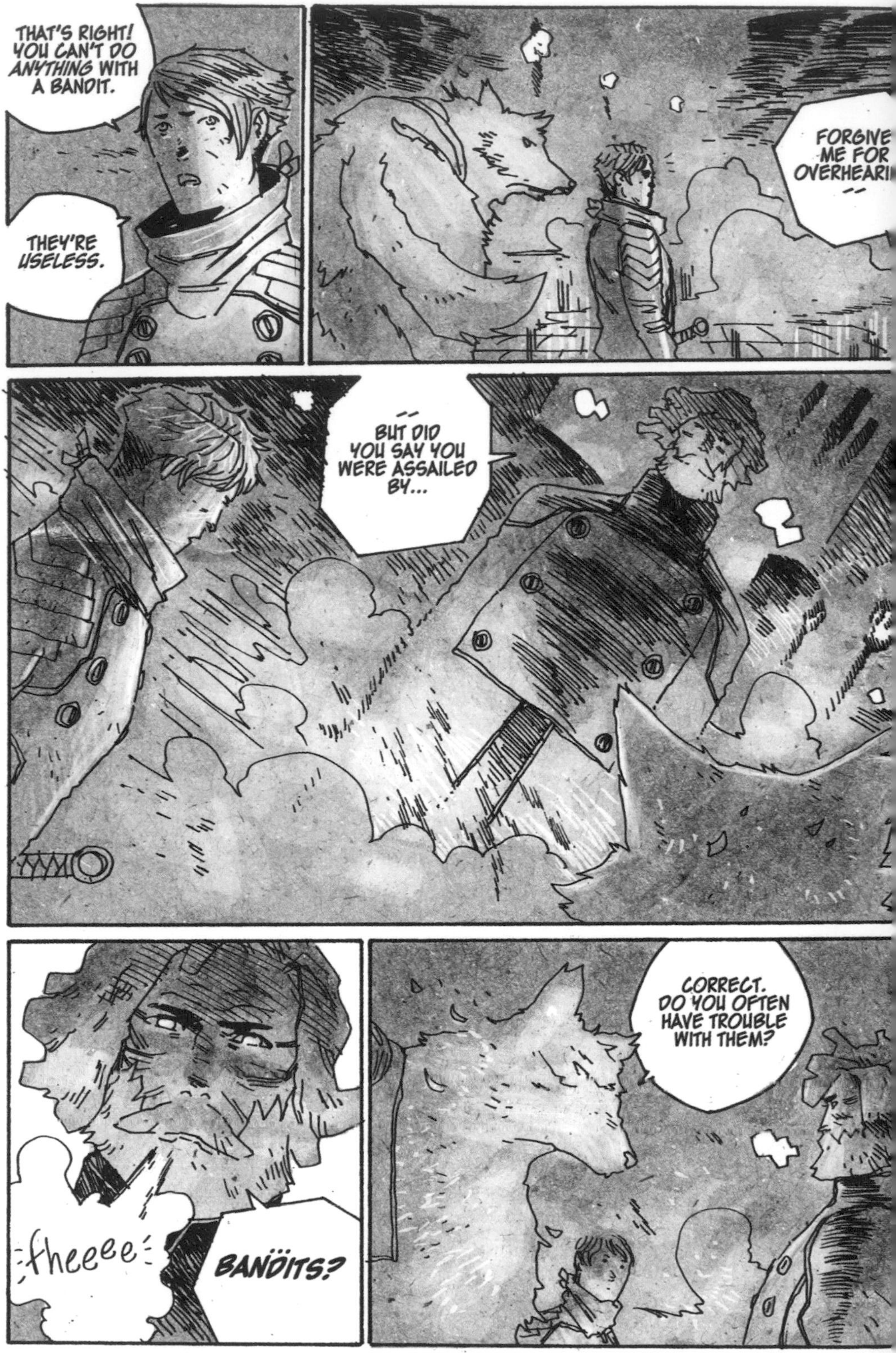
THAT'S RIGHT! YOU CAN'T DO ANYTHING WITH A BANDIT.
THEY'RE USELESS.
FORGIVE ME FOR OVERHEARI --
-- BUT DID YOU SAY YOU WERE ASSAILED BY...
fheeee
BANDITS?
CORRECT. DO YOU OFTEN HAVE TROUBLE WITH THEM?

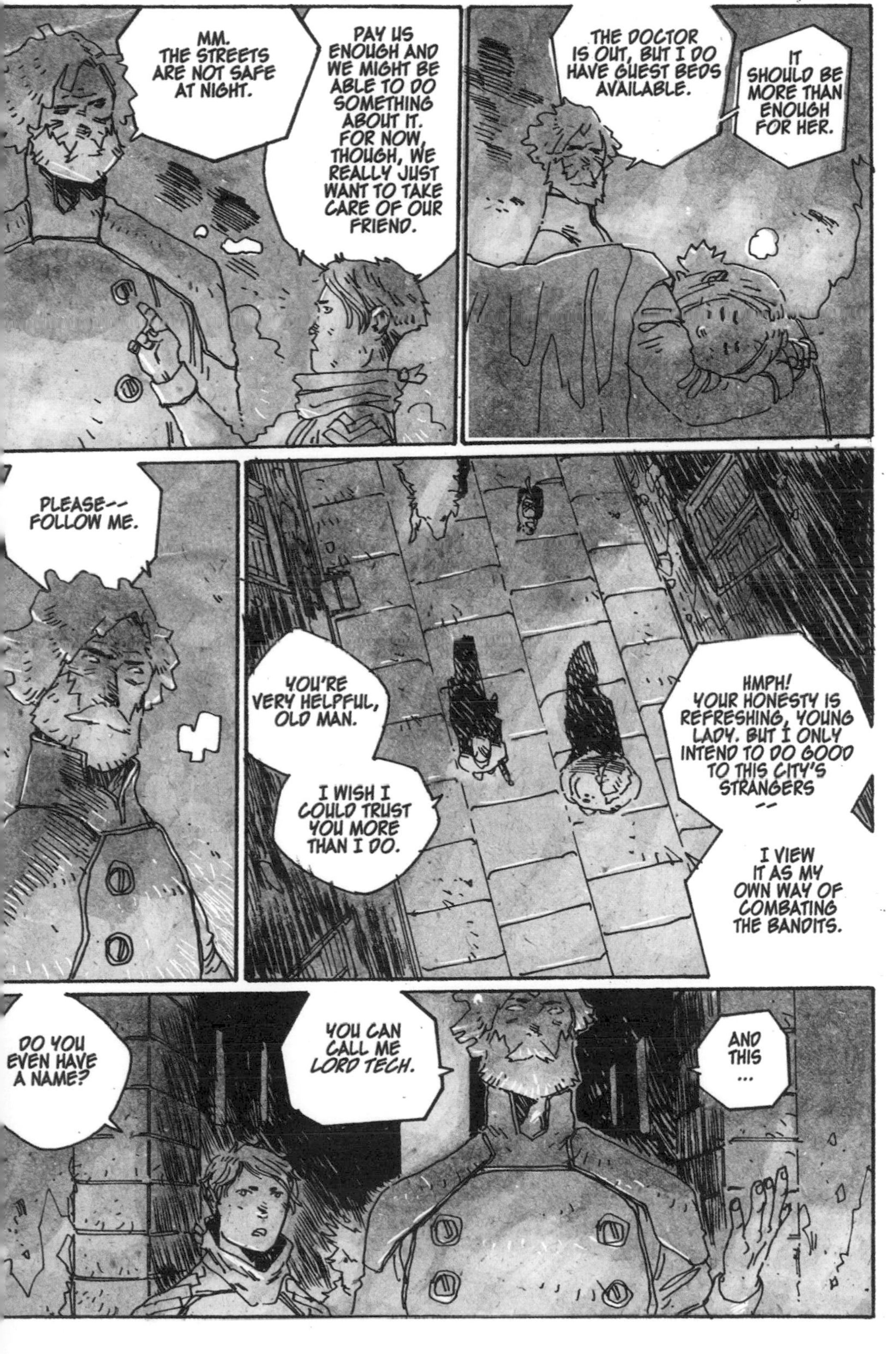
MM. THE STREETS ARE NOT SAFE AT NIGHT.
PAY US ENOUGH AND WE MIGHT BE ABLE TO DO SOMETHING ABOUT IT. FOR NOW, THOUGH, WE REALLY JUST WANT TO TAKE CARE OF OUR FRIEND.
THE DOCTOR IS OUT, BUT I DO HAVE GUEST BEDS AVAILABLE.
IT SHOULD BE MORE THAN ENOUGH FOR HER.
PLEASE-- FOLLOW ME.
YOU'RE VERY HELPFUL, OLD MAN.
I WISH I COULD TRUST YOU MORE THAN I DO.
HMPH! YOUR HONESTY IS REFRESHING, YOUNG LADY. BUT I ONLY INTEND TO DO GOOD TO THIS CITY'S STRANGERS --
I VIEW IT AS MY OWN WAY OF COMBATING THE BANDITS.
DO YOU EVEN HAVE A NAME?
YOU CAN CALL ME LORD TECH.
AND THIS ...

...IS MY HOUSE.

SMELL ANYTHING OFF ABOUT THIS GUY, YONDER?

I'VE BEEN DETECTING SOOT, GREASE AND METAL... BUT NOTHING PARTICULARLY STRANGE, CONSIDERING THE CITY.

STILL, HE'S A BIT DIRTY FOR A LORD, NO?

COME IN, COME IN!

WE MUST GET THE GIRL TO BED.

YOU NEVER TOLD ME YOUR NAMES...

I'M PIRA AND OUR FRIEND IS LONO.

THE DOG IS YONDER. CHOBO IS THE CAT.

DELIGHTFUL.

WE'LL CHECK ON HER IN TIME.

FOR NOW WE SHOULD PREPARE NOURISHMENT FOR WHEN SHE WAKES.

DON'T YOU HAVE ANY SERVANTS?

I DO, BUT THEY'RE RESTING. THEY'VE HAD A BUSY DAY.

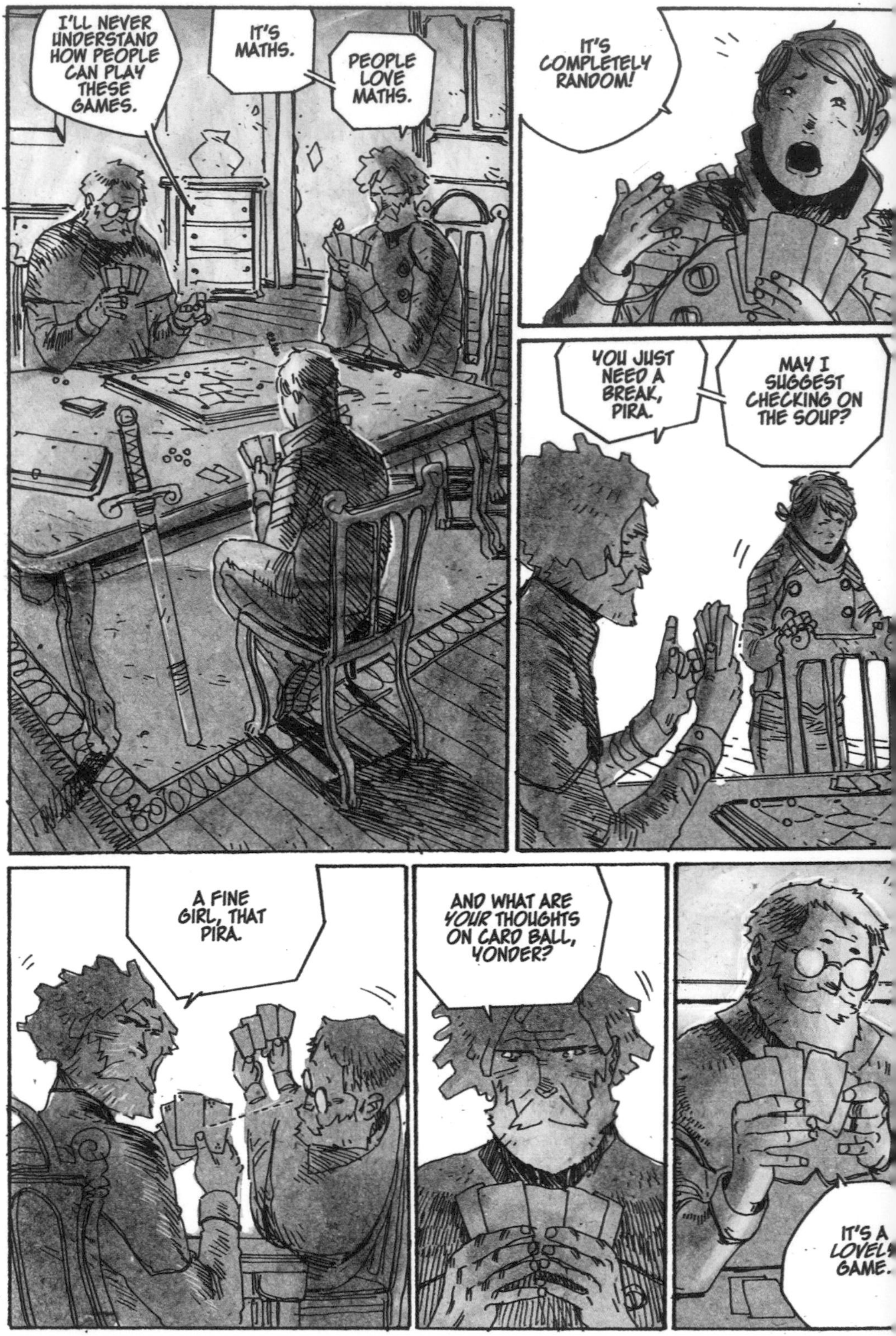
I'LL NEVER UNDERSTAND HOW PEOPLE CAN PLAY THESE GAMES.
IT'S MATHS.
PEOPLE LOVE MATHS.
IT'S COMPLETELY RANDOM!
YOU JUST NEED A BREAK, PIRA.
MAY I SUGGEST CHECKING ON THE SOUP?
A FINE GIRL, THAT PIRA.
AND WHAT ARE *YOUR* THOUGHTS ON CARD BALL, YONDER?
IT'S A LOVEL GAME.

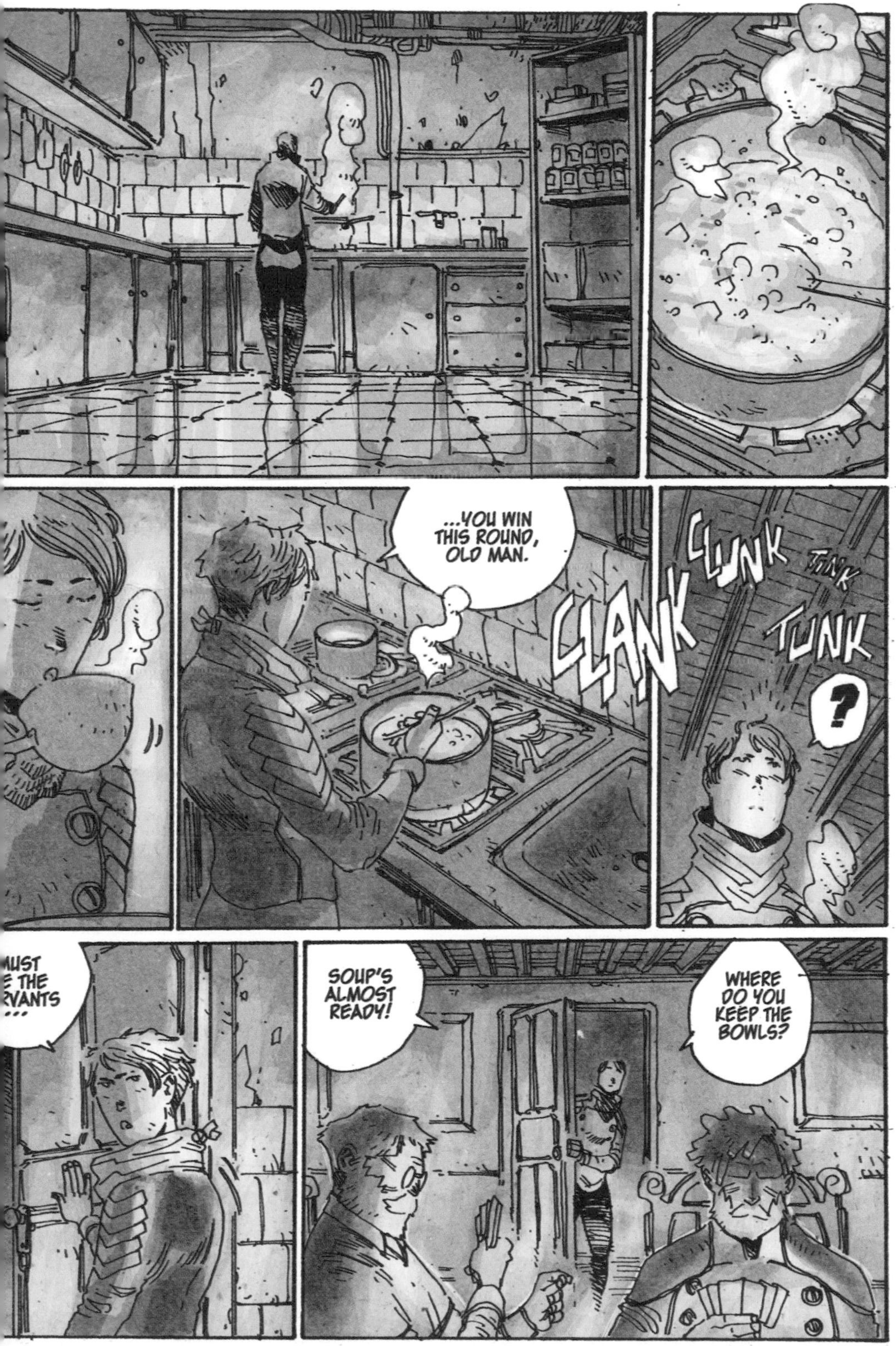
...YOU WIN THIS ROUND, OLD MAN.
CLANK
CLUNK
TUNK
TUNK
?
MUST
E THE
RVANTS
...
SOUP'S ALMOST READY!
WHERE DO YOU KEEP THE BOWLS?

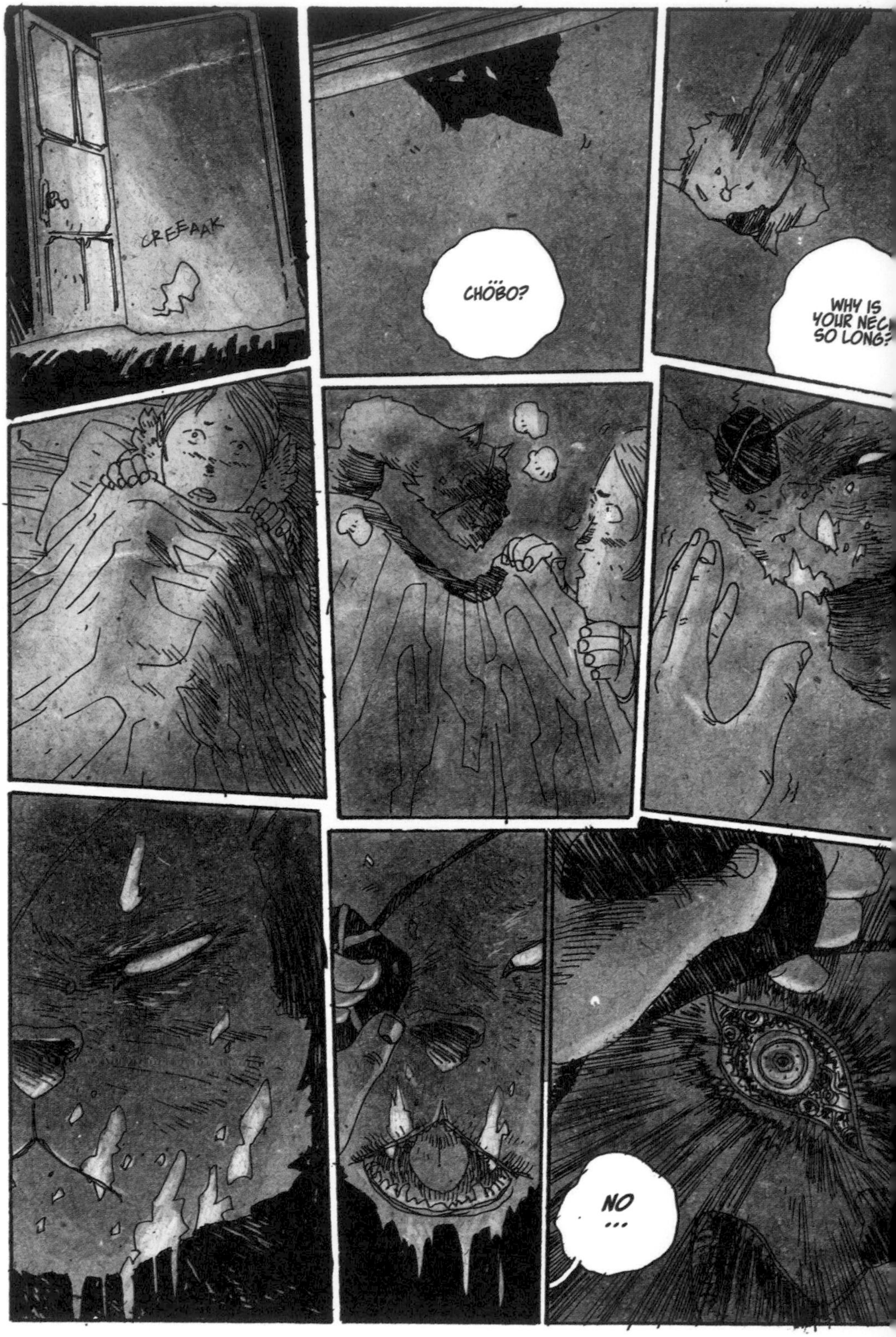
CREEAAK
...CHŌBO?
WHY IS YOUR NEC SO LONG?
NO ...

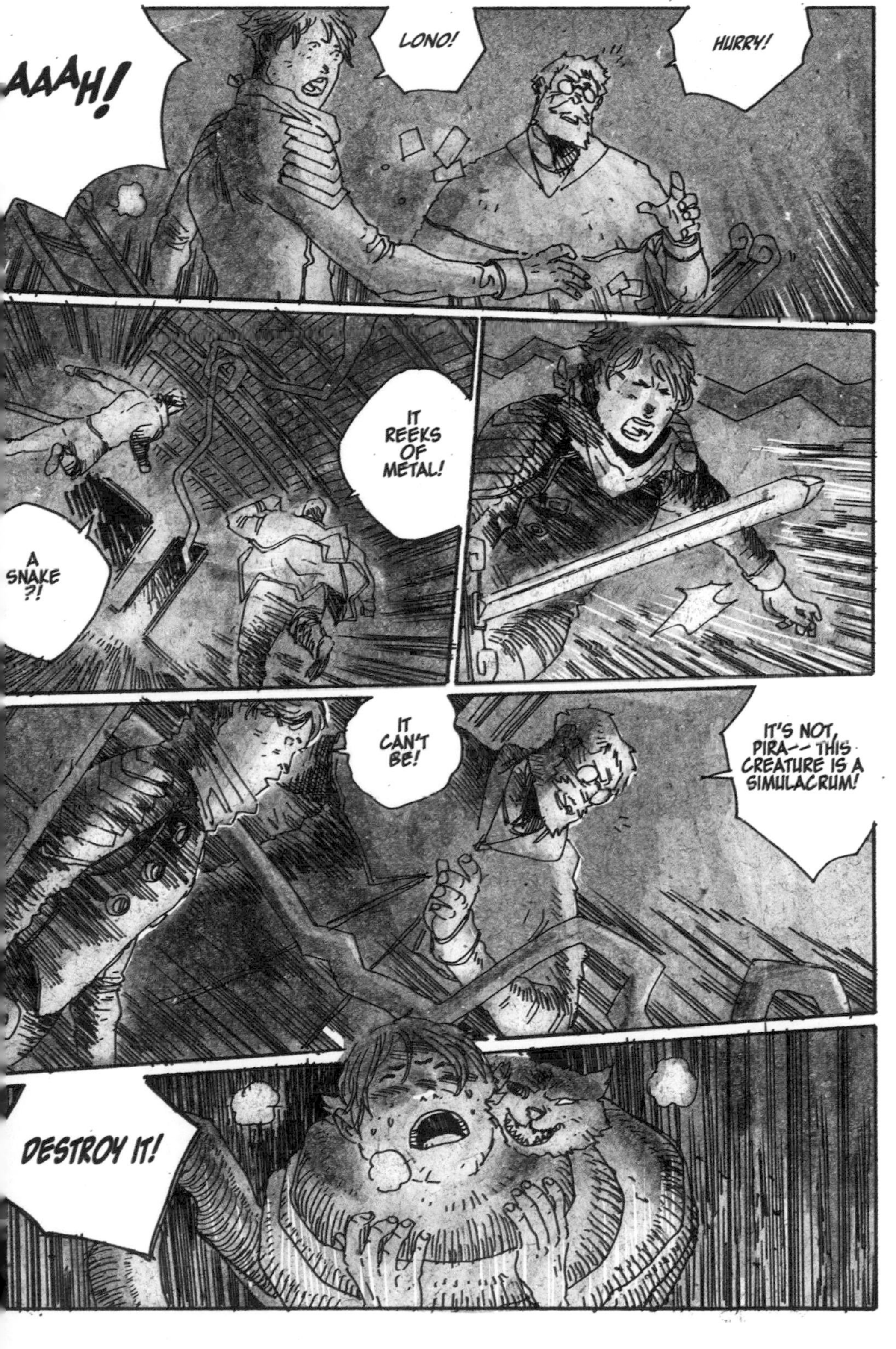
AAAH!
LONO!
HURRY!
IT REEKS OF METAL!
A SNAKE ?!
IT CAN'T BE!
IT'S NOT, PIRA-- THIS CREATURE IS A SIMULACRUM!
DESTROY IT!

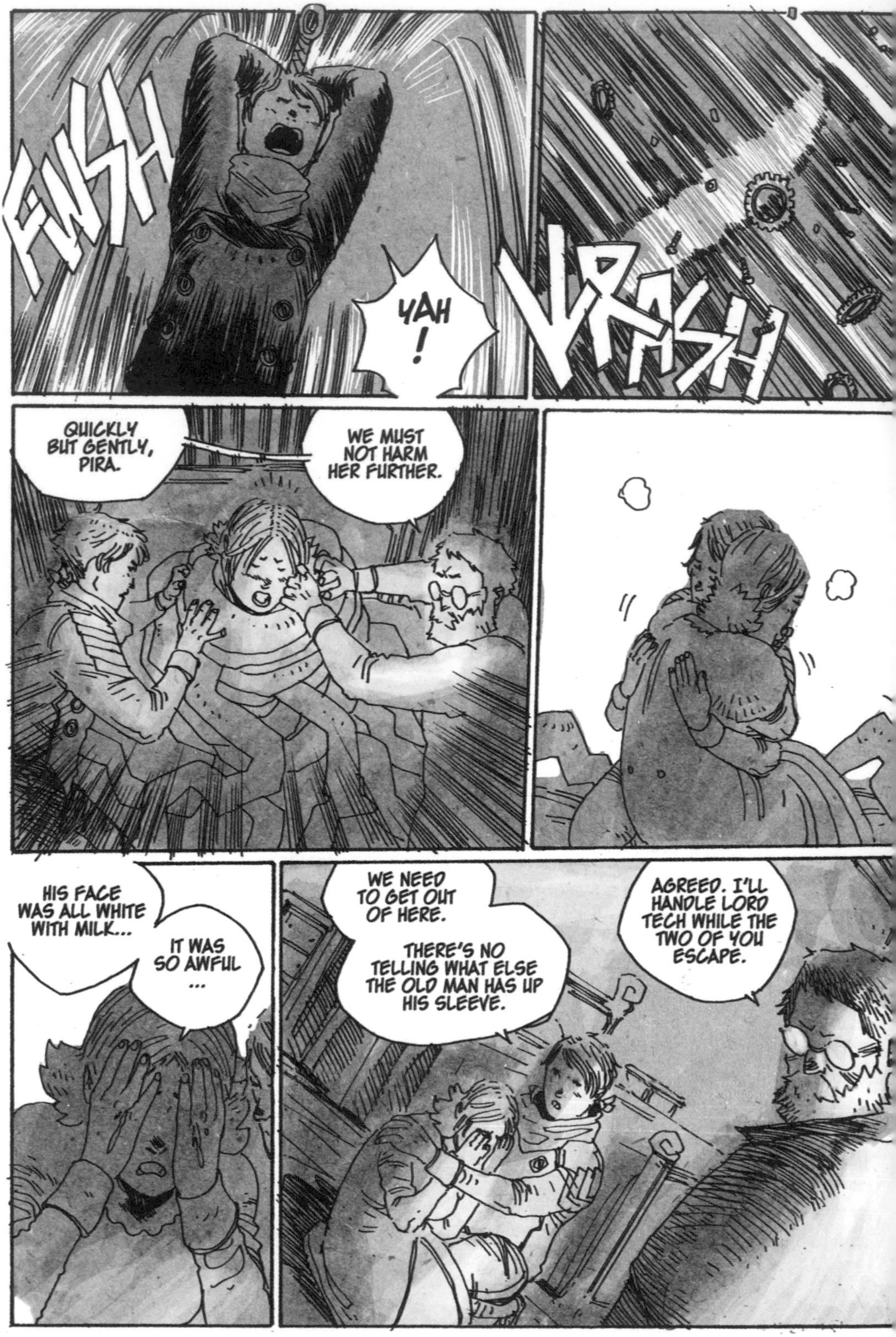
FWSH
YAH !
VRASH
QUICKLY BUT GENTLY, PIRA.
WE MUST NOT HARM HER FURTHER.
HIS FACE WAS ALL WHITE WITH MILK...
IT WAS SO AWFUL ...
WE NEED TO GET OUT OF HERE.
THERE'S NO TELLING WHAT ELSE THE OLD MAN HAS UP HIS SLEEVE.
AGREED. I'LL HANDLE LORD TECH WHILE THE TWO OF YOU ESCAPE.

IS IT YONDER?

IT IS. AND THANK THE *GODS* FOR THAT.

ORD TECH CAPED, BUT I MANAGE TO FIND THIS.

I HAVE A FEELING LORD TECH WAS UP TO SOMETHING MUCH WORSE THAN COPYING CATS.

INDEED.

WE MUST LOCATE THE LOCAL AUTHORITIES IMMEDIATELY. THE REMAINDER OF THE NIGHT WILL BE SPENT ON RESTING.

CHOBO!

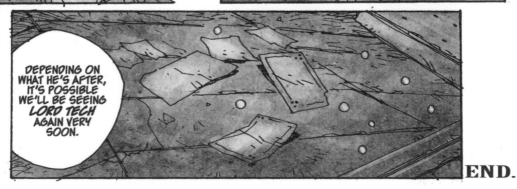

DEPENDING ON WHAT HE'S AFTER, IT'S POSSIBLE WE'LL BE SEEING *LORD TECH* AGAIN VERY SOON.

END.

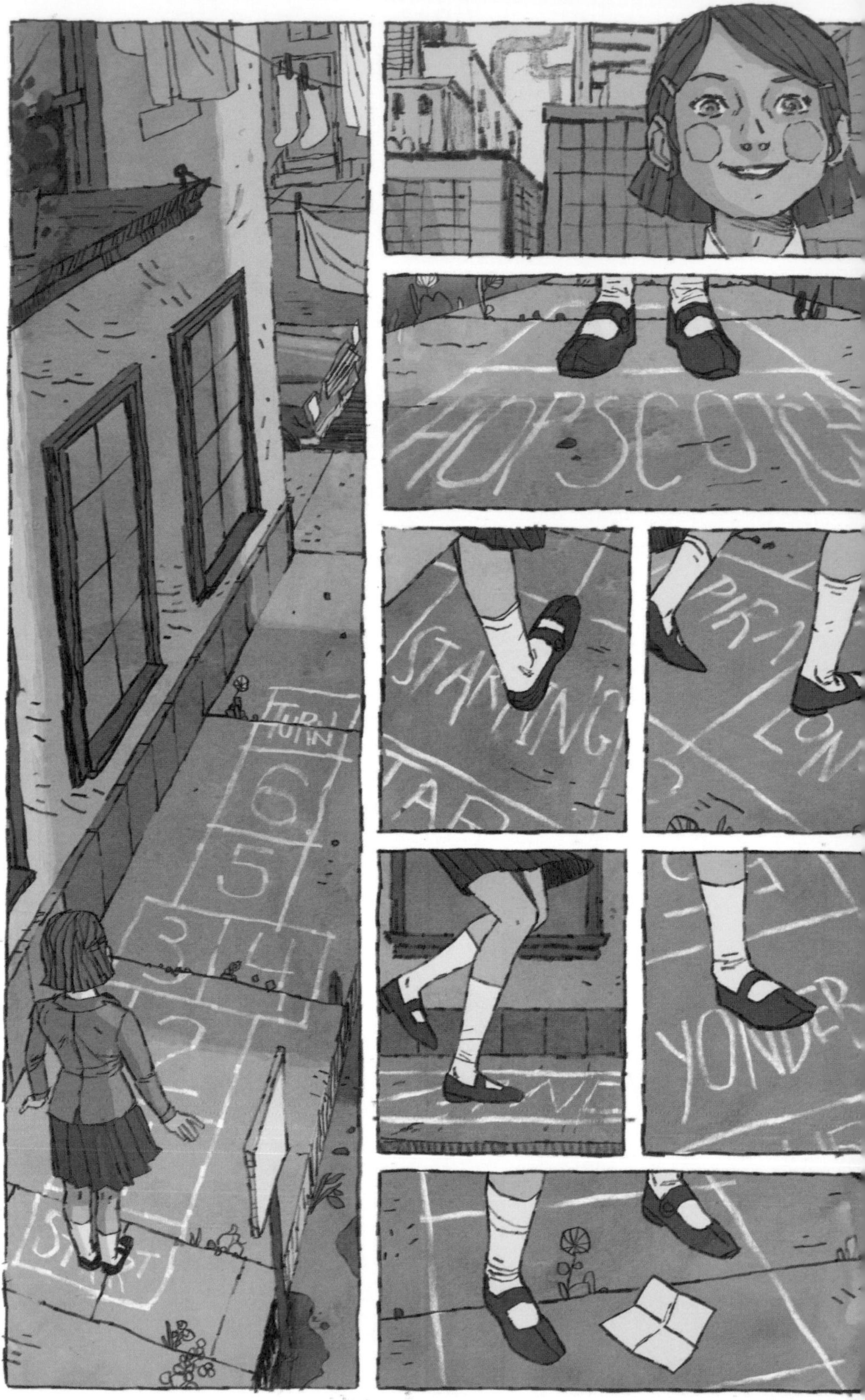
TURN
6
5
3
4
2
STARTING
YONDER

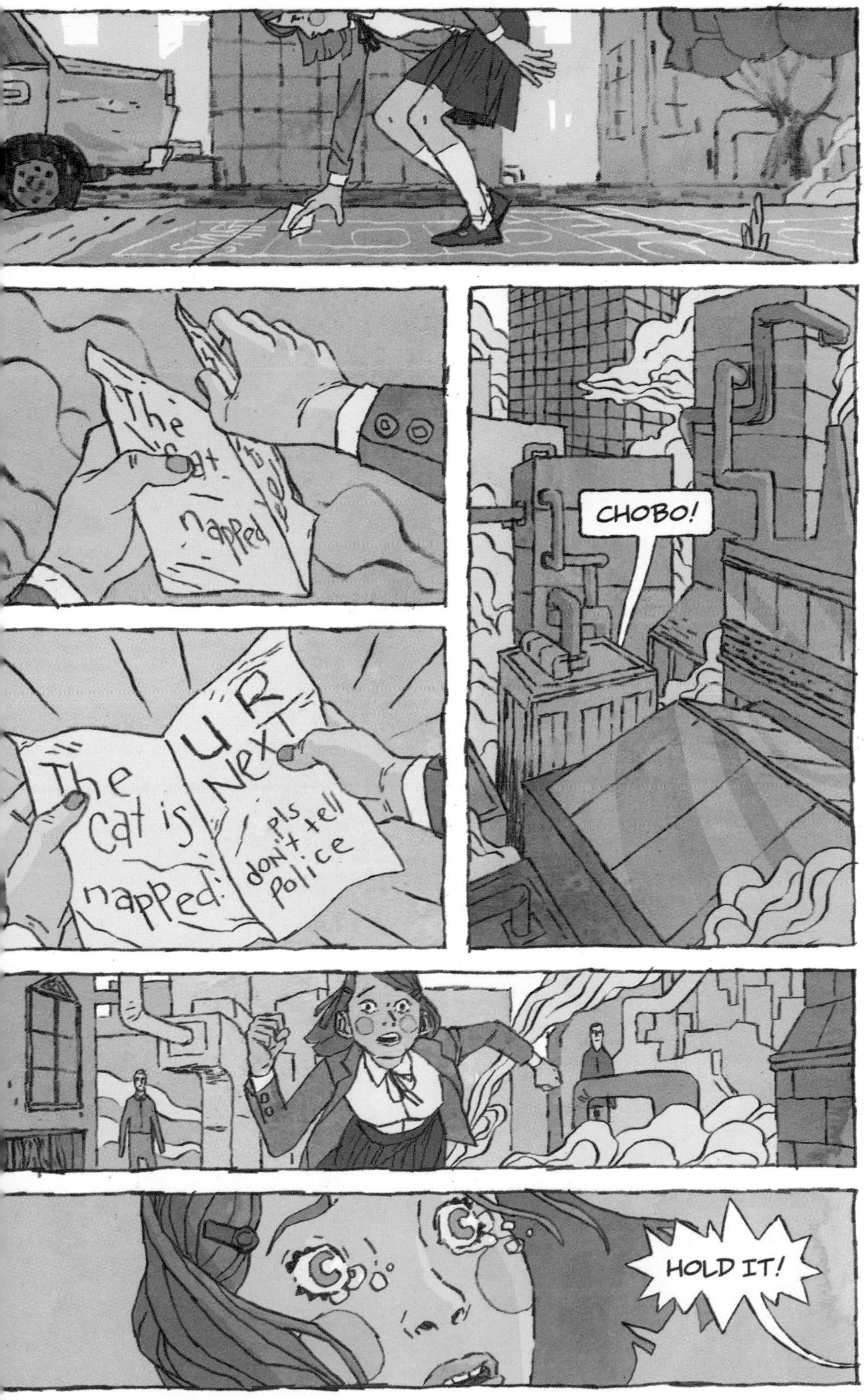
The
napped
CHOBO!
The cat is napped:
U R NEXT
pls don't tell police
HOLD IT!

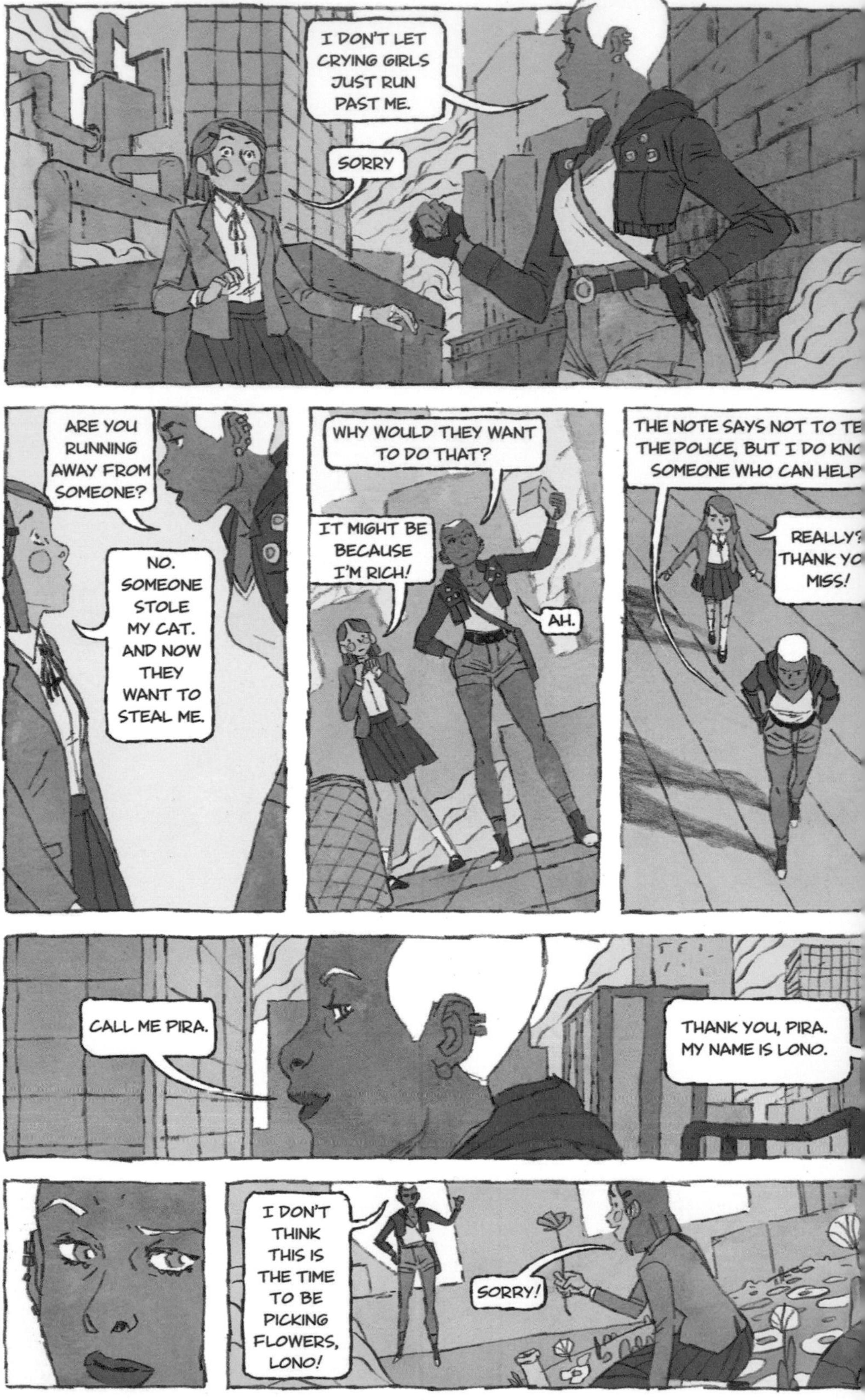
I DON'T LET CRYING GIRLS JUST RUN PAST ME.
SORRY
ARE YOU RUNNING AWAY FROM SOMEONE?
NO. SOMEONE STOLE MY CAT. AND NOW THEY WANT TO STEAL ME.
WHY WOULD THEY WANT TO DO THAT?
IT MIGHT BE BECAUSE I'M RICH!
AH.
THE NOTE SAYS NOT TO TE
THE POLICE, BUT I DO KNO
SOMEONE WHO CAN HELP
REALLY?
THANK YO
MISS!
CALL ME PIRA.
THANK YOU, PIRA. MY NAME IS LONO.
I DON'T THINK THIS IS THE TIME TO BE PICKING FLOWERS, LONO!
SORRY!

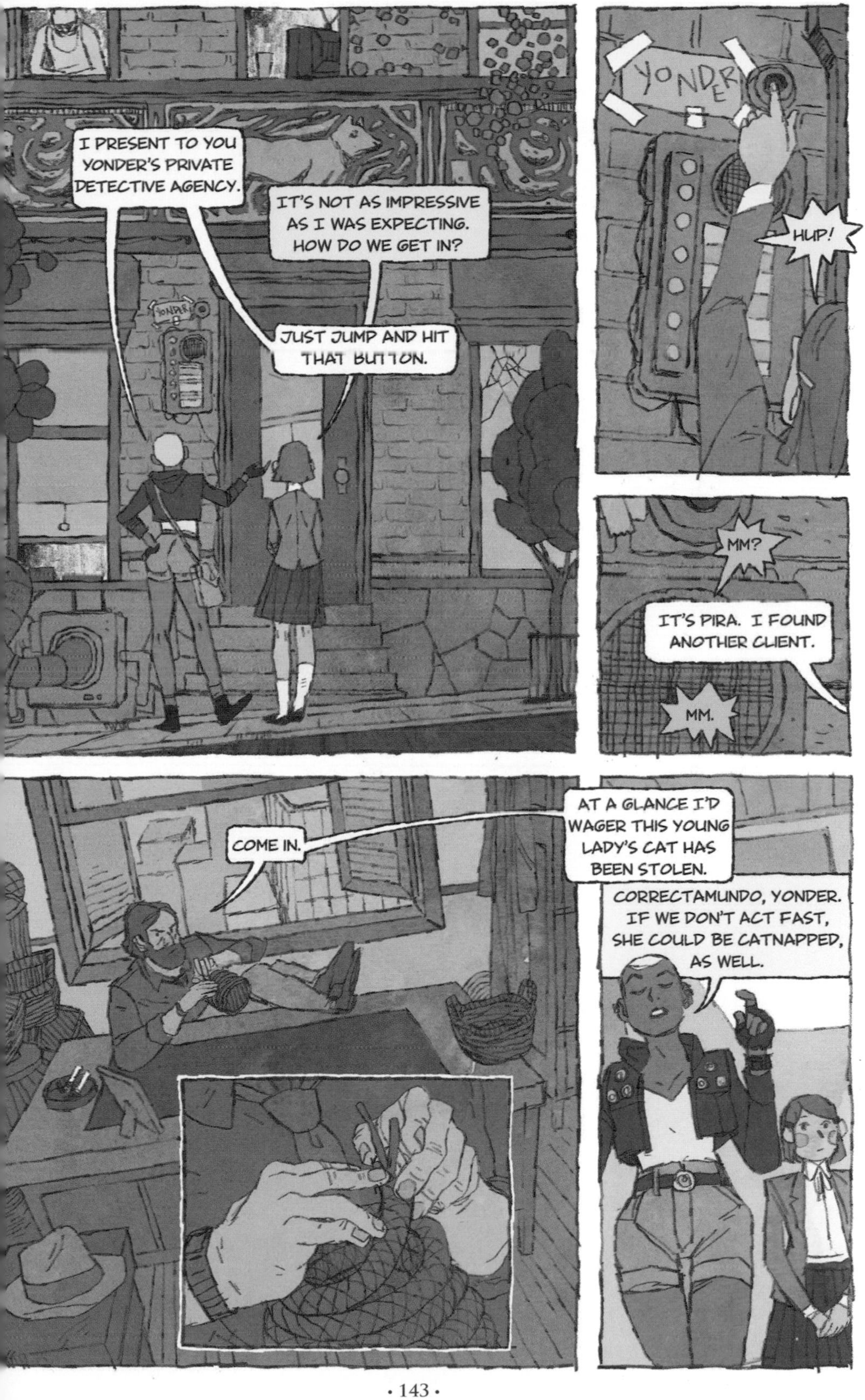
I PRESENT TO YOU YONDER'S PRIVATE DETECTIVE AGENCY.
IT'S NOT AS IMPRESSIVE AS I WAS EXPECTING. HOW DO WE GET IN?
JUST JUMP AND HIT THAT BUTTON.
YONDER
HUP!
MM?
IT'S PIRA. I FOUND ANOTHER CLIENT.
MM.
COME IN.
AT A GLANCE I'D WAGER THIS YOUNG LADY'S CAT HAS BEEN STOLEN.
CORRECTAMUNDO, YONDER. IF WE DON'T ACT FAST, SHE COULD BE CATNAPPED, AS WELL.

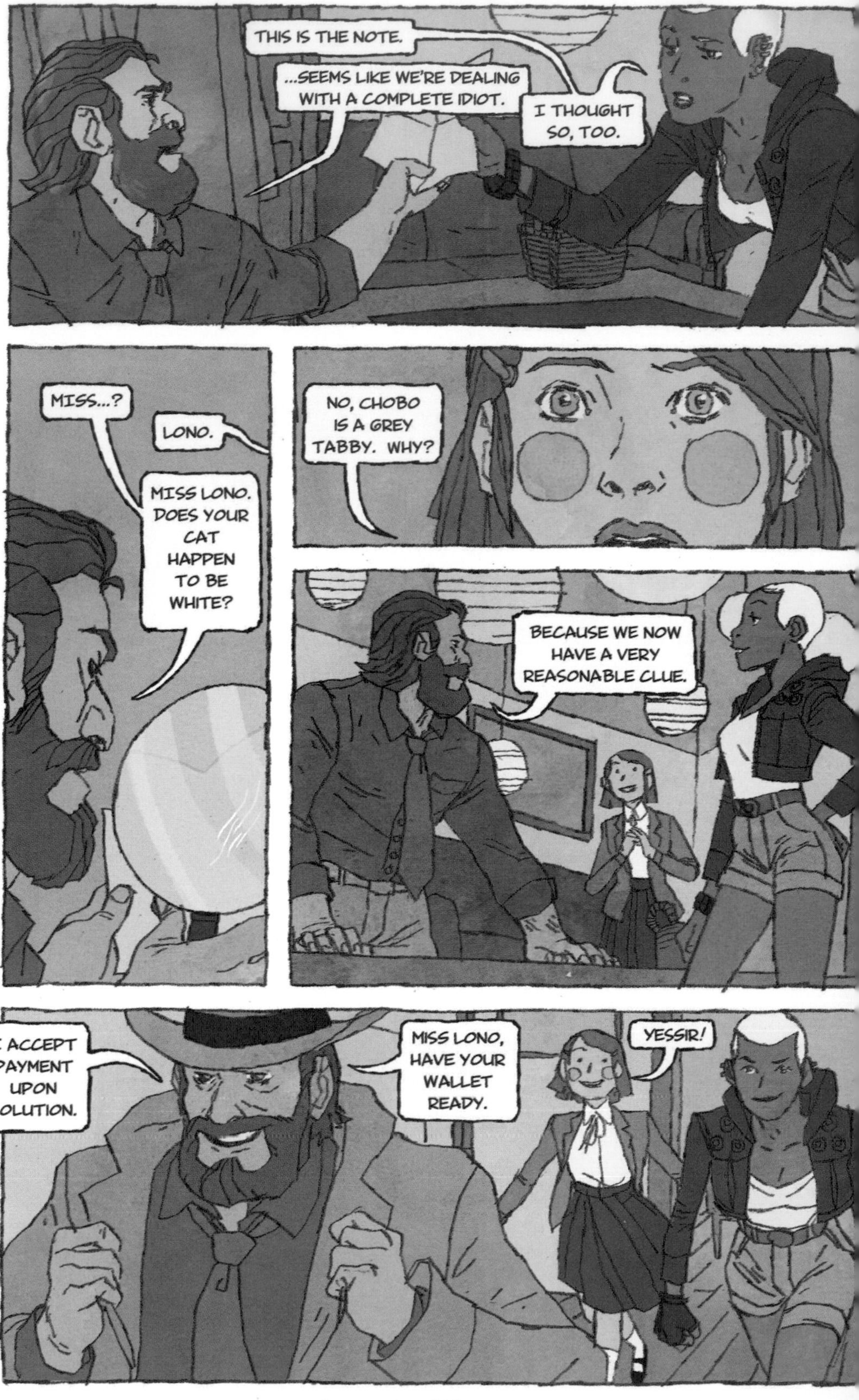
THIS IS THE NOTE.
...SEEMS LIKE WE'RE DEALING WITH A COMPLETE IDIOT.
I THOUGHT SO, TOO.
MISS...?
LONO.
MISS LONO. DOES YOUR CAT HAPPEN TO BE WHITE?
NO, CHOBO IS A GREY TABBY. WHY?
BECAUSE WE NOW HAVE A VERY REASONABLE CLUE.
I ACCEPT PAYMENT UPON SOLUTION.
MISS LONO, HAVE YOUR WALLET READY.
YESSIR!

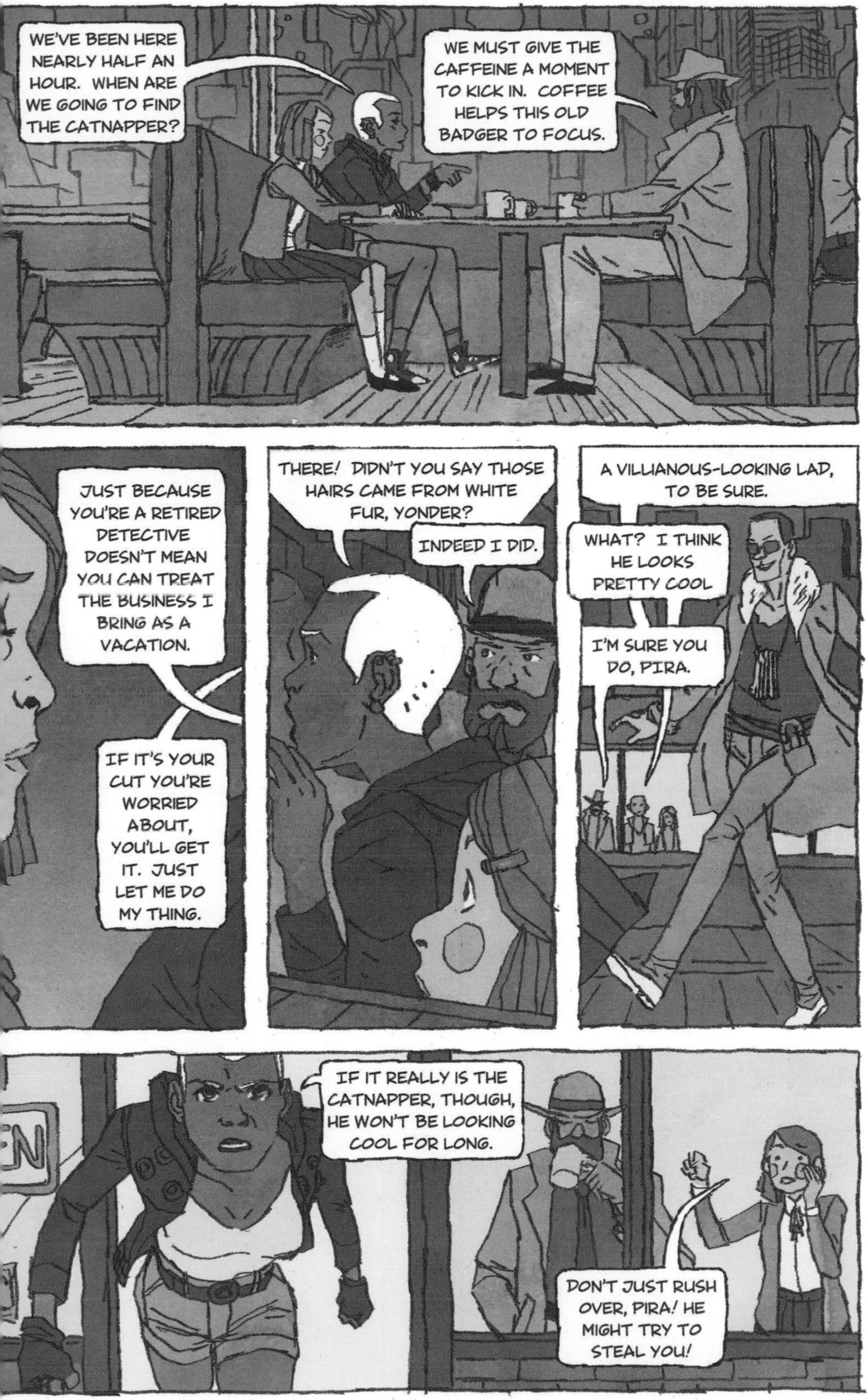
WE'VE BEEN HERE NEARLY HALF AN HOUR. WHEN ARE WE GOING TO FIND THE CATNAPPER?
WE MUST GIVE THE CAFFEINE A MOMENT TO KICK IN. COFFEE HELPS THIS OLD BADGER TO FOCUS.
JUST BECAUSE YOU'RE A RETIRED DETECTIVE DOESN'T MEAN YOU CAN TREAT THE BUSINESS I BRING AS A VACATION.
IF IT'S YOUR CUT YOU'RE WORRIED ABOUT, YOU'LL GET IT. JUST LET ME DO MY THING.
THERE! DIDN'T YOU SAY THOSE HAIRS CAME FROM WHITE FUR, YONDER?
INDEED I DID.
A VILLIANOUS-LOOKING LAD, TO BE SURE.
WHAT? I THINK HE LOOKS PRETTY COOL
I'M SURE YOU DO, PIRA.
IF IT REALLY IS THE CATNAPPER, THOUGH, HE WON'T BE LOOKING COOL FOR LONG.
DON'T JUST RUSH OVER, PIRA! HE MIGHT TRY TO STEAL YOU!

HEY!

HULLO, DARLING.

IT'S A BIT DARING TO BE CALLING ME DARLING, BUT THAT'S BESIDE THE POINT. YOU RECOGNIZE THE GIRL COWERING BEHIND ME?

NOT IN THE SLIGHTEST.

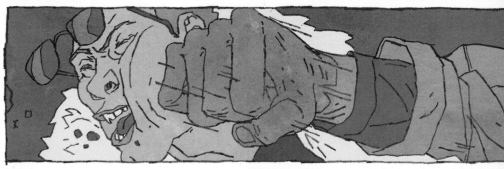

HOW ABOUT NOW?

...MIND EXPLAINING YOUR ACTIONS BEFORE THE MATTER ESCALATES, OLD MAN?

WE'RE CURRENTLY HAVING ISSUES WITH THE FUR BANDITS. THERE'S NO POINT IN DENYING YOU'RE A MEMBER.

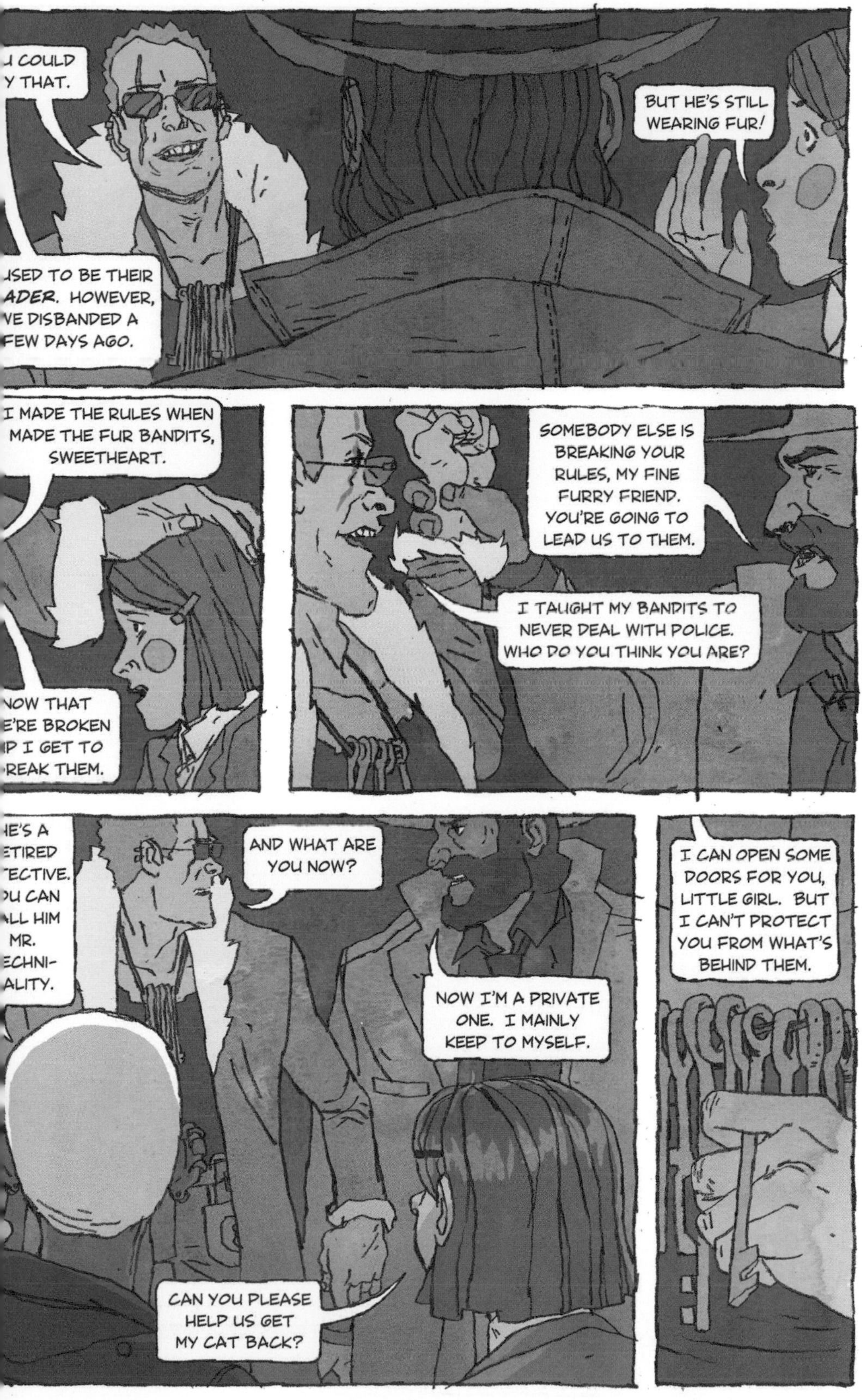

U COULD
Y THAT.
BUT HE'S STILL WEARING FUR!
USED TO BE THEIR ADER. HOWEVER, VE DISBANDED A FEW DAYS AGO.
I MADE THE RULES WHEN MADE THE FUR BANDITS, SWEETHEART.
NOW THAT E'RE BROKEN P I GET TO REAK THEM.
SOMEBODY ELSE IS BREAKING YOUR RULES, MY FINE FURRY FRIEND. YOU'RE GOING TO LEAD US TO THEM.
I TAUGHT MY BANDITS TO NEVER DEAL WITH POLICE. WHO DO YOU THINK YOU ARE?
HE'S A ETIRED TECTIVE. OU CAN ALL HIM MR. ECHNI- ALITY.
AND WHAT ARE YOU NOW?
NOW I'M A PRIVATE ONE. I MAINLY KEEP TO MYSELF.
CAN YOU PLEASE HELP US GET MY CAT BACK?
I CAN OPEN SOME DOORS FOR YOU, LITTLE GIRL. BUT I CAN'T PROTECT YOU FROM WHAT'S BEHIND THEM.

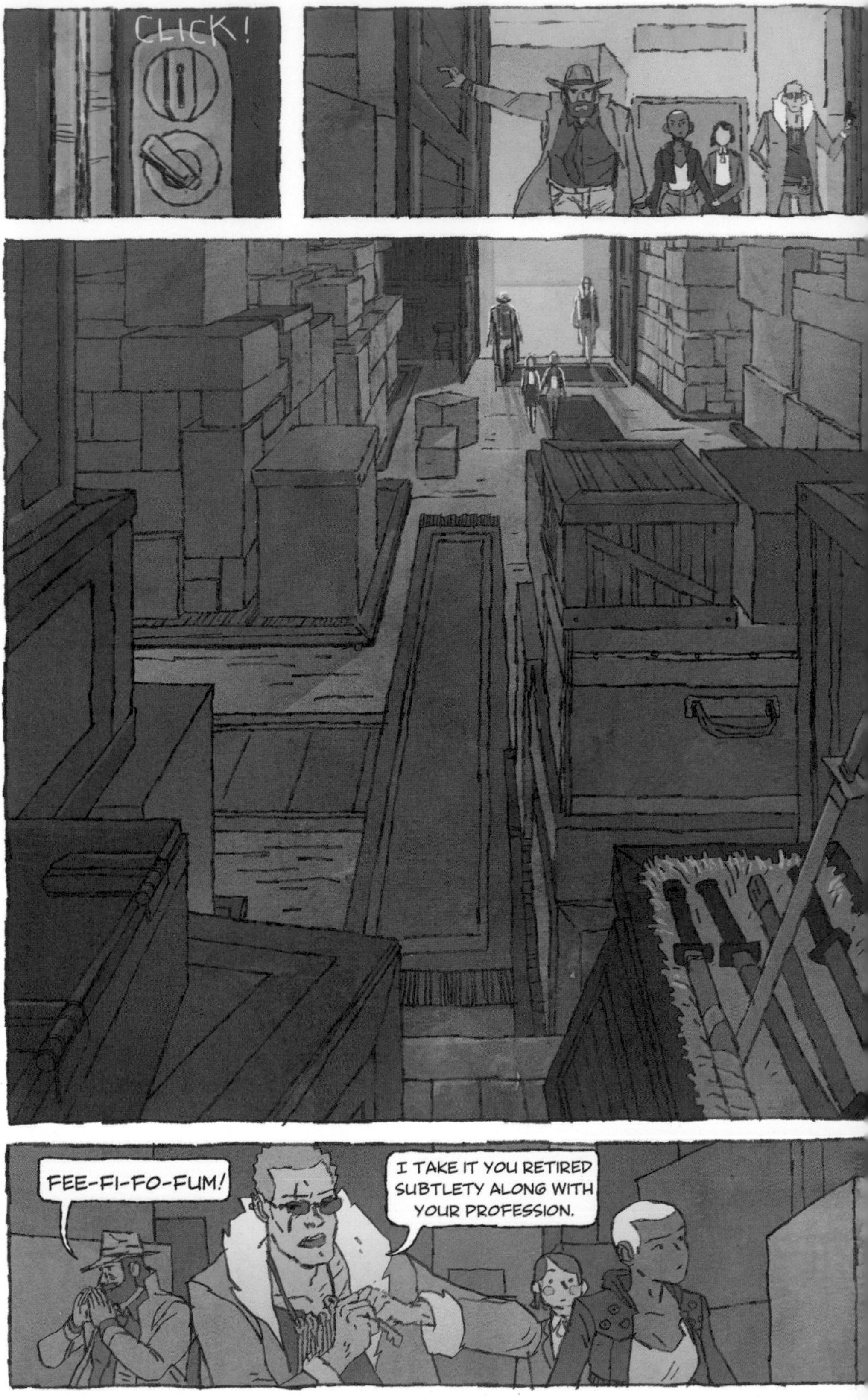
CLICK!
FEE-FI-FO-FUM!
I TAKE IT YOU RETIRED SUBTLETY ALONG WITH YOUR PROFESSION.

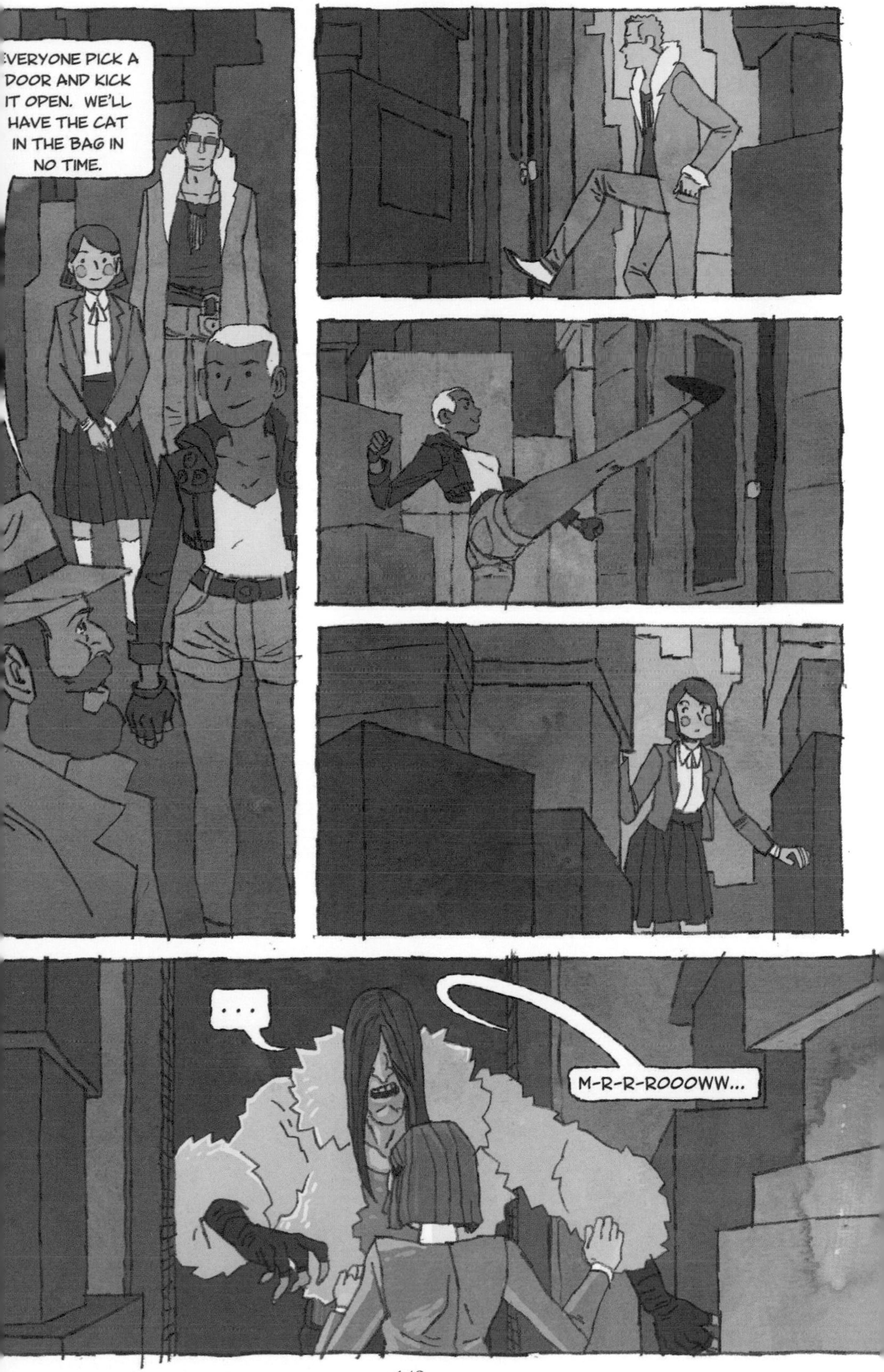
EVERYONE PICK A DOOR AND KICK IT OPEN. WE'LL HAVE THE CAT IN THE BAG IN NO TIME.
...
M-R-R-ROOOWW...

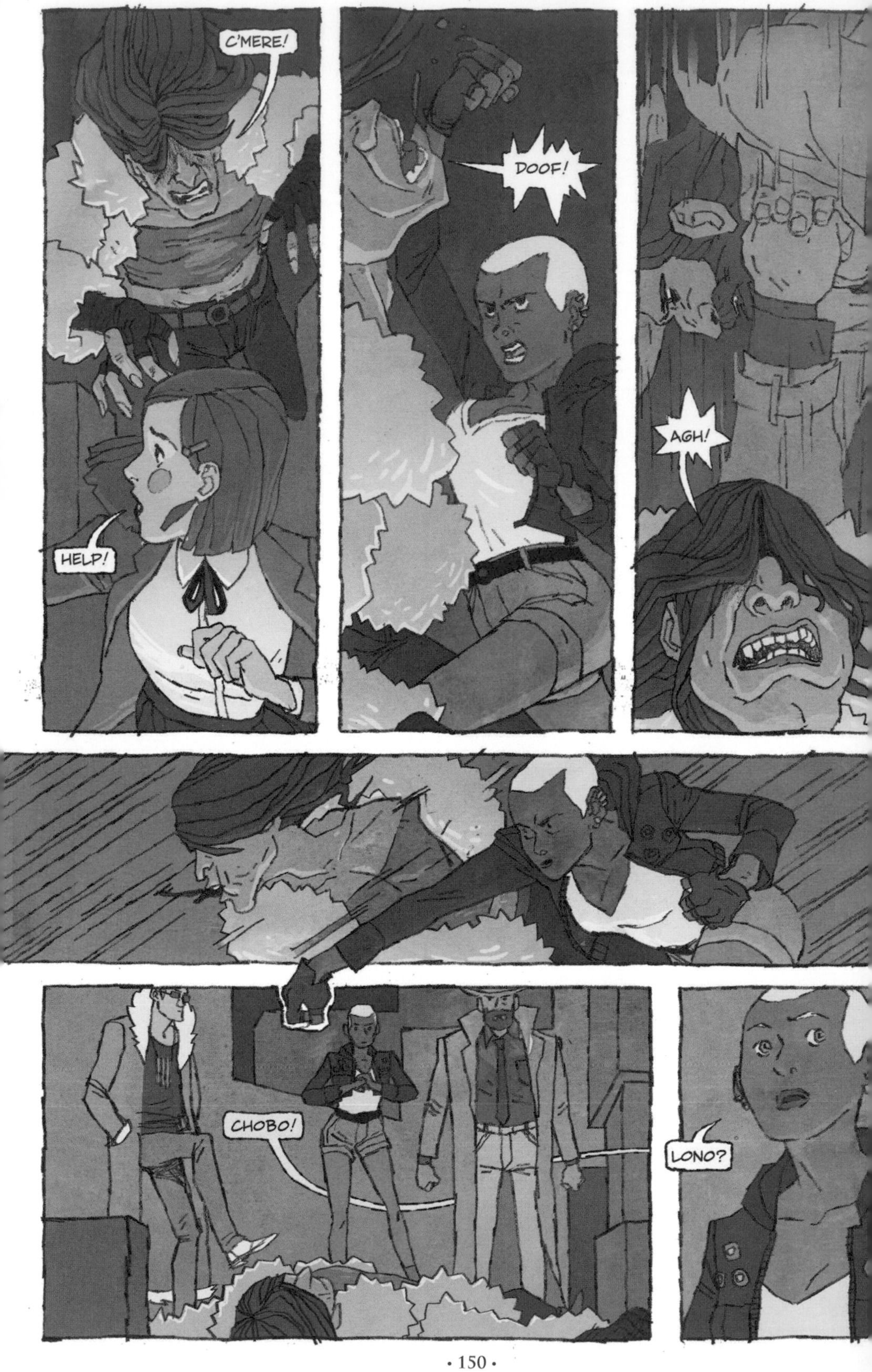
C'MERE!
HELP!
DOOF!
AGH!
CHOBO!
LONO?

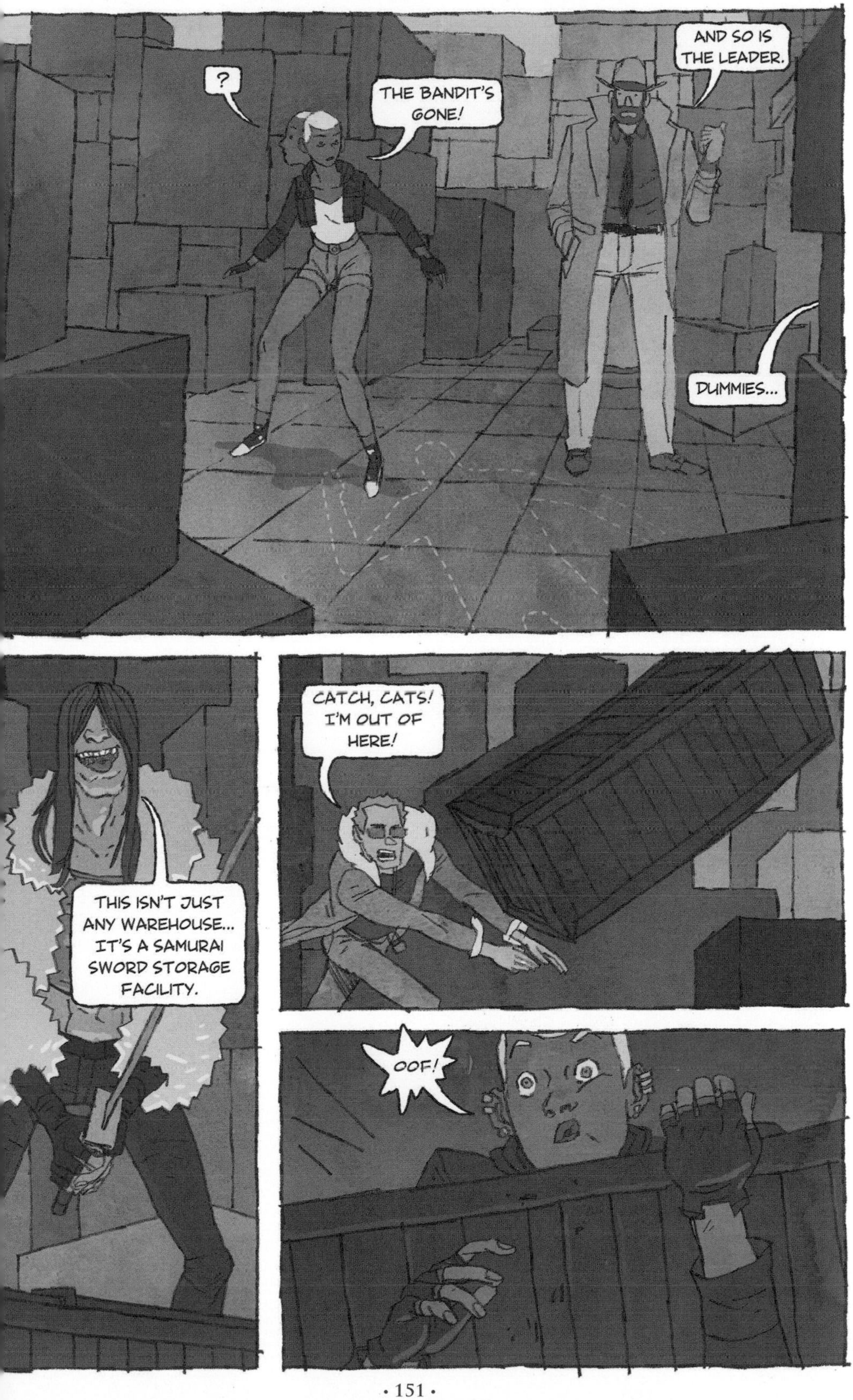
?
THE BANDIT'S GONE!
AND SO IS THE LEADER.
DUMMIES...
THIS ISN'T JUST ANY WAREHOUSE... IT'S A SAMURAI SWORD STORAGE FACILITY.
CATCH, CATS! I'M OUT OF HERE!
OOF!

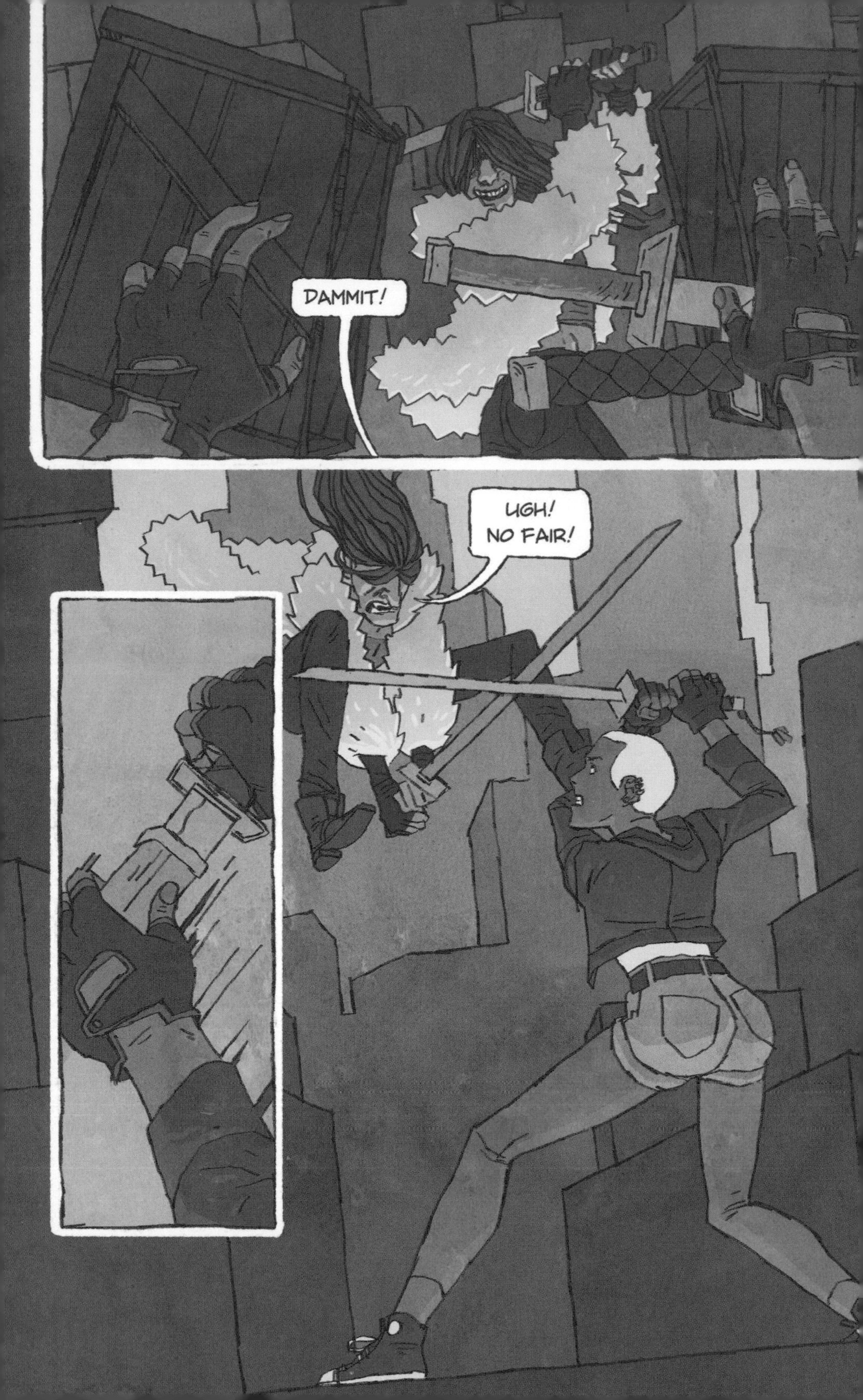
DAMMIT!
UGH! NO FAIR!

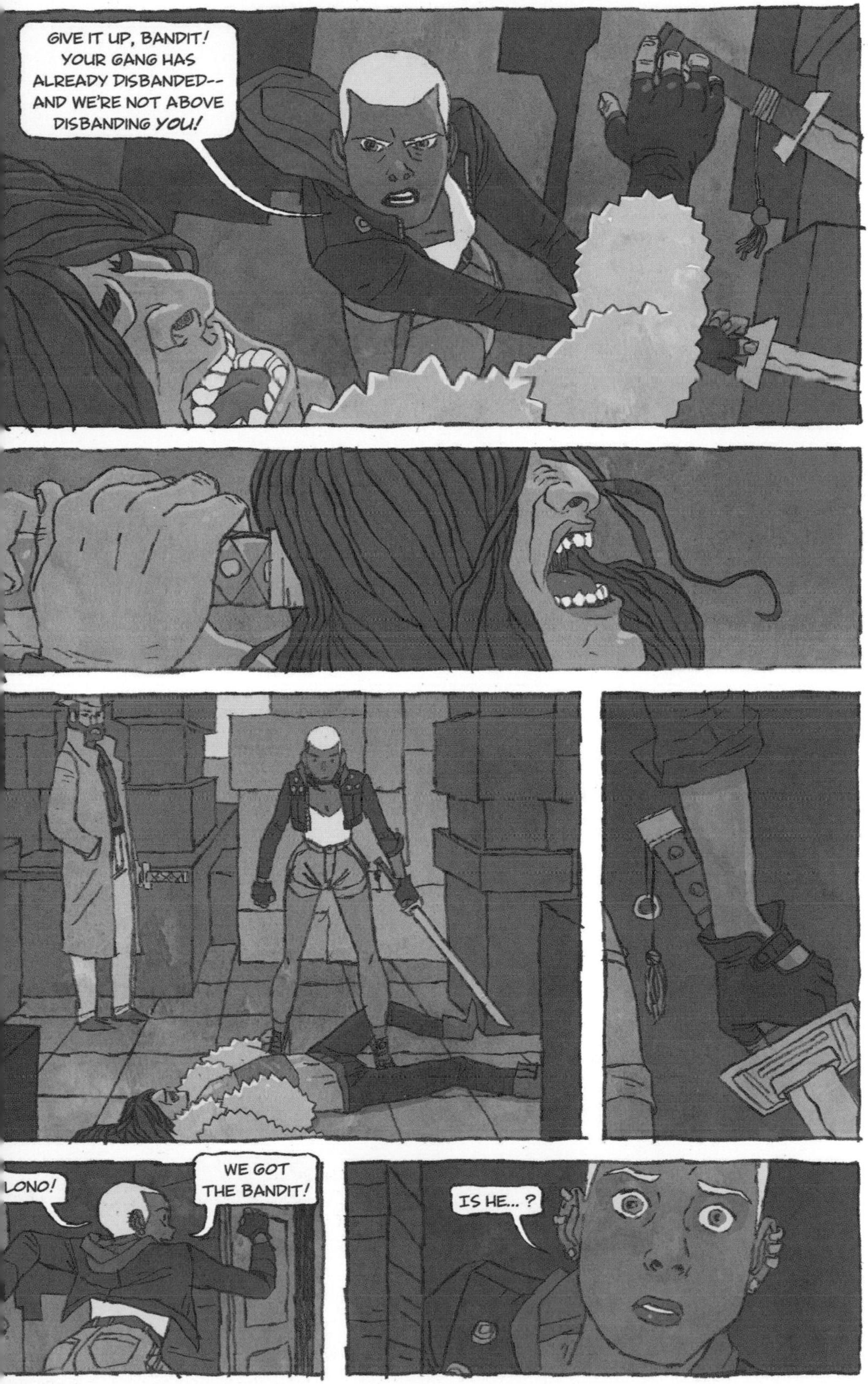
GIVE IT UP, BANDIT! YOUR GANG HAS ALREADY DISBANDED-- AND WE'RE NOT ABOVE DISBANDING *YOU!*
LONO!
WE GOT THE BANDIT!
IS HE... ?

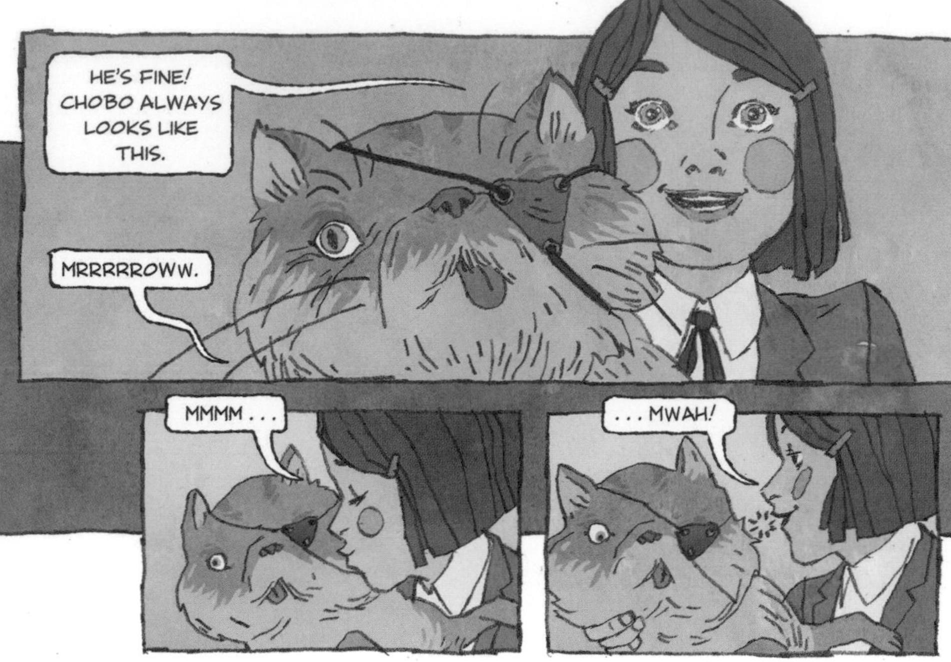

HE'S FINE! CHOBO ALWAYS LOOKS LIKE THIS.
MRRRRROWW.
MMMM . . .
. . . MWAH!

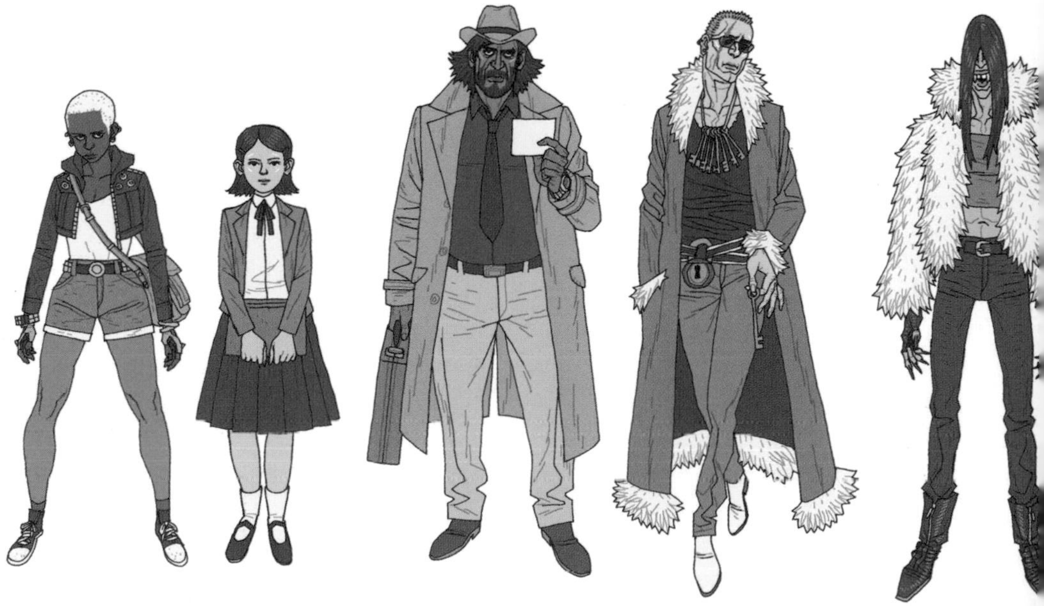

Spera Punk character designs
AFU CHA

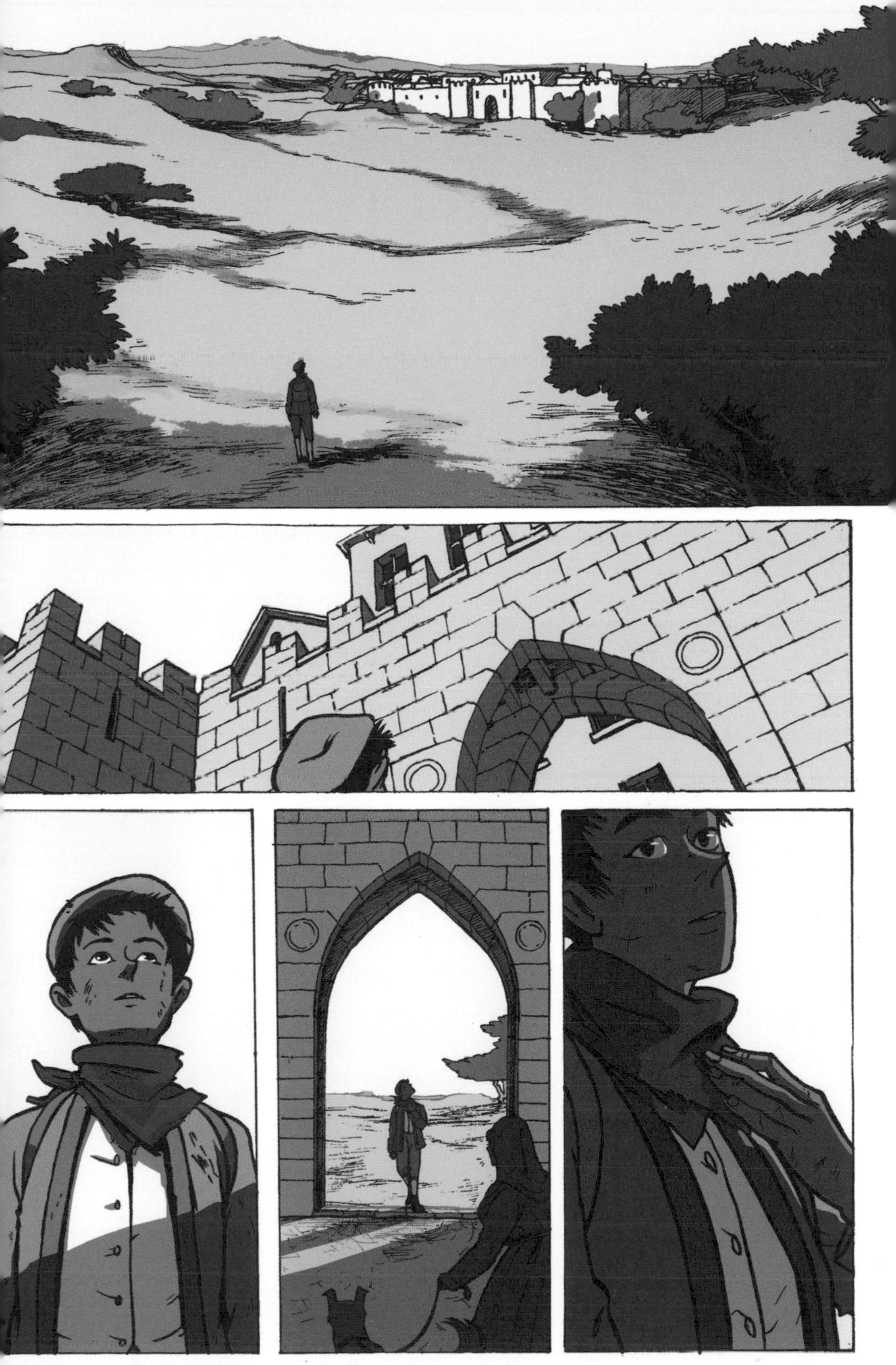

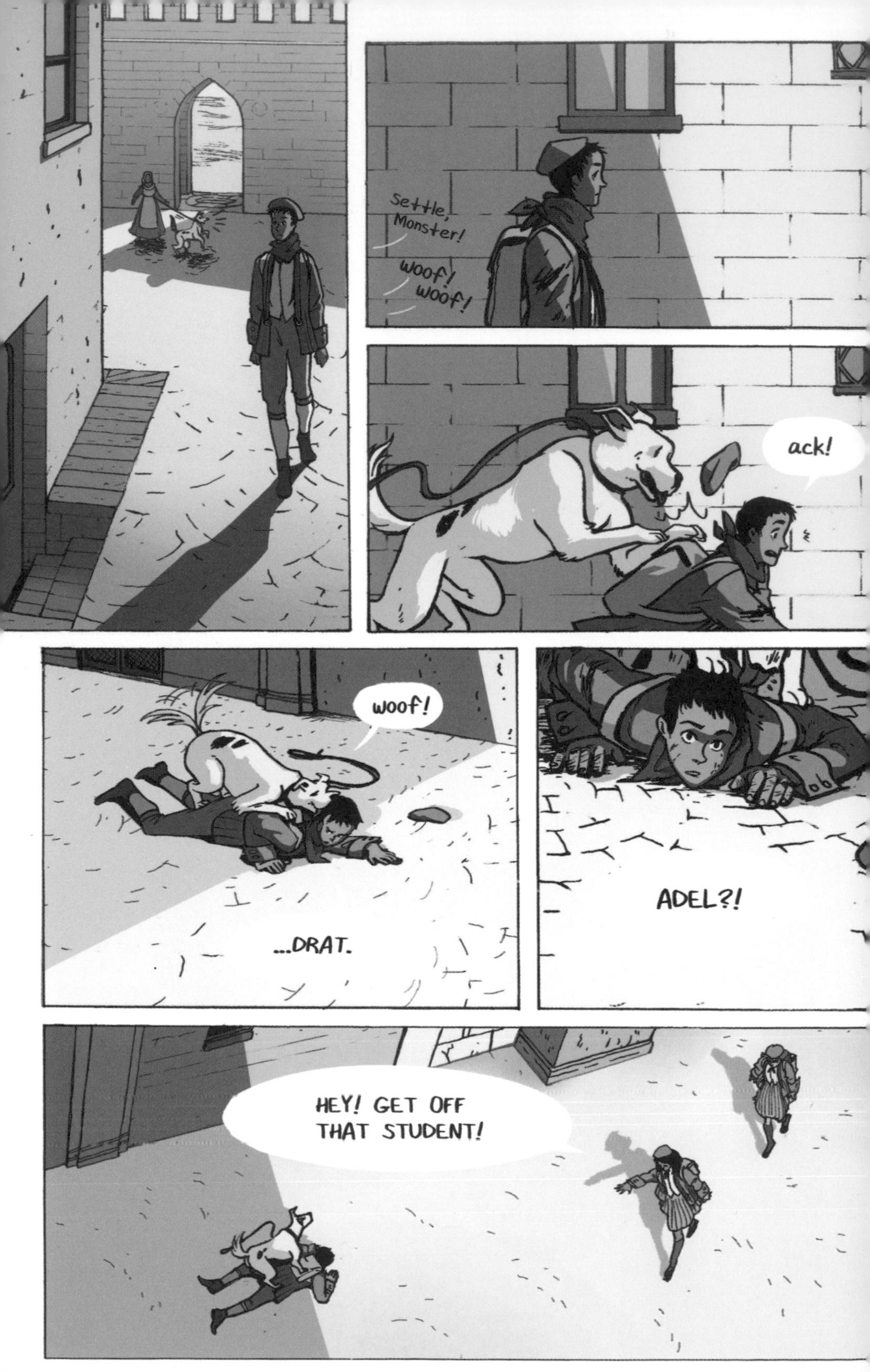
Settle, Monster!
woof! woof!
ack!
woof!
...DRAT.
ADEL?!
HEY! GET OFF THAT STUDENT!

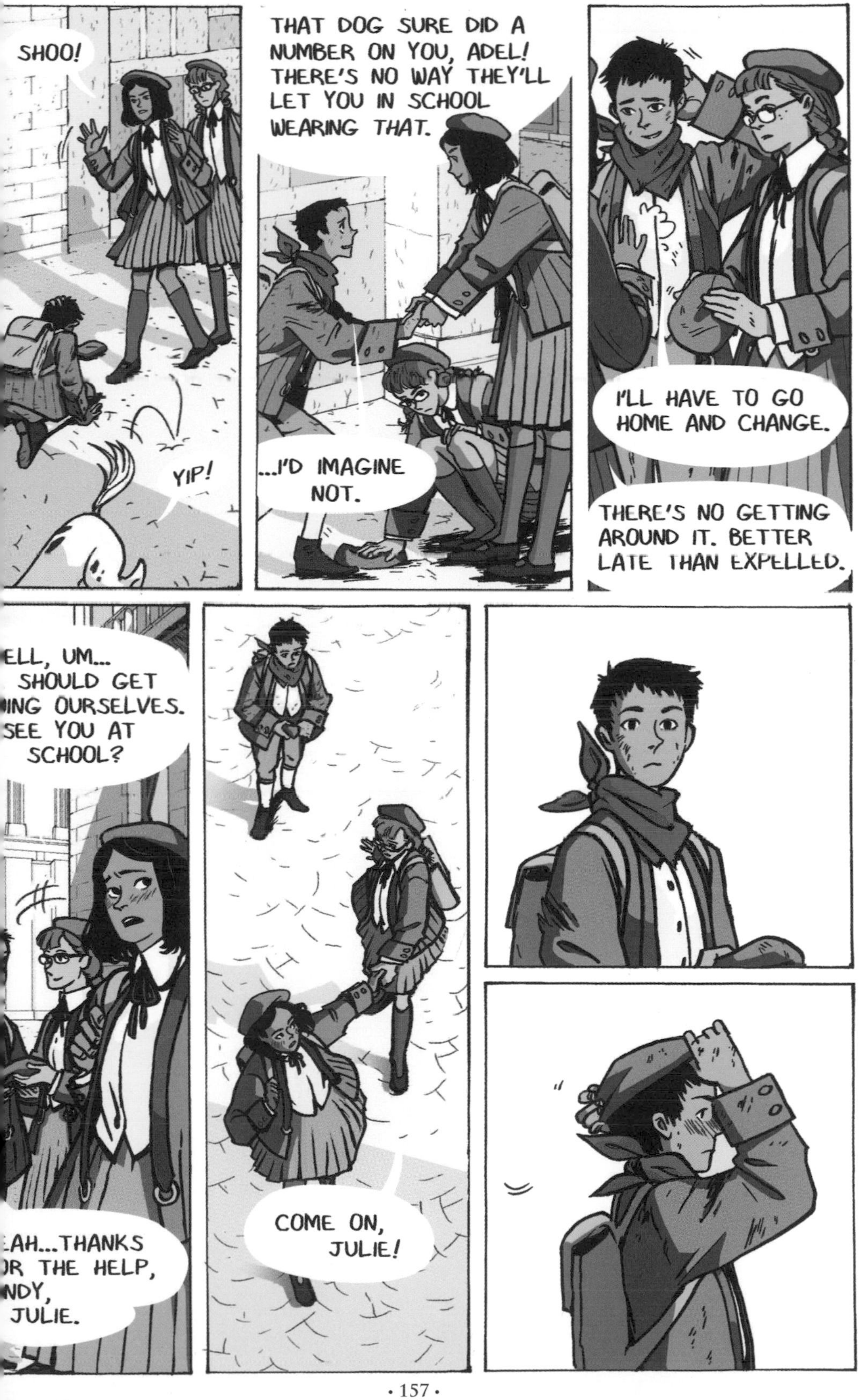
SHOO!
YIP!
THAT DOG SURE DID A NUMBER ON YOU, ADEL! THERE'S NO WAY THEY'LL LET YOU IN SCHOOL WEARING THAT.
...I'D IMAGINE NOT.
I'LL HAVE TO GO HOME AND CHANGE.
THERE'S NO GETTING AROUND IT. BETTER LATE THAN EXPELLED.
ELL, UM... SHOULD GET ING OURSELVES. SEE YOU AT SCHOOL?
EAH...THANKS OR THE HELP, NDY, JULIE.
COME ON, JULIE!

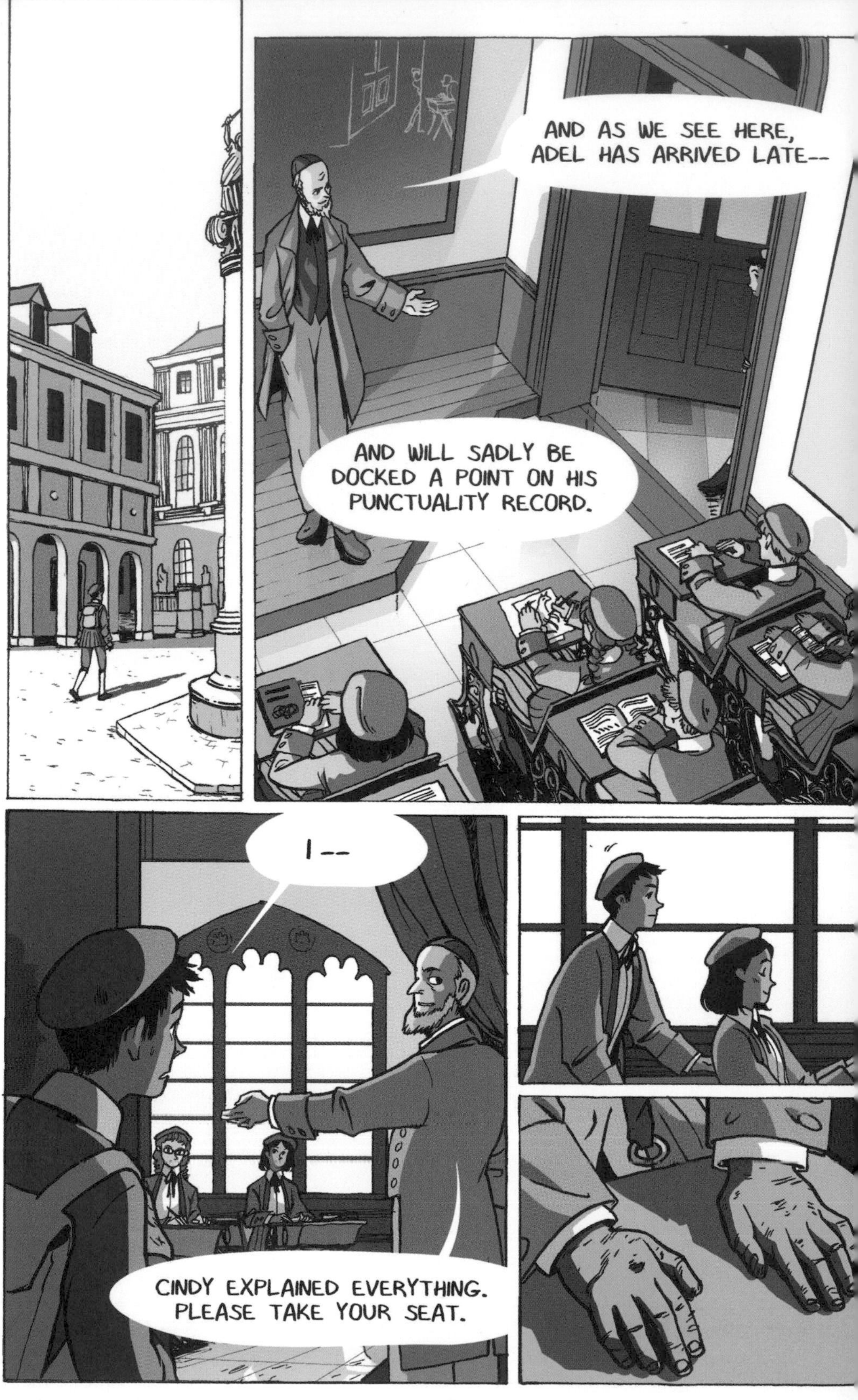
AND AS WE SEE HERE, ADEL HAS ARRIVED LATE--
AND WILL SADLY BE DOCKED A POINT ON HIS PUNCTUALITY RECORD.
I --
CINDY EXPLAINED EVERYTHING. PLEASE TAKE YOUR SEAT.

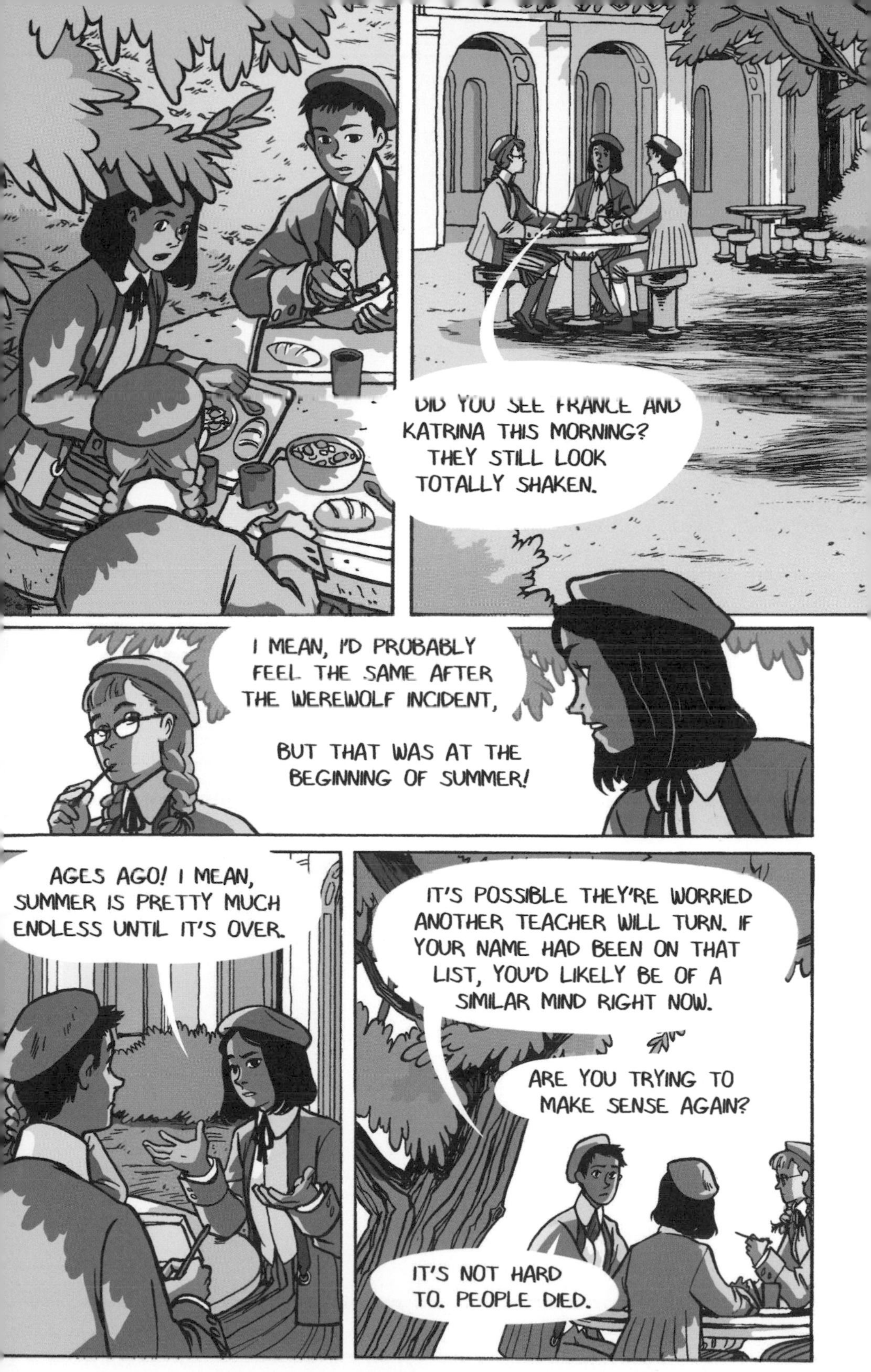
DID YOU SEE FRANCE AND KATRINA THIS MORNING? THEY STILL LOOK TOTALLY SHAKEN.
I MEAN, I'D PROBABLY FEEL THE SAME AFTER THE WEREWOLF INCIDENT,
BUT THAT WAS AT THE BEGINNING OF SUMMER!
AGES AGO! I MEAN, SUMMER IS PRETTY MUCH ENDLESS UNTIL IT'S OVER.
IT'S POSSIBLE THEY'RE WORRIED ANOTHER TEACHER WILL TURN. IF YOUR NAME HAD BEEN ON THAT LIST, YOU'D LIKELY BE OF A SIMILAR MIND RIGHT NOW.
ARE YOU TRYING TO MAKE SENSE AGAIN?
IT'S NOT HARD TO. PEOPLE DIED.

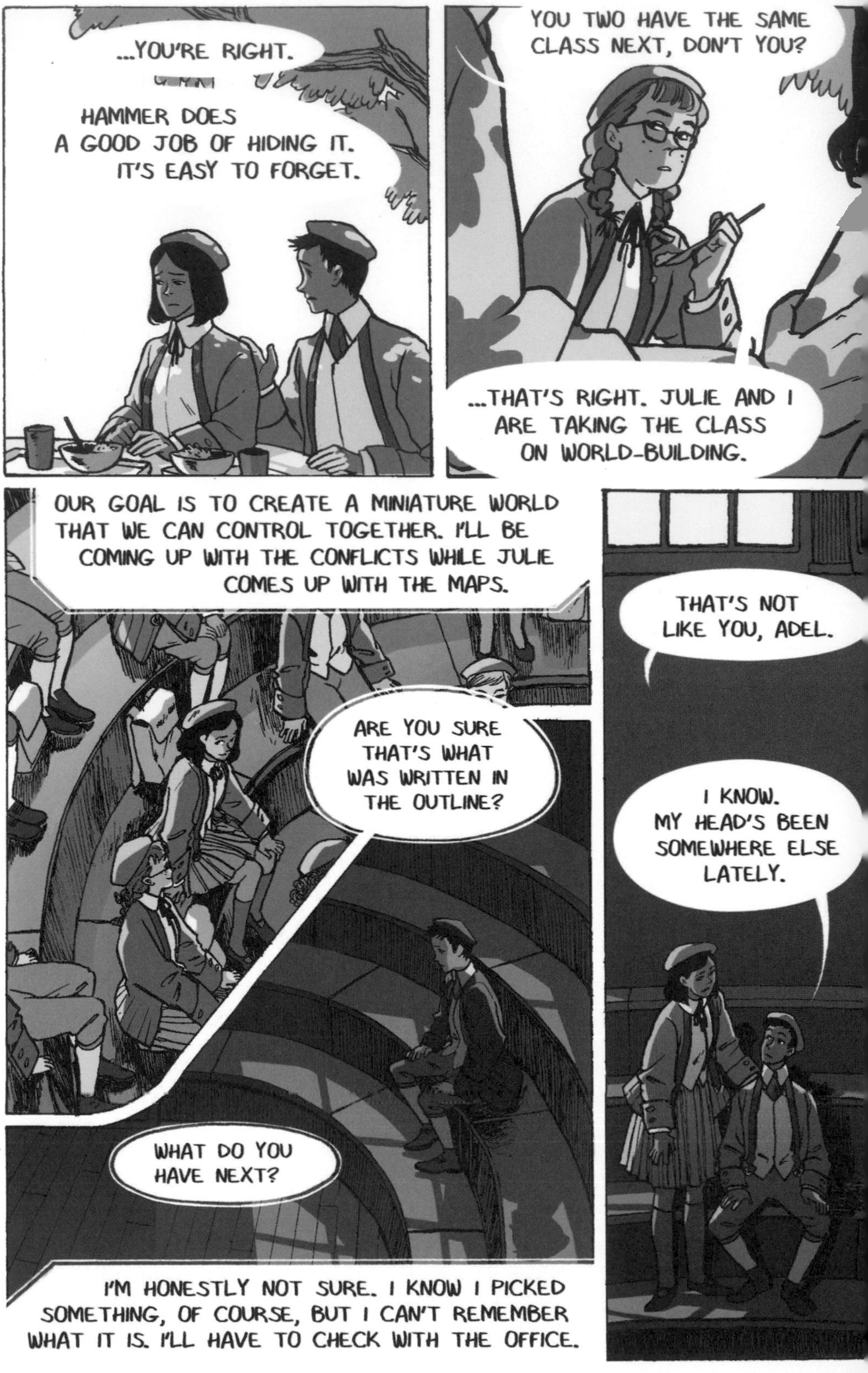

...YOU'RE RIGHT.
HAMMER DOES A GOOD JOB OF HIDING IT. IT'S EASY TO FORGET.
YOU TWO HAVE THE SAME CLASS NEXT, DON'T YOU?
...THAT'S RIGHT. JULIE AND I ARE TAKING THE CLASS ON WORLD-BUILDING.
OUR GOAL IS TO CREATE A MINIATURE WORLD THAT WE CAN CONTROL TOGETHER. I'LL BE COMING UP WITH THE CONFLICTS WHILE JULIE COMES UP WITH THE MAPS.
ARE YOU SURE THAT'S WHAT WAS WRITTEN IN THE OUTLINE?
WHAT DO YOU HAVE NEXT?
I'M HONESTLY NOT SURE. I KNOW I PICKED SOMETHING, OF COURSE, BUT I CAN'T REMEMBER WHAT IT IS. I'LL HAVE TO CHECK WITH THE OFFICE.
THAT'S NOT LIKE YOU, ADEL.
I KNOW. MY HEAD'S BEEN SOMEWHERE ELSE LATELY.

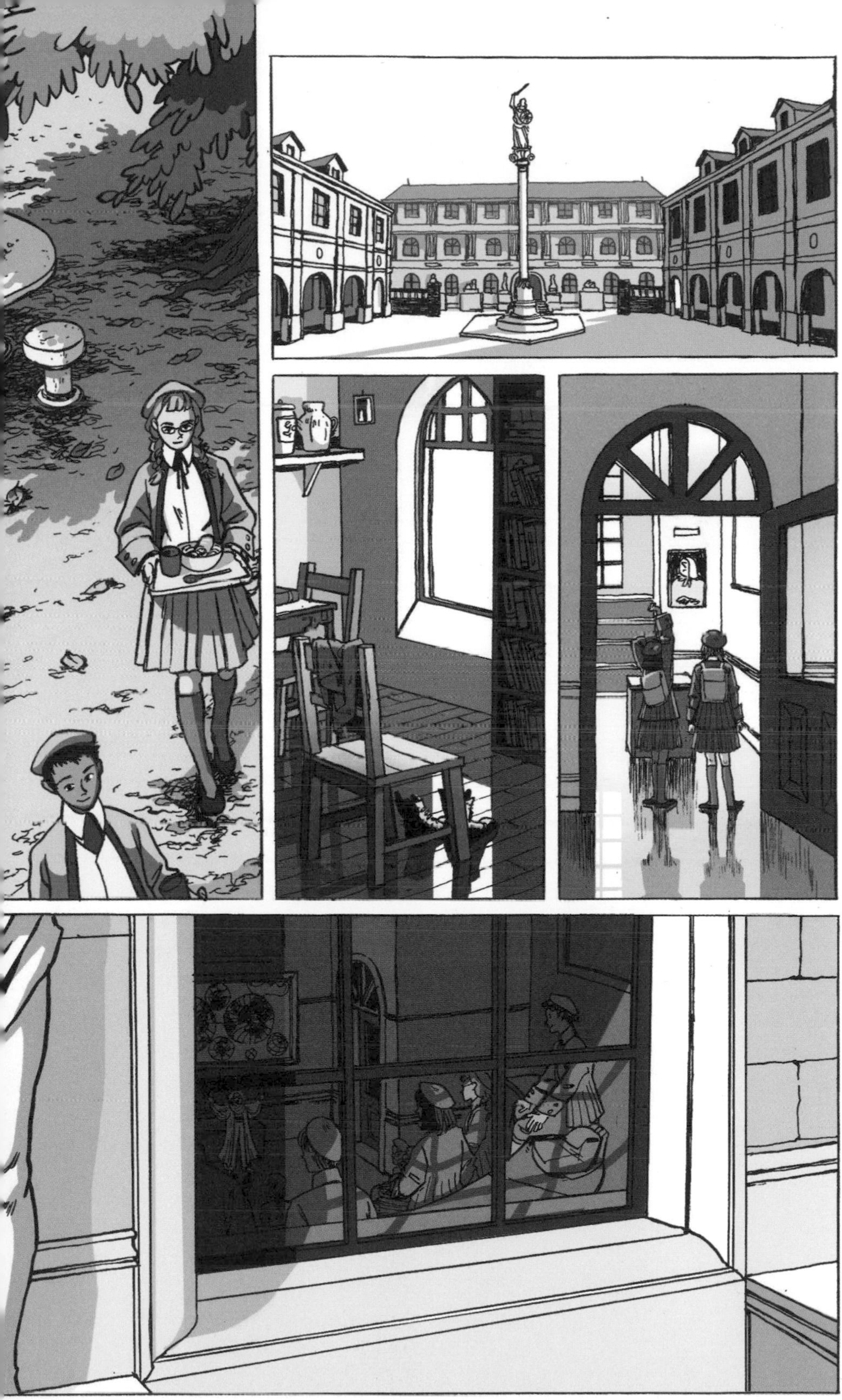

WELCOME TO WORLD-BREAKING.

HERE YOU WILL BE TAUGHT HOW TO DISMAN AND DIMINISH THE WORL BEING CRAFTED IN WORLD-BUILDING.

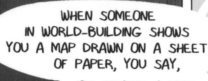

WHEN SOMEONE IN WORLD-BUILDING SHOWS YOU A MAP DRAWN ON A SHEET OF PAPER, YOU SAY,

'OH, THAT'S A NICE SHEET OF PAPER'.

WHEN SOMEONE IN WORLD-BUILDING PRESENTS YOU A SUMMARY OF THEIR WORLD, TRACE BACK THE INSPIRATIONS AND INFLUENCES, AND TREAT THEIR WORLD ONLY AS A COMBINATION OF THOSE SOURCES.

WHEN A STUDENT OF WORLD-BUILDING TELLS YOU THEY ARE IN WORLD-BUILDING PRETEND TO CARE.

THIS MIGHT JUST BE THE MOST IMPORTANT STEP.

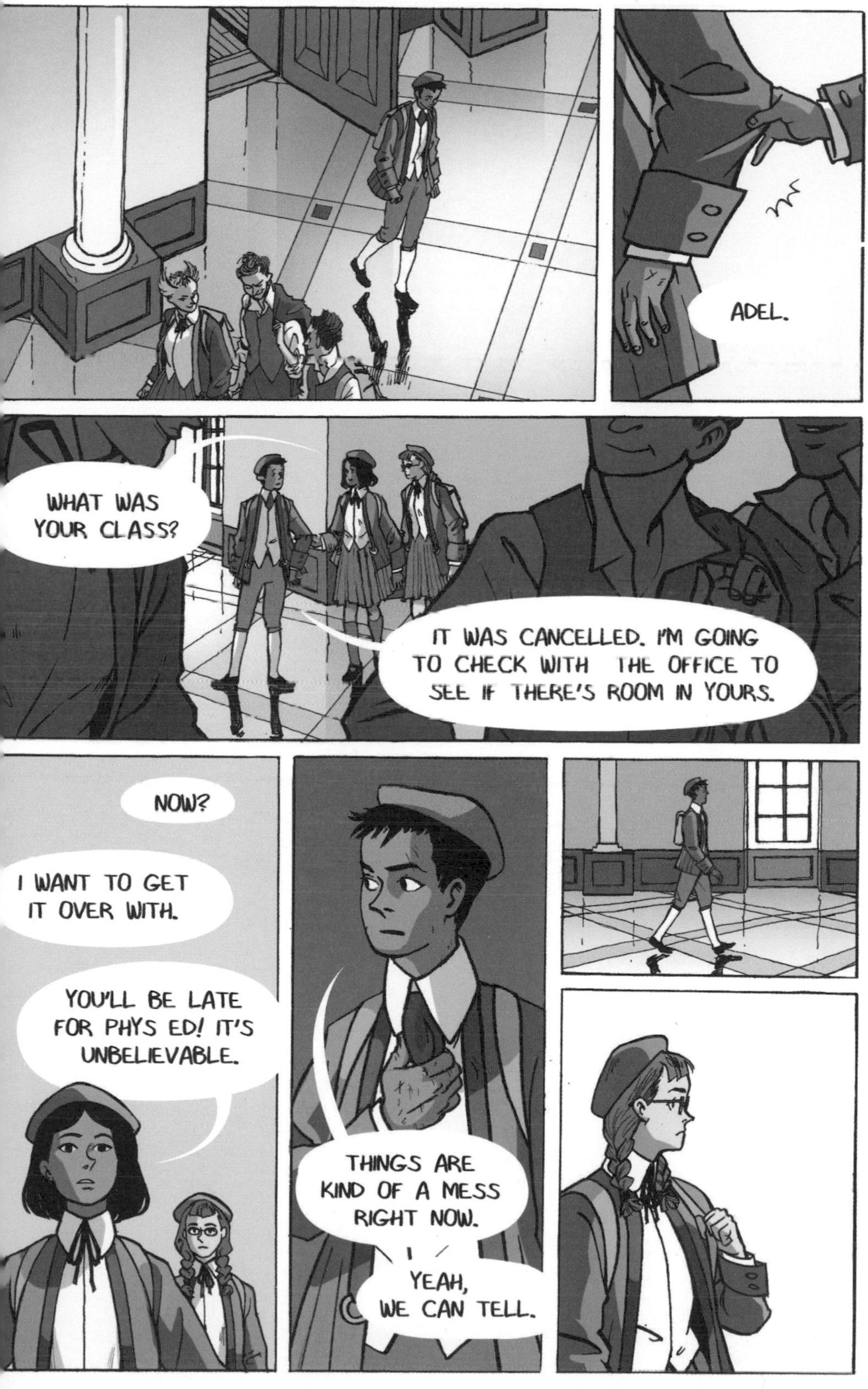
ADEL.
WHAT WAS YOUR CLASS?
IT WAS CANCELLED. I'M GOING TO CHECK WITH THE OFFICE TO SEE IF THERE'S ROOM IN YOURS.
NOW?
I WANT TO GET IT OVER WITH.
YOU'LL BE LATE FOR PHYS ED! IT'S UNBELIEVABLE.
THINGS ARE KIND OF A MESS RIGHT NOW.
YEAH, WE CAN TELL.

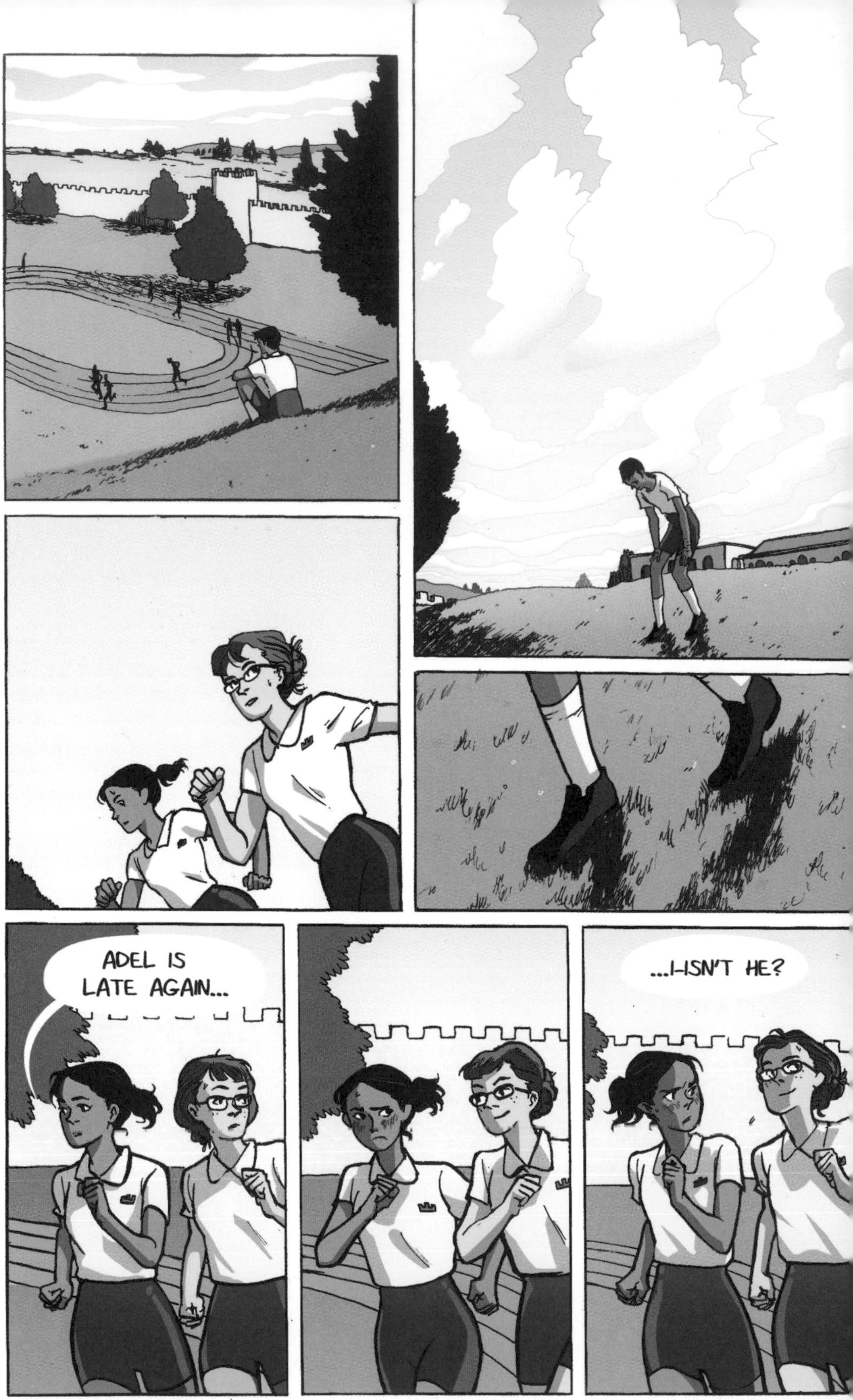
ADEL IS LATE AGAIN...
...I-ISN'T HE?

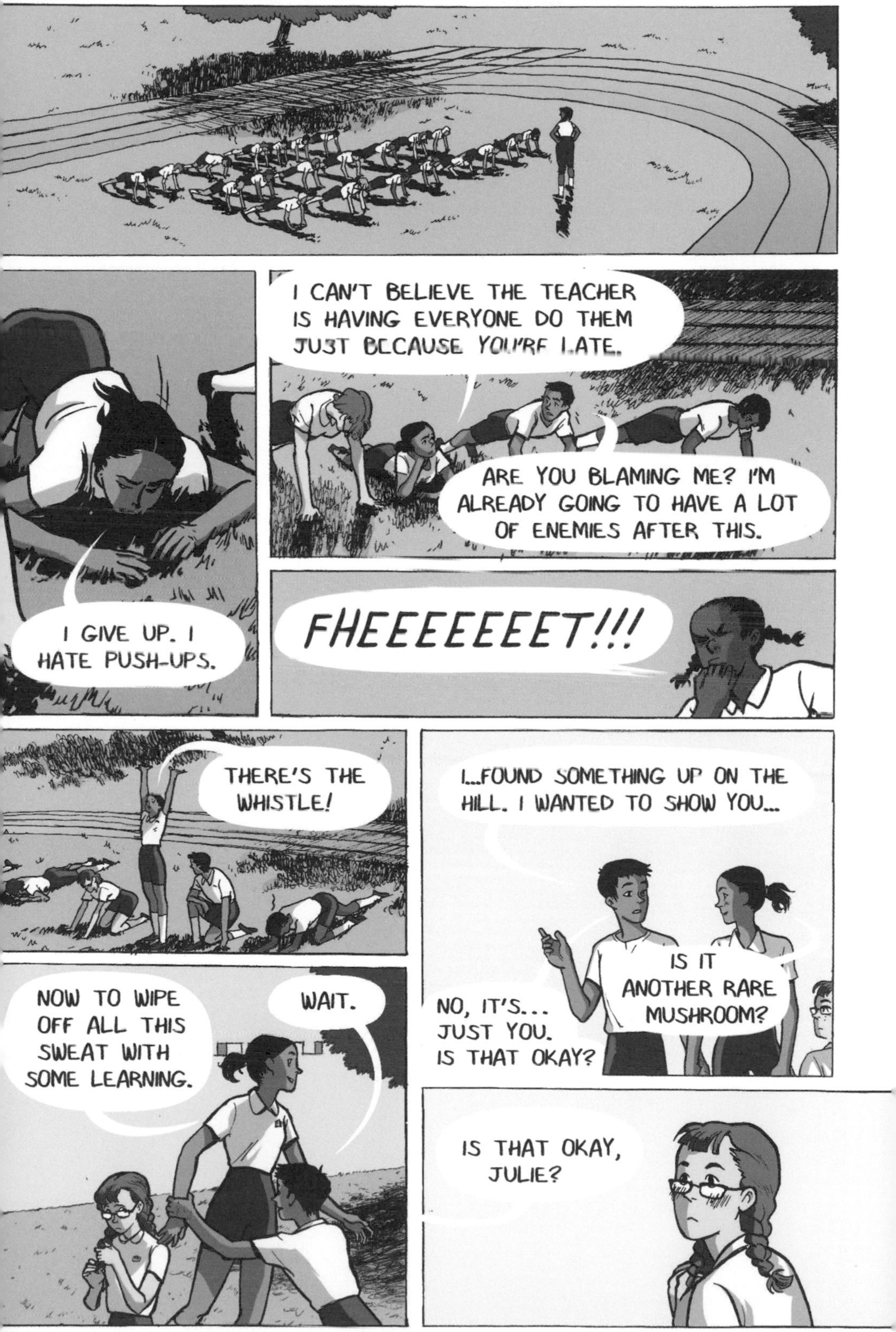
I GIVE UP. I HATE PUSH-UPS.
I CAN'T BELIEVE THE TEACHER IS HAVING EVERYONE DO THEM JUST BECAUSE YOU'RE LATE.
ARE YOU BLAMING ME? I'M ALREADY GOING TO HAVE A LOT OF ENEMIES AFTER THIS.
FHEEEEEEET!!!
THERE'S THE WHISTLE!
NOW TO WIPE OFF ALL THIS SWEAT WITH SOME LEARNING.
WAIT.
I...FOUND SOMETHING UP ON THE HILL. I WANTED TO SHOW YOU...
IS IT ANOTHER RARE MUSHROOM?
NO, IT'S... JUST YOU. IS THAT OKAY?
IS THAT OKAY, JULIE?

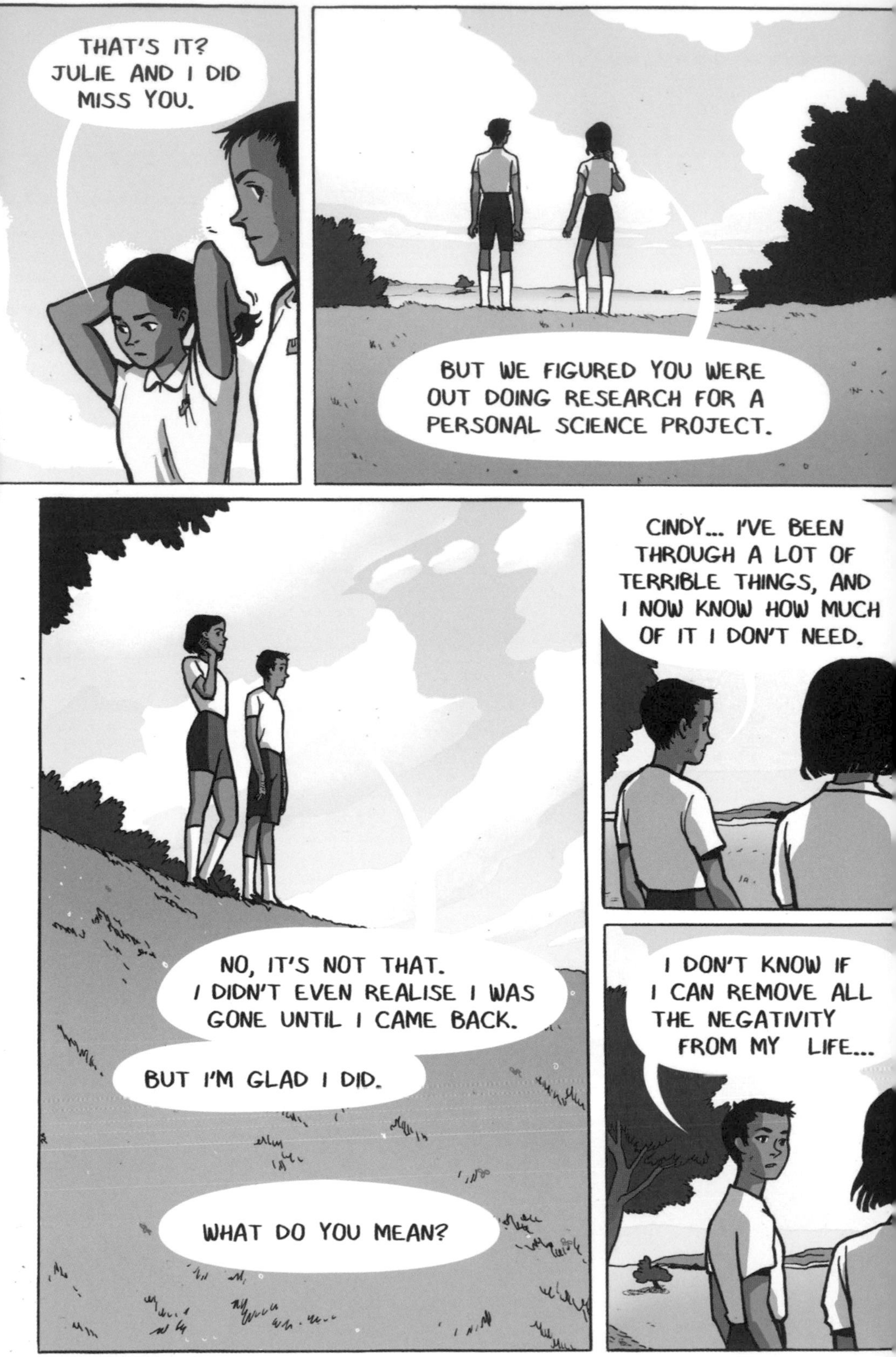
THAT'S IT? JULIE AND I DID MISS YOU.
BUT WE FIGURED YOU WERE OUT DOING RESEARCH FOR A PERSONAL SCIENCE PROJECT.
NO, IT'S NOT THAT. I DIDN'T EVEN REALISE I WAS GONE UNTIL I CAME BACK.
BUT I'M GLAD I DID.
WHAT DO YOU MEAN?
CINDY... I'VE BEEN THROUGH A LOT OF TERRIBLE THINGS, AND I NOW KNOW HOW MUCH OF IT I DON'T NEED.
I DON'T KNOW IF I CAN REMOVE ALL THE NEGATIVITY FROM MY LIFE...

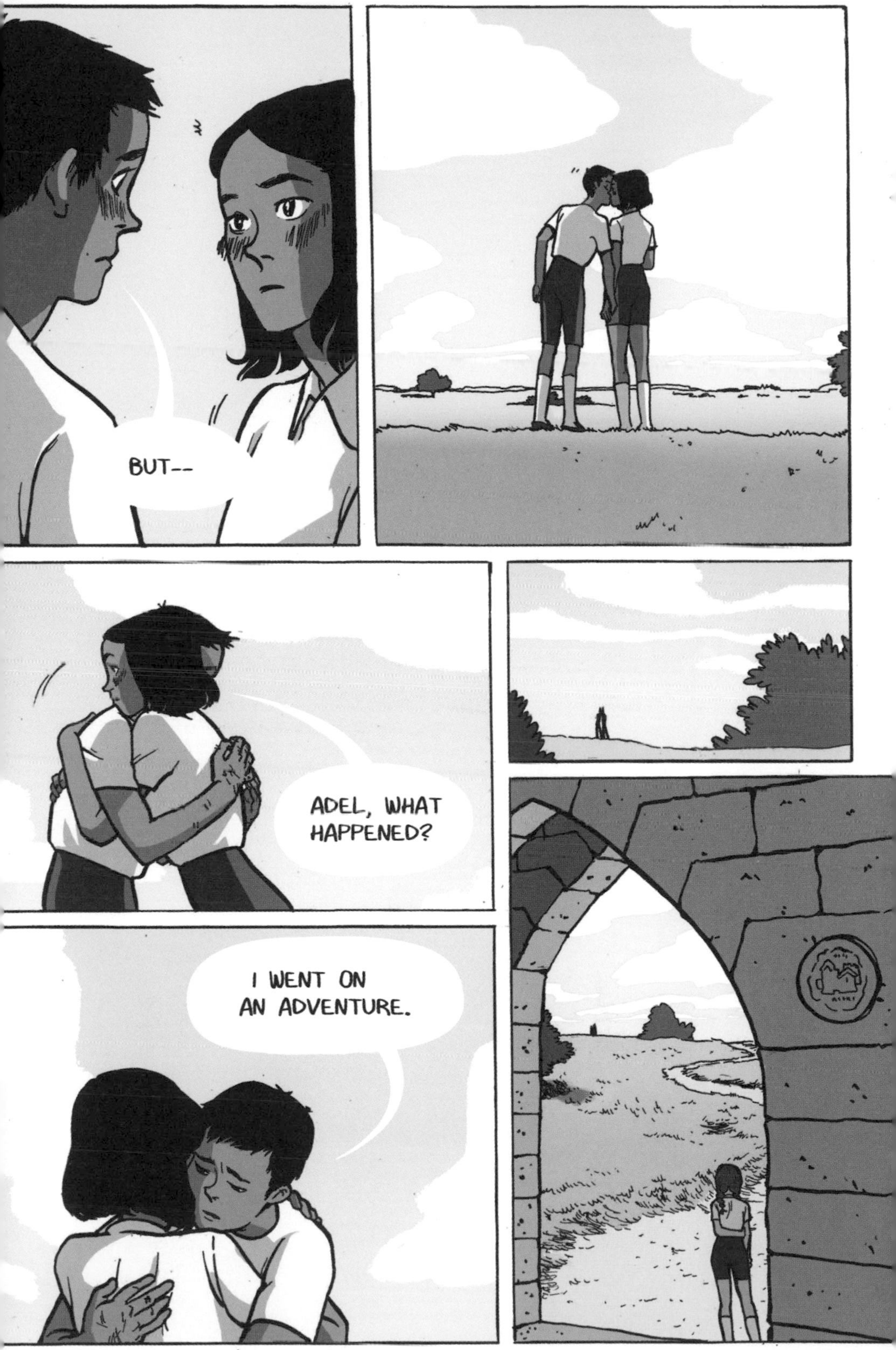
BUT--
ADEL, WHAT HAPPENED?
I WENT ON AN ADVENTURE.

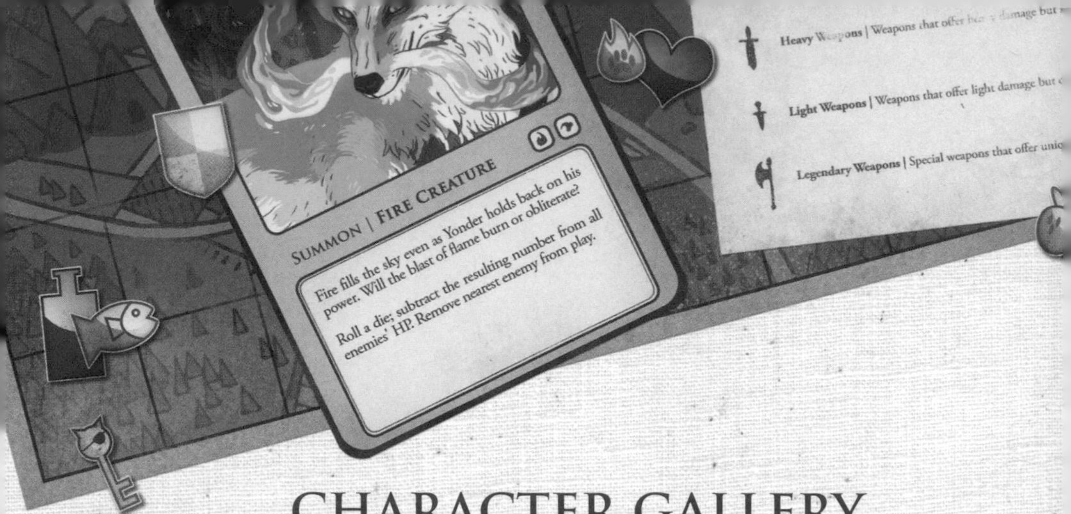
Summon | Fire Creature
Fire fills the sky even as Yonder holds back on his power. Will the blast of flame burn or obliterate?
Roll a die; subtract the resulting number from all enemies' HP. Remove nearest enemy from play.
Heavy Weapons
Light Weapons | Weapons that offer light damage but
Legendary Weapons | Special weapons that offer

CHARACTER GALLERY

character designs and illustrations by
AFU CHAN

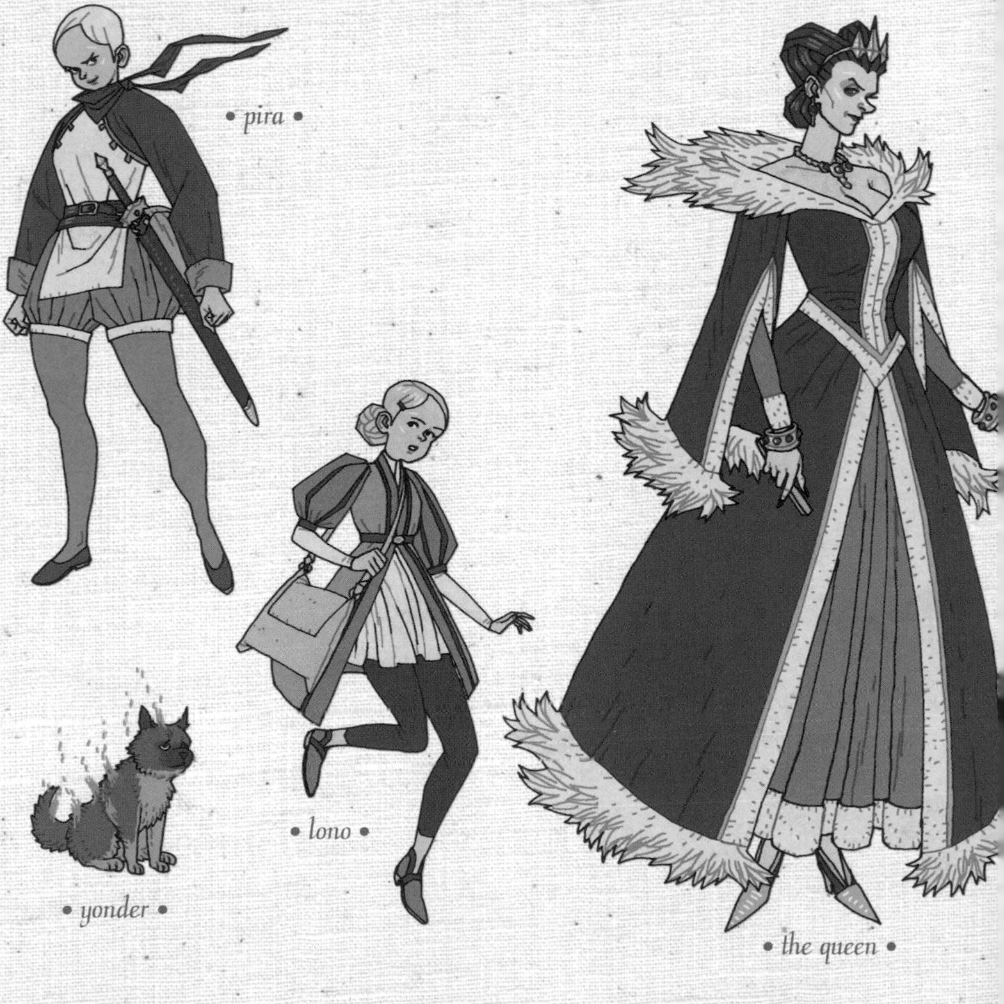
• pira •
• yonder •
• lono •
• the queen •

Earth Element | Elemental classification for creatures, weapons and spells.

Nature Element | Elemental classification for creatures, weapons and spells.

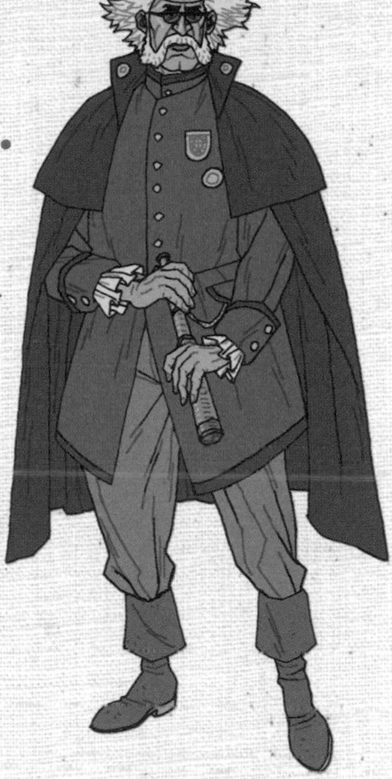

• *the lighthouse keeper* •

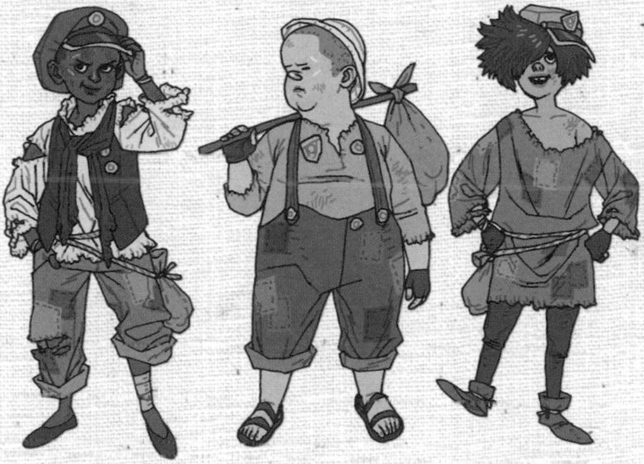

• *urchins* •

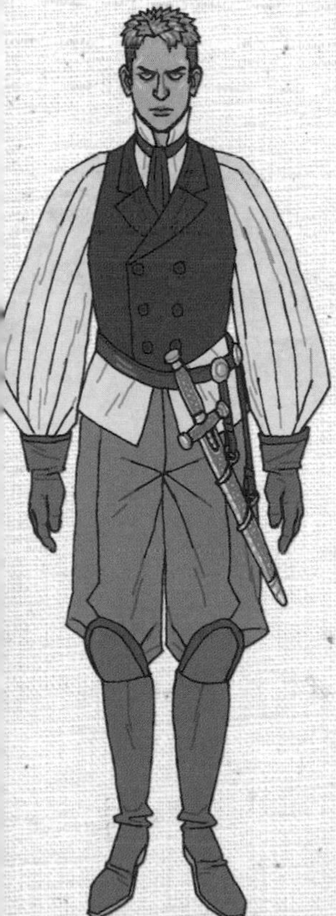

• *nole* •

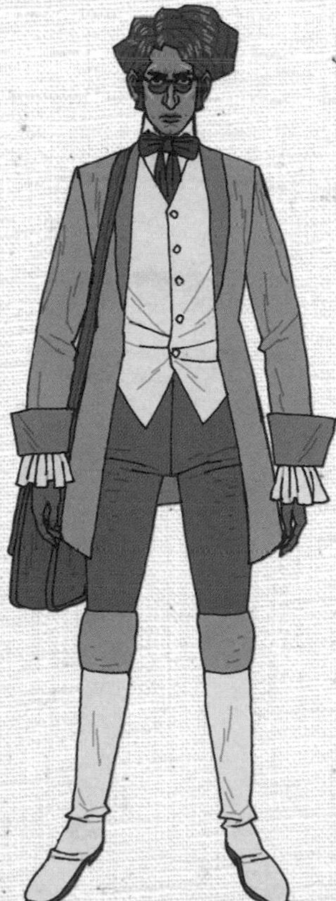

• *kyle* •

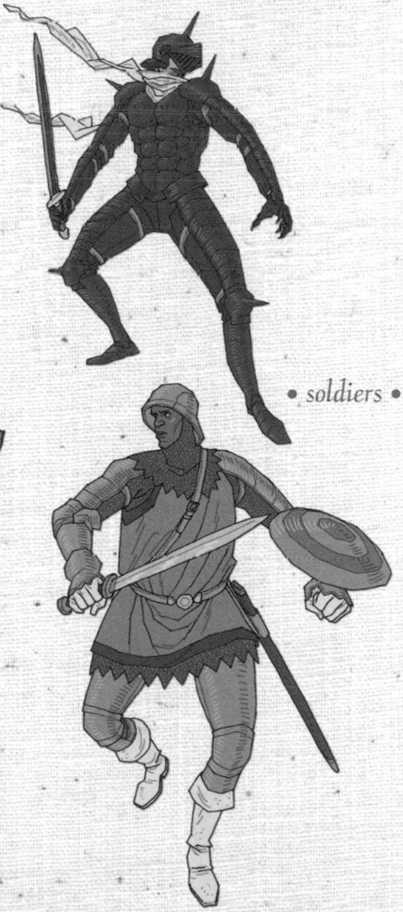

• *soldiers* •

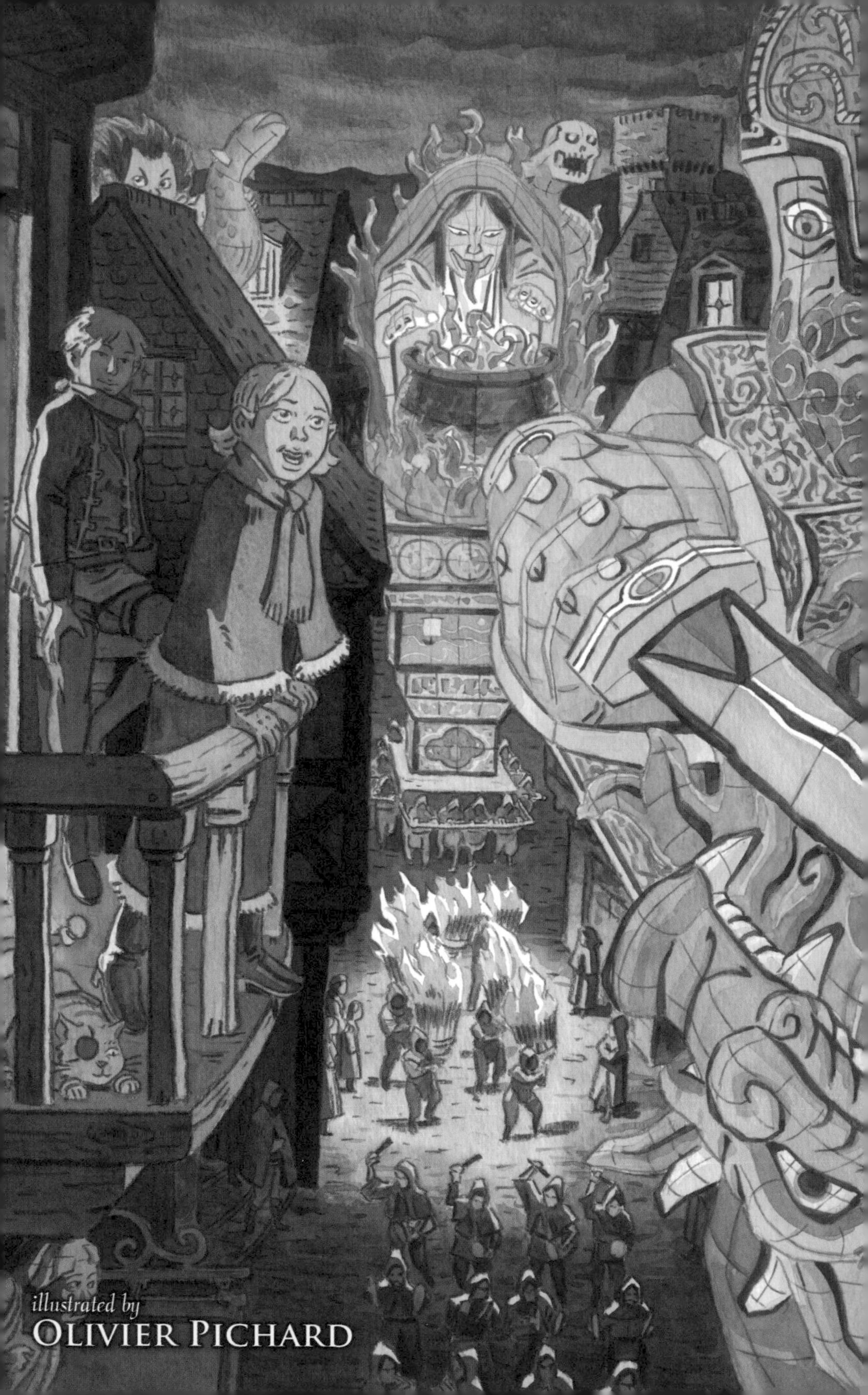
illustrated by
OLIVIER PICHARD

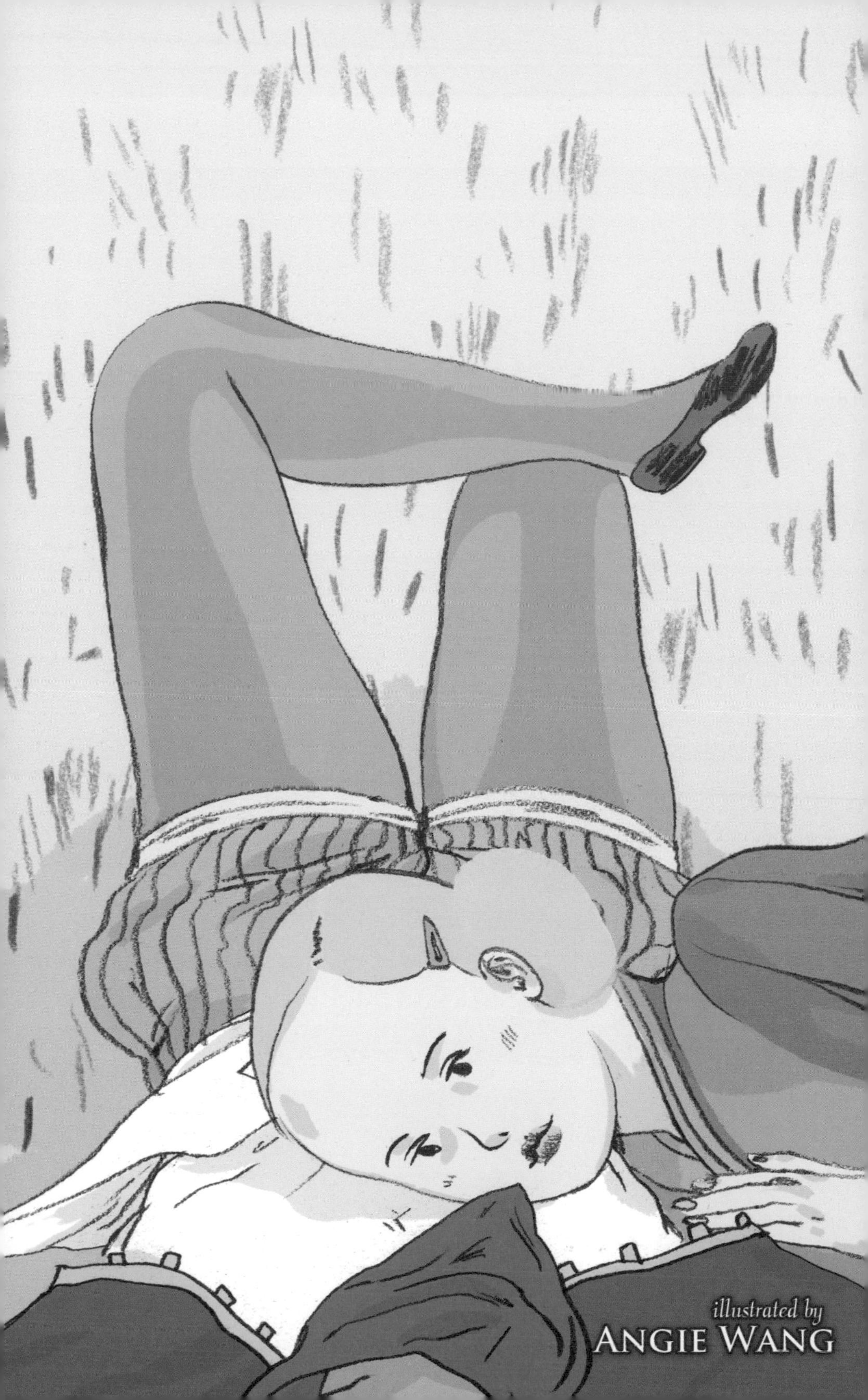

illustrated by
ANGIE WANG

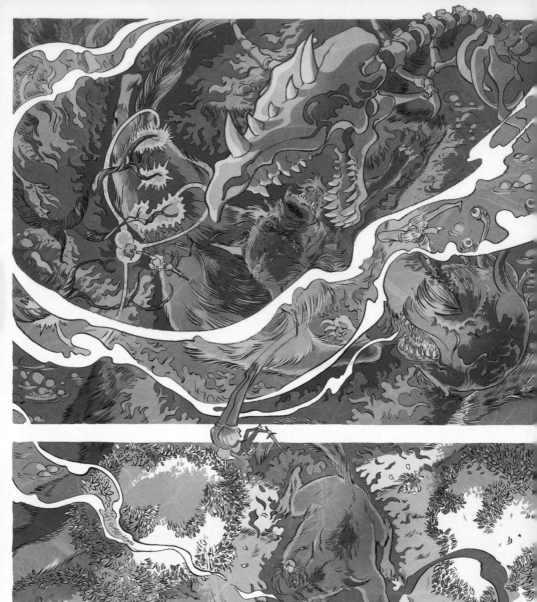

illustrated by
EMMA RIOS

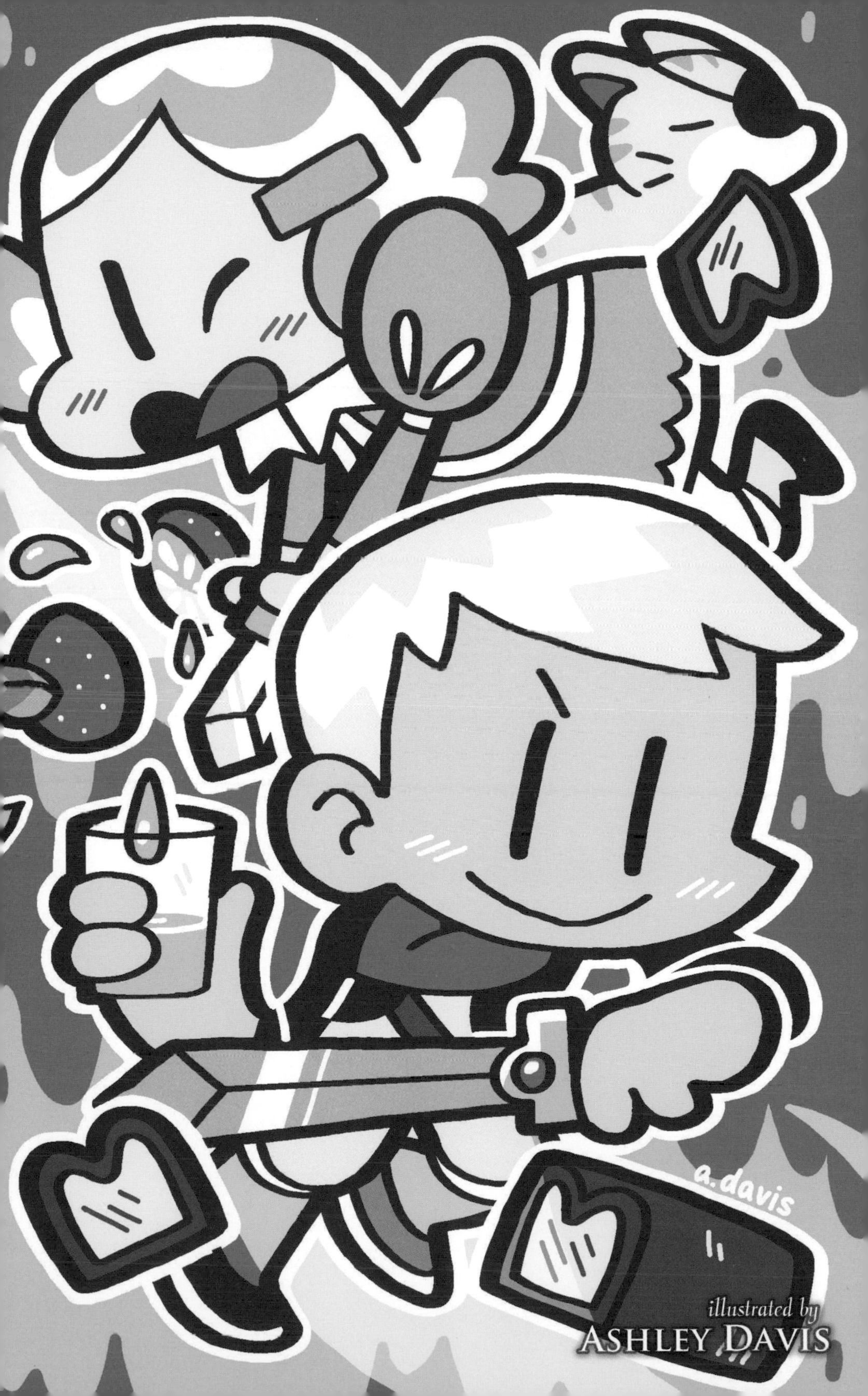
a.davis
illustrated by
ASHLEY DAVIS

ABOUT THE AUTHORS

the storytellers who have spun our tales...

JOSH TIERNEY resides in Ontario, Canada with his wife, daughter and cat. In addition to writing and editing the *Spera* series of books for Archaia, Josh runs *Spera-Comic.com* with the help of Olivier Pichard.

MICHAEL DIALYNAS is an illustrator and comic artist that resides in the exotic land of Athens, Greece. In his native tongue he has published a book by the name of *Trinkets* and a series called *Swan Songs*. He is also the co-creator and artist on *Amala's Blade*, published by Dark Horse. You can find more about his work at *WoodenCrown.com*.

MEG GANDY lives in a small city with a tall husband and a variable number of tiny cats. She makes comics – including webcomics – and her work can be found at *shatterlands.com*.

CORY GODBEY lives and works in Greenville, SC, USA. His comics résumé includes work for Archaia and the Jim Henson Co. (*Fraggle Rock*, *Labyrinth*) as well as David Petersen's *Mouse Guard* and the award-winning *Flight* anthologies. Cory seeks to tell stories with his work. He also likes to draw monsters. *CoryGodbey.com*.

AMEI ZHAO draws pictures and comics about her ongoing existential crisis. During the day she works in animation or biomedical science. It depends. Visit her at *ameizhao.com*.

SAM BOSMA is an illustrator from Baltimore, Maryland. He spends most of his time drawing swords.

KYLA VANDERKLUGT is a Toronto-born freelance illustrator and comic artist now working out of her ramshackle little studio in the country. She takes inspiration from her surroundings, and mostly the things she is surrounded by these days are animals and trees — and the tottering piles of books of her overflowing library. You can visit her online at *www.kylavanderklugt.com*.

KEN NIIMURA was the lonely owner of a Mega CD. Now that the teenage years are over, he's happy to claim that the countless hours playing "Lunar" have served for something. He currently writes and draws comics in Tokyo, where by the time you read these lines he'll have finished "Mother 2" and/or "Chrono Trigger". Ken's website is *niimurablog.blogspot.com*.

AFU CHAN is a freelance illustrator and comic artist. He also loves designing characters of all types and races, including monsters. To check out more of his work, visit *www.afuchan.com*.

GIANNIS MILONOGIANNIS makes comic books on his own and with others. You can find his work in **Old City Blues** and **Spera** from Archaia and **Prophet** from Image Comics. Giannis' favourite things are coffee and samurai robots.

JAKE WYATT is from Places in America. He currently lives in exotic Burbank, CA with his wife, Kathryn, where he draws things for film, television, comics and fun. Sometimes Kathryn helps. Like when she flatted all the pages for the Hopscotch short in this book. You can follow Jake's work at: *jakewyattriot.tumblr.com*.

REBECCA MOCK is a freelance illustrator, comic artist and corny movie enthusiast working from her home studio in Brooklyn, NY. She has done freelance work for Rockstar Games, the comic **Adventure Time: Fionna and Cake**, the **New York Times**, and **Wired Magazine**, among others. She hopes to draw more comics, travel the world, and attend plenty of comic conventions.

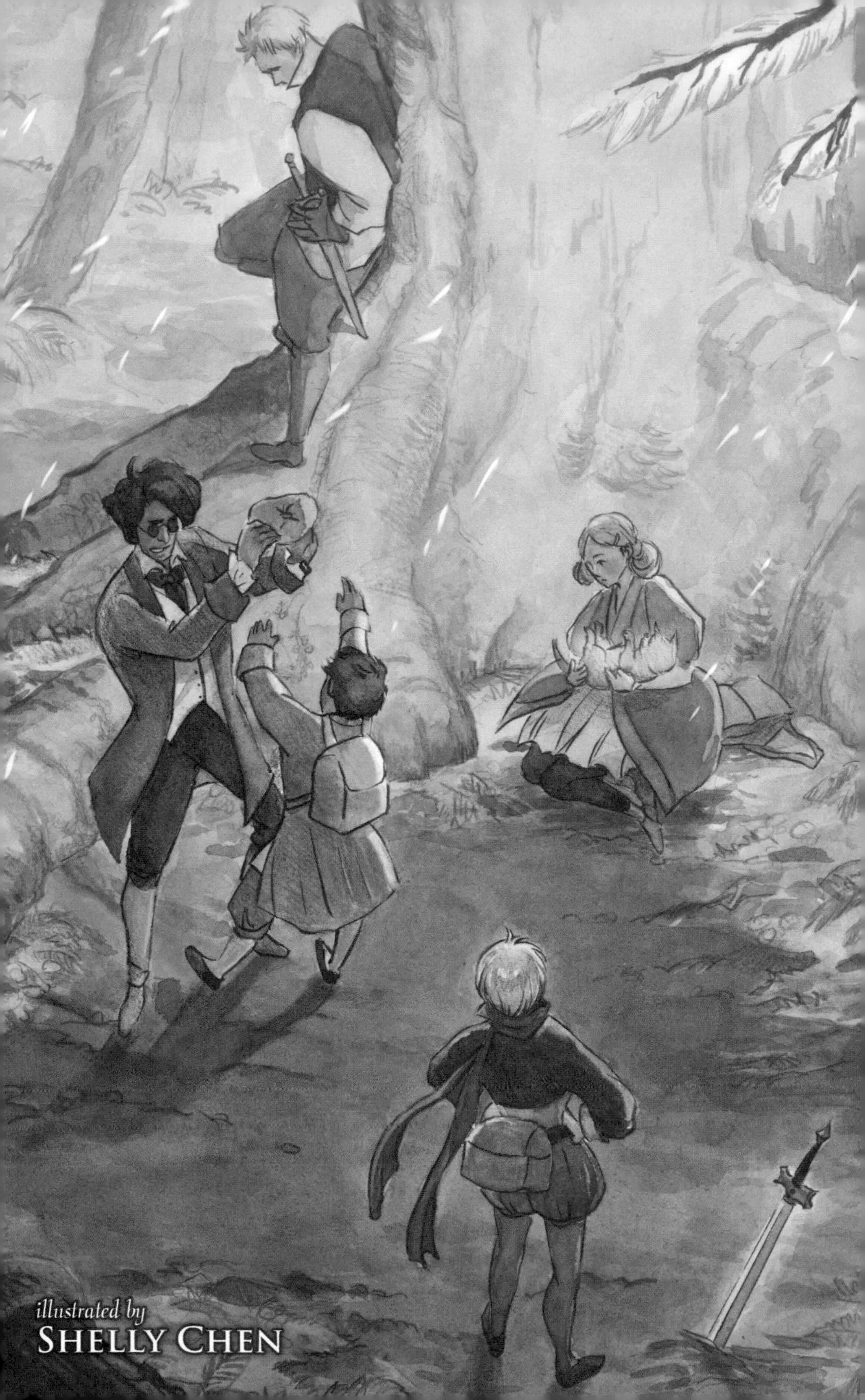

illustrated by
SHELLY CHEN

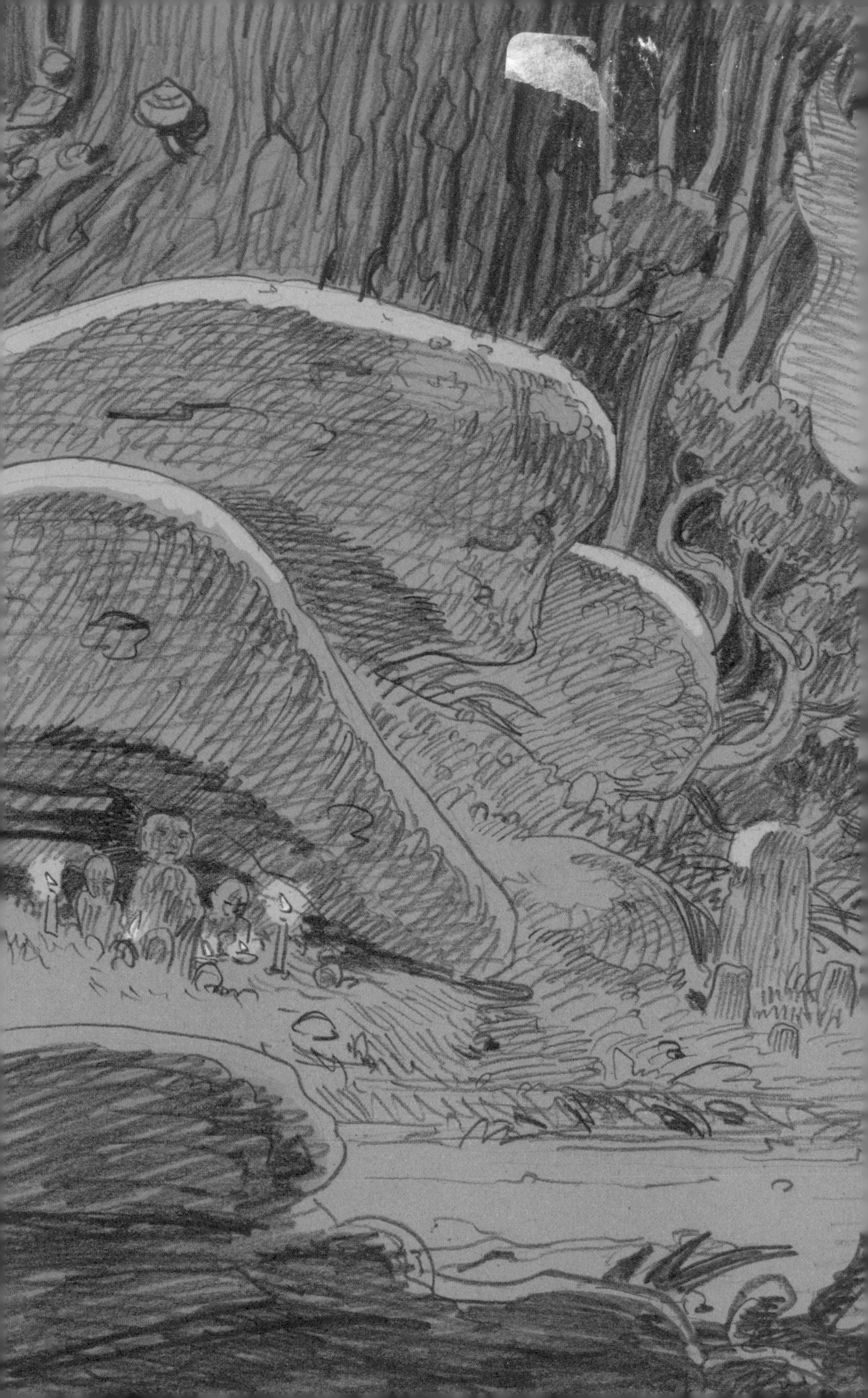